CULTURE

UNDER CANVAS

THE STORY OF TENT CHAUTAUQUA

BY

HARRY P. HARRISON 1878-

AS TOLD TO

KARL DETZER

HASTINGS HOUSE, PUBLISHERS, NEW YORK

TO
MY WIFE, ETTA PARSONS HARRISON

Introduction

Mark Twain was walking on a San Francisco street one misty evening in 1866, when a bibulous stranger halted him and announced: "My name's Sawyer." His tongue was thick, his voice loud, and there could be no doubt that he was unhappy. "Hear you're goin' to give a talk." To steady himself he grabbed Mark Twain's lapels. "I haven't got a cent, but if you knew how bad I wanted to laugh, you'd give me a ticket."

Mark Twain considered. His proposed lecture, first of the uncounted thousands that he would deliver in the course of forty years, was only three nights off. His pockets were nearly empty. He could find no steady work in either of his trades as printer or reporter. He had done a little writing here in the west, but he had not used his real name, Samuel Langhorne Clemens.

The Sacramento Union recently had published an account of Twain's trip to Hawaii. Readers had found it amusing and an editor friend, seeking to be helpful, had suggested, "Hire a hall, advertise. Sell tickets at a dollar each and give a funny talk."

As the date approached, Twain did not feel funny. He felt distressed. What if no one came? If no one laughed? But this drunken stranger, appearing out of the night, actually wanted to hear him and wanted to laugh. Twain gave the man a ticket and detailed instructions. Next day he gave tickets and similar instructions to four hearty friends. The night of the lecture the five were scattered through the "Opera House" that Twain had rented for $50—to be paid later. At each secret signal from the stage, they guffawed until the audience joined them. The evening was a huge success.

Mark Twain thereafter talked his way around the world, usually to roars of merriment. Usually, not always. Five years after his first attempt, he wrote to his booking agent, James Redpath of Boston, refusing a date.

"I never made a success of a lecture in a church," he explained. "People are afraid to laugh in church."

This shrewd observation called attention to a national characteristic that was to worry lecture managers for nearly half a century before they did something constructive about it. That something was called "Chautauqua." It separated the pulpit and the platform and substituted footlights for the religious dimness of the Sunday-school room. To accomplish this, it went outdoors. Once launched, it became a mighty influence in American entertainment and education, in politics and the nation's culture.

In the intervening years, while Mark Twain was making a million dollars on the platform, and losing it all in fantastically bad investments, America was a lecture-loving nation. In churches and halls from the Alleghenies to the Rockies, a people thirsty for culture and hungry for information paid its dimes and dollars for an evening's program. Often the society into which they grouped themselves was called a "Lyceum."

The Greeks had coined the word. Aristotle taught in the walled garden of the "Temple of Apollo Lyceus." In the streets nearby, Athenian crowds gathered to listen to their philosophers and poets, foot-loose and unpaid. Until one day some entertainer became so popular that the citizens were willing to pay to listen to him, and on that day "Lyceum" was born.

In America in the first quarter of the nineteenth century, a Yale graduate, ambitious Josiah Holbrook, used the word to name his "association of adults for the purpose of self-education." Boston had subscribed to the idea in 1830, with Daniel Webster as its first leader, and the Massachusetts and New York legislatures had even formed state Lyceum boards. Their purpose, to improve schools, organize libraries and museums, provide classes for adults, was purely educational, with no idea of a return in dollars for anyone.

In 1831 the American Lyceum Association was founded to unite a chain of societies for weekly lectures and debates. "A good pulpit," Ralph Waldo Emerson called it. It was a pulpit for men only; women were not invited to speak. The system flourished for years; then the meaning of the word gradually changed and "Lyceum" became the organized lecture business that it is today.

Migrating homesteaders had little room to carry books. New England culture had centered in the schoolhouse and meetinghouse where a few fluent men aired their views and many other persons listened. Oratory was the literature of the masses. Most of it was solemn, stemming from long, grim sermons like those of Cotton Mather and Jonathan Edwards. America's first stump speech was not delivered from a stump but from Plymouth Rock, which spread its gloomy shadow far across the land, all the way to the plains of Kansas, almost to the end of the nineteenth century.

Between 1850 and 1900, New England remained the revered heart of American culture. Boston, Cambridge and New Haven, and to a lesser degree Philadelphia, were the seats of learning most highly respected in the prairies. The bleak philosophy of Cotton Mather and the gray Quaker conscience had ridden west together in homeseekers' flatboats and Conestoga wagons. New England, never slow to take advantage of a profitable opportunity, soon was sending its long-winded sons in droves to talk to the muddy back country.

Under this influence the new west, weary of listening to its unlettered self, tried to recapture some of the intellectual splendor and the spiritual expression it had left behind the mountains. If it did not have the eloquent New England clergyman for daily fare, or the sight of white steeples above a village green, next best was to embrace the evangelistic "camp meeting." Morality was a topic for any platform. Exhorters, riding tirelessly in search of souls to save, turned naturally to the south which was not yet on the social defensive and was more interested in plain religion than in talk of "democracy" or "Yankee land." Back-hill folk, in particular, acquired a taste for exhortation under the stars. The "camp-meeting" joined the literary club as a social institution.

Each raw settlement tried to minister to the spiritual and intellectual needs of surrounding woodlands and newly broken prairies. Fast-growing Cincinnati, sloshing through its mud streets, called itself, and seriously considered itself, "The Athens of the West." Its Young Men's Mercantile Library Association and its equally active Mechanics' Institute sponsored most of the eloquence. In six years, between 1850 and 1857, the members of its Lyceums listened to twenty-six lectures by Amos Bronson Alcott, "most transcendental of the New England transcendentalists," whose daughter, Louisa May, would outshine him in the post-Civil War era with her best-selling *Little Women*.

Across Ohio, from the Maumee to the Muskingum, forty-five other communities boasted lecture courses which, in twenty years, brought Alcott and more than a dozen other famous New Englanders to hundreds of ecstatic audiences. In Toledo the sponsors were a dedicated group of women in a Suffrage Association, cooperating with a daring crowd of young men who called themselves the Radical Club. In Zanesville a Young Men's Literary Association imported speakers; in Sandusky it was an Arts Association, in Warren a Polemics Club. Chillicothe, combining physical and mental cultures, depended on a Gymnasium and Library Association.

Speakers usually stuck to safe subjects. Most sponsors, in their serious quest for the Better Life, slammed their doors with equal finality on both the controversial and the frivolous. Therefore Alcott, in his lectures and "conversations" delivered all over the new "Northwest," as far even as Michigan, avoided vegetarianism which he practiced, slavery which he deplored and temperance which he approved. He also neglected to mention several of his alarming innovations in New England schools.

Among these were the facts that as a teacher Alcott had spared the rod to a point that shocked stern pedagogues, had introduced the "honor system" of discipline, experimented with organized play, started a parent-teacher club, even tried to educate white and Negro children in the same class. Neither did he discuss from the platform his ideas on agriculture, to which he clung stubbornly, despite the fact that his failure as a farmer had been spectacular. Sympathy for dumb beasts had caused him to substitute manpower for horses in the fields; for reasons which he never quite made clear, he also refused to use manure as a fertilizer. He raised only "aspiring vegetables" which grew upward, eschewing the lowly onion and potato, that lived in darkness under the ground. All these ideas he believed in enough to fight for them in New England, but not enough to discuss them in the middle west.

Carlyle, after meeting Alcott, wrote to Emerson of "the good Alcott, with his long, lean face and figure, his gray, worn temples and mild, radiant eyes; all bent on saving the world by return to acorns and the golden age . . . a venerable Don Quixote, whom nobody can laugh at without loving."

But there was no Don Quixote jousting in Alcott's lecture titles; in Ohio he talked safely about *Friendship, The Family, Social Life, New England Authors,* and *Health and Beauty.* In each, no doubt, he stood resolutely on the side of the angels.

Fluent Henry Ward Beecher, who at home could shake Brooklyn's pious foundations with scholarly or moral contention, in Ohio lectures, between 1855 and 1862, also confined his discourses to *Patriotism, Beauty, Social Manners, Table Talk* and *Immortality.* For each of these he received a staggering sum ranging from $50 to $150, and some of his listeners suspected that he had talked just for the money there was in it.

Beecher was not a stranger to western country. Born in Massachusetts —younger brother of Harriet Beecher Stowe of *Uncle Tom's Cabin* fame —he was graduated first from Amherst, then from an Ohio seminary. His first charge, in 1837, at the Ohio river port of Lawrenceburg, Indiana, was a struggling Presbyterian congregation of nineteen women and one man. Even then the ladies liked Henry Ward Beecher! Lawrenceburg today has slight interest in remembering him; it is too busy turning out millions of gallons of Seagram's Seven Crown Whiskey to bother its head about a struggling preacher—and a "dry" at that—who lived there more than a century ago.

From that first struggling church Beecher, still a Presbyterian, moved to Indianapolis. Here, with patches on his homespun pants, he joined the volunteer firemen. Here, too, began his reputation as a lecturer, and he was in demand throughout Indiana with his discourses on *Industry and Idleness, Gamblers and Gambling,* or *The Twelve Causes of Dishonesty.*

At Indianapolis the young man developed his talents as a showman-

preacher. Later, in Brooklyn, after he had shifted from the Presbyterian
to the Congregational faith, he would use this showmanship to lure 2500
persons into Plymouth Church each Sabbath morning. He was of less
than medium height, of more than medium girth, with a ruddy face and
long hair that hung over his shoulders, yet according to all reports, he
was "dramatic." For one thing, he stood not in a pulpit, but on a platform
in the semicircular hall, and shifted rapidly to face first one part of his
audience, then another. Not only his delivery, but his subject matter was
exciting, and New York newspapers sent reporters across the East River
on the ferry to keep the public informed on what Clergyman Beecher was
saying. Among other things he preached in favor of woman suffrage, advised disobedience of the fugitive slave law, and railed at gamblers. Several
Sundays this fervent anti-slavery orator engaged handsome young Negro
women to cringe in chains on the platform, below a box that represented
an auction block, while he went through the spectacle of a slave auction.

After eight crowded years, Beecher returned to the middle west for a
series of lectures. Even out here he was famous now, and among the friends
who had helped make him so was Oliver Wendell Holmes, with a limerick
that all America recited:

> "The Reverend Henry Ward Beecher
> "Called a hen a most elegant creature.
> "The hen, pleased with that,
> "Laid an egg in his hat . . .
> "And thus did the hen reward Beecher."

In 1855 when Beecher took to the road on his second lecture series, another Brooklynite travelled the same territory with a livelier subject. Phineas
Barnum was everything that Beecher was not and, undoubtedly to the
churchman's chagrin, Ohioans welcomed him with enthusiasm. Barnum,
reared in a Connecticut inn, not in the Beecher family's Puritan atmosphere,
was manager of Scudder's fantastic American Museum in New York. His
dabbling in lotteries, his delight in hoaxes, his exploitation of colored
Joyce Heath—who, when she died, was more nearly eighty years old than
Barnum's advertised one hundred and sixty—were already in the public
record.

Barnum had presented Midget "General Tom Thumb." Songster Jenny
Lind's 1850 concert tour had been under this showman's spectacular direction. Like Beecher, he offered Cincinnati a speech on philosophy. But
his was *The Philosophy of Humbug,* in which realm he was already known
as "The Prince."

Beecher had annoyed the Ohio public by arriving as a lecturer under
the auspices of an agent, a Chicagoan named Wells. Enraged local associations, accustomed to monopolizing the field, had started a newspaper
campaign against him. Agent Wells demanded $125 for one evening. Cin-

cinnati, Cleveland and Columbus boycotted the series, with only a handful of the faithful turning out to hear the idol of the east, and Beecher wrote letters to the newspapers defending the use of a lecture agent.

The next year, unencumbered by the grasping Mr. Wells and once again handling his own bookings, Beecher returned and all seemed forgiven. He talked one night to twenty-three hundred persons who jammed an auditorium and sent away disappointed hundreds who could not get through the doors. His subject was the old standby, Patriotism.

Another lecturer who remained extremely popular for a long period was globe-trotting Bayard Taylor. He was twenty-eight years old when he first set out on the Lyceum road, but he had more experiences to talk about than most men twice his age. In the inky tradition of so many lecturers, he had begun life as a printer's devil, but at nineteen already had a book of verse to his credit. By the time he was twenty-one he had covered Britain, France, Italy and Germany, most of the way afoot, on a journey of two years that cost him five hundred dollars. He made more than that from his travel articles in the New York *Tribune* and the Philadelphia *Saturday Evening Post,* then collected the material in a book that sold well.

At age twenty-four Taylor was on his way again, this time crossing America ahead of the railroads and, after filling many notebooks in the California gold camps, he returned to New York by way of Mexico. His volume based on this experience, entitled *El Dorado; or, Adventures in the Path of Empire,* sold ten thousand copies in America, three times as many in Britain. Also, from the trip he brought back many soft Spanish phrases for use in later verse, and some rollicking ballads of the gold camps.

Without tarrying long enough to see the new book, the young man crossed the seas and began working his way up the Nile and into central Africa: object, travel literature. He was twenty-seven when he sailed from Egypt for Calcutta. After a brief sojourn in China, where he scribbled notes endlessly, he fell in with Commodore Matthew Perry, who was about to open the door to Japan. Naturally Taylor went along.

Arriving home at Christmas, 1853, with two more books and sheaves of new verses ready for the printer, the traveller set out at once on fifteen years of lecturing, in which time he gave eighty-five talks in Ohio alone, several thousand others all the way from Maine to Wisconsin and the Carolinas. Between tours he found energy to accept several diplomatic posts, each of brief duration, which permitted him to add Russia to his far-flung subject matter and the River Neva to his poetry.

On Taylor's lecture tours, in which he discussed *The Arabs, Japan, India, Moscow* and *The Philosophy of Travel,* he was described in the newspapers as "handsome, six-feet, four-inches tall, with ruddy complexion and bright blue eyes." Women adored him.

Like Barnum's, Taylor's style was informal; "easy and gentlemanly," a newspaper wrote, "a man of and from the people who put on no airs." His travel talks eventually gave way to more abstract discussion of American society.

In contrast to its hat-tossing reception of Taylor, audiences in the midwest welcomed Dr. Oliver Wendell Holmes with restrained enthusiasm. Despite his humorous writings, the people did not find him witty on the platform.

Perhaps at the moment the good doctor did not feel witty. He followed the practice of delivering several lectures in succession; after all, travel to this remote area was not too easy in 1855, and if one jounced and rolled all the way on a sooty train from the "Hub of the Universe," as Dr. Holmes had christened Boston, it should be for more than one hour's appearance.

Humorists of the era were a race apart. Mark Twain, having bought his first success with five free tickets, was able to maintain it by entirely orthodox means. He had reversed the trend. Instead of coming from the east, he travelled across country toward it. Handsome, urbane, even better dressed than the best-dressed-man-in-town—he introduced the cream-colored silk formal evening suit—Twain poked fun at himself and at the foibles of the human race in general. But he pushed home his punch lines with a sabre, rather than with the dull barnyard shovel employed by many well-paid humorists of the period.

Usually humorists had made their reputations with the printed, misspelled word. The more exaggerated the misspelling, the more devastatingly funny it was considered. This type of humor, naturally, was hard to translate from the printed page to the lecture hall. So comedians on the platform substituted gross mispronunciation and backwoods Americanisms. They posed as midwestern villagers or New England farmers, shrewd and iconoclastic, but with verbal hayseed in their hair.

Except for Mark Twain, the most successful dispenser of platform humor in the decades following the Civil War was Henry Wheeler Shaw, who called himself "Josh Billings." His big, far-reaching voice and New England country twang were come by honestly, for in his younger years he had been an auctioneer in Lanesborough, Massachusetts. His *Essa on a Muel,* published in 1860 in *The New York Weekly,* was widely quoted and gave him some celebrity along the Atlantic seaboard. When he first wrote it, he spelled the words properly—and no one read it. But "mule" became "muel" in the second edition and sales zoomed. Later he recited the "essa" on the lecture platform, together with *What I Kno about Hotels* and *The Pensive Cockroach,* which might have been grandfather to the "archy" of Don Marquis.

Billings' *Farmers Allminax* were full of his sound, unsoundly spelled philosophy. "Most people," he wrote, "repent ov their sins bi thanking God they aint so wicked as their nabors."

There was a great deal of deep discussion of "manifest destiny" among politicians at the time, to the confusion of most of the people. So Billings wrote a piece about it, calling it "the science ov going tew bust, or enny other place, before you git thare." He also gave it as his considered opinion that "manifest destiny . . . is like the number ov rings on the rakoon's tale, ov no great consequense only for ornament."

Another humorist of the era was New York-born David Ross Locke, a printer and editor who, in 1860, became a columnist on the *Toledo Blade*. There he invented an ignorant, bigoted, letter-writing character whom he called "Rev. Petroleum Vesuvius Nasby, Confident of President Andrew Jackson," and it was as "Nasby" that Locke became famous on the platform. Like Josh Billings, his outrageous spelling tickled the nation's fancy. One book, *Swingin' Round the Cirkle,* became a best seller.

Nasby's humor had a ragged and painful cutting edge and he used it mercilessly in attacks on slavery and on the Democratic party. According to the *Nation,* "His humor, apart from the Democracy, is not remarkable . . . and sometimes coarse."

Another humorist in the Josh Billings-Petroleum Nasby tradition was Charles Farrar Browne, famous as "Artemus Ward." Born in Maine, he had gone to work at thirteen as a printer's devil in New Hampshire, then followed his trade through a dozen cities until, like so many Lyceum favorites, he settled in Ohio.

Artemus Ward not only went to work young, became famous young, but he died young. He had spent four years on the platform and had written five books, when "consumption" took him off in 1867, at the age of thirty-three. He had had fun, burning uncounted candles at both ends. Inspired misspellings marked his writings, and he even applied it to his original name, adding the final "e" to plain "Brown," he once explained, "as an afterthought." On the platform he was gawky and ungainly, and he delivered his funniest lines with a blank expression and a quiet, almost hesitant style that enriched their humor.

One of Artemus Ward's best-remembered remarks was that "Old George Washington's fort was not to hev eny public man of the present day resemble him to eny alarmin extent." Writing from "Pitsburg," in 1858, to the "Cleeveland Plane Deeler," he offered to take "a show" to the city beside Lake Erie. His display consisted of "a Calforny Bare two snakes tame foxies & also wax works my wax works is hard to beat, all say they is life and nateral curiosities among my wax works is Our Saveyer Gen taylor and Docktor Webster in the ackt of killing Parkman."

That was funny enough to make Artemus Ward famous a hundred years ago.

Meanwhile, throughout the south, religious camp meetings were taking the place of the humorous fellows and the staid lecturers in the north. The man who, more than any other, was responsible for these hallelujah gatherings was a Connecticut zealot named Lorenzo Dow, who began his

Redpath & Fall
Feb 7ᵗʰ 1873

I want the night of
Feb 22ᵈ to use for a
picnic purpose. = Is there
any reason why I cant
have _her_ =

Josh

P.S

Dont put me
down for any more
work that is not near
home, I ame done up =
Josh

Facsimile of a letter from Josh Billings to Redpath.

preaching career in 1794 at the age of seventeen. He always put on a good show under the stars and as many folk came to hear him tear into the Pope as came to get their souls saved.

Dow was first a Methodist preacher, but the church suspended him after three months and he became a non-denominational shouting evangelist. He preached the first Protestant sermon ever heard in Alabama and spread the Gospel, as he interpreted it, all the way from the Carolinas—where he was convicted of libel—to Tennessee. When he was twenty-one, he went to Ireland "to save it from Catholicism," but after eighteen months he retired in disorder toward home.

Before long the itinerant Dow attacked Methodism, which he found "tainted with Popery"; then, giving up the camp meeting platform, he retired to New England, where he invented a nostrum which he insisted would "cure biliousness." In Lorenzo Dow the outdoor pulpit and the medicine show walked hand in hand. He made some converts, but his oratorical and theological excesses also tickled the American funny bone.

The people, like Mark Twain's drunken stranger, wanted to laugh. They also wanted to be uplifted and edified. Lyceum managers tried desperately to supply both needs. In the end, the preachers and poets lectured in churches, "atheneums" and libraries, while the humorists often were relegated to the less refined "opera house" or village hall.

The twentieth century was four years old, and Mark Twain was once more almost penniless, when comedy and culture finally met on equal terms. To achieve this, a showman named Keith Vawter, like Twain a product of the middle west, put the two forms of entertainment on the same platform in a travelling tent. He married the respectability of the Lyceum to the spangles of the stage, naming the union "Chautauqua" after an institution established permanently on Chautauqua Lake, New York.

For a quarter century thereafter, Chautauqua and Lyceum covered the same geographical area, fed on the same deep passion for uplift, shared the same taboos, used the same talent, often were operated by the same men. Chautauqua, as Vawter and his followers developed it, was Lyceum cavorting in the fields, minus its long winter underwear. In Chautauqua the pulpit was out of sight, though never out of mind.

If Lyceum chose to be amusing, it did so with scrupulous decorum. It laughed, but never boisterously. Chautauqua, on the contrary, was show business, genteel, prudent, more respectable than Phineas T. Barnum, but show business just the same. Lyceum, appearing in church, school and library, with an occasional side trip to the Odd Fellows Hall, used a platform. Chautauqua boldly set up a stage. There was a subtle difference.

Chautauqua tents rolled back and forth and up and down America for nearly thirty years. Pitched in pastures, school yards and courthouse squares, they offered not only the soaring oratory of a William Jennings Bryan, but also music, drama, magic, art lessons, cooking classes, low comedy and high-minded debates. Millions of eager listeners under the "big top" canvas, hot with summer's sun, perspired freely and soaked up both erudition and amusement.

Famous men and women, statesmen and politicians, explorers and adventurers, actors and opera stars, heroes and an occasional well-publicized heel, each season covered the long summer trail. A few of them still hailed from New England, but a Beacon Hill background no longer assured a program spot.

"Chautauqua week," in hundreds of communities, became the most important five or six or seven days in the whole year. "The most American thing in America," Theodore Roosevelt called it, a statement that few tried to challenge in the first quarter of the century.

Those persons old enough to remember it think fondly of the frosting on this Chautauqua cake and forget the intellectual calories underneath. They remember the handsome Singing Hussars, the *Mikado* opera companies, the magician's white rabbits or the cute little number with blond curls singing *Tipperary,* and forget the debates, the arguments over legislation.

Men talked freely from this new, informal platform. Taboos that had made the nineteenth-century Emersons and Alcotts stick to ringing praise of "Beauty" and "Kindness" were abandoned. To be sure, a few honeyvoiced speakers clung to the inspirational line. Another New Englander, Judge George Alden, still urged a man "to know himself"; Robert Parker Miles pleaded for man "to let his light shine." In and out of Congress, oratory was still the favorite form of literature, but it was a new kind. A new kind of speaker planted his feet firmly on the platform in the tent— and said exactly what he believed. Independent thinkers like Catholic Bishop John Ireland of Minnesota did not dodge the subject of temperance as Yankee Alcott had felt compelled to do. Sponsors of daring ideas uttered them freely and all America went home to think. The Edward Amherst Otts and the Judge Ben Lindseys discussed marriage, the Harvey Wileys dared demand pure food, "Fighting Bob" LaFollette attacked "Special Privilege" and Senator Albert Cummins the railroads. Inside the big brown tents, millions of Americans first heard impassioned pleas for a Federal income tax, slum clearance, free schoolbooks, world disarmament.

Travelling Chautauqua, which took to the road in 1904, had a glamorous and footloose life. It died in 1932 under the hit-and-run wheels of a Model-A Ford on its way to the movies on a new paved road. Radio swept it into the ditch, and the Wall Street crash and the subsequent depression gave it the *coup de grâce.*

It is important to realize that Chautauqua tents went up at that moment in history precisely half way between Pickett's cavalry charge at Gettysburg and the bomb run over Hiroshima. The frontier had moved; railroads spanned the continent. But there still remained in the southwest a few blank spaces on the maps. Horsepower still meant horses. The America that watched the first Chautauqua tent rise in an Iowa meadow in 1904 and the America that saw the last tent come down, twenty-nine years later in a little Illinois village, were separated by a period that marked swift changes in a people's thinking, in concepts of both humor and morality, in public and private manners.

Early Lyceum had endured a Civil War; tent Chautauqua survived the Argonne and Belleau Wood. The movement had reached from T.R. to F.D.R., from the surrey with a fringe on top to a speedometer that could register seventy miles an hour. In that fraction of history the nation had experimented nobly with prohibition and made education universal, as the old Lyceums had dreamed it should be. It had wrapped radio bands around the continent, taken to the skies in airplanes, fallen madly in love with Mary Pickford, and as quickly forgotten her.

Tornadoes wrecked Chautauqua tents. In Kansas, one summer, winds blew pianos off the stage. Artists dodged falling tent poles. The lights went out. Floods washed away bridges the troupes were trying to cross to reach the next town by curtaintime. Cows bellowed and freight trains hooted in the midst of soprano solos. Backers lost their shirts and railroads lost tents and stage sets.

But the show went on. . . .

K. D.

Acknowledgments

The authors are particularly indebted for assistance to Carl E. Backman and Miss Amy M. Weiskopf of the Chicago office of the Redpath Bureau; to former circuit owners Crawford A. Peffer, Charles F. Horner, Louis J. Alber and Benjamin Franklin; to Librarians Dorothy Higbie of Cornell College, Clyde C. Walton, Jr. of the University of Iowa, Opal Carr of the University of Oklahoma, Stanley Pergellis of the Newberry, Chicago; and the staffs of the Library of the University of Arizona, of the Public Library of Traverse City, Michigan, and the Reader's Digest Research Department, and to Professor Albert T. Cordray of Michigan State College.

Former Chautauqua talent who generously contributed many facts include William Rainey Bennett, Ailene Pettit Collmer, Dean Jagger, Blanche Pinkerton Jones and the late Hilton Ira Jones, Everett C. Kemp, Fay Pettit Maddy, Caroline McCartney, Magdalen Massmann, Jess Pugh, Clyde Tull, Jewell Bothwell Tull, and William W. Weatherwax.

Thanks go also to many former Chautauqua staffers, including Don Alford, Oscar Allanson, Oliver E. Behymer, O. O. Bottorff, Herbert Boughey, Richard R. Eddy, Earl H. Gammons, Rall I. Grigsby, the late Hugh T. Gruell, Raymond Harrington, Charles Hedges, William Knox, C. B. McIntyre, Joseph Meade, H. Z. Musselman, Hugh Orchard, Paul K. Scott, Richard A. Taylor, H. R. Templeton, Miss Jean Thompson.

Others who assisted include Editors J. H. Smith of Pulaski, Tennessee and A. W. Hamblin of Bedford, Iowa, J. Elder Blackledge of Indianapolis, Mrs. Arthur Esgate of Washington, D.C., Mrs. Mathilda Anderson, Mrs. Carl Nelson and Fred Send of Suttons Bay, Michigan.

H. P. H. AND K. D.

Contents

List of Illustrations

Illustrations inserted between pages 130 and 131:

Bishop John H. Vincent

James Redpath

President Woodrow Wilson and William Jennings Bryan

William Jennings Bryan arrives at a Chautauqua stopover

Edgar Bergen in his Chautauqua days

The White Hussars

Typical audience outside the tent

Season-ticket holders at Marengo, Illinois

A tent-Chautauqua audience

A tent on the circuit

A Chautauqua boosters parade

Ladies Harp Ensemble

Daddy Groebecker's Swiss Yodelers

CULTURE
UNDER CANVAS

Strike Up the Band

1

The Community Band was playing on the depot platform, waiting for the train. The Big Chautauqua Special, bringing crowds from Northport, Omena and Peshawbetown, was due at seven o'clock. Band Leader Theodore Esch pulled out his big watch and looked at the time uneasily. Seven P.M. exactly, and no sight nor sound of the train.

His men were beginning to be uncomfortable in their Sunday shoes. For thirty minutes they had been waiting in a stiff half circle, fifteen serious musicians in brand-new uniforms, blue coats with brass buttons and choker collars fastened tight around perspiring necks. Except for Jim Hogan, first trombone, every player was on hand. Hogan had got bad news this morning about his boy, in a base camp overseas just two weeks. He didn't feel like any skylarking tonight.

Everyone else did, though, everyone in town. Excitement had been mounting for a week and now that the big night actually was at hand, people were half wild. Even the air tingled; you could feel it. It made you want to sing, laugh, dance, slap your neighbor on the back, wave at your friends, cry "Hello, there! By gosh, this *is* something . . . nothing like it before in *this* town. . . ."

It was Tuesday evening, August 7, 1917, Chautauqua's opening night in the old lumber port of Suttons Bay, Michigan, and no ordinary Chautauqua, either. This was the ultimate, the last glittering word in exciting grandeur, the world-famous Redpath DeLuxe Seven Day Circuit, coming to Suttons Bay fresh from artistic and civic triumphs in the state capital at Lansing, before that in South Bend, Indianapolis, Louisville. Next week it would even open in Chicago, in Jackson Park, site of the '93 World's Fair. Suttons Bay . . . population 400 . . . was justly proud, every member of the local committee especially so. Proud, but a bit uneasy, too,

1

of course. Proud because this, by all odds, was the smallest community in which the great DeLuxe Circuit ever had hoisted its big tent. Uneasy because so many unexpected things could pop up to mar what should be a glorious week.

Within the hour, over at the Hose House, committeemen had held a last-minute meeting. They could think of nothing else to do. Everything was as ready as it ever could be. And with this big, expectant crowd . . . they tried to count it. Scores of single admissions were milling here near the station. The Committee had guaranteed a fat $2000 ticket sale out of their own pockets and several hundred singles tonight at fifty cents each would help. Of course they had sold the season tickets. That had been easy, even six hundred at two dollars and a half each, after the advance copies of the program arrived. First-night attraction was the "world-famous Bohemian orchestra" and smart local merchants were quick to take advantage of that happy fact. A world-famous Bohemian orchestra!

So up to the Bohemian Hills men had gone, by twos and threes, pockets full of the elegant pasteboards, to extol in a hundred parlors the glories of the coming show. Carl Lund, the cobbler, and Barber Fred Send had been most successful; if they skirted close to the edge of truth with their description of an orchestra full of "Bohemians fresh from Bohemia," it was certainly in a good cause. Those Bohemian farmers, most of them with eighty acres and big families and solid bank accounts, had not been too hard to sell on the proposition that it would be a disgrace to the memory of the old country to leave anybody in the family at home. One man on the Gills Pier road, sampling his black cherry wine when Lund arrived, felt so mellow and nostalgic that he shelled out $62.50 for twenty-five tickets. . . . "Bohemians should stick together." There had been many other incidents to enliven that ticket campaign. The Redpath Chautauqua office in Chicago had sent up a most personable young lady to help with the sale. Her name was Springsted, and it had been the town's most eligible bachelor, hypnotized by her charm and beauty, who inadvertently introduced her at the pep meeting as "Miss Bedstead."

Band Leader Esch looked again at his watch. Five minutes past seven.

The special train was still four miles from town, thumping southward through the long, soft Michigan twilight. Its single day coach and the caboose were jammed. People sat three to a double seat or stood swaying in the aisles, big families with wide-awake babies, moon-eyed couples, gay young blades, old folks, grinning high-school kids. There were lumbermen, fishermen, storekeepers, farmers, teachers; Norwegians and Swedes and Bohemians, a few Frenchies and Chippeway Indians—two hundred in all.

Only the Indians sat silent. Everyone else was singing. The car windows were opened wide and happy voices floated out past the new cherry orchards and across the Michigan countryside, while the flat wheels of the day coach ticked away like a giant metronome.

"K-k-k-katie, beautiful Katie,
"You're the only g-g-g-girl that I adore. . . ." [1]

The festive spirit of the occasion touched even Conductor Charley Decker, a man not easily stirred out of his immense, square-jawed dignity. To his surprise he found himself singing lustily along with the rest and up in the locomotive, Engineer Lee Mann threw frugality to the winds and wasted steam joyously, tooting the throaty whistle.

He tooted more loudly and long at the county road north of town. The crowd waiting at the Suttons Bay depot heard, this time, and began to cheer. In their excitement they even mauled up one of the committee members, but he didn't mind. Why should he? The crowd was good-natured. And getting bigger. Editor K. Gus Smarey of the *Provemont Courier,* who had hitched a five-mile ride to be on hand, vowed that this was the greatest, happiest, finest-looking lot of people ever collected in the whole county. They had poured in all day, sweltering hot though it had been, home folk and resorters from all over the area arriving in wagons, cars, spanking new Maxwells, Reos and Model-T Fords, even one old White Steamer manned by a Frenchie from over Provemont way. Farmers from as far as Good Harbor and Cedar City had driven in long before noon, with tents and cooking gear piled in their buckboards, and were camping along the bay shore. There wasn't an empty bed in the town and the livery barn had been doing a rushing business filling straw ticks.

The town looked fine, too. It still was light enough for visitors to see how really pretty Main Street was, with everything polished and shined up and strings of Chautauqua pennants stretched across the road. Up and down the entire two blocks from Lars Sogge's grocery to Nixie Steimel's Suttons Bay House Hotel, merchants had draped their stores with bunting and had not been stingy about it either; and along the walks on both sides of the street the G.A.R. and the Spanish-American vets had set up new poles with brand-new American flags. Their color still showed even now in the twilight; so did the classy red and green felt hats that the young ladies were wearing, with the words "Redpath Chautauqua" printed on them . . . those Chautauqua folks certainly could think of everything!

George Smeltzer, the village drayman, who yesterday had hauled the heavy tent from the depot to the Chautauqua grounds, had dressed up his old gray horse in a gorgeous green-and-white cotton blanket with the word "Redpath" painted on it and tonight he still found it necessary to clop-clop busily up and down the street. Today George had hauled the piano and the xylophone from the noon train and reported later that the xylophone fellow was mighty pleased with the careful way George handled his precious instrument.

The orchestra and most of the artists had arrived earlier on the noon

[1] *K-k-k-katy* by Geoffrey O'Hara. Copyright 1918/Copyright Renewal 1945, Leo Feist, Inc. Used by special permission Copyright Proprietor.

train. A reception committee, headed by Township Supervisor Oliver Hanson and Village President Ernest Hughes, had welcomed the group at the depot. Mr. Hughes, the popular undertaker, was a man who knew human nature, and he said that they all, four men and three women, seemed like very nice people. He did think, though, that Mr. Giuseppi Bartolotta, the tenor soloist, looked more like an Italian than a Bohemian, in spite of the name "World Famous Bohemian Orchestra."

At noon also, there had been a crowd here at the track and John Ott, the Maxwell dealer, had certainly put one over on the Dodge agent, Frank Clark. Ott turned up in a shiny new Maxwell touring car with its top strapped down and Chautauqua pennants floating out behind, and before Clark knew what was going on, all the famous artists rode off in the Maxwell to the houses where they were to be entertained.

Ten minutes past seven. In exactly thirty-five minutes the curtain would open in the tent on the vacant lot on the nameless "back street" behind Gronseth's shoe store. It had gone up once already. There had been a short musical program this afternoon and an entertainment for the kids. The heroic woman who called herself the "Story-Hour Girl" had begun her frantic task of training all the children for an evening performance of the "Mother Goose Festival" later in the week. But tonight was the *real* beginning.

Leader Esch lifted his silver cornet. Here came the train. The slow sweet notes of *A Long, Long Trail* swelled out against the noise of the engine. Visitors piled off front and back platforms, on both sides of the track. They were in a hurry, but two hundred is a big crowd of people and it took time to unload. Charley Decker helped the last woman off carefully, old Mrs. Dunlap with her two canes. She was eighty-five if a day, but she had taught music forty years and she wouldn't miss a feast like this for the risk of a dozen broken hips. She had with her two great-grandchildren, girls in sashes and plenty of starch, who were supposed to give her a hand but who were so goggle-eyed at the Community Band that they forgot great-grandmother.

The band had broken circle and lined up four abreast. The snare drummer gave a couple of long rolls and *The National Emblem* filled the air and bounced back in a thrilling echo from Larson's Point across the bay. At the first blast, half a dozen farmers had to leap down from their wagons and hold their horses' heads. The crowd shied off for a moment, then straightened out and followed the band, troops of bare-footed boys in the lead.

Up at the Chautauqua grounds a long line stretched out at the box office. Superintendent and crew boys, sizing it, already had rolled up the canvas walls of the tent and put plank benches around the outside, enough for four hundred extra persons. The planks had come on loan from Mr. Chadsey's lumber yard and the superintendent had agreed generously to announce that fact when he addressed the crowd.

The Community Band halted in a circle in the road before the tent. The last two numbers were to be *Put on Your Old Gray Bonnet* and *I Want a Girl* and the men certainly gave everything they had, playing them. People cheered and again wiped their faces beaded with perspiration from walking so fast and funnelled excitedly into the gate. It might be even hotter inside the tent, but who cared? There was no delay. As soon as every seat was taken, all the elegant new folding chairs as well as the planks, the stage lights flashed on and the curtain opened on the handsome young Redpath superintendent standing there in fresh white duck pants and blue coat, smiling and showing all his teeth.

Folks said afterward that the fellow certainly knew how to talk. He began by saying that Suttons Bay was the greatest little town in the world; everybody knew that, why otherwise had the Redpath Seven Day DeLuxe Circuit stopped here? Then he went on to tell enthusiastically about all the wonderful attractions which would fill the big stage the coming seven joyful afternoons and seven gala nights. A few choice season tickets might still be for sale, he added. Just a few. Then he introduced the crew boys, except the one sitting on a paper sack full of cash in the box office, and explained that these young men were well-known college athletes working to make money for next year's school. When he suggested that they deserved a hand, the audience responded loudly.

Now the famous Bohemian orchestra took its place on the stage. Joseph Mach, the polite young director who also played the violin, had his three young ladies take a bow first . . . they were the cellist, violinist, and the pretty one at the piano. Then the clarinetist had a turn and James Hurt, an artist with the xylophone, who could play the drums, too. You could hear the old farmer from Gills Pier road, who had bought the twenty-five tickets, clapping harder than anybody else for the three young ladies. This, because they were wearing real Bohemian costumes with a lavish lot of color and plenty of embroidery on their aprons and caps, in contrast to the men in sober black tail coats and white ties.

Mr. Bartolotta, the tenor, a handsome fellow with a big, dark mustache, announced his own numbers. It was true, he had an accent that certainly wasn't Bohemian, just as Undertaker Hughes had thought. A Neapolitan, somebody else said he was, but it didn't really matter after the crowd once heard him sing *Silver Threads Among the Gold*. "Soul feeling," the newspaper described it next day. He had a few numbers with foreign names, but chiefly good American songs like *The End of a Perfect Day* and *Somewhere a Voice Is Calling*.

The orchestra opened with *Hungarian Rhapsody*. Then it played *Water Lilies* by St. Clair, a Beethoven minuet which old Mrs. Dunlap applauded for all she was worth by knocking her canes together, and then a Kela Bela waltz and other numbers which the Bohemian audience liked. For his own solo Mr. Mach offered Kreisler, but the high point of the evening was Mr.

Hurt's athletic rendition of *Finniculi, Finnicula* on the xylophone, "accompanied by the entire orchestra." He must have been a tired man that night, for the crowd liked it so much that he generously repeated it three times.

The evening's speaker was the Reverend Martin D. Hardin of Chicago. People had read about him in the advertising folders and so some of them, particularly the young folks, were a little disappointed in his looks. He had been billed as "a man looking for peace with a gun in his hand," and he not only had no gun but he was quite mild in expression. His subject was *America and the World of Tomorrow*. It was a deadly serious speech and the platform superintendent, introducing him, said that William Jennings Bryan had once called it "the greatest appeal to the Christian conscience made during this world crisis." The audience agreed that it was quite a speech and not *very* much too long.

Motion pictures of Yellowstone Park finished the evening. When the crowd left the tent, people were saying that the following six nights would have to be mighty choice to equal this opening performance.

They *were* choice, too. The Beulah Buck Ladies Quartet dressed in colonial costume, a Spanish cellist, and the Oratorio Artists all were on hand for one night each. The Artists were a mixed quartet out of New York. Its baritone, a pleasant-looking young man named Frederick Wheeler, had a solid chin, big hands, a pearl in his black necktie and an idea that this crowd would like the *Road to Mandalay,* and he wasn't wrong. The second evening Harry L. Fogelman of New York—his friends called him "Gattling Gun Fogelman" because, they said, he could deliver three hundred words a minute—talked on *An Analysis of Success and Failure.* Mr. Fogelman, the leaping, athletic type, also was known as "the Billy Sunday of Business," and he told the Suttons Bay merchants that he had small sympathy for those unpleasant muckrakers who cast aspersions on captains of industry.

Of course, the afternoon crowds were not so large, women for the most part, who had to hurry when the program ended to get home and fix supper and be back on time for the evening performance. One of the afternoon speakers was George L. McNutt, "the Dinner Pail Man," with a lot of good, sensible ideas on *How to Meet the High Cost of Living.* Another was the Reverend B. F. McDonald of Newark, Ohio. His title was *Moonshine,* and some people thought he didn't make it too clear as to what kind he was talking about.

Every afternoon there was a half hour of community singing, led by another acrobat, this one a former clergyman, who also helped the Story-Hour Girl ride herd on her young charges in the forenoons. Because the nation was at war, the songs for the most part were martial, like *Maryland, My Maryland* and *Hail, Columbia,* but every day when the leader asked the audience what it wanted, the same bass voice from somewhere down in front demanded *Rocked in the Cradle of the Deep.* Folks could sing it pretty well before the week was over.

As the days went on the programs became even better. The fourth night opened with the Spanish cellist, followed by beautiful and aristocratic Princess Watahwaso. She was a full-blooded Penobscot Indian from Maine, "flower of one of the last pure Indian families," the program said. She sang tribal songs, told tribal legends, and danced in tribal costumes, including a feathered war bonnet, to the astonishment of the Chippeways from Peshawbetown, who always sat huddled together in the rear of the tent. Suttons Bay remembers the Princess to this day as a charming, gifted young lady. "Bright Star" her name meant. Mrs. Carl Petersen, at whose house she was entertained, says she never had a more appreciative house guest.

As if two attractions were not enough for one evening, Fräulein Marie Mayer of Oberammergau, Germany, a woman in her upper forties, lectured next on the *Passion Play,* in which she once had taken the part of Mary Magdalene. It seems that the Redpath management had felt some worry about whether or not this *fräulein* would appear. Even if she was a first cousin of Anton Lang, the *Christus,* America was at war with Germany. But she proved to the satisfaction of Washington that she hated Kaiser Wilhelm, so here she was.

There was no Sunday evening performance, which was just as well, for people and artists needed a day of rest. Saturday night the crowd had overflowed the tent to hear Gilbert and Sullivan's *Mikado,* with "an all-star New York cast of thirty, including the orchestra." Arthur Aldrich, who actually had played on Broadway, took the part of Nanki Pooh, and single admissions went up to seventy-five cents.

This was a big night for everybody, particularly for Lars Sogge's daughter. The Sogge house stood across the street from the Chautauqua grounds and his daughter, Rose, a musician of great talent everybody knew, was very ill. Hearing of her desire to see the play, the Redpath superintendent kindly took down the canvas wall opposite the house and Miss Rose watched and listened from her bed by the window. It was a memorable night, too, for Mrs. Charley Abbott of Detroit, whose husband owned the power plant that supplied the county with intermittent current. She lost the big diamond out of her engagement ring somewhere in the tent and superintendent and crew helped hunt it, unsuccessfully, until dawn. No one ever did find it, not even the small boys who scrounged through the grass all the next week; one reason, it had rained torrents Sunday night, almost in itself a catastrophe. Water poured down until the little creek meandering past the grounds overflowed and spread like a flood toward the tent. Crew boys at dawn had thrown up a low dike and, as the water ran off, spread straw so that not one lady at the next performance even soiled her best shoes.

Monday night's program opened with the *Mother Goose Festival,* in which platoons of local children took part. The crowd was immense, what with loyal uncles and aunts and cousins and grandparents and all the neighbors dutifully attending. They thought it splendid, even though the dark-haired young Story-Hour Girl sat down on the ground behind the stage when it was over and told the superintendent that she had passed the limit of human endurance.

A good, solid, "vital" lecture had been scheduled for that evening, too, by Congresswoman Jeannette Rankin of Montana, "subject to congressional duties." Congress was in emergency session so she did not appear. Some people thought it was just as well, for Suttons Bay was a patriotic village and had small sympathy for anyone who talked about peace at any price. Miss Rankin, a leading pacifist, had voted against war, and Spanish-American veterans in several cities had passed flag-draped resolutions against her. Instead of presenting the Congresswoman after the children's show, the superintendent ran off two special reels of moving pictures. The women were disappointed, even if the veterans were not.

There was no let down, however. The last night not only brought the special train from the north again, but a dozen chartered boats from Traverse City, sixteen miles up the bay. Again tickets were seventy-five cents for this program, and cheap enough, too, to hear the great Giuseppe Creatore in person directing his world-famous band. No one argued Creatore's nationality, nor his musicianship. A swarthy man with a headful of upstanding black hair and a mustache of heroic proportions, he seemed to pull magic sounds out of his troupe by physical effort. No one else, not even the Bohemian xylophone player or Gattling Gun Fogelman, had half approached his energy. The red, white and blue folder claimed his direction was "cyclonic," which indeed was no exaggeration. He lunged and leaped. He swung his baton like a baseball bat, jabbed it like a javelin, sank almost to the floor as he pleaded for *andante tranquilino* effects. His men responded. The only rest they got all evening was when the Redpath superintendent stepped out to talk persuasively about next year's contract. For the final number the entire audience rose and, led by the sensational Creatore, sang *The Star Spangled Banner,* then applauded so wildly and so long that the conductor made his worn-out men play it over again.

Thus ended the visit of the great DeLuxe Circuit. If there had been a show the next day, people would have staggered back to hear it, but since this was the last, they just folded their souvenir programs carefully, nodded good nights and went home to bed. It would take weeks to digest all they had heard.

Most of the children had to be carried aboard the train back to Northport. There was no singing. Except for folks saying enviously that Suttons Bay certainly was to be congratulated for putting on such a glorious treat, there was little talk. The engineer blew his whistle only once for a grade crossing. Nearly everyone, even old Mrs. Dunlap, slept.

That was Suttons Bay. That was Chautauqua. That was small town America in 1917.

"Ladies and Gentlemen . . ."

2

I heard my first lecture, the first of ten thousand, in 1893 in the little opera house at Anita, in western Iowa, in the heart of that vast midwest area known later as "the Chautauqua belt." It was a snowy night. A dozen bright kerosene lamps lighted the room, smoking slightly as hanging lamps were wont to do, when a fat young man in a stylish Philadelphia suit bounced up to the platform and said, "Ladies and Gentlemen . . ."

His name was Ralph Bingham. He had hopped off the Rock Island local that afternoon, wearing fawn-colored gloves, a big fur collar on his coat and a pearl stickpin in his elegant flowered-silk tie. Everyone in Anita and the surrounding country who could scrape together the twenty-five-cents admission fee, in that year of panic, had crowded into the room. I had three nickels and a dime, so I was there. I had just turned fifteen.

Ralph Bingham was more than a lecturer. He was actor, humorist, musician, storyteller, philosopher, and gentleman. He played the piano and violin, sang, acted out amusing stories. He was droll, debonair, beaming, sparkling with good humor. He began his program that night and many nights thereafter with a gay song called *Ta-ra-ra Boom de-ay* and, off to that hilarious start, kept up the same pace for an hour and a half.

Ta-ra-ra Boom de-ay already had survived two seasons on Broadway. I don't remember the name of the musical show in which it first was sung, or who was the dashing lady in red who lifted her long skirts, daringly displayed her petticoats, and gave a can-can kick with every "boom." Of course, it was new to Iowa, and though there were no red skirts, Bingham kicked up his heels when he sang it and impressed and delighted all of us, in little Anita. In fact, the crowd enjoyed everything he did. Whether he winked, scowled, yawned, whistled or hummed, the people liked it; but they laughed hardest when he laughed, which was much of the time.

9

The first story was *Brother Jones' Sermon*. Bingham was a southerner, born in Richmond, Virginia. Probably half the stories of his long, successful platform career were pleasant tales of colored folk. "Darky" vernacular was popular in those days. There was no sting in its humor; to the people in my town it was simply the way some folks happened to talk, as a Swede "just over" from the old country or a Yankee peddler from down-east might "talk funny." The Victor Company later made records of this Bingham monologue, and of many Bingham acts, and all sold widely. They are typical of the kind of humor that drew uproarious laughter before the turn of the century.

"Brother Jones," as Bingham told it, took his text from "the 14th verse of the 14th chapter according to the gospel of etomology." It read: "And de Lord cured the multitude of divers diseases."

Bingham sat at the piano for most of the "sermon," strumming out chords as the spirit moved him, reciting some lines, sing-songing others:

"My beloved brethern and sistern, de Lor' cure de multitude of divers diseases! Does you all get dem words? . . . Let me 'lucidate . . . *divers diseases!* Does you notice? It don't say nothin' bout *plu*-ral-a-sis or '*nu*-mon'ya, nothin' 'bout jan-dice or yaller fever. Nothin' 'bout little ol' common mis'ries like m'laria, or *ty*-phoid, or chills an' fever. . . .

"An' de Lor' cure de multitude of divers diseases! Oh my chillen, my lambs, my pillars and bolsters o' de church! If you get de jan-dice, little ol' tube o' salve kin cure you . . . '*nu*-mon'ya, little ol' pill box kin cure you . . . n'ralgee, little ol' sawbones kin saw you . . . but oh-h, my brethern! If you once get de *divers,* unh-unh, you're gone! You're de dead cock in de pit!

"Nobody but de Lor' hisself kin cure de *divers!* Nobody but de Lor', my lambs . . . k'chew! . . . nobody but de Lor' hisself . . . k'chew! . . . k'chew!

"Brethern an' sistern, we will now take up a c'lection . . . K'chew! . . . an' disband de meetin', for some o' dem lowdown white trash sittin' back dere has done throwed red pepper on de stove . . . K'CHEW!"

Sneezing was a favorite expression of humor in the 90's and even much later. Jess Pugh, the entertainer, made a sneezing act famous in later Chautauqua. The people in Anita, Iowa, in 1893, laughed at Bingham's outburst just as hard as they were expected to and he beamed and went rollicking on to another story. This one, also a popular Victor record later, had to do with a possum hunt.

It seems that a crowd of men down south went possum hunting one night. "Grandpaw," who couldn't walk very well, wanted to go, too. His sons didn't like the idea but the old man insisted, so they finally carried him all the way in a chair. They treed a big bear, thinking they had a possum, and when the bear dropped to the ground, everybody ran, dogs, men, rabbits, everybody. Half way home one son suddenly slowed and said, "Why, gosh sakes, we done forgot gran'paw!"

"That's sure too bad," his brother said, keeping right on running. "We can't go back atter him, though. Poor gran'paw! The bear'll sure eat him up!"

But when they got home, there sat grandpaw rocking.

"How you get home, gran'paw?" they asked.

"Me?" grandpaw said. "I come home 'head o' the dogs."

People back east were singing *The Bowery* and *After the Ball* that first winter of Grover Cleveland's second administration. The mid-west had heard echoes of such light-hearted songs, but this was straight-laced, God-fearing Iowa. My parents kept a deck of playing cards in our parlor, even though we discreetly put them out of sight when certain neighbors came to call, but a "Bow'ry ablaze with lights" and dancers not starting home till "break o' morn" smacked in our part of the country of plain wickedness. Bingham, being smart, left out some New York songs. Instead he sang *Daisy Bell.*

Even in our small town the bicycle had arrived, presumably to stay. None of our neighbors wore black tights and none of them went scorching off cross-country on a "century-run," a hundred miles between dawn and dusk of a summer day. But occasionally when the roads were dry we had seen a crowd race by. There were plenty of bicycles in our village, nevertheless, and one young married couple had even skylarked around the preceding summer on a tandem. So everybody knew what this young man was singing about when he banged the keys and launched into:

> "Daisy, Daisy, give me your answer true!
> "I'm half crazy, all for the love of you!
> "It won't be a stylish marriage,
> "I can't afford a carriage,
> "But you'll look sweet
> "Upon the seat
> "Of a bicycle built for two!"

Bingham sang all the stanzas and repeated the chorus and men whistled and stomped their feet. Here was something brand-new and up-to-the-minute, their kind of song, American to the core and their kind of America. He had many more songs and more stories, the last one about a colored picnic. To get to the picnic spot, a crowd of young people rode on a train for the first time in their lives and it bounced, and to illustrate the bounce, fat Bingham hopped away from the piano and jumped up and down, singing, on the stage.

Here ended the comedy. He closed his program with a serious three-minute sermon, a practice he continued in one form or another all his long career as an entertainer. "The lecture platform stands for good clean fun," he said. "I've never yet used a story in Lyceum that I couldn't tell with my mother and sister in the audience. Dirt isn't funny.

"If anybody tells you young men that you can't have fun without indulging in dirt," he advised, "look him straight in the eye and tell him in plain English that he's a liar."

Looking back on it, that speech may sound a bit corny, but in the declining days of the 19th century it appeared to be plain Iowa horse sense. It was the brief echo of the New England sermon, whispering its way across the prairies. It was the spirit of Lyceum. It wasn't yet smart to be cynical in rural America. Everyone in our audience was impressed.

Bingham was in his early twenties. He had started on the platform as a six-year-old "boy wonder," touring the states and Canada under his father's management; at twelve he was a star in his own right and continued as a top-notch performer for thirty more years. He died in 1925. I little guessed that night in Anita, Iowa, that some day I would manage this intriguing man's Chautauqua and Lyceum bookings, sending him out to cast his hilarious spell on other country boys. I probably saw him perform hundreds of times, one of the last occasions at the Lamb's Club in New York. I still believe him to be one of the great entertainers of our era and his short speech that night in Anita set an antiseptic standard for Chautauqua programs with which I was concerned, from beginning to end. He was the proverbial "funny man" who could laugh and grow fat, always fastidiously dressed, with his hair parted in the middle and slicked down tight. He was a hero, particularly in Philadelphia, in later years. He made his home there between lecturing trips, and the sports writers used to say that the Phillies' ball team would wait to crack a three-bagger until beaming "Bing" came into the stand to take his seat.

Ralph Bingham charged the batteries of one boy's ambition, at least, and by the time I was nineteen years old I was principal of the Wiota, Iowa, school, just seven miles southwest of Anita. I stood six feet, two inches tall and was capable of keeping order in the classroom, if nothing else. But my most exciting duty for two years was to manage Wiota's winter Lyceum course.

Our committee had $150 to buy four glorious evenings of information and entertainment. That was a lot of money, with the price of Iowa corn in Chicago both of those winters averaging between nineteen and twenty-one cents a bushel. The speakers cost $25 to $35 each, depending on their fame, so before we signed the contracts we had to be sure we were right. Years afterward, when Chautauqua was big business and I was managing four lively circuits, if I found myself impatient with some small-town committee unable to make up its collective mind, I used to remember those Wiota days and that $150.

Of course Ralph Bingham was the star of the Wiota course and he beamed with the same good spirits and was as funny as ever. He was billed as an "entertainer" this time, not as a "lecturer," and therein lay a subtle difference. One could laugh freely at an "entertainer" and his nonsense without ever having to worry about laughing in the wrong place. In those days the more pompous speakers usually proclaimed somewhere in their perorations that "this is the message I bring," expecting everyone to listen solemnly and profit by it. Not Ralph Bingham. Instinct told him that even here on the half-empty prairies, a speaker had best poke fun at stuffiness. So he bounced up on the platform again, faced an already-smiling audience—about two hundred and fifty there must have been, most of them having driven ten miles in open sleighs—and announced in mock-serious tones, "I don't have a message for you tonight." Then added, "I'm not a messenger boy."

There'll Be a Hot Time in the Old Town Tonight was just coming into its own as a popular song. It reached its peak as the men returned from the Spanish-American War. But even before the war, and even as far west as Iowa, young men in barbershops on Saturday night were singing it.

In Anita that night, for the first time, I heard Bingham play it as a hymn, then as a march, then as a dirge, and finally as ragtime, a stunt he kept up for many years to the glee of hundreds of audiences. He called this act *Bill Johnson and His One Tune,* explaining how Johnson, a bashful lumberjack, stumbled into a church that needed an organist and admitted, "Yeh, I kin play," and he could—one tune. So he played it for a church service, then for a funeral, then at a wedding, finally for a wedding dance.

The piano in the Wiota school was new; it had replaced the old reed organ that fall at a cost of $97. It was an upright, of course, and its elegant golden-oak case had that glassy polish which in those days was the last word in decoration. Squatting on a round piano stool with his fashionable long coattails flaring out behind, Bingham always looked like a gnome, particularly to the newspaper cartoonists with whom he was a great favorite; not a sober, shriveled gnome, but an enthusiastic fellow whose highest purpose in life was to make the world happy. Years later, one summer in Chautauqua in South Dakota, he was playing the piano so hard that he fell off the stool. It was not intentional, but the people, who came to look upon everything he did as a prank, thought it was, and he let it go at that. He didn't intentionally split his trousers, either, the night he was appearing at Billy Sunday's Winona Lake Chautauqua, but the dreadful having happened—it happened so frequently to agile performers that they faced the catastrophe in their dreams—Bing simply sat down on the floor, beamed, and said, "I'll do the rest of the show from here," and did.

One of Bingham's most popular monologues after the advent of the Ford automobile was *Mrs. Rastus Johnson's Joy Ride.* This also was recorded by the Victor company. In this act a young colored boy named Wesley is taking his best girl for a ride in his new car, saying, "Ain't she a lolly-paluzer! Lissen to her purr, honey! Some kyar, I'll tell the world . . ."

He is singing, "This little flivver with a funny little liver is good enough for me . . . ," when the car stops and the boy tries to crank her. Bingham, for his sound effect in this particular monologue, in addition to a hammer and dishpan and what not, used the two old reliable tin cans and rosin on a string.

The boy is saying, "Doggone ol' self-starter's balkin' on me, honey lamb! . . ." when there comes a "knock, knock, knock . . ." and he cries, "Whew, that's hard work . . . whew! Harder'n pickin' cotton. . . ."

The girl suggests, "Mebbe you is out of gas, Wesley. . . ."

"Mebbe you is out your head!" he shouts back. "I oozed five gallons in yest'idy! Where you 'spect I been since then? San Franfornia? Califrisco? . . . don't talk, woman, don't talk. . . ." Bang, bang . . . "I'se the doctor a'tendin' this infant . . . she got enough gas to drown a pottahippamus. . . . Oh, Lord, oh Lord . . . well, mebbe she do need a gill or two of gas . . . h'm, it's dark in here, woman . . . can't see . . . gimme a match. . . ."

BANG! BANG! BANG!

"Whoa, whoa, Henery! She done exploded!"

The girl says, "Nev' mind, Wesley, she's insure for $60. . . ."

"But I ain't insure . . . you git a ladder, woman! Get me down outten this h'ar 'simmon tree quick!"

Laughter again was uproarious.

One winter the Wiota lecture course had a magician, nameless now. The prospectus described him as "mystifying" and "refined" and he certainly proved to be both. He was the first man who ever made a rabbit do anything worth while in prairies plagued with too many rabbits, and his refinement was apparent to all. For our magician not only knew how to bow from the waist, but he was rigged up in formal court dress with knee breeches, silk stockings, buckled patent-leather pumps and a swallow-tailed coat which no doubt was amply supplied with hidden inside pockets.

The magician's fee is no longer a matter of record, but the male quartet cost $50, a sum which gave pause to even the most spendthrift members of the committee. But when the four bushy-haired young singers had rendered *Good Night Ladies* as their final encore and taken their last bow, everyone agreed that it had been worth the high price. The baritone was short and plump and what he could do to the low notes in *Old Black Joe* was beyond belief, and the tenor was tall and lean and, like the magician, refined.

Of the three lecturers on those winter Lyceum courses, I was later to manage two on circuit Chautauqua. They were "Colonel" George Washington Bain and Lou J. Beauchamp. The other, the Reverend L. B. Wickersham, a valiant Methodist clergyman from Atlantic, Iowa, appeared the second winter with his famous tear-jerker, *Chickens Come Home to Roost*. I say "valiant" because twenty years later Mr. Wickersham was still delivering the same speech, for Britt Chautauqua at that time, in almost the same territory. Taking no stock in the comforting theory that what is past is past, he preached the unhappy gospel that whatever wickedness a young man does in his youth, he pays for. If he has wasted his early life, any attempts to make good later are doomed. Laziness, extravagance, the use of tobacco, a taste for beer, fooling around the pool hall, loafing on street corners, all are homing birds that will fly back eventually to their original hen coops.

"Colonel" George Washington Bain was billed as a "temperance speaker from Kentucky," which state everyone in Iowa at that time suspected was a whiskey-drinking, horse-racing region with strong Confederate leanings, a state that usually voted Democratic. At any rate, in Kentucky or else-where, "Colonel" Bain had acquired first-hand information on the demon rum and he revealed it in Wiota under the title *The Safe Side of Life.* He changed that title afterward to *If I Had to Live My Life Over Again* and spent another quarter of a century elaborating on it. Wiota approved heartily of his bone-dry talk. One of his later speeches he called *Boys and Girls, Naughty and Nice,* and the young people, crowded together in the back rows of the tents, laughed as loudly at it as he did himself and took it to heart. Bain was middle-aged when I first advertised him, had been lecturing even then since the Garfield administration, and he lived to see Herbert Hoover become President.

Genial Lou Beauchamp was billed in later years as the "original humorous philosopher," but like "Colonel" Bain, in my early days he was a temperance speaker. The reformed drunkard had a special appeal in the 90's. The latest gubernatorial campaign in Iowa had involved "temperance." The "dry" Republicans had unseated, after four years, what they called the "Demi-john party." The state never yet had made actual prohibition stick, but it had local option and audiences in general heartily approved the character, who after years of bibbing, could turn his back on the demon rum. Beauchamp not only frankly described himself as this type of shocking, and therefore fascinating, person, but he glossed over no horrid details of his story. An Ohio product, self-educated—he had spent his early years among the Creeks and Choctaws—he was a poet of sorts and liked to sprinkle his eloquence with his own homespun verse. He was an impressive looking man, with wavy hair and handlebar mustaches, and he gave our little community a good moralizing speech packed with gentle humor, called, by a stroke of genius, *Take the Sunny Side.*

Like Ralph Bingham's serious words, Beauchamp's remarks undoubtedly would be classed as corny today. Styles in speeches change about as often as styles in hats, and perhaps for just as obscure reasons. One man's corn, I was to learn later, can be another man's inspiration. Beauchamp in Wiota did use one shocking simile which caused many a decorous citizen to keep his eyes straight front. Describing a speech he had heard, he said it was "like a Mother Hubbard, covering everything and touching nothing." That was daringly close to indelicate in the midwest in those days, when anything remotely suggestive was banned not only from public entertainment, but also from polite conversation. Beauchamp's remark took, however. More than one speaker used it later as his own product, Congressman Adam Bede among them, in his debates with Emil Seidel.

As the years went on, Lou Beauchamp delivered *Take the Sunny Side* thousands of times, in almost every summer Chautauqua across the land, over and over in winter Lyceum, often two or three times in the same city, covering altogether 1,300,000 miles, an enterprising mathematician once figured. So far as his managers could determine, he was one of a handful of lecturers who never in his whole career had a bad press notice. He was particularly popular in Cincinnati, where as a young man he had edited one of the dailies, but so far as reappearances went, cities like Chicago and Washington, D.C., called him back fifty and sixty times. He offered an assortment of titles in later years—phrases like *The Age of the Young Man, Blunders of Humanity, New Ideas on an Old Subject,* this last one offered particularly for Sunday programs. All of them told how to make the best of life, but none of them ever was as catchy as *Take the Sunny Side.* Beauchamp made thousands of dollars in Chautauqua and Lyceum, spent much of it on book collecting, lost everything he owned in an Ohio flood, lectured feverishly after that, but died as he started, with little money. His sense of humor carried him through many a platform crisis. It was probably the same quality that influenced him, the reformed drinker, at the peak of his career, to refuse an eldership in the Presbyterian church, "because," he said, "looking back on my life I realize I am not sufficiently dignified for such an exalted position."

Citizens in the prairie states learned a great deal from these speakers who visited their dimly-lighted platforms before the Spanish-American War. A restless yeast was at work in America. People west of the Mississippi, in fact all the way from Kentucky to the far Dakotas, felt uneasiness, many of them discontent. That discontent was to grow, before the 1890's ended, into a steadily moving social and political upheaval that lasted almost to the First World War, and to put that upheaval into convincing words and attempt to correct its causes, great speakers took to the lecture platforms.

The same year that an ambitious young school teacher in Wiota, Iowa, was excitedly spending $150 for a lecture course, William Allen White in nearby Emporia burst out with his angry editorial, *What's the Matter With Kansas?* People in Iowa and Kansas and a dozen other states were aware that something was seriously wrong. They were restless as only pioneers can be. It was restlessness that had sent many of them into the Plains states in the beginning, with free land as a secondary lure.

Now most of the free land was gone. The restlessness remained. Back east, great fortunes were being built out of railroad empires into which the western farmer believed he was paying too much for his freight. Rockefeller had joined the kerosene-producing companies into a single unit that could charge what it wanted to fill the farmer's coal-oil lamps. Whiskey, sugar and metals prices were dictated by a few men in New York.

Farmers seethed. They organized. In the west and south the rural anger fused impatient groups into Granges, a Greenback Party, a Colored Farmers' Alliance, a People's Party of Kansas, until finally, at Omaha, Nebraska, in July, 1892, representatives from thirty-two states had formed the Populist Party.

Editors along the Atlantic seaboard recoiled in horror at the new party's platform. It demanded a graduated income tax, direct election of senators, conservation of natural resources, a postal savings system, a shorter working day in industry, and as if all this were not un-American enough, the government ownership of railroads. Among local leaders who flirted with the Populists was an obscure young Nebraska politician-editor named William Jennings Bryan. In every western state other challengers of the old order lifted angry voices while half the continent listened.

New words came into the language and old words took new, sinister meanings. "Wall Street," in western ears, had a dirty sound. "Monopoly," "the Trusts," and a little later "the Octopus" and "the System," all of which referred to evil "Big Business," were the subjects of unflattering speeches, editorials and cartoons. The Populists did not win the election. Democrat Grover Cleveland went into the White House in 1892, but there were a million Populist votes.

In Iowa and Kansas, Nebraska and the far Dakotas, rural and small-town folk read whatever they could find about the new movement, sweeping the prairie and Plains states, for freedom and a fairer share of the national wealth. They wanted to know what all the shouting was about, and they wanted their own yearnings and indignations put into ringing words by eloquent prophets of social reform. Weary of mud-road isolation, they thirsted for knowledge, for the exposition of new ideas not accessible to them in the ordinary course of their reading—in the daily or weekly newspapers. And above all, they were hungry for escape from their own flat horizons into the fascinating world that lay beyond. If they could not see it with their own eyes, they could perhaps behold it with that "inner eye" of the imagination of which the poet speaks. Lecturers who "had been there" could evoke these exotic scenes for their enjoyment. These were the people for whom circuit Chautauqua was finally conceived, the kind who supported it with quarters and half dollars, who got the most out of it, who unconsciously shaped its moral concepts and established its intellectual levels, and when the time for the annual guarantee for next summer's program came around, signed on the dotted lines. These were the people who caused a period of twenty-five years to be known as "the Chautauqua era."

Talent for Sale

3

The infant 20th century found America in an argumentative mood. Argument blossomed into oratory and oratory sold tickets, not only to the widely advertised debates in the east, but to Lyceum courses in the prairie states. When naval heroes of the Spanish-American War began to quarrel loudly over the credit for victory, the people immediately took sides. The Army "embalmed beef" scandal, the unsanitary recruit camp at Chickamauga which caused more casualties than did the Spanish guns, efforts of politicians to ride Admiral George Dewey into the Presidency on his wartime popularity, all led to strenuous debate.

Then, in 1901, Queen Victoria died, ending an era for the British Empire but not for rural towns in mid-America. There, as the entertainment business learned unhappily, Victorianism long outlived the Queen. However, that same year, in September, another death did affect the lecture platform. A madman assassinated William McKinley, a cautious President who never rocked the boat. His vigorous successor, throwing caution out the White House window, set a pattern for political debate that lasted a long generation.

Theodore Roosevelt gloried in battle. When he cried out against "those poor spirits . . . in the gray twilight that know not victory or defeat," a robustious crowd of dedicated reformers with strong voices and convictions flocked immediately to his banner. Audiences cheered these orators who, with Roosevelt, attacked "the doctrine of ignoble ease," the "idle rich," "malefactors of great wealth." The wide midwest was waiting for that kind of talk and willing to pay the price, within reason, to hear it.

Men had a little money in their pockets in that spring of 1901. Iowa corn had gone up to thirty-six cents a bushel, but by the same token a good three-piece suit cost six dollars and a half. So as spring advanced, boys like myself, working their way through school, began to think about summer jobs to pay next year's expenses. What to do? The harvest fields offered a dollar a day and board, for twelve hours of hard work. A barn carpenter's gang earned about the same money. There was little else to choose.

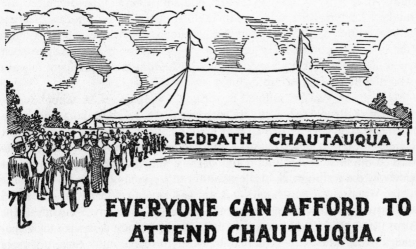

EVERYONE CAN AFFORD TO ATTEND CHAUTAUQUA.

Drawn by Alton Packard

Then in April, as vacation neared at Cornell College, in Mount Vernon, Iowa, a lecture manager named Keith Vawter came to the campus searching "live wire salesmen" to work that summer signing up communities for next winter's lecture courses. Such a job certainly sounded better to most students than one with a sweaty threshing crew. For one thing, it meant travel in far places, away out beyond the state line. And the only journey I had ever made up to this time had been a trip to Chicago with two carloads of cattle.

Keith Vawter had the best room in the village hotel. He was a small, brisk, pleasant, well-dressed man of thirty-two. I stood six feet, two inches in my not-to-well-pressed campus clothes. He listened politely to my unexciting story, but when I mentioned the Wiota Lyceum courses, he questioned me about the way I had handled them, what talent I had chosen, how the local ticket sales had developed. Then he made his proposition. He would pay ten percent commission on all programs an agent sold, guaran-

teeing train fare as a minimum. Would I try my hand in a few towns, not
next summer, but at once, during the ten days of spring vacation?

Thus began a splendid association, which in one form or another, was
to stretch through three decades. Vawter's background was curiously like
my own. We both were sons of Civil War soldiers. Our families, like those
of most other Iowans, were Protestant Republicans. My father was a
farmer who also ran the village grain elevator; Vawter's was a clergyman
who, the story goes, under the pseudonym of "Sergeant Oats," had written
the once-famous *Prison Life in Dixie,* memories of a Confederate prison
camp. After a try at college his son had sold books, then organized the
Standard Lecture Bureau, a one-man effort operating out of Des Moines.
He booked talent, hired lecturers, wrote publicity and letters in swift long-
hand, swept the office floor, collected the commissions. Yet despite such
varied labors, he was a glass of midwest fashion, urbane, confident, always
giving the impression of professional success.

My task, as Vawter outlined it, seemed a simple one. A school superintendent at Brookings, a county seat in eastern South Dakota and home
of the new state college, had already inquired about a Lyceum course. I was
to go there, try to sell the town a full winter program, then venture westward on the new Huron, Pierre and Deadwood division of the Chicago and
Northwestern Railroad, on the lookout for other good business.

Here was adventure! South Dakota was an infant state. Except for a
few towns sprinkled along its eastern border and the roaring gold camps
in the Black Hills to the west, it was raw frontier. Only yesterday there had
been Indian battles. The Rosebud and Yankton Sioux, blasted out of their
choicest hunting grounds, still were retreating sullenly into the badlands.
Righteous homeseekers, unrighteous traders, shrewdly visionary railroads
were pushing north and west, spreading the cultural benefits of civilization
and at the same time appropriating from the Indians a million and a
quarter acres of virgin soil.

Looking back on it, this would seem an unpropitious place and time to
try to sell oratory or introduce the niceties of life. The star attraction on
Vawter's list was, strangely enough, a persuasive, honey-voiced orator
named Russell H. Conwell, whose benign philosophy it was that a man
need not seek afar for money or success; they lay in his own back yard.
I say "strangely," since for some reason this philosophy appealed to those
South Dakota frontiersmen who had done just the opposite with their own
lives. They had not stayed in their own back yards. They had gone west.

In that era the Reverend Mr. Conwell, with his *Acres of Diamonds,*
was the world's most famous lecturer, now forgotten by most of the world.
In 1901 he already had delivered the speech more than 5000 times, in a
score of countries besides his own, and was to repeat it on still another
thousand occasions. It was purely a sermon, but a surprising one, because
it turned the tables on most sermons and took as its theme, "You have no

right to be poor." Larded with anecdotes, it gave name, date and place to prove in the best Horatio Alger manner that a man was foolish not to make money. He should get rich and help his fellows.

Conwell himself had done exactly that. With the fees from *Acres of Diamonds*—later there were royalties from a million reprints—he had founded Temple University in Philadelphia and helped thousands of boys to attend it; before he was done, he had given them half a million dollars, all from lecturing fees. His purpose never changed; neither did the speech. He tried other titles as time sped on, but like Lou Beauchamp with *Take the Sunny Side,* Conwell found that the public wanted only *Acres of Diamonds*.

It is impossible to guess what this indefatigable man felt when he stepped out on a platform to deliver that same lecture he had already delivered time and time again. His was a brilliant mind; before he took to lecturing he had been a soldier, foreign correspondent, lawyer, then a great Baptist preacher, with such crowds coming to his Philadelphia church that admission finally had to be by ticket. He had associated with Longfellow, Beecher, Holmes, Emerson, Whittier, Grant, Garfield, remaining to the end a humble man who never in his fabulous life could supply a manager with a newspaper clipping about himself, because he never saved them.

Certainly Conwell knew as well as others that *Acres of Diamonds* was neither a great literary work nor a masterpiece of oratory. It is entirely possible that he was as baffled by its appeal as were the students who dissected it, seeking some clue to its fantastic popularity. Among these curious students had been Vawter himself when he signed Conwell. Why, he asked, was this particular lecture so popular? If a Lyceum agent could discover what was hidden in its words or delivery, why thousands and thousands of adult men and women crowded in again and again to listen, if that agent could find other such speeches and other such speakers, and pour them out across the nation, his fortune would be made.

What was the key? Was it the sentence, "Your wealth is next to you. You are looking right over it."?

"Wherever there is human need," Conwell advised, "there is always a fortune . . . greatness consists in doing great deeds with little means, in the accomplishment of vast purposes from the private ranks of life."

Or was the key possibly in the phrase "Get rich"? Instead of scoffing at wealth, as most "inspirational" speakers did, Conwell was urging people to *make* money, actual cash in hand, not just treasures laid away in heaven. The men and women listening so avidly to him had worked hard. They not only remembered the pioneers' struggle for survival, many of them still were experiencing it. True, he exhorted them all, fathers and mothers, boys and girls, particularly the boys, to be good citizens. But also rich citizens.

Money wasn't the root of all evil, he argued. He dared anyone to find any such foolish statement in the Bible. The evil lay in the *love* of money.

Get rich by honorable and Christian methods and use the wealth for good. And that wealth, those acres of diamonds, lay at one's feet. "Money has power!" he shouted. "For a man to say, 'I do not want money,' is to say, 'I do not wish to do any good to my fellow man.'"

So it wasn't wicked to be rich after all? Was this the pleasant doctrine that the crowds thronged to hear? Keith Vawter pondered, but never could be sure. And even if it were, what other "inspirational" lecturer would be bold enough to use such an unorthodox theme? Neither Vawter nor any other lecture manager ever discovered the answers and Conwell carried on to the end in a class by himself and no one succeeded him. A few tried. In 1926 a complacent young man, hearing that the great Conwell had died the year before, came into the Chicago office of the Redpath Bureau and announced, "I have come to take his place."

Conwell was a big man physically, who slouched as he walked out on the stage. His lecture was two hours long. He put vigor into its delivery; cajoled, scorned, argued, imitated; then he took his fee, mailed a share of it promptly to a boy who needed it, caught the first train out of town and the next night uttered the identical words with identical gestures and identical effect to another audience. Redpath Manager Crawford A. Peffer tells how, after ending a tour, Conwell would come into the Philadelphia office and relate harrowing tales of this hardship and that, of poor hotels and early morning trains. "I would be at the point of tears," Peffer relates, "when suddenly he would stop and say, 'Well, that's that. Where do I go next?'"

Conwell was fifty-eight years old that summer when I booked him in South Dakota. He had delivered his first lecture in Westfield, Massachusetts, in 1862, when he was nineteen years old, and from then on until he died he spoke on an average of 150 to 200 nights every year. In a period when many orators and entertainers were content to pay their own expenses and receive $75 to $100 a week, Conwell sometimes received a thumping $200 for a single appearance. He had been a poor boy. A bowl of oatmeal often had been all he had to eat. He hadn't liked poverty. He put a high price on himself and got it, and then gave the money away.

I never had heard *Acres of Diamonds* when I started out to sell it. If I feared difficulties in handling such an expensive product, I soon learned differently. The school superintendent in Brookings, South Dakota, and his lecture course committee had heard of the great Conwell and they itched to see him in the flesh. Theirs was a lively town of nearly 3000 persons. It had stout wooden sidewalks on both sides of mud streets, and in addition to its state school, it boasted two newspapers and several banks and was the trading center of a great wheat- and flax-growing area. Naturally it yearned to be a cultural center as well. So it did not take long to get the signature of a banker, a teacher and a land lawyer on a binding contract with Vawter's Standard Lecture Bureau, which I proudly countersigned as agent.

The railroad ran west out of Brookings across flat, treeless plains, already broken here and there for corn and good Dakota wheat. The new Huron, Pierre and Deadwood division had not yet reached Deadwood in 1901. It was a single-track line with flimsy bridges over shallow creeks, and along the broad open reach of country between Brookings and the Missouri River, occasional new towns spotted the right of way. Every few miles an intrepid band of pioneers, full of rosy confidence in the bright future of the western plains, had laid out the beginnings of a settlement. Sometimes these new towns were only a dismal cluster of sod-roofed houses, with a short muddy street, but there were a few "cities"—Huron, also with a small college; Miller, Highmore and the new state capital of Pierre. Huron had nearly 3000 people and Pierre, chartered as a city only the previous year, claimed 2000.

Having slain the dragon at Brookings, I started west excitedly, my pockets full of Vawter's blank contracts, my heart full of hope. The fare, handed over to the conductor on boarding the train, was two cents a mile. With such a scattered population, it did not pay the railroad to operate passenger trains; passengers must ride the freights in the sun-baked comfort of the caboose. At the few "eating houses" scattered along the right of way, meals cost twenty-five cents. Since I slept in the caboose, expenses remained low.

The train, being an "accommodation," kept no regular schedule, simply halted anywhere as long as necessary for the crew to unhitch the locomotive, shunt cars along sidings, haul package freight out of the boxcars or enjoy a meal. This meant that in some towns the stop was thirty minutes, in others three or four hours.

The crew, interested in any errand that took a traveller into this half-empty countryside, was excited with my success in Brookings. So, leaning heavily on the men's kindness, I made a practical arrangement. As we neared a town I washed my face in the tin basin in the caboose, put on my collar and necktie, slicked down my hair and leaped off before the wheels stopped turning.

On Main Street I made for the bank, if the place boasted one, and introduced myself as a "travelling representative of the Standard Lecture Bureau of Des Moines, Iowa." If there was no bank, I chose a lawyer by his shingle or the proprietor of the most prosperous-looking store. I had a brief speech ready. Certainly, I pointed out, this beautiful new community, which had progressed so far so fast, deserved the cultural advantages of a Lyceum course next winter. I brought out my list of personalities, brochures on their specialties, explained the way a Lyceum course was set up, with a local committee of prominent citizens in charge.

Ten minutes before the train was ready to leave, the engineer would signal with three long blasts of the whistle. This gave me a chance to end a conference and run for the siding, telling my prospect that if he would go ahead and form his committee, I would be back in a few days. At the next stop I made another contact and, at the locomotive signal, ran again. When the slow train retraced its route east-bound, I revisited the towns. The men to whom I had talked on the trip out did not disappoint me. In a matter of minutes or hours, I had the necessary signatures on the dotted lines.

South Dakota grew into fertile Chautauqua ground. Among our crews and talent in the big years, this region became famous for the worst storms, the worst transportation difficulties, all kinds of problems, from rattlesnakes to Indian audiences that didn't understand an English word. Hilton Ira Jones, a scientific lecturer in the golden days of Chautauqua, used to tell a story about going out on a summer circuit to Buffalo Fort Indian Reservation to make a speech to the Sioux. The session was held in a big frame council house and on the back wall, Jones noticed, was a long row of sixty penny spikes, too high for anyone to hang his hat on, so what their use was he couldn't imagine. When the Indians arrived, however, each squaw with her papoose strapped to a board, Jones to his amazement saw them hang up the babies on the spikes; then to a string six or eight inches long on each child's wrist they tied a piece of fat meat as a pacifier.

Jones was just well started with his speech, giving each sentence to an interpreter, when a commotion started among the papooses. A baby had swallowed his meat. It stuck in his throat and, choking, he began to fling his arms back and forth. Finally, still with no attention from the squaws, the infant waved his hand so hard that the meat came up, with a sound like a cork popping out of a bottle. The papoose gasped, then went back to sucking the meat, but all through the rest of the lecture, one child after another exploded his cork. Jones finished, a little envious undoubtedly of Russell Conwell, who in the early 1900's had had few Indians in his audiences.

Besides Conwell, on those first programs, Vawter offered, and I sold, Jacob A. Riis, the Danish immigrant friend of Theodore Roosevelt. There was no mystery about the success of this speech as there was about the great Conwell's. Riis, who had turned public attention to the horror of city slums, was not only a great humanitarian, but also an orator of great skill. His subject that year, and many later years, was *How the Other Half Lives,* which also was to be the title of his first book. Though I had not heard Conwell's lecture before I sold it, I had had opportunity, in Iowa, to hear Riis. His was an ugly, frightening story of political corruption.

Riis was a lean, sad-faced man of fifty-two the first year I booked him. A slight Danish accent, which he kept to the end of his life, helped rather than hindered his oratory. He knew how to "soften" an audience into tears, then launched into denunciations of his—and the plain peoples'—enemies. One story no audience ever forgot concerned "my little dog." Riis had come to New York from Denmark in 1869, the "Black Friday" year when the gold market crashed. He was twenty years old, friendless, poor, and all that first cold winter his only true friend was a pitiful stray dog. They huddled together in doorways, keeping each other from freezing, and the bewildered young immigrant shared with the dog the scraps of food he collected. Finally, one bitter night, he applied for shelter at a police station near the Bowery.

The brutal lieutenant in command told the stranger to come in, but to leave his dog outside. Riis demurred. He explained in broken English that the dog and he must stay together.

"The lieutenant, before I could stop him, picked up my little dog that I loved so much, and swinging him by the hind legs, beat out his brains on the stone steps of the station house. 'Now come in,' he said. 'No reason you cannot be comfortable tonight.' I walked the streets until morning, weeping."

The audience by this time was sobbing. Then Riis related how, after he became a reporter for *The New York Sun,* he told the tragic story to Theodore Roosevelt, when he was police commissioner in New York City. Roosevelt was touched. The tale, "T.R." often said, influenced him in running his department, and Riis and he became close friends.

Like Conwell, Riis talked of rich men. But not Conwell's kind. Riis's rich men took brutal advantage of the poor. *How the Other Half Lives* caused angry listeners to want to tear down the temples of heartless wealth and cruel injustice, just as Riis's earlier written words, exposing conditions in New York's festering "Five Points" area, near the foot of the Bowery, had sparked the city's great slum clearance crusade.

Riis had jabbed the public conscience with sharp words and pictures of filth and wickedness, hungry old folk, wan listless children, crime and politics and fat landlords hand in hand, until the city destroyed the Five Points slum. A park occupies the spot today.

Every Riis lecture appearance was a call to arms. He urged the plain people to organize against looters in high places, so that America could become a land of equality. There was enough work, food, money to go around. Why allow a selfish minority to grow wealthy at the expense of the majority?

Riis fitted well into the social and political thinking of the hardy South Dakota settlers at that particular time, for they had become annoyed at the standpat Republicans. Though most of them were of solid Republican stock, not only had they voted a Populist governor into office, but the year before they had lined up overwhelmingly behind William Jennings Bryan in his second unsuccessful joust for the Presidency. Jacob Riis was their kind of speaker. He talked of the here-and-now, of men's pocketbooks and the feed sacks in the back of the wagon. I had no trouble selling him.

The next year when I booked Riis he was beginning to stress the ballot box. Appearing in South Dakota his second season, he argued that as an American he didn't care what ticket men voted, if they sent fearless representatives to their state capitals and to Washington. Actually Riis did care deeply what ticket men voted. When Theodore Roosevelt bolted the Republican party ten years later, Jacob Riis used any platform he could get, including Chautauqua's, to urge the election of the Progressive candidate. After "T.R.'s" defeat, Riis continued doggedly with the same theme, lecturing steadily; in fact, his last illness began while he was speaking in New Orleans.

Among other attractions on the 1901 Vawter list were vivacious Katherine Ridgeway and Leland T. Powers, one of the most accomplished actors of his day and the first "play reader" to take to the Lyceum road. Miss Ridgeway, as usual, was to give short readings of poetry, prose and drama, a "miscellaneous program" it was called. The fact that she recently had come back from England, where Londoners, with the Prince of Wales in the audience, broke all records for encores, was enough to sell her in the wilds of South Dakota.

There were more important reasons, to be sure. In her field Katherine Ridgeway was already as popular as Conwell in his. She had first tried her wings in 1896 with the Temple Quartette of Boston, but within two years she was heading her own Concert Company of reader, pianist, soprano and tenor. By the time she toured South Dakota for Vawter—in fact, all the years from 1900 down to her last stage appearance during Franklin D. Roosevelt's first administration—she put on a hefty two-hour program alone except for an accompanist.

Competition was keen among readers. They tried to keep their program numbers their own property for a year at least and Miss Ridgeway often retitled hers—they were chiefly cuttings—so that her rivals could not locate them for their own use. One method was to omit the name of the author, occasionally even the title itself. Miss Ridgeway's recital always opened with a long number, usually a selection opposing war. She had tasted the bitter aftermath of war as a child in Georgia, and besides, her intention was not just to "entertain" an audience, she wanted it to do a bit of thinking. She used Negro dialect frequently; with her antecedents such stories were naturals for her.

One of the best-known Ridgeway Chautauqua programs later on was a condensation of a "peace" play, *In the Vanguard,* by Katrina Trask. The short recitation most often requested was a four-stanza poem by Thomas Bracket, for which Miss Ridgeway's husband, Percy F. Hunt, later of the faculty of the New England Conservatory, composed music which he played as she read. This was called *Not Understood* and is typical of the moralistic type of verse the public liked in that day. It began, slowly, to music:

> "We move along asunder,
> "Our paths grow wider, as the seasons creep
> "Along the years. We marvel and we wonder
> "Why life is life and then we fall asleep—
> "NOT UNDERSTOOD.

"We gather false impressions
"And hug them closer as the years go by,
"The virtues often seem to us transgressions
"And thus men rise and fall and live and die—
"NOT UNDERSTOOD.

"How trifles often change us,
"The thoughtless sentence or the fancied slight
"Destroy long years of friendship and estrange us,
"And on our souls there falls a freezing blight—
"NOT UNDERSTOOD.

"Oh, God, that men could see a little clearer,
"Or judge less harshly where they cannot see—
"Oh, God, that nations would draw a little nearer
"One another. They'd be nearer Thee—
"AND UNDERSTOOD."

Miss Ridgeway had her tear-jerkers, of course, and the one old Chautauqua audiences still sometimes quote is *Christmas Morning at Home,* a poem that her friends claimed would send any wayward young man stumbling out from the lecture hall determined to write his mother that night a long overdue letter. In those forty years of trekking hither and yon, winter Lyceum, summer Chautauqua, Miss Ridgeway often explained her reputation as a good trouper by saying that one-night stands were the life of Riley after what she had endured as a girl. Her father, a penniless Confederate officer named Ridgeway Hogan—hence the daughter's stage name —had left Georgia after the Civil War for the mountains of Washington State. At fifteen smart Katherine was teaching school in the lumber camps, "boarding 'round" the district, sharing a bed with as many small children as happened to be in her host's family. At Whitman College, a Presbyterian school in Walla Walla, she chanced to hear an elocutionist, and, possessed from then on with the idea of becoming one herself, she managed to get to the Boston School of Oratory where she earned part of her keep by leading a blind man on his walks. Riding a railroad division like the Huron, Pierre and Deadwood wasn't too trying after that beginning.

One experience I had with Katherine Ridgeway, while I was still a young booking agent, permanently influenced my own ideas about good speakers—political, clerical, or any type. Our bureau was already listing the Reverend Newell Dwight Hillis, called about that time from Chicago to famous Plymouth Church, Brooklyn, where the congregation apparently hoped that the eloquence of Henry Ward Beecher and Lyman Abbott would descend upon him. I happened to be in Boston when Miss Ridgeway and the clergyman were there and the three of us met for lunch. In the course of the meal Miss Ridgeway asked whether we would like to go to the theatre that night to see Joseph Jefferson in *Rip Van Winkle.* I answered that the house was sold out.

"I'll get tickets," Miss Ridgeway said. "Mr. Jefferson is a friend of mine."

This incident itself shows how the long battle between church and stage was shaping up, in the east at least. Newell Dwight Hillis went unquestioningly with us to the theatre that night, whereas the great preacher whose pulpit Hillis had just inherited had waited most of his life before he dared attend a play. It had not been too many years before, in 1885, at a banquet for Sir Henry Irving, that Beecher, liberal theologian though he was, confessed that he never set foot inside a playhouse until he was seventy years old. He was then seventy-two.

At the final curtain of *Rip Van Winkle,* Miss Ridgeway said, "Let's go backstage. Mr. Jefferson will be delighted to meet both of you."

The great actor greeted us warmly. I was thrilled, of course; I was a country boy, just out of an Iowa classroom, and Jefferson, still in the white beard and tattered clothes of Rip Van Winkle, was the most famous actor of his day. But the Reverend Mr. Hillis obviously was unhappy about something. We had hardly got into the actor's dressing room when he asked:

"Mr. Jefferson, how does it happen that *you,* who perform in what frankly is fiction, are turning people away every night, while *we,* who present Eternal Truths, must preach to empty houses?"

Wise old Joe Jefferson put down the rag with which he had been wiping off make-up. "That's easy to understand, sir," he said. "You see, we present fiction as if it were the eternal truth. And you, I am afraid, present eternal truth as if it were fiction."

A certain ambitious young booking agent learned a lesson from that remark, whether anyone else in the party did or not: find speakers who make truth sound like truth and there would be no trouble about return engagements for them.

Miss Ridgeway's poverty-stricken beginnings may have conditioned her to the ham-and-egg life of a trouper, but there certainly was no hint of them in her ravishing appearance on a stage. When she walked out into the lights, a long expressive "ah-h-h" was wont to escape involuntarily from the women in her audience. Play readers always wore elegant costumes—their own, not those of any character being impersonated—and Miss Ridgeway's tall, statuesque figure, draped often in billowing yards of chiffon or lace, usually white with a long train, her arm-length white kid gloves, the elegant feather boa around her shoulders, the enormous ostrich plumes on her big hat, when she wore a hat, caused envy in every feminine heart.

Leland Powers, another real actor from the top of his erudite head to the tips of his shining patent-leather pumps, was to give readings from Beau Brummel the first year I booked him in South Dakota. His practice was to condense the play to less than an hour and, without costume or make-up, footlights, props or scenery, take all the parts, acting as well as speaking the lines. Like Conwell, he was a $200-a-night man. In comparison, Ralph Bingham, in spite of the demand for him, drew only $60 to $75 at that period.

Powers, who had gathered his first laurels in Boston and Chicago, also became a tremendous hit in South Dakota. It probably was a first experience in real drama for nine out of ten of his listeners that winter, accustomed only to muddy versions of *Uncle Tom's Cabin*. Local pride there on the edge of the badlands probably helped Powers' popularity. His pristine white tie, his "full dress suit" gave blue-jeaned villagers a moment of glamor. The sidewalks might be wooden and the streets deep in mud, but Powers stood there for all to see, proving by his elegance that nothing was too good for a raw, proud town. They approved of his formal clothes just as they did of Katherine Ridgeway's beautiful gowns.

When the ten-day spring vacation ended that year, I had sold $4900 worth of entertainment. My commission was $490. I was the richest undergraduate in eastern Iowa. What I did not guess was that I had a job that would last almost a lifetime.

When Vawter sent me out to South Dakota again in 1902, after my sophomore year in college, he added western and northern Iowa to the territory and, if that region lacked erudition the following winter, it was not the fault of Vawter's Standard Bureau. The headliners were the same: Conwell and Riis repeating their lectures, Powers with readings from *David Copperfield* and *The Rivals,* and again lovely Katherine Ridgeway. She was commanding $75 a date that year, fabulous for a woman reader, and could have appeared six nights a week if the train service had permitted. Within five years, for herself and her pianist, she was getting $200 for an appearance.

Dr. John B. DeMotte of DePauw University at Greencastle, Indiana, was also on the 1902 list for a deadly serious lecture on the power of habit —bad habit. DeMotte, like Conwell, had been lecturing up and down the land for many years; his career ended in 1904. His offering was called *Python Eggs,* and it was his grim contention, delivered in dramatic fashion, that small bad habits, nurtured in the breast of an unsuspecting victim, are like the eggs of the python: they finally hatch into serpents that destroy their hosts. South Dakota and western Iowa evidently thought they needed that sort of advice, for they were willing to pay for it. DeMotte received $50 a night.

On that second trip in 1902 I again expanded not only my pocketbook but my horizon. It was a fine year and a fine place to watch America grow. I remember arriving at Geddes, South Dakota, on the day new land was to be opened to settlers. The little town was a cauldron of excitement. This was one of the last openings; free land was almost gone. Pouring in were hopeful people in wagons and spring carriages, all with fast, lean ponies.

The homestead area lay southwest of the village, down along the Missouri River bottoms, and as dusk fell the settlers lined up facing the future.

Land agents had stretched a rope; at midnight a pistol shot signalled them to drop it and the thunder of hooves and the rattle of wagons filled the night. Dust rose in a cloud that caught at the throat. Long after the impatient adventurers had left the town, plunging forward in the darkness to unknown destinations, one still could hear the distant rumble of their charge. It was the sound of a nation exploding. Here was virgin land, in quarter sections of sandy loam, enriched by the blood of its original owners. This land was to make homesteads, wheat fields waving yellow in the afternoon summer sun, grain elevators standing high against flat horizons. It took little skill to sell a lecture series in that time or place. Food, shelter and water were the first concern until the stakes were driven and the land claims filed, but after that came something else. The people, soon weary of lonely emptiness, of dust and endless distances, wanted to see the lights twinkle, hear and look at men who wore elegant clothes like Leland Powers, women who spoke in soft voices like Katherine Ridgeway. They wanted to laugh, and along came a young man with a handful of tickets.

That is how most Chautauqua managers got into the business of talent, tickets and tents. Lyceum was only a step on the way, for only two years after my second South Dakota trip the fertile mind of Keith Vawter began to think about revolutionizing Chautauqua by taking the programs in tents to the people. The circuit plan was Vawter's creation, but the foundation and background for Chautauqua itself had been long in building.

Three Americans before Vawter were responsible for it and each in his own way contributed genius, imagination, courage and hard work. They were James Redpath, John Heyl Vincent and Lewis Miller.

Mr. James Redpath

4

One frosty evening in December, 1867, Novelist Charles Dickens appeared in Boston's Tremont Temple and in the immense audience sat a bearded crusader, pamphleteer, war correspondent and shrewd promoter named James Redpath.

This was Dickens' second American visit. He was world famous, a controversial personality. His *American Notes* had irked people in the United States by its acid comments on life and manners in the young republic. It was a habit of visiting celebrities to criticise us severely. Mrs. Trollope rubbed us the wrong way, too. But Dickens' caustic comments had evidently not diminished his popularity. Speculators anywhere in America could buy up blocks of tickets to lectures by the author of *David Copperfield* at three dollars each and then sell them for fifteen.

Authorities differ on how much Dickens himself netted on this hectic trip to America. Some put it at $60,000. Paul Pearson, a Chautauqua manager, once figured that Dickens' share for his sixty-seven appearances in 1867–8 came to $228,000, an average of $3000 a reading, considerable money for the post-Civil War years. Whatever it amounted to, Dickens was unhappy.

In print and on the platform the visitor complained about the discomforts of the lecturer's life. He "caught American catarrh." He experienced a bad fire in Boston, a flood in Albany, a snowstorm in New York. Gas jets in the halls where he appeared gave a "garish light." The railroad trains on which he rode were "truly alarming . . . we were beaten about . . . the train either banged up hill or banged down hill."

The handling of his baggage Dickens called "outrageous" and in the middle of his tour President Andrew Johnson distracted the thoughts of even the most literary minded by getting himself impeached. All this, Charles Dickens let it be known, left him "much disgusted."

James Redpath already had discussed the practical problems of the tour with Dickens' manager. But after listening in Tremont Temple to the unhappy novelist himself, Redpath put his agile mind to work overnight and at breakfast next morning he outlined to his family an idea that had come to him in the night.

"There should be a general headquarters," he is quoted as saying, "a bureau for the welcoming of literary men and women coming to our country for the purpose of lecturing. They should be made to feel at home among us and the business of arranging routes of travel and dates for lectures should be in charge of competent workers and an established fee agreed upon."

Redpath discussed his own idea that December day with Dr. Samuel G. Howe, in the physician-philanthropist's office at 36 Bromfield Street, Boston. Dr. Howe, in turn, consulted his wife, Julia Ward Howe, author of *The Battle Hymn of the Republic*. Naturally, the idea of any kind of lecture bureau appealed to that flaming abolitionist. She herself was a lecturer. Among her close friends were the leading platform figures of New England, individuals valuable indeed to anyone thinking of building a string of famous speakers. Dr. Howe was rich and open-handed. Why not, his wife suggested, offer the inventive young Redpath a desk in the Bromfield Street office? The doctor agreed and presently that desk became the first headquarters of the Boston Lyceum Bureau, before long to be known as the Redpath Bureau.

Born in Scotland in 1833, Redpath was seventeen when his family came to southern Michigan, where the parents settled on a raw, new farm—but not ambitious James. The son neither settled nor turned his hand to the plow. A born crusader, already a writer of sorts, he soon found himself a job on a Detroit daily newspaper, and before he was nineteen, Horace Greeley, learning somehow of this young man's evangelistic zeal, and reversing his usual advice to youth to "go west," summoned this particular individual east instead, to the powerful New York *Tribune*.

Journalistic restraint was a virtue rarely practised in those days. Like oratory, much current newspaper writing, including James Redpath's, could be extravagantly grandiloquent. The young man was also of a positive nature; the world was always black or white, never gray. Therefore, since he hated slavery he hated it violently, and so he soon contrived for himself an assignment in the slave-holding south.

Redpath's press dispatches were sensational. They endeared him to the anti-slavery faction in New England and apparently also to Mr. Greeley, for in the next few years Reporter Redpath travelled recklessly north to south, east to west, picking up extravagant gossip or unhappy facts, all in favor of freeing the slaves. When the Kansas-Nebraska bill opened those territories to the possibility of slavery, he rushed at once to "Bloody Kansas," there took sides vehemently, wrote, harangued, organized, joined in the fist fights, became a dedicated partisan of Captain John Brown, whose moldering body soon would become a battle song. When war finally arrived, young Redpath, as a New York *Tribune* correspondent, attached himself to Sherman's army, eventually sent the first dispatch on the fall of Charleston.

Admirers of the Redpath family credit it with inspiring the first "Decoration Day." Some give the honor to James, some to Mary Cotton Redpath, his wife. At any rate, near Charleston, South Carolina, in 1865, while Redpath was superintendent of education for the freedmen, either Mary or he chanced to see an uncared-for military cemetery. Its "rows of half-filled graves" held two hundred and fifty-seven Union soldiers, and angry at the neglect, Redpath enlisted the aid of enough newly-freed slaves to raise and clean the mounds, and on May 1, while Lincoln's body lay in state in Chicago, Showman Redpath, in Charleston, held one of his first spectacles.

Flags waved, drummers drummed. A clergyman, a general, thirty startled colored men and Redpath himself, spoke, and the exercises ended with a review of a full army brigade—all of this, the Charleston *Courier* related next day, before "an immense gathering, fully 10,000 persons." The colored men had erected a "fine substantial fence," the newspapers reported, and "the graves at the close of the procession had the appearance of a mass of roses."

So at the ripe age of thirty-two, with the war ended, Redpath had returned north to discover himself famous among the very people he wanted to impress, the writers, poets, preachers and teachers of New England. He went back to his writing; it was two years later that he happened to listen to the controversial Dickens.

From the beginning James Redpath's lecture bureau was a success. The great and the near-great, who had been journeying to Ohio and other accessible corners of the land, suddenly discovered that here was a man who for a small fee would eliminate much of the risk and some of the hardships of the lecture business. Moreover, he could promise most speakers six paid engagements a week, and if one happened to be an ordained minister, there could be a Sunday engagement as well.

In Redpath's first booking season of 1868 he shared, at least to some extent, in the management of Mark Twain's east-bound tour. Next year a few cautious New Englanders were ready to join his bureau. Bayard Taylor, Barnum, Humorists Billings and Nasby, other purveyors of entertainment, who up to now had "managed" their own western trips, turned their troubles over to Redpath. Beecher, whose 1855 experience with an agent had been unhappy, found that Redpath, on the other hand, eased the way, partly because he cooperated with local groups instead of trying to ignore them.

By 1871 Redpath's growing lists included Charles Sumner, Wendell Phillips, Edward Everett Hale, James G. Blaine, and a dozen other scholars and public figures. From the not-so-frail group of "feminists," who already were agitating for women's right to vote, he offered such names as Lucy Stone, Mary A. Livermore, Anna Dickinson.

Lucy Larcom for a number of years had given readings of her poems. New England respected dark-haired Miss Larcom as a self-made woman; in her childhood she had worked in the Lowell, Massachusetts, cotton mills. In her readings she always included her famous title, *Hannah*—"poor lone Hannah, sitting by the window binding shoes . . . faded, wrinkled . . . 'Is there from the fishers any news?' . . . old with watching . . . Hannah's at the window, binding shoes."

School children of the period committed *Hannah* to memory. No program of recitations was considered complete without it. A prolific versifier, Miss Larcom had hundreds of published poems and ballads to draw upon, including a stirring nineteen-stanza defense of spinsterhood.

Many of the lecturers, no matter how restrained they managed to be on their trips west, were controversial figures on the Atlantic seaboard. None was more so than Senator Sumner of Massachusetts, the successor to Webster in the Senate as leader of the abolitionists. His violent *Crime Against Kansas* speech, with its opening words, "The wickedness which I now begin to expose . . ." had so roused one southerner that he clubbed its author almost to death and for three years Senator Sumner made no speeches. To make matters worse in the minds of certain editors, Sumner also was not only a Free-Soiler, but also talked recklessly about prison reform. Notoriety, of course, made him a box-office success, despite the fact that audiences in some localities might have difficulty fathoming the Greek and Latin phrases with which he sprinkled his prose.

It is apparent that James Redpath, the flaming agitator of the John Brown days, sent out to lecture men whose opinions, for the most part, coincided with his own. Another reformer, as controversial as Sumner, but with diction easier to understand, was Wendell Phillips, most outspoken of all the abolitionists. Phillips used a new platform approach. Instead of following the popular ornate style, he spoke in a quiet, conversational tone, larding his speech with homely colloquialisms. But he pulled no punches. He had happened to see Editor William Lloyd Garrison mobbed in Boston in 1835 because of his opposition to slavery. The incident made an agitator of the well-born Phillips. But not only his outspoken defense of the abolitionist cause made him suspect among many politicians. To their dismay, he had the effrontery to go out among the people and recommend a new method of picking public employees, without reference to party loyalty. Some day it would be called "civil service."

James G. Blaine, the "Man from Maine," was a mere political fledgling when he permitted Redpath to place his name on his list of lecturers. In later years the "plumed knight," as Colonel Robert Green Ingersoll dubbed

Blaine in the 1876 Presidential race, was to become the most controversial figure on the American political scene. Despite Ingersoll's eloquence, Blaine was defeated in the first try by Rutherford Hayes, largely because of the now long-forgotten "Mulligan Letters" scandal. However, in 1884, he actually won the Republican nomination. The campaign that followed was studded with billingsgate; Cleveland, his Democratic opponent, was held up to general opprobrium as the alleged father of an illegitimate child. Blaine's prospects were ruined almost at the last moment when a hotheaded Protestant cleric dubbed the Democrats the party of "Rum, Romanism and Rebellion," and Blaine, by neglecting to disavow him, lost the Irish-Catholic vote. Blaine lost to Cleveland by the narrow margin of 1149 votes in New York State, which put that great commonwealth into Cleveland's column. Of course, Blaine's adherents screamed, "We was robbed."

When Blaine began his swing around the Lyceum circuit, bitterness over freeing the slaves had been followed by bitterness almost as vehement over allowing them to vote. Blaine, in his lectures, aroused public support for his defense in Congress of impartial suffrage. Actually, the Fourteenth Amendment of the Constitution was substantially his idea.

Steadily James Redpath pushed up his clients' rates. The records show that Emerson, for one early appearance, had accepted five dollars, plus three quarts of oats for his tired horse. Thanks to the new bureau, before the New England philosopher said farewell to the platform, he was earning five hundred dollars a night. The one thousand dollars that Beecher received for a lecture on the Boston Lyceum course is said to have been the highest guaranteed fee James Redpath ever paid.

The business department continued to be difficult for Redpath to handle, however. Money details worried him. Most of these, from the start, he left to the judgment and decisions of a friend in nearby Malden, George L. Fall. Neither of them ever became rich from bureau receipts. But public education profited and for Redpath that was enough. If speakers benefitted too, well and good. The goal was improvement and new and happy direction for the American platform. Although not a frivolous man, neither was Redpath a glum one, and he knew that the public wanted its risibility tickled, as well as its intellect improved.

"The Lyceum lecture is a failure," he said, "if it succeeds in imparting instruction alone. It should afford pleasure as well." He had in mind clients like Josh Billings who imparted little instruction and much pleasure.

Edward Everett Hale, pastor of Boston's Old South Congregational Church for more than forty years, certainly was not listed as a humorist, but his droll speech and whimsical side remarks delighted everyone, particularly when he spoke extemporaneously or read from his own fiction. His stiff-necked home town of Boston came in for not-so-gentle spoofing, and occasional sharp jibes, from cities less reserved and less sure of themselves. In the west and south it was the disrespectful habit of local humorists to say that Boston exported no articles of native growth except granite and ice.

"We have improved," Hale replied in one speech, taking amused note of the charge. "We have added roses and cabbages, and I assure you that the granite is hard granite and the ice is very cold ice."

In spite of Hale's reputation as a wit, his most quoted words, over the years, became an uplift motto, out of one of his short stories: "Look up and not down, look forward and not back, look out and not in, and lend a hand."

Half a dozen "do-good" groups appropriated the words. From a story essentially romantic, *In His Name,* came similar missionary-society inspiration. Religious overtones notwithstanding, audiences found Hale entertaining. His *Man Without a Country* had first made him famous; to Redpath's own satisfaction, it had given strength to the Union cause in the North. Of all the personalities handled by the Redpath agency, Hale more than any other transferred his enthusiasms later to the Chautauqua movement as it was to be launched in New York State.

In 1875, at the age of forty-two, Redpath wearied of the confinement of an office and sold his Boston bureau to two employees, George H. Hathaway and Major James B. Pond. However, Redpath did not retire. He shortly was managing a headline-making tour for Colonel Ingersoll, the Congregational minister's son whose silver-tongued atheism caused pulpits to quiver and good folk to pray in public for his benighted soul. It was in the midst of this tour that Ingersoll nominated James G. Blaine for the Presidency at the Republican convention in Cincinnati on June 15, 1876. His brief address, full of patriotism and lofty sentiments, counteracted somewhat his more lurid reputation as an atheist.

"James G. Blaine," Ingersoll declaimed, "has . . . the audacity of genius . . . the grandest combination of heart, conscience and brain . . . beneath the flag. Like an armed warrior, like a plumed knight, he marched down the halls of Congress and threw his shining lance against the brazen foreheads of the defamers of his country. . . . In the name of the great Republic, in the name of all her soldiers dead upon the field of battle, in the name of those who perished in the skeleton clutch of famine at Andersonville and Libby, whose suffering he vividly remembers . . . Illinois nominates that prince of parliamentarians, that leader of leaders, James G. Blaine."

The lecture tour ended without the anti-church orator being struck dead, as many pious citizens had predicted would happen and Redpath, possibly thankfully, gave his attention again to the arts. He organized several opera companies and sent them through the east. Then, in 1880, he turned his back on oratory and the stage both, and resuming his connection with the New York *Tribune,* he went to Ireland as a correspondent.

In Ireland, as in Kansas before the Civil War, instead of reporting objectively, Redpath leaped actively into the fray. He not only wrote violently of the violent deeds of Captain Charles Boycott and other heartless land agents, but he rushed back to America and himself took to the platform to tell the sad story of "the holy land of Connaught and Munster." While doing so, he collected $125,000, which he forwarded to Ireland to relieve its suffering. It was in these speeches, he later claimed, that he made Boycott's name into a common verb.

Meanwhile the Redpath bureau, without Redpath, found itself marking time while its new owners tried, without too much success, to adjust themselves to one another. Australian-born Hathaway was a solid citizen; he booked safe and respectable lecturers and maintained an excellent set of books. The reputation of the bureau was in his hands and he intended to keep it unsullied.

The other partner, Major Pond, was by nature a showman. Thirty-seven years old when he bought into the agency, he had until now drifted from one adventure to another. Son of a New York blacksmith who had taken his family to central Illinois by way of a Great Lakes schooner and a covered wagon, young Jim Pond had struck out for himself at fifteen. First, like so many wanderers of the time, he learned the printing trade; then, like Redpath, he went to "bloody Kansas."

When war came, Pond enlisted with the Third Wisconsin Cavalry and soon found himself in Kansas again, a lieutenant fighting guerrillas. At Baxter Springs in 1863, he repelled an attack by the notorious "Quantrell's Band." Confederate General William C. Quantrell, believing that "anything's fair in love and war," had dressed his riders in captured Union uniforms and carrying a Union flag, had infiltrated into the Northern lines. Pond was commended for gallantry in action and left the army a major.

After the war the young veteran worked his way west to Utah and into a reporter's job on a Salt Lake City newspaper. While there, a rich lecture possibility dropped into his eager hands. Ann Eliza Young, a somewhat confused young woman who claimed that she was Brigham Young's nineteenth wife, sued Young for divorce. Pond quickly signed her for a lecture tour.

The lady paved the way for huge audiences by bursting into print with scandalous stories of secret goings-on in "Mormon harems." Her semiliterate letters to the press and public figures were full of piety and sex. So far as curious crowds went, it was a triumphal tour, and at its end James Redpath recognizing showmanship when he saw it, had asked Pond to join the Boston bureau.

Friction betweeen Pond and Hathaway did not openly develop after Redpath went his way, but in 1879 Hathaway bought Pond's share in the company and the younger man moved to New York and opened his own office. A number of personalities on the old Redpath list went with him, among them Henry Ward Beecher. From then, until the clergyman's death in 1887, Pond travelled almost continuously with him—300,000 miles in twelve years, he once figured.

For more than twenty years Hathaway, as sole owner, carried on the Redpath name and tradition in Boston, but with shrinking success. He believed in solid meat-and-potatoes fare and that is what he offered, without glamor or excitement. Then in 1901, evidently convinced that younger blood was needed in his organization, he cut the business into three slices. He kept one slice and made it the head office in Boston with himself as president. Another slice went to Crawford A. Peffer, a man of both vision and vigor, who was to run the Philadelphia headquarters with the title of vice-president.

The third slice was bought by Keith Vawter, who closed his own bureau in Des Moines and moved to Chicago as western manager. James Redpath was out of the picture and Vawter, the man who was to put high-class entertainment into a travelling tent, was in.

Redpath himself did not live to see Vawter's Chautauqua circuits. But the pioneer's influence on them, when they came, was two-fold. He had created American Lyceum in the sense that it is known today. This in time inspired Chautauqua circuits and he gave them both his name. Actually he gave more. He bequeathed to both movements a practical foundation, a taste for controversy and an abiding sense of decency. His ideals and prejudices, enthusiasms and taboos guided them.

Chautauqua Lake

5

In the meantime, the church had not been idle. Slowly, in a rural county in western New York, it had been establishing its own medium for enlarging the horizons of the people. Where Pennsylvania and Lake Erie squeeze the Empire state into a jut of land, lies an inland lake, some eighteen miles long, shaped like an uneven crescent. The lake is called "Chautauqua," a word which a local historian, Obed Edson by name, claimed was of Seneca Indian origin and meant "jumping fish." In 1788 George Washington, who often spelled by ear, referred to the lake, in a letter, as "Jadaqua."

On its northwest shore, a hundred years ago, lake steamers called at the stubby dock of a hamlet known as Fair Point. There in a grove a band of Methodists held camp meetings, the same kind of religious gathering that was to spread through the south and the west, festivals full of sound and fury, dedicated to the laudable purpose of saving souls. Each summer farmers from miles around hitched up their teams, piled their families, tents and cooking supplies into buckboards and drove to the lake for a few days of swimming and salvation. They erected an "assembly tent," later built a "pavilion" with a good stout roof, still later a cookhouse and dining hall. But after a dozen or more seasons, the attendance declined. Why, no one knew.

Among the financial backers of the Fair Point institution was an Akron, Ohio, manufacturer of farm machinery named Lewis Miller, a man of inventive bent who had made considerable money. Years later his daughter was to marry another inventor named Thomas Alva Edison. More important to the sleepy town of Fair Point on Chautauqua Lake, Miller was deeply religious. He regretted the decline of the camp meeting and when one summer it finally did not open, he became a trustee to manage the idle property.

Miller, from early youth, had been an enthusiastic teacher in Methodist Sunday schools and in the late 60's there came to his attention a series of articles in a church magazine urging better education for Sunday-school teachers. These articles were signed by the Reverend Dr. John Heyl Vincent of the Methodist Episcopal church.

Vincent had long shown signs of religious leadership; at eighteen he was licensed in Pennsylvania as a Methodist "exhorter and preacher." By twenty-five he became an "elder," and with a copy of Dante in his pocket went out to preach in Illinois, taking over presently the church in Galena, where lived an obscure whiskey-drinking veteran of the Mexican War, named Ulysses S. Grant, who was clerking in his father's leather store.

Merchant and minister became close friends. It was Vincent, standing on a freight car, who delivered Galena's official oration when Soldier Grant left for the Civil War. It was Vincent who welcomed the returning general home, and then, when this hero could find no words of his own, orated for him. The tongue-tied Grant appreciated Vincent's flattering remarks that day at Galena, and years later, as the eighteenth President of the United States, repaid him for them handsomely—at Chautauqua Lake.

Vincent was an able speaker. By 1864 he was minister of growing Chicago's Trinity Methodist Church and here he became distressed by the mediocrity of the Sunday school. Children in uncomfortable Sunday clothes, confined for an hour a week on hard chairs in dimly lighted rooms, recited like parrots dull lessons from the church's "Question Books." The teachers were uninspiring, the lessons dreary, and Vincent, determined to do something about such a disappointing business, established in Chicago "a correspondence course" for Sunday-school teachers.

Back in Ohio, Lewis Miller read the Reverend Dr. Vincent's writings with continued satisfaction. The two men, with so many ideas in common, met at last and in their conversation Vincent repeated his conviction that the discouraging Sunday-school problem in the end must be solved by the proper education of teachers.

"There should be a summer school in Akron or New York or Philadelphia," he is quoted as saying, "where we could give our teachers a short course in Biblical history and geography, in interpretation of the Scriptures and in moral philosophy."

Here was Lewis Miller's long-awaited opportunity. If he could combine the Lord's work with getting the camp site on Chautauqua Lake out of its financial hole, why not? He pointed out to John Heyl Vincent that classes there, under God's open sky, would permit students to concentrate away from the city's gas-lit temptations. Vincent demurred. The fact that Fair Point had been a camp-meeting ground caused him uneasiness; he disliked noisy, razzle-dazzle evangelism. But at last he agreed and the two churchmen made plans for training teachers at a "Sunday School Normal Institute."

Thus Vincent and Miller, six years after the night in Boston when James Redpath listened to Charles Dickens, embarked on a venture which, joined later to Redpath's booking agency, eventually would develop into the tent Chautauqua circuits.

The Sunday School Assembly at Fair Point on Chautauqua Lake opened August 12, in 1874, lasted sixteen days and was attended by forty eager young men and women who paid $6.00 each for bed and board, instruction and inspiration. As superintendent, Dr. Vincent took vigorous charge of the academic program, led the singing and prayers, taught classes in Bible reading, and to aid the study of Biblical geography, built on the sand a great relief map of Palestine, possibly one of the first attempts in this country at visual education.

As the school grew, the rigidly chaperoned recreation that had been promised parents became an enlarging problem. Miller and Vincent, fearful that some scandal beyond their control might develop in the sylvan glades, agreed that a regular program of entertainment must fill the idle time after lessons. Before long this innovation became part and parcel of the institute, and more and better teachers were hired. These included William Rainey Harper as educational director.

Ohio-born Harper filled the post at the school on the lake for six years, until he became president of the University of Chicago. Never a man to oppose an idea because it was new, Harper immediately revolutionized Chautauqua Lake's educational program; later, at Chicago, he did likewise. Conservative critics, who had watched Harper suspiciously in the east, in the west were to find him outright radical; in an irreverent press, Chicago's new and later distinguished institution of learning became known for a period as "Harper's Bazaar."

As college president, Harper did not drop his interest in Chautauqua. His talents as a scholar were offered regularly to the independent assemblies. Once, with clergyman Franklin Weidner, president of Chicago Lutheran Seminary, he gave an evening's lesson in Hebrew. The two men, both students of Oriental languages, set up a blackboard on which they wrote, in Hebrew, the first verse of *Genesis*. They coached their audiences to read in unison; when the first verse was learned, they went on to the second.

Vincent, who found all dullness most distasteful, had not objected when Director Harper enlarged the Lake's curriculum to offer knowledge, not only of the Bible, but also of the modern world. He agreed to classes in the arts and crafts, literature, science, physical education, even in what today is known as home economics. Music remained sacred, of course. Not until 1880 is there any record of any music not sacred at Chautauqua Lake. In that year a brave soul dared play Carl Maria von Weber's romantic *Invitation to the Dance*.

The great sand map depicting Holy Land geography was abandoned as the enrollment grew, with one unseemly episode probably speeding its demise. Passengers, landing one dark night from a lake steamer, were searching for their sleeping quarters when one man lost his way. Good Chautauquans later pointed out that this was a "travelling salesman" perhaps not in complete harmony with the moral philosophy of the camp. At any rate, as the stranger wandered in outer darkness, his wayward feet led him straight across the Reverend Dr. Vincent's elaborate sand map. He struggled up the steep Judean mountains and having attained their height, he lost his footing and plunged face first into the Dead Sea.

In time, the name of the school also changed. Students and summer visitors, swarming to the lake shore in ever-larger numbers, filling its orderly rows of tents, packing the new frame hotels, did not bother to say "Assembly," or "Institute," or "Normal School." They merely were "at Chautauqua." Visitors to the spot in current years find a classic touch in its main building, a Grecian temple in a grove of hard maples and long-leafed pines, its front elevation a façade of pillars. Its buildings represent millions of dollars in investment today; thousands of persons still patronize its summer programs and schools, continued successfully over the years on a non-profit basis.

John Heyl Vincent eventually became Bishop Vincent, which surely did not hurt his institution, but in the meantime his quick mind had raised the question: Why should teaching be confined to a summer session and nine months of the year be left a cultural desert? So he started the Chautauqua Literary and Scientific Circle, a home reading course and correspondence school.

Naturally someone had to furnish the books. Therefore the Chautauqua Press was set up, governed by an unsalaried "committee of six." In 1885 its catalogue listed ninety-three titles. They were "paperbacks," undoubtedly the first ever printed in the country, smaller than today's, however. They measured three by five inches, approximately the size of the "little blue books" that E. Julius Haldeman was to make famous in later years in Lawrence, Kansas. They numbered seventy to one hundred pages and sold for ten cents. They included poems by William Cullen Bryant, a beginners' astronomy, a life of Socrates, the educational theories of Horace Mann, a history of art, readings from the classics and a half dozen historical titles by Bishop Vincent himself.

"Chautauqua Literary and Scientific Circles," meeting to discuss books, sprang up in several thousand towns; their members usually were women, though in Arkansas, the records show, an ambitious country storekeeper recruited the men loafing on his cracker barrels. As a measure of the circles' popularity, in the late nineteenth century and on into the twentieth, is the fact that in distant Iowa alone, where some fifty towns participated, cities as large as Des Moines had to be divided among several "circles." At one time this state capital had thirty groups in action.

The Miller-Vincent enterprise had a host of imitators throughout the country. By 1900 upward of two hundred copies of the New York original were popping up like toadstools, most of them beside lapping waters, from New Jersey and the Maine woods to California and Oregon.

Owners of these summer institutions did not beat about the bush. They called them "Chautauquas" and neither Miller nor Vincent objected. Programs at these "independents," as they came to be known, were planned primarily for customers in the immediate neighborhoods and they lasted each summer from a few packed days to a month. For talent the managers

A letter from Thomas A. Edison to the Chautauquas,
September 15, 1923

Greetings to all the Chautauquas who have set aside one day in recognition of the original movement started by those two men of imagination, Lewis Miller and J. H. Vincent; a movement based on an idea which has now spread over the whole of our country and, in fact, over the world; an idea which has been and will continue to be of immense educational value to all the people, and, therefore, of first importance to their welfare.

Thos A. Edison.

turned to the winter Lyceum bureaus, enlisting the great and famous, the in-betweens, sometimes the notorious. They billed the best musicians, orators and humorists available, all the time eyeing enviously the star-studded talent that constantly distinguished the boards at the "mother" institution.

Undeniably more famous men and women, including Presidents of the United States, have appeared at Chautauqua Lake in eighty years than in any other spot in America. For despite its Wesleyan ancestry, the Chautauqua Lake Assembly became not only non-denominational, but, more important, it reached beyond the pulpit for exciting orators, men of ideas, be they orthodox or not, popular or unpopular. Both Vincent and Miller had small sympathy for unreasonable sectarianism, so the great outdoor assembly under the trees—today it would be called a bowl—soon responded to the voices of ministers and laymen of almost every Protestant faith. If they were thinking men and had good, carrying voices, that was enough.

But it also helped, Vincent well knew, if their names were in the news. Names attract crowds and the good clergyman established the policy, then and there, for all later types of Chautauqua, that it was much more profitable culturally, and was also within the proper spirit of his organization, to offer a program to a large crowd rather than to a small handful of already enlightened faithful.

By Vincent's time the "star system" already controlled the theatres, just as it dominates movie and television screens today. New York and Philadelphia audiences might be mildly enthusiastic about Shakespeare, but they were wildly so about Shakespeare plus Edwin Booth, or Shakespeare plus Henry Irving, or Shakespeare plus Edwin Forrest. Vincent had been twenty-five years old when American loyalty to Forrest, in opposition to a popular British actor, led to the Astor Place riots in New York, with Forrest's admirers dying for him. Whether the good clergyman was consciously aping the theatre when he introduced the star system at the Chautauqua Lake assembly may only be surmised today. At any rate, in the second year he prevailed upon the President of the United States to make an appearance.

Stiff-necked churchmen were shocked and practical politicians startled when the newspapers announced that Ulysses S. Grant would spend a week "participating" at Chautauqua Lake. That he actually was a second choice was not mentioned at the moment. The famous personality Vincent had planned to use to put his institution into the headlines was Henry Ward Beecher. But to Vincent's dismay, the clergyman made headlines of his own.

Beecher at the time had served the Plymouth Church for twenty-five years. He was fifty-nine years old, one of the most respected men in the nation, when a strange, unhappy, vindictive woman named Victoria Woodhull, a member of his church, published a leering story in which she linked

Beecher's name with that of the wife of his friend and fellow lecturer, Editor and Poet Theodore Tilton. Not only was Tilton also a member of the Plymouth congregation, but he had been Beecher's house guest many times and the two had travelled together on their Lyceum rounds.

At first Tilton refused to believe the story; gossips persisted, and nearly two years after the Woodhull "disclosure," Tilton sued Beecher for $100,-000, charging him with adultery. Mrs. Tilton, never strong mentally, thereupon gave out a series of contradictory "voluntary confessions," which from time to time she withdrew. The lawsuit lasted six months. After the jury had been out nine days, it stood nine to three for acquittal, and agreed that it never could agree. A church body, after hearing the evidence, cleared Beecher of the charge. The case cost him $180,000; he took to the road at once on a new series of lecture tours to pay off the debt.

At Chautauqua Lake, meanwhile, Bishop Vincent had reconsidered his choice of a speaker. The invitation that he had prepared for Clergyman Beecher, went instead to President Grant.

Certainly the Civil War hero was controversial enough. Politicians blamed him, probably unjustly, for the panic of 1873 and for the upsurge of the "greenback" movement for cheap money that followed it. They hammered at him for the "Whiskey Ring" scandals in which several of his appointees defrauded the government, and which finally reached his own office where only his intervention saved his private secretary. As if all this were not enough, the Senate impeached his Secretary of War for taking bribes. Grant stopped this proceeding by quickly accepting his Cabinet officer's resignation.

Outside the political arena, Grant had detractors who attacked him on "moral" issues. Prohibitionists loudly resented his whiskey drinking and anti-tobacco crusaders never allowed him to smoke a cigar in peace. He had been known, under stress of war, to break the Tenth Commandment in a loud voice. Also he belonged to no church.

Vincent shut his eyes to such objections. He could be fairly certain that the President would accept. The inarticulate Grant had favors to repay, dating back to Vincent's speeches for him in Galena, Illinois. "The fact that he is the President," Vincent told his associates, "will make a point for our cause," no matter, apparently, how tenuous the President's connections with religion.

Grant's visit on Saturday, August 15, 1875, gave the Chautauqua Lake assembly the nation-wide publicity it needed. He travelled by slow train to Jamestown, New York, then he boarded the side-wheeler *Josie Belle* for the trip up-lake. In later years in circuit Chautauqua there were gala parades aplenty, but certainly nothing like this. Young ladies of the church had draped the little *Josie Belle* with red, white and blue bunting until, according to one reporter, "it looked like something out of fairyland." Be-

hind the steamer, with the President of the United States sitting conspicuously in its bow, trundled a procession of other craft, these, too, "gaily be-
decked and carrying thousands of cheering enthusiastic watchers."

Republican party leaders in New York state lent willing hands to the
celebration. In fact, this widely publicized union of the Republican party, the
Protestant church, the White House and Bishop Vincent's cultural enterprise pleased everyone except the Democrats. New York newspapers estimated that the crowd waiting at the Chautauqua assembly grounds numbered 30,000, a figure possibly padded by the excitement of the moment.
But no matter how many persons witnessed the event, all America read
about it. From that day on, the nation knew about Chautauqua Lake.

Grant did not make a long speech, though it was not as short as the one
his young son Jesse had play-acted about a few years before in the White
House. The child, seven years old, had set out to entertain his family with
a portrayal of "How papa makes a speech." It was unwittingly acid, and
Grant's feelings, always hiding near the surface, had been hurt.

The boy, striking a stiff attitude, had said: "Ladies and Gentlemen . . ."
and then a pause. "I am very glad to see you. I thank you very much. Good
night."

Grant reminisced at Chautauqua Lake about his carefree days with
Bishop Vincent at Galena, Illinois. When he sat down, he knew that he
had done better than usual. Talking about old friendships was pleasant compared with the endless insoluble problems, the backbiting and political
wrangling that filled his mind most of the time in Washington; also, he
could talk better out-of-doors.

Grant was only the first of a long line of Presidents, former Presidents,
Presidents-elect and Presidential candidates to speak at the "mother"
Chautauqua, and later at the scattered independent assemblies, and finally
in the canvas tents. In 1880 the Republican nominee, General James A.
Garfield, arrived at the Miller-Vincent quarters and again Republican cam-
paign managers played up the visit for all it was worth.

Garfield, like Grant, approached the New York grove by steamboat, but
it was night and he slept instead of sitting nobly in the bow. The next
morning he piously attended Sunday morning devotions and was introduced.
He did not speak. For one reason, his voice was worn out from campaigning; for another, it was the Sabbath and even the most anxious politicians
in that period knew that it would never do to mix politics with the Lord's
Day worship. Garfield simply bowed and sat down and immediately the
audience, rising enthusiastically to its own feet, startled the visitor with a
"Chautauqua salute."

Mr. Garfield was accustomed to tromping, hollering political crowds.
This was silent applause and he never had met anything like it. Nor had
anyone else, except men speaking on the Miller-Vincent programs. Good
folk in the Chautauqua Lake audience considered hand-clapping and cheers

a bit uncouth, particularly on the Sabbath. Also it was often difficult to determine whether a visiting clergyman's remarks constituted a sermon, which you didn't applaud, or an inspirational address, which you did. Lurking in the background of the whole idea was the thought that, as Mark Twain had expressed it to James Redpath, "people are afraid to laugh in a church." So at Chautauqua Lake someone had suggested that an approving audience wave its handkerchiefs.

Those doctors present who had heard the echoes of the new germ theory were highly critical of this practice of waving handkerchiefs about in a tabernacle full of innocent people. But those to whom the "salute" was an emotional safety valve pointed out that the handkerchiefs for the most part were clean, so why be fussy?

A newspaper reported that Monday, when Mr. Garfield's party prepared to leave, a "great throng" crowded the dock. Since it was no longer the Sabbath, the Republican nominee could indulge freely in politics. After tossing a few barbs at the discredited "party of slavery," without mentioning the Democrats, he rolled up his sleeves and attacked the "idle rich."

Dr. Vincent had invited the Fisk Jubilee Singers from the fledgling university at Nashville, Tennessee, to take part in the program. This lusty musical group had been on the road only half a dozen or so years; for the next half century its succeeding members would be familiar figures on hundreds of platforms. They sang now for the departing Garfield:

> "This is the Year of Jubilee,
> "You shall gain the victory,
> "The Lord has set His People free,
> "And you shall gain the day."

The Book of Leviticus tells that twice each century, in the ancient system of "Jubilee Years," a Hebrew sold into service must be freed. This held particular meaning for these young colored singers. The war to free the slaves was no by-gone memory. The crowd, however, saw political implications for the 1880 Presidential campaign. The "great throng" took the song as a prophecy and the "pent-up enthusiasm of the previous day demanded vent." Not only did they cheer both Mr. Garfield and the Jubilee Singers, but the white handkerchiefs came out again, until, in the reporter's words, "the fluttering linens made the lake shore look as if a magical snowstorm had fallen on the forest."

In the early 1900's another entertainer whose platform appearances spanned almost the whole life of tent Chautauqua, Poet-humorist Wallace Bruce Amsbary, read Riley one summer evening to seven thousand people at the Lake assembly. The "salute" he received he compared to "an immense cauldron of pop-corn exploding all over the vast auditorium." For decades the practice of waving handkerchiefs persisted. Not until just before the First World War did a Chicago doctor, lecturing on a Chautauqua

circuit on causes of the common cold, finally succeed in putting a stop to
the practice. Bishop Vincent had tried. Alert to criticism in the press, he
finally had set a rule that he alone, from the platform, could "start" a handkerchief salute and even he only "a few times a season." In spite of him,
his delighted audiences had continued to break out the handkerchiefs.

A refinement of the practice cropped up in 1956 in Leningrad. While the
American company of *Porgy and Bess* was playing there, eight or ten Negro
members of the cast attended Sunday services at the Leningrad Baptist
church and at the request of the minister sang several Negro spirituals. When
they had finished, the Russians, like the Americans at Chautauqua Lake,
showed their delight with "fluttering linens." Finally, as a special accolade,
they rolled the handkerchiefs into balls and pelted the singers with them.
The pelting was symbolic, no doubt. Roses are hard to find in the Russian
winter and word of Bishop Vincent's ideas about germs may not have arrived in Leningrad.

In 1881, Schuyler Colfax, an Indiana radical who was Vice-President
in Grant's first administration, lectured at the lake, the first of many Vice-
Presidents to appear in independent assemblies or circuit tents. From Indiana, too, came "T.R.'s" mate, Charles Fairbanks, and one of Bryan's several
fellows in defeat, John Kern. Benjamin Harrison, Cleveland, McKinley,
Theodore Roosevelt, Taft, Wilson, Harding, Coolidge and Franklin Delano
Roosevelt all were distinguished Chautauqua Lake orators before or after
their terms of office, and in the case of the two Roosevelts each appeared
there once while living in the White House. Their own homes were not too
far from Chautauqua Lake, and "T.R.," who liked to fill his lungs with fresh
country air, appeared five summers as a speaker, "F.D.R." four times.

As for defeated Presidential candidates, they were legion. Democrats
Alton B. Parker, Alfred E. Smith, James M. Cox and Henry Wallace,
Socialist Eugene V. Debs, Progressive Robert M. LaFollette, Republicans
Charles E. Hughes and Wendell Willkie, all, at one time or another, mounted
Bishop Vincent's stage, and of course the greatest attraction of them all was
that Democratic aspirant, William Jennings Bryan.

The tent Chautauquas, although they never entertained a President while
he was in office, were to book several before or after their residence in the
White House—Taft with his chuckle and heavy valise, scholar Wilson,
first-rate speaker Harding. Vice-Presidents Tom Marshall, of the memorable epigram, "What this country needs is a good five-cent cigar," and Calvin
Coolidge both took to the road while in office. It was the fate of the usually
non-loquacious Coolidge to be hissed off a platform, one suffocating day in
Minnesota, by a crowd impatiently waiting for the horse races; they thought
one hour and twenty-five minutes too long for a dull speech—a state fair
platform, it happened to be, in between Mr. Coolidge's Chautauqua dates.

Mr. Taft, with his triple chins, chuckled his way once through a less ig-
nominious incident. In Washington Heights in 1916, in the only Chautauqua

ever attempted by any system within the limits of New York City, the genial ex-President arrived in a hard rain storm to find only a handful of persons occupying a few scattered seats in a vast tent. He joined the audience in a hearty laugh and made his speech as if the tent were full and the handful of listeners went home satisfied.

Tent circuits welcomed governors by the dozen, ambassadors and United States senators in platoons, congressmen in such numbers that members of mere state legislatures found themselves left out in the cold. Managers of the travelling Chautauquas had learned their lessons well from Bishop Vincent and Lewis Miller. Not only had these two pioneers made the New York assembly so respectable that even chiefs of state were glad to appear there, but like crusading James Redpath, they also taught their successors the publicity value of big names. If the names were controversial, so much the better.

Vawter Has an Idea

6

In the early summer of 1904 I bought a pair of white duck pants. I needed them in my new role as platform superintendent in Iowa Falls and general superintendent in Bedford, Iowa. Vawter was taking the daring plunge that year from winter Lyceum into summer tent Chautauqua. I was delighted, naturally, by the assignment, but scared, too. It was one thing to talk fast to a small committee on the Dakota frontier and quite another to address an audience of several hundred from a stage.

It was an auspicious year, 1904, for Keith Vawter's new venture. The country was enjoying considerable prosperity. Chicago, capital of his Redpath Lyceum principality, was booming, making big wages, putting up big buildings, amassing big fortunes, shouting its greatness in a big midwestern voice. As western manager for the Redpath Lyceum Bureau, Vawter was now in a position to offer culture in wholesale lots to all the middle west. He not only could sell all the eastern Redpath list of famous orators and entertainers; he also had the clients of his original Standard Bureau, that he had operated by himself in Iowa. Moving from Des Moines to Chicago, he had honored me with a splendid title: "Manager of the City Department." I transferred my college credits to the University of Chicago and for a little longer attended law school while I sold lectures.

Business was plentiful. In addition to the great field of winter Lyceum bookings, there were the independent Chautauquas which operated across the country; during the summer months they all needed platform talent. However, as Vawter studied their loose organizations, he observed what time and effort they wasted, and Vawter hated waste. He realized that the individual summer groups had no over-all plan. Instead of combining to funnel available talent from town to town, on a well-oiled schedule, each manager attempted to do a job alone.

50

To be sure, there had been a few efforts at cooperation. In 1897 three managers in Iowa, Kansas and Colorado had tried unsuccessfully to combine in a single circuit, but after stupendous effort they had signed only nine widely scattered towns. George E. Vincent, son of the Bishop of Chautauqua Lake, later a president of the University of Minnesota, also had joined with four other managers to establish a loosely-knit association that they hopefully called the International Chautauqua Alliance. By 1904 it had acquired twenty-four members in fourteen states, but these, too, were spread too thinly to take advantage of mass bookings or economical travel time.

More important, perhaps, was the fact that each assembly manager, possibly an ex-schoolteacher or a clergyman, was an individualist, working for no one but himself. His personal preferences, and often his own hidebound prejudices, dictated his choice of program. Usually he insisted to the booking agent that "My people demand" this or that. As Vawter well knew, the truth was that his people got the type of Chautauqua fare that the manager or the president of the Ladies' Aid Society, who happened to be chairman of the Chautauqua committee, thought would be good for their souls.

Thus, when the Reverend Billy Sunday was the energetic moving spirit of Winona Lake Assembly in northern Indiana, he discovered a never-satisfied yearning among his customers for equal parts of loud gospel music and evangelical orators charging in a solid phalanx against tobacco, the Demon Rum, "bad" language, short skirts and Sabbath-breaking.

On the other hand, the committee responsible for the program at Bay View Assembly on Little Traverse Bay in northern Michigan thought the people who swarmed into its unfenced grounds, that once had been a camp-meeting site, were more interested in poets and poetry, art, literature and polite travelogues. The manager of Old Salem Chautauqua, down in Lincoln country near Petersburg, Illinois—its seats were on the site of one of Lincoln's early homes—leaned toward patriotic subjects, patriotic music, novelty acts that waved the flag. But at the great Miami Valley Assembly on the old Miami and Erie Canal, at Franklin, Ohio—where sometimes six hundred tents housed families during the course—programs had to adhere closely to the tone of the mother institution at Chautauqua Lake.

Vawter, for his part, believed that people everywhere were pretty much alike. If given free choice, audiences at all the assemblies scattered through the middle west would be interested in much the same fare. A program with enough variety would appeal to both Bay View and Winona Lake, Miami Valley and Old Salem, or any other locality where some visionary or alert businessman had planted his idea.

So with map, calendar, railroad timetables and his list of available Redpath talent, Vawter planned a new kind of summer season. He built a sample program with proper balance of serious lecturers, humorists, magicians, popular music companies, play readers and a few famous preachers, to operate on an eight-day schedule. Being a realist, he did not offer a complete "package" in the beginning. Instead, he would break down resisting local managers slowly, allowing them to decide on their own serious lecturers, to be selected, of course, from Vawter's list. But he alone would choose the entertainment features, the musical companies and quartets, the magicians and all specialty acts that carried heavy baggage.

Thus he could send those portions of the program that cost more to transport, on a regular route, planned in advance to take advantage of short railroad hops and to avoid open dates. This would reduce overhead for his bureau and fatigue and frustration for the talent. His own winter lecture experience had proved that it was too hard on his pocketbook to move a single lecturer, say from the permanent tabernacle at Clarinda, Iowa, back across two states to southern Ohio to Miami Valley Park; then, as he had done his past season, west again four or five hundred miles to Kansas to the old building at Ottawa, also a one-time tabernacle, and finally down across Missouri to Mark Twain's town of Hannibal.

This was bad enough. But it cost a great deal more to shift a magician and his wife, their two assistants and five or six heavy trunks over the same haphazard route. The new Vawter plan would eliminate extra travel and extra baggage costs and keep a larger portion of the Chautauqua dollar where it belonged, in the pockets of talent and booking agents, not in the cash drawers of railroad stations.

Vawter also knew that, under the system then in vogue, the average independent operator, who probably had met few big payrolls himself, was spending every summer around $5000 for a two- or three-week program. By selling a partial package deal, eliminating rival advance men and concentrating all advertising, Vawter figured that he might put together a lively eight-day program for $2000. But to do this he would need a test run with at least a dozen towns. For this experiment he chose his native Iowa.

With the help of J. Roy Ellison, a former Nebraska Lyceum agent already in Vawter's employ, and Lee H. Maus, a Cherokee, Iowa, school principal with experience in running a small assembly, (he later became a Redpath lecturer), Vawter booked his first tent assembly.

The first bold spirit willing to plunge into the scheme was Elijah B. Jones of the independent Chautauqua in Marshalltown, Iowa. Jones signed for a series of programs to open July 1, 1904, and in the agreement guaranteed a $2000 ticket sale. Of total gate receipts, Vawter was to receive the first $2500, plus fifty percent of everything above it; in turn, he would pay all talent and be responsible for their train fares and expenses. Not wanting to endanger the respected Redpath bureau's reputation should he fail, he did not use its name. He still owned the Standard title, so for this adventure he converted himself into the "Standard Chautauqua Bureau of Chicago."

By late winter, seven independents had joined the plan. But seven were not enough. Nor did softening the contract help. It was May before Vawter secured a total of eleven. And no other towns would join. So to fill out a seven-weeks' season, he himself plunged: he would provide his own tents and give the show under his own auspices in four other communities.

Two of these towns were Iowa Falls and Bedford, both county seats. In each he organized a committee of "prominent citizens" to be responsible for the ticket sale and to guarantee a $2000 minimum. He surmised again, and as it proved, rightly, that a local group would be able to stir up enthusiasm as no professional from outside could hope to do. Not only that year, but from then on until the last tent came down, this "committee of citizens" carried the load locally and kept the flags flying in the Chautauqua towns. A live committee meant a good show, and a reasonable profit. A poor committee often resulted in financial loss and a complete lack of interest among the people of the community.

Before Vawter started his adventure, he talked it over with his Redpath partners, Peffer in Philadelphia and Hathaway in Boston. If they objected, it was mildly. Besides, it was Vawter's own money he was wagering. Although the Redpath corporate set-up still theoretically was a single institution, the three partners, Vawter, Peffer and Hathaway, to all practical purposes were independent operators. All through Chautauqua history the parent Redpath Lyceum Bureau functioned as a single corporation. If a manager of a Lyceum office wished to establish a Chautauqua circuit, he created a separate organization and for the privilege of using the corporate name, he paid a royalty to the Redpath Lyceum Bureau, usually three percent. So even in this first venture, profit or loss would be Vawter's own. But in either case, the scheme would provide pay checks through midsummer doldrums for Redpath winter Lyceum talent and operating employees. This prospect could only find approval in both eastern offices.

Vawter booked his talent carefully. As starting date approached, however, flaws began to appear. His determination to break the crust of opposition by independent managers to any kind of travelling circuit had caused him to temporize at the end. His fourteen towns, as finally mapped, sprawled not only across the whole of Iowa, but took in one small city over the Minnesota line and four in eastern Nebraska. Moreover, their dates fell into awkward sequence. The resulting miles of back-tracking, the very mistake Vawter had been trying to avoid, would so swell railroad fares that he must have realized even then that although, like Crusader James Redpath, he might be launching a new idea, he would not get rich from it. Many local managers for years had used specific favorite weeks for their programs. Why should they shift dates, they protested now. If this crazy man Vawter wanted to furnish talent, he could do so at precisely the moment it suited his customers' convenience.

Years later, in 1915, on the Redpath-Columbus, Ohio, circuit, the jump of seven miles between Bellevue and Clyde was the shortest I ever heard of in Chautauqua's history. Vawter, unfortunately, had no such good fortune in this first season of tent Chautauqua. Marshalltown, the county seat where the season would open July 1st, was almost precisely in the middle of Iowa. But instead of moving on swiftly to the nearest town on the list, talent, that probably did not feel too fresh even at the start, must angle up to the north, on three railroads, to MacGregor Heights. There was sure to be a good crowd here, for it was a vacation spot on the Mississippi River.

There would be no vacation for the talent, however. All they could do was pack up and go back over the same three railroads to Marshalltown, where they had started, and on down to the state capital at Des Moines; from there north again to little Iowa Falls, where I was to have my baptism of fire as a platform manager; thence almost straight west eighty miles on a milk train to the new packing plants at Sioux City. The next jump, longest of all, swung the caravan northeast, with half a dozen transfers, this time to Albert Lea, ten miles inside Minnesota.

Busy Albert Lea, on its chain of lakes, would be another good spot. Like MacGregor, it not only was vacation country; it also had two little colleges, twelve churches and a host of business people to back the Chautauqua project. But then came Iowa again. For a third time companies must back-track to Waterloo, stopping now for a program in "Chautauqua Park"; next a visit to Marshalltown again and the Des Moines coal fields, to get to the pretty little riverside village of Chariton; thence west to Bedford, where I was to be general superintendent.

Beyond Bedford, the tiring trail led down to Glenwood, a county seat in the Missouri River bottoms that had six churches—just half as many as Albert Lea but enough for members to get out a good crowd. This was the last stop in Iowa. Jumping the river, the route ended in the four fairly adjacent eastern Nebraska towns of Frémont, Fullerton, Lexington and Auburn, all with grain elevators, all signed by Roy Ellison.

In the experienced later days of the travelling tents, a circuit manager, for that matter the manager of any public entertainment, from circus to concert stage, merely would have shuffled the dates into a logical geographical sequence, saving travel fatigue as well as money. Fatigue was important, and those who suffered most from it were the entertainers.

There were three "musical companies" in this 1904 experiment, all quartets, vocal or instrumental. Unlike the lecturer, who spoke his piece once on any platform and took off for home or another date in some other community, the entertainers must stay several days in every town, then plod on over the whole seven-week route. This, by itself, the companies could have endured. They were seasoned troupers, accustomed to one-night stands, to snatching a hot cup of coffee or the fabled ham sandwich. What they really objected to, loudly, was the need to keep shifting their programs.

For among the other points that Vawter had not meant to surrender to the independent managers, but actually had surrendered, was his rule as to how many days a series of attractions would last in any community. In Des Moines, they were to stretch over ten. In Iowa Falls and Bedford it was a nine-day program, in all others eight. With this irregular schedule no company could march out on the stage with a tested production. It must present this here, and add something else there, constantly improvising, and this sort of drawback was very frustrating to professionals.

Vawter thought matters over carefully as summer approached. He was a stubborn man. He had to admit that there were obstacles, but a few things were on his side—to begin with, the condition of the country. People, on the whole, were in a fairly good mood. Even the fact that the winter of 1903-04 had been unusually cold might help; folks who had stayed in more than usual would be glad to get out and about as summer came. Nor was money particularly tight. Iowa corn prices were not doing so well as they might, but wheat had come up.

It seemed to Vawter, too, that the general public was more than usually music conscious. The newspapers, even as far west as Iowa, had been full all winter of enthusiastic stories about Signor Enrico Caruso, the new Italian tenor, who in the autumn of 1903 had started his first tour of America. He had made his debut at the Metropolitan Opera House in New York as the Duke in *Rigoletto,* and people were talking about him and about music in general.

A Presidential campaign also was at hand. The Republicans were to meet in Chicago in June. It was almost certain that they would nominate Theodore Roosevelt. The Socialists, in May, had renamed railroader Eugene Victor Debs. In July, after the first programs started, would come the Democratic convention. No one was sure what the Democrats would do, but probably they would accept the gold standard and Judge Alton B. Parker. All these free political speeches would give considerable competition to paid lecturers, Vawter reflected. But they also had the virtue of putting audiences in a questioning mood.

So, rationalizing, Vawter rented his tents and with no precedents to guide him started out on the long Chautauqua road.

The Curtain Rises

7

"My grandfather's clock was too large for the shelf
"So it stood ninety years on the floor;
"It was taller by half than the old man himself,
"Though it weighed not a pennyweight more."

A quartet named the Chicago Lady Entertainers led off Vawter's program in 1904. They were a sprightly group of vocalists under the leadership of Mrs. Estelle Clark, who also was a "reader." Their repertoire was cheerful and extensive. In three afternoons and evenings the four doughty women, keeping in step as they marched out to the platform in their high-buttoned shoes, their white starched shirtwaists and long black skirts, without once repeating themselves put on six shows, each at least forty-five minutes long and one of them a full afternoon.

Henry Clay Work, whose inventive genius ranged from knitting machines to popular music, has several songs that have lived to his credit, among them *Marching Through Georgia* and *Father, Dear Father, Come Home with Me Now*. In 1904, his *Grandfather's Clock* was still a favorite. It struck a nostalgic note that the middle-aged especially enjoyed. Hadn't most settlers, venturing into the west, brought their big clocks with them and set them up in the front parlors? The Lady Entertainers sang the song with proper sentiment. They followed it, in most of Vawter's towns, with *Blest Be the Tie*. Appreciative crowds applauded the one as much as the other.

Bedelia was the hit in New York and Chicago that year, but the discreet ladies did not sing it in Iowa Falls. Not that it was wicked, it just smacked of the big, gas-lit cities. The words, by William Jerome, certainly would not have given pause to the most priggish listener. They were written to

56

be sung in a lilting Irish, were full of Killarney and Erin's Isle and a Tipperary smile. The author of the lyric modestly offered himself as Bedelia's Chauncey Olcott, if she'd consent to be his "Molly O'."

It was tuneful, light as a thistle, but who in Iowa ever had heard of Chauncey Olcott? True, he had been packing them in on Broadway, as he sang his way through a confection called *The Minstrel of Clare,* but no one west of the Mississippi ever had heard of him or it. And no one cared.

The Lady Entertainers kept their feet on solid ground. Like Ralph Bingham at Anita, ten years earlier, they stayed properly away from anything that suggested the raffish Broadway stage.

Their popular numbers included *The Old Oaken Bucket, Ben Bolt, Sweet and Low, Listen to the Mocking Bird;* such Civil War favorites as *Father Abraham* and defiant *Shoo Fly, Don't Bother Me.* They sang *Annie Laurie,* which a few persons still considered a little doubtful, and *Comin' Through the Rye, Loch Lomond,* ballads the people knew and loved. *Sweet Adeline* was almost brand new; many in the audience never had heard it before. Dresser's *Banks of the Wabash* could stir up as many pleasant memories here on the Iowa River as it could in Indiana. Certainly the moonlight was as fair, the breath of hay as sweet in Iowa as anywhere else.

As for hymns, church people were singing *Love Divine* just as piously in 1904 as their parents had, and so therefore did the wise Lady Entertainers. They trilled and rejoiced in everything they should, and for their third and last appearance brought down the house with Mrs. Howe's triumphant *Battle Hymn,* flaming words set to a familiar camp-meeting air.

Mrs. Clark's reading selections ran in the same proper vein. The first day she recited Bryant's *Thanatopsis,* repeating the stanza that began: "To him, who in the love of Nature holds Communion with her visible forms . . ." One afternoon she used Longfellow's *Excelsior,* next day James Whitcomb Riley's *Out to Old Aunt Mary's.* Her climax for one program was *The Charge of the Light Brigade,* and this was an innovation, since women readers usually left Tennyson's vigorous narrative for the males to handle, but the versatile Mrs. Clark did it with splendid gusto.

She "interpreted" a short passage from *The Hoosier Schoolmaster,* Edward Eggleston's popular tale of the trials of a frontier teacher before the Civil War; and another from *Mrs. Wiggs of the Cabbage Patch,* by Mrs. Alice Hegan Rice of Louisville, Kentucky.

Iowa still liked the bearded Eggleston, no matter what stuck-up Hoosiers said about his slandering Indiana in his fiction. *Mrs. Wiggs* was a new best-seller. It had appeared first in the *Century Magazine* and had so pleased Theodore Roosevelt that he entertained the author and her poet-husband, Cale Young Rice, in the White House. The line in *Mrs. Wiggs,* in which the little girl becomes so confused over her "hat" and her "walk" that she says, "So we left our short walk to home," was good every time for a ringing laugh. Young and old, the audience applauded Mrs Clark.

Except for *Mrs. Wiggs,* which the coming fall was to open on Broadway as a play with Madge Carr Cook in the title role, these were recitations and songs that the men and women in the audience had known in school, so what could be better? The tried and true still was good entertainment and certainly the safest from the viewpoint of a program director in 1904.

After their three days' appearance the Lady Entertainers tied big veils down over flapping hats and trouped on to Sioux City, and into their places on the creaking Iowa Falls stage marched an aggregation called the Giant Colored Quartet. On one program or another, this group rendered all of Stephen Foster's melodies, from *O Susanna* and *Nellie Was a Lady* to *Old Black Joe.* They sang *Massa's in the Cold, Cold Ground* and *John Brown's Body,* written to the same Sunday-school tune as Mrs. Howe's *Battle Hymn.* Finally, to the delight of everyone, for one encore they offered:

> "Oh, my poor Nellie Gray,
> "They have taken you away
> "And I'll never see my darling any more;
> "I'm sitting by the river and I'm weeping all the day,
> "For you've gone from the old Kentucky shore."

G.A.R. buttons were conspicuous in every audience in this period. The Civil War still colored much of the thinking, and *Nellie Gray* and emotional songs of the freedmen belonged as truly to the rural west as to the rural south, were as American in thought or sentiment as *Daisy Bell* or *Good Night, Ladies.*

The singers on the final three days of the 1904 series were the famous Temple Male Quartette of Boston, assisted now by Reader Victoria Lynn instead of Katherine Ridgeway. Thus Vawter opened each program with music. He had counted on the country being music-conscious. Children still "sang" their geography lessons, even their multiplication tables. Gathering 'round the family organ or piano was a certain part of any evening's entertainment, at least in the midwest. Everybody sang, which may account for the fact that musicians as a class were paid less than other entertainers. Records show that the men in the Temple Male Quartette were performing at about that time for $25 a night for the group, and out of this they paid their own expenses.

Opening the Chautauqua program with music eventually became a pattern. No matter who the speaker might be, with rare exceptions he followed a musical prelude lasting from fifteen minutes to an hour. "We pre-luded," companies used to say, coining a good Chautauqua verb, cousin to the later movie verb to "pre-meer." Few individuals ever objected to the custom. Humorist Strickland Gillilan did in later years; he wanted no frivolous distractions before he took the stage. But in general, speakers, from William Jennings Bryan down, liked the musical prelude. It quieted folk, let them get settled in their not-too-comfortable seats and forget any chores left undone at home. Perhaps it even put them in the right mood for a message.

A copy of that program in pleasant little Iowa Falls, where I occupied the exalted position of platform superintendent, still exists:

IOWA FALLS CHAUTAUQUA
Program Furnished By
THE STANDARD CHAUTAUQUA BUREAU

July 10–19, 1904.

Mrs. Roudebush,   H. P. Harrison,
   Morning Hour Lecturer   Platform Manager

1st DAY
Afternoon—Concert, CHICAGO LADY ENTERTAINERS
           MRS. ESTELLE M. CLARK, Reader
Evening   —Prelude, CHICAGO LADY ENTERTAINERS
           Lecture, REV. JOHN ROACH STRATTON (*sic*)

2nd DAY
Afternoon—Prelude, CHICAGO LADY ENTERTAINERS
           Lecture, DR. D. F. FOX
Evening   —Prelude, CHICAGO LADY ENTERTAINERS
           Moving Pictures by DR. W. ROBERTSON
                (travel talk with slides)

3rd DAY
Afternoon—Prelude, CHICAGO LADY ENTERTAINERS
           Lecture, DR. CASPER W. HIATT
Evening   —Drama, "HIAWATHA," illustrated by Moving Pic-
           tures.

4th DAY
Afternoon—GIANT COLORED QUARTETTE
           Entertainment, EDWIN M. BRUSH, Magician
Evening   —Prelude, GIANT COLORED QUARTETTE
           Joint Debate, "The Political Issues of the Day,"
                CONG. J. ADAM BEDE and
                JUDGE MARTIN D. WADE

5th DAY
Afternoon—GIANT COLORED QUARTETTE
           Musical Novelties and Juggling, GEORGE W.
                GARRETSON.
Evening   —Prelude, GIANT COLORED QUARTETTE
           Lecture, "Moving Pictures," W. ROBERT GOSS

6th DAY
Afternoon—GIANT COLORED QUARTETTE
           Lecture, "Flying," DR. T. BAIRD COLLINS
           Musical Novelties, GEORGE W. GARRETSON
           Lecture, GEORGE L. McNUTT
Evening   —
           (This was Sunday, so there was no evening program
           planned.)

7th DAY
Afternoon—Concert, TEMPLE MALE QUARTETTE
           Readings, MISS VICTORIA LYNN
Evening   —Prelude, TEMPLE MALE QUARTETTE
           Lecture, "The Key to the 20th Century,"
                DR. THOMAS E. GREEN

<table>
<tr><td rowspan="4">**8th DAY**</td><td>Afternoon—Prelude,</td><td>TEMPLE MALE QUARTETTE</td></tr>
<tr><td>Lecture,</td><td>GEORGE L. McNUTT</td></tr>
<tr><td>Evening —Prelude,</td><td>TEMPLE MALE QUARTETTE</td></tr>
<tr><td>Lecture,</td><td>DR. FRANK G. SMITH</td></tr>
<tr><td rowspan="4">**9th DAY**</td><td>Afternoon—Prelude,</td><td>TEMPLE MALE QUARTETTE</td></tr>
<tr><td></td><td>Chalk Talks by ASH DAVIS</td></tr>
<tr><td>Evening —Prelude,</td><td>TEMPLE MALE QUARTETTE</td></tr>
<tr><td>Lecture,</td><td>BISHOP JOSEPH CRANE HARTZELL</td></tr>
</table>

In addition to this particular group appearing at Iowa Falls, Vawter offered local committees a choice of twenty-five other numbers that season, chiefly serious lecturers, with a few entertainers thrown in to lighten the diet. The list was made up heavily, one realizes now, of churchmen and Democratic bigwigs. It included Rabbi Leon Harrison of St. Louis, Methodist Albert B. Storms, "General" Zach Sweeney, shouting southern evangelist Sam Jones, clergyman Frank Gunsaulus of Chicago and William Jennings Bryan, hero of the lecture platform since the 1896 Democratic convention; Methodist Bishop Charles H. Fowler and Congressman Champ Clark of Missouri; Baptist clergyman Kerr Boyce Tupper and the Honorable James K. Vardaman of Mississippi; finally Congressman Charles Grosvenor of Ohio, a Civil War general with thirty years in Congress, who, to give a little balance to Vawter's undoubtedly accidental political picture, happened to be a Republican. This may sound as deadly as a museum catalogue, but actually these were all flesh-and-blood, highly amusing and interesting personalities.

The nine days in the town on the Iowa River were hot—hot enough, as the saying went, to bake biscuits on the stage. In those years Iowa Falls, with its 4000 people in the middle of rich farm territory, had two railroads, a spur line of a third, and, as was to be expected in a prairie state, a half dozen wooden grain elevators. Ellsworth College, with three buildings in midtown, was a going concern with an especially good music department, and the town and faculty for several years had supported a permanent Chautauqua assembly. They had invested hard-earned dollars in a frame building on grounds just across from the town, reached by a footbridge a little up-river from the road bridge. So, though this might be my first Chautauqua, it was not Iowa Falls'.

Our series opened on Tuesday. The stores closed at one o'clock and, by half after the hour, the dusty streets and roads began to show that air of excited activity which I came to know in later years as "Chautauqua bustle." Ladies with parasols, carrying cushions under their arms, began to walk slowly across the footbridge. There had been a study session in the morning, with textbooks from the Chautauqua Lake Reading Circle. A school teacher had lectured on the care and feeding of infants and two middle-aged women, both of them with big hats, arriving now at the ticket booth, had not agreed with what the teacher had said. "What does a spinster know about infants, anyway?" one was objecting.

I put the remark away among other items to report to Vawter and leaned into the ticket booth and looked hopefully at the cash box. It held probably two hundred and fifty stubs from season tickets and $26.50 from cash admissions, at thirty-five cents each.

"Keep a sharp eye on the money," I warned the ticket boy.

I was not being fussy. I worked for Vawter, and to him, carelessness with money, or with anything that cost money, was an unforgivable sin. He took no chances and expected no one else to take any. A green crew boy, who didn't know Vawter by sight, challenged him at the ticket gate one night in western Iowa and compelled him, the owner, to buy a ticket before he could enter the tent. This made such a good impression on Vawter that he eventually promoted the youngster to circuit auditor. If you worked for Vawter, you took care of his money and his property.

I recall an incident years later, in Maryville, Missouri, when William Jennings Bryan was speaking. Since it was the famous Bryan, the crowd started to gather at five o'clock. By six-thirty all seats were filled inside the tent and the superintendent rolled up the canvas and began selling space outside. Vawter arrived at seven. He opened the door to the box office where a young Cornell College student was working as cashier. Money, mostly silver dollars, was stacked high on the twelve-inch shelf.

"Hang up a sign saying 'sold out,' " Vawter directed, "there's not enough space to get anyone else in the tent." Then he called a carriage, scooped all the money into a suitcase, took it and the cashier to the town hotel, and, without waiting to hear Mr. Bryan, the two climbed into a double bed, with the precious suitcase safely between them, and went to sleep.

No such problem faced me in Iowa Falls at half after two that opening afternoon, even if the crowd did look stupendous when, arrayed in my new white pants, I mounted the platform. There may have been four hundred in the audience, mostly women. They stared at me expectantly while their palm-leaf fans waved back and forth in unison.

As a manager I was to wrestle later with the worrisome fact that afternoon audiences often fanned more for the purpose of keeping awake than of keeping cool, but I did not anticipate any such problem that day. I merely welcomed the crowd heartily in the name of Keith Vawter and his lecture bureau, told them what a wonderful town Iowa Falls was "here beside its beautiful river," invited the embarrassed chairman of the local committee to stand and take a bow, asked all the ladies please to remove their hats, put in a plug for the Reverend John Roach Straton, the evening speaker, and fled to the back of the building to wipe my perspiring brow. The show was on!

The crowd was larger at night. A breeze had blown up from the river and the naphtha lights flickered and buzzed under the roof gables. The barefoot children of the afternoon stayed at home, but husbands in white shirt sleeves accompanied their wives to hear Fundamentalist Straton talk on *Sin.* He did not disappoint them. Straton was a spectacular speaker and had a reputation as such, a tall, lank man with a zealot's eyes and a granite face. When he told the people in Iowa Falls that the whale actually swallowed Jonah, he could have been the whale himself, with all his fascinating gestures. His lecture was a no-holds-barred attack on dancing, divorce, prize fighting, atheism, beer saloons and wicked city politicians—but chiefly on liquor and atheism, which latter, in his mind, might be anything that was not Fundamentalism.

Straton, a Chicagoan at that time, was to achieve considerable notoriety twenty years later when his fiery debates in Carnegie Hall with the Reverend Charles Francis Potter caused near-riots on New York City streets. Unitarian Potter was a champion of evolution, Baptist Straton was not, but in Iowa Falls, in 1904, no one disputed anything he said. That would have been heresy and there were old rails waiting in Iowa fences for heretics to ride.

The Reverend Frank Smith, who followed Straton a few nights later with *Hero of the Age,* a serious speech on the "ideal man, honest in his political life," was to continue many years with Redpath after his Iowa Falls beginning. Pastor then of a Chicago Congregational church, he was more practical than most clergymen. He wanted good government and didn't just preach about it. Half a dozen years later, prior to the Bull Moose campaign, he ran for the Illinois legislature on an independent ticket, won against both old parties, and served one term, while still holding down his pulpit. On Chautauqua programs he leaped very early into the suffrage fight. Gratified women didn't rise and give him the old "Chautauqua salute," when he assured them that they had as much sense as men and "were entitled to the same blessings and benefits"—this was no news to them—but they hospitably invited him back to lecture again and again.

Frank Smith for a long time opened with the same story in every town. In the previous community, he would say, he had noticed that the big advertising poster with his picture, standing in a restaurant window, had slipped down from its place and lodged so that all that could be seen was Smith's name, and under it a sign painted on the window—"Frank Smith . . . Open All Night." It started things with a big laugh from every audience. Such was the humor of the times, such the readiness to laugh.

The night before I introduced Frank Smith in Iowa Falls, the Reverend Thomas Green delivered his lecture. I use the word "delivered" designedly. It was a polished oration, dignified, poetic, oft-repeated, called *The Key to the Twentieth Century.*

The *Key* was Peace. There never would be another war, the Reverend Mr. Green promised that night, because civilization had reached too high a peak. This was a happy assurance to Iowa and Minnesota and Nebraska villagers. The Spanish-American War had not been such a holocaust as the Civil War, but sons and fathers had died, from disease, if not in battle, and people wanted no more war. Ever. If this very distinguished-looking speaker was right, if the world had moved forward and another war was impossible, he was telling them just what they yearned to hear. They left the tent with wet eyes and great hopes.

The Reverend Mr. Green, bearded, fluent rector of an Iowa diocese of the Protestant Episcopal church, delivered that oration in Iowa Falls in 1904 and in twenty-seven other assemblies that same summer in twelve states; its "pre-meer" had been in Emporia, Kansas, in 1902. Ten years later, right through the evening of July 31, 1914, he was still delivering it, by that time on a western circuit, still assuring his listeners that there could not be another war. But that date ended the speech abruptly, for World War I began the next day.

Mr. Green's next topic for the Chautauqua audience was as pregnant: *The Truth about Japan.* "I talked with the Emperor," he said in that later speech dealing with a trip to the Orient. "He assured me, there will never be a war between the United States and Japan." Of course, we had not billed him as a prophet.

Ash Davis, on the final day in Iowa Falls, entertained with what down the years would prove to be one of the most popular of all offerings in the tents. I believe it can be said truthfully that Chautauqua "invented" the chalk talk. I have heard the same claim for the male quartet. There had already been a number of "chalk" artists appearing on independent platforms. Thomas Francis ("Frank") Beard, Civil War cartoonist for *Harper's Weekly,* had been one of the first. But Ash Davis developed the idea into an interesting study in mass psychology.

Chautauqua was to send great artists and poor scrawlers around its circuits as the years flew by, and almost without exception the scrawlers proved more popular. As a rule, great artists with brush, crayon or clay are not particularly articulate human beings. They say what they have to say through the medium of their art. On the other hand, a glib, amusing speaker sometimes has a small knack for drawing which can be an afternoon's entertainment. The American people proved time and again that they preferred good lively talk illustrated by inferior art, to great art accompanied by a dull speech.

Redpath managers tried both kinds. W. M. R. French, the first director of the Chicago Art Institute, had been setting up an easel on indoor Chautauqua stages as early as 1902, chatting urbanely on *Wit and Wisdom of the Crayon.* He appealed to the very literate; he was too much of an artist to be uproariously popular.

Marion Ballou Fiske, clever New Englander billed as "cartoonist and crayon lecturer" who toured the summer stages just a few years after

Mr. French, had a readier tongue. She liked to have her audience "join in," and to accomplish this she developed a character named "Uncle Zeke." When the drawing was completed, she presented it to the man the crowd had voted the homeliest in the room. In 1908, as a finale, she was doing a sketch of William Howard Taft, flattering the Republicans in the room with the tag, "Our next President," and after a moment getting the Democrats' cheers by adding, "IF he is elected!"

By no stretch of the imagination was chalk-talker Ash Davis a great artist, but the people loved him. In forty-five minutes, chattering gaily beside his flag-draped easel, he could turn out scores of platform masterpieces, landscapes, animals, sketches of people real or imaginary. The crowds liked the real ones best. The high point came when with deft strokes Ash smeared his paper with streaks of color, then whisked it upside down to disclose a noble reproduction of the "Statue of Liberty Enlightening the World." The applause shook the tent, as it did for a sketch of "Teddy Roosevelt in Rough Rider Hat," showing all his teeth.

The magician making the rounds for Vawter that summer was Edwin Brush, a performer who kept his name before the public for another fifteen years. He called himself an "illusionist," a high-sounding word fashionable in those days, and he mystified Iowa Falls with what purported to be Hindoo magic. This included snakes, of course. Brush was a circumspect man. When his dates fell on Sunday, he piously built up a special program called *The Other Man's Game,* in which he discussed spiritualism, gambling, confidence tricks, with emphasis on "the game of life from a Christian magician's viewpoint." In later years we used magicians chiefly on the children's programs, knowing many adults were bound to accompany them.

Country folk, crowding into the Iowa Falls pavilion on single admissions that Saturday afternoon in 1904, watched George F. Garretson in another one-man production. Billed as offering "musical novelties," which meant that he performed on a variety of instruments, Garretson was a juggler, too, able to keep six sparkling balls in the air as nonchalantly as he played *Home, Sweet Home* on the cornet. Jugglers were familiar, inexpensive entertainment. In the century just ended they had plied their trade first on the street, along with the organ grinder. Garretson had nothing new. But the speaker that followed him did.

T. Baird Collins is credited with being the original lecturer on aviation in America; whether this is true or not, he certainly was among the earliest. Orville Wright had made his first twelve-seconds flight at Kitty Hawk just six months prior to Vawter's 1904 trial run. Foreseeing, ahead of many others, that before long men and boys in small towns would be rushing out to the nearest big field to watch a crazy barnstormer, Collins in Iowa Falls gave fabulous information to an incredulous audience. With due credit to the Wright brothers, he strung a wire across the little stage, suspended a model airplane from it and discussed wing surfaces, "speeds upward of forty miles an hour," mysterious wind tunnels, and an aileron, a fancy word not yet in the dictionaries. His lecture was a "stunt" of course, scheduled on the same afternoon with a similar one by George L. McNutt.

George McNutt, after his 1904 start, became a Redpath headliner, a likeable, fast-talking crusader who in the hey-day of travelling Chautauqua could average one speech a day from June until September and, after a quick breath, begin months of winter Lyceum. Eventually it became our practice to use McNutt as "first day opener," since opening and closing days were most important. By 1915, for instance, we were to advertise that in the three years just passed, McNutt had opened three hundred and thirty-six Redpath Chautauquas. We billed him as George L. McNutt, "D.P.M.," meaning "Dinner Pail Man."

McNutt's nickname of "dinner pail" referred to a speech that he made about cooking. It also emphasized for the sake of the audience that he himself had carried a dinner pail. A Presbyterian preacher, in the late 90's, he suddenly had walked out of his pulpit in Urbana, Illinois, determined to find out why many church pews were empty. He put on overalls, at the age of forty-two, bought himself a dinner pail, took his wife and sons and went to work as a laborer in the steel mills.

Satisfied after seven years that he knew a few basic facts about the working man's point of view, George McNutt started out in Chautauqua with a missionary speech on the needs of labor. He was not a Jacob Riis, but he could take Riis's famous title of *How the Other Half Lives* and twist it into a challenging talk on *How the Other Half* Ought *to Live.* He branched into the subject of food by linking poor food with crime and in Iowa Falls in July, 1904, he prepared a meal on the platform to demonstrate his various ideas.

McNutt had a contraption related to the modern pressure cooker, except that it did its cooking only with hot water, without any fire. Into the pot, on a table on the stage, he stuffed potatoes and cabbage, onions and celery, clamped on the lid, pulled out his handsome big watch on its long chain, determined the exact time and, paying no more attention, apparently, to the pot, began to talk about the "dawn of a social conscience" and "labor as an art." Finally he uncovered the steaming kettle, produced plates, forks and spoons, ladled his vegetables into dishes and offered them to the somewhat suspicious audience. The crew boys ate it, if the audience did not.

In between engagements over the years McNutt was likely to disappear into the nearest machine shop, put on overalls and work with the men again for a week or two, "getting the feel of new facts." Chautauqua people found him not difficult, just "different." When mealtime came and the others went to the hotel, McNutt preferred to sit down under a tree, take a spoon from his pocket and enjoy a can of tomatoes and a pint of ice cream, "a perfect meal." If he disappeared overnight, friends did not worry. He probably had put on his overalls and gone out to the nearest farm and asked the surprised farmer for permission to sleep in the oat or wheat bin. "To rest my nerves," he would explain.

The big name at Iowa Falls that July was saved for the last night. Bishop Joseph Crane Hartzell, of the Methodist Episcopal church, known as the "Bishop of Africa," had already been appearing in the permanent Chautauquas for years, talking excitedly about the Dark Continent, branching from that to Negro rights in the United States. He was sixty-two years old that summer, and he travelled the circuits for eight or ten more years and even in his old age he pulled no punches. A spade in his lexicon was a spade and he never avoided a subject for fear of offending someone. His life, dogged by violence, was a Chautauqua saga.

A graduate of Garrett Bible Institute in Evanston, Illinois, Hartzell had first made headlines as a young student, when, alone, he rescued the crew of a schooner breaking up in Lake Michigan. After he was ordained he had headed south and into trouble. He enraged southerners by crusading in the New Orleans area for civil rights for Negroes, offended northerners by slashing out at still-existent carpet-bagging. The Methodist church naturally found him difficult to handle, but it appreciated his oratorical gifts, his integrity and his crusading zeal. So what could be more natural than to make him a bishop with all Africa his field, where he would run afoul of neither northern Republicans nor southern Democrats?

A first trip to Africa taught Bishop Hartzell that American dollars were needed to save the black man, so he came back for a money-raising campaign. To be sure, he did not ask for money from the tent platform. Such a practice was frowned on in Chautauqua, except by our own privileged agents the last day, importuning what we prayed were satisfied citizens to sign up for the next year's course. Bishop Hartzell merely created a climate in which dollars would come in easily later. In twenty years he made thirteen trips to the United States and on almost every trip he took to the Redpath road.

He was a "platform personality," a man who stirred up controversy merely by opening his mouth, who packed drama into his lectures. One minute an audience froze with him in an Atlantic gale, next cringed before wild African tribesmen attacking a back-country mission. As I have said, violence dogged the Bishop. He finally had retired when, on his eighty-sixth birthday, robbers invaded his Blue Ash, Ohio, home and since, as usual, he refused to run from the fight, they beat him to death.

Although the Iowa Falls course lasted nine days, only eight night performances were scheduled, for a good reason. Any nine-day program included at least one Sunday. This created a problem. So far as over-all organization went, Vawter naturally needed to put on a Sunday afternoon show, but he knew well enough that no matter how pious in tone a Sabbath entertainment might be, many local church people would line up against it. He surmised, though, that here in the midwest where any Sabbath entertainment more lively than a buggy ride was frowned upon, an innovation such as Sunday Chautauqua would bring out a crowd tired of boredom.

So Vawter offered a compromise, whether it then was recognized as one or not. If the local committee would permit him to sell tickets for a Sunday afternoon program which in no way would affront their religious scruples, he, in turn, would make tent and talent available at no cost for a Sunday evening union service. Iowa Falls in that period had one Catholic and three Protestant congregations—Methodist, Baptist, and Congregationalist. Under Vawter's plan each local clergyman would have a chance to make a platform appearance and utter at least a few words before what proved, when Sunday night came, to be the largest crowd in the town's history.

Once the local committee acquiesced, Vawter did not pussyfoot about his program. So far during the week there had been a parade of clergymen on the platform, and more were to follow. So he omitted the clergy altogether on Sunday afternoon. McNutt, a former clergyman to be sure, gave his "dinner pail" speech. Garretson entertained again musically, but did not juggle. Collins predicted the airplane age.

The Sunday afternoon program was a sell-out and Iowa Falls churches joined enthusiastically in the evening union service. The Giant Colored Quartette led the singing, and without benefit of loudspeaker, paeans of praise rolled in volume across surrounding hills. Everybody came, parents with sleepy children, boys with their hair slicked down for their best girls. It was impossible to get them all into the tent, so we rolled up the canvas sides and hundreds sat in the field.

There was bound to be frequent discussion over the years about Sunday performances. The south in particular disliked them. Congressman J. Adam Bede of Minnesota solved the problem, for himself at least, by saying, if his date happened to be on Sunday, "I'll take as my text this morning . . ." and then after reading it, add, "As the text says," and go on from there with his regular speech.

Usually managers provided musical talent with a list of numbers suitable for Sundays. Occasionally a company, notably the Ben Greet Players, would specify in a contract that there would be no Sunday work; a few individuals at times insisted on the chance to rest. On some circuits at later dates, for various reasons, the Sunday program was abandoned entirely. Particularly was this true after Broadway plays were presented. But on the whole, over the years, managers utilized the device Vawter introduced that first summer.

I remember a Swarthmore circuit program one Sunday in 1922 at Harrisonburg, Virginia, in which a Jewish rabbi, a Catholic priest and twelve Protestant clergymen sat on the platform while Greek-born Julius Caesar Nayphe gave his interpretation of the Twenty-third Psalm. Occasionally there was clerical criticism. *A Pair of Sixes,* for instance, with

which the talented Tull Players from Cornell College, Iowa, fought Dakota
storms in the 1920's, had to do with a poker game. That fact in itself was
bad enough and for Sunday performances all the worse. A few local committees frowned at it, and once in the director's home town a clergyman
used it as a basis for a condemning sermon. Until the final years, however,
when the quality of programs on many circuits deteriorated, clerical opposition to selling tickets for a Sabbath program rarely got a gaitered foot
into the tents.

THE FAST EXPRESS, TWO HOURS LATE, MAKES A SPECIAL STOP AT SWANSON'S MILLS
TO PICK UP THE LYCEUM ENTERTAINER, AT 4 A.M. BELOW ZERO.

Bedford in the Mud

8

The Iowa Falls course closed the night of July 19 and I hopped the next train to Bedford in Taylor County, one hundred fifty miles southwest on the Missouri state line, where the nine-day series of which I was to be general superintendent would open the 26th. It was raining as I arrived. The East Fork of the muddy Hundred and Two River that flows through Bedford had spread over its low banks, and the village streets, for the most part listed merely as "graded," were already bottomless pools of rich, black Iowa mud.

It looked like catastrophe to me. But that was my inexperience. One learned to expect "weather" in Chautauqua. Let our fluttering banners appear over any Main Street and skies seemed to weep and areas parched for months became quagmires. Let the tent be half staked and clouds swelled black with wind, strong enough, the crews used to say, to rip the feathers off a chicken. In fact, one lecturer returned from a summer windstorm in Hallock, Minnesota, claiming that the chickens in that isolated town near the Canadian border wore blankets to keep their feathers on.

It rained hard for three days. Except for this I found no serious problem. One of the newspaper editors met me at the station. There were two weeklies in Bedford at that time, a national bank, a state bank and five churches serving the spiritual needs of some 2000 persons. The editor reported that the season-ticket sale was lagging; if we could create what later psychologists were to call "a climate of enthusiasm," that, too, could be overcome. We did create it. Citizens began selling tickets door-to-door. This meant farm doors, too, all over Taylor County and a few across the line in Missouri, so that before the first program I could report to Vawter that the necessary number of season tickets had been sold. In this case

69

it was a thousand at $1.50 each, for a full series of seventeen programs, a sum less than nine cents a performance.

The grassy knoll which the editor suggested for the tent, only a few hundred yards beyond the last picket fence at the end of Main Street, seemed the logical place for Chautauqua grounds. It was high enough above the river bed to be safe from flood and it had what looked like a good stand of grass. It also was within easy walking distance of every house in town and the nearby open fields offered plenty of space for farmers to tether their horses and park their buggies and spring wagons. In fact, as it turned out later in the week, some of them even set up camp there.

Tent and poles were to arrive on the morning train on the branch line of the Chicago, Burlington and Quincy—the expanding CB and Q already had absorbed the old Burlington and Missouri River Railroad that first served this section of the county. So I hired a drayman with a two-horse team and a solid-bedded wagon, and at the livery barn I found a couple of muscular young men who craved a dollar each for eight hours' work. Thus fortified, I met the train.

We had used a permanent pavilion at Iowa Falls the previous week. Bedford, later an enthusiastic Chautauqua town, was to build itself a wooden auditorium three years after our visit. Three years too late for me, however. In Chicago, before I started out, I had spent considerable time thoughtfully studying Vawter's drawings of a tent, but I was unprepared now for the vast bundle of soiled canvas and the enormous coils of rope which we dragged off the Burlington local. We hauled it to the Chautauqua grounds and spread it on the damp grass.

Somehow we got it up. But after the last stake had been driven into the mud and the last guy rope tightened, there came the business of seats and stage. In later years circuits carried their own folding seats, but in 1904 seating arrangements had to be improvised. There was very little in the budget for it or for the stage. The superintendent's ingenuity, plus a few carefully spent dollars, must do the trick.

Luckily the lumber dealer was a member of the Bedford Chautauqua committee. Yes, he agreed when he heard the problem, he would lend me at no cost the necessary two-by-ten planks, provided we did not drive nails into them or saw off any ends. Those were the days of cedar shingles, packaged a quarter square to the bundle. He would lend us those, too. The bundles, laid flat, made uprights on which to put the planks.

The stage was another matter. About nine feet by twelve and nearly three feet off the ground, it had to be nailed together, but if we carefully drove the nails only part way, making them easy to pull, and did not seriously damage the planks, the dealer would take them back also.

As opening day approached, I began to have misgivings about the place where we had set up the tent. It was on high enough ground, but to reach it from town people must cross a field, and even our own tramping around had started to reveal the deep Iowa mud under the sod. If weather continued to plague us, by the time the last stragglers for the first day's performance reached the tent the field would be a slimy puddle. Something had to be done, cost or no cost.

So I pitted courage against the memory of Keith Vawter's fine frugality and ordered several hundred more planks. The morning of the opening day I laid them, two wide, from the edge of the village to the main entrance of the tent. The ladies would have dry feet whether they liked our programs or not.

Then began the fretful period of waiting that every Chautauqua superintendent was to know. With all those thousand tickets sold and the whole countryside keyed up, what if a railroad wreck should block the line ahead of the local train bringing the talent? What if Ash Davis broke his wrist and couldn't "chalk talk"? What if the Chicago Lady Entertainers fell into a quarrel at Chariton, the last stop up the line, and called off the tour and went home? What if wild animals, a visiting skunk, a wandering herd of cows got into the tent and broke up the show?

Such dire things could happen. One later summer, just before the First World War, we were appearing in western North Carolina and at a boardinghouse in the town the night before there had been a rape case and the sheriff had brought bloodhounds to find the scoundrel. At our evening performance Wells Watson Ginn, the monologist, was reciting, with musical background, *The Man from Home,* by Booth Tarkington and Harry Leon Wilson.

The spotlight was playing on Mr. Ginn and strains from *Sweet Genevieve* drifted in melodiously through a window in the stage set, when the sheriff's pack of bloodhounds roared into the tent, down the center aisle, veered off to the left and plunged out under the canvas, with the sheriff's posse after it. The brief intrusion spoiled the effect of the soft music and annoyed Mr. Ginn no end.

None of these catastrophes occurred in Bedford. The show opened on schedule. Even the piano was in place on the stage. In those early days the piano was a problem for every superintendent, because Chautauquas did not carry their own. Later on, the Kimball piano company of Chicago supplied us, furnishing the instruments free for the advertising and we were criticized for it, I think unjustly. But in 1904 each piano had to be begged or borrowed in each town, and in Bedford I made the important discovery that there always were owners who found it flattering to lend their golden oak uprights for famous entertainers to use. The one to choose was that which the lady music teacher, personally acquainted with every piano in town, said was in best tune.

On opening night I slipped out of my muddy shoes and overalls, somewhere found a citizen who kindly allowed me to take a bath, put on my white duck pants, a clean shirt and a necktie. The tent was crowded. The two naphtha lamps on the center poles were sputtering loudly, it seemed to me, so that some of the people nearest them apparently were straining to hear what was said. There was nothing I could do about that, and I could find nothing else wrong. The Chicago Lady Entertainers, sedate and lovely in their shirtwaists and long skirts, opened again with *Grandfather's Clock* and put their hearts in it. They responded to six encores and the crowd went home happy. So did I.

Among the lecturers at Bedford was one who for many years would be a popular Chautauqua attraction. I had never met him before that night. "General" Zachary T. Sweeney was a Campbellite preacher from Columbus, Indiana, who derived his military title from the fact that in the early 90's, in payment for staunch party regularity, President Benjamin Harrison had appointed him American consul general at Constantinople. A consul general was one kind of general, wasn't he, and if audiences preferred to think of Zach Sweeney as a military man, wasn't it their privilege? His lecture, with proper overtones of patriotism, concerned the Middle East and the Terrible Heathen Turk, who liked plenty of women around his house and resented all fine Christian efforts to teach him otherwise. The audience found it impressive.

Rabbi Leon Harrison of St. Louis and the Reverend Albert Boynton Storms, who followed "General" Sweeney, talked of things perhaps less fascinating, but considerably closer to Bedford, Iowa, experience. Storms, a Methodist clergyman, was the new president of Iowa State College of Agriculture and Mechanical Arts, now known more simply as Iowa State College, at Ames. Naturally, his theme was education, and he presented it with pedantic earnestness. There was nothing pedantic, however, about Harrison, the English-born rabbi of the Temple Israel in St. Louis, nor about Bedford's interest in him.

Bedford was just eight miles from the Missouri line, close enough to be familiar with Rabbi Harrison's fame as an orator. In his late thirties, he still spoke as eloquently as he had at twenty-one, when he delivered an oration at Henry Ward Beecher's funeral. He was primarily interested in the poor, particularly in their living conditions, and he discussed the subject passionately.

The word "passionate" also described the evening address by the Honorable James K. Vardaman of Mississippi, though the two men otherwise could not be compared. Many times in years to come I listened from the back of a tent to U.S. Congressman, later Senator, Vardaman. I remember him as a tall and impressive-looking gentleman with a voice trained in cottonfield political oratory. His long black hair cascaded over the shoulders of an immaculate white suit and, like Fundamentalist John Roach Straton, he had the flashing eyes of a zealot.

Vardaman had a horror story of political corruption, and he told it well,

but, in looking back on it, one wonders how many pertinent facts he left
out. He claimed to represent on the platform what he called the "liberal
element of the Democratic party in the south," and he complained bitterly
that his opponents in rural Mississippi, "the reactionaries," had fought him
by every foul means. But he neglected to tell, outside his own state, that
he was accused there of extending the spoils system and of battling to
prevent the education of the Negro because "the educated Negro would
threaten the political dominance of the White Man."

As with some speakers in every era, Vardaman's voice, full and rich
and soft with the accent of the southland, was musical to the ear whether
or not it actually informed. He stayed on the Chautauqua circuits even
after he became a member of the Senate, where in 1917 he was one of the
six men who voted against the declaration of war on Germany.

Another speaker appearing in Bedford in 1904 was shouting Sam Jones,
the evangelist. He, too, was a southerner, but there any similarity to James
K. Vardaman ended. Jones was a fervent crusader for the Lord who could
speak in simple, clear, careful English in a Sunday morning sermon and
on any other day use salty hillbilly jargon bordering on the vulgar. He
came from Georgia, not in Vardaman's immaculate white suit, but a
tobacco-chewing, spitting spectacle in baggy trousers, unpressed and ill-
fitting black alpaca coat, cheap shirt with celluloid collar and black string
tie.

Jones made a practice of starting his speech with a few rude remarks
aimed at the bald-headed elderly men in the first row, cupping their ears
with their hands. "Old Roosters," he called them. One of the thousand jobs
assigned the harassed superintendent, eventually, was to keep the children
out of the front seats and to fill them with oldsters whose hearing was on
the decline. Jones not only made the men hear, but he made them grin
and feel sheepish and at the same time like what he said.

"How long's it been since any of yo' ol' scamps has kissed yo' wife?"
he would shout. "Used to be a habit when she was young an' purty. Good
habit. Better git it again. Jes' go slow a bit to start, though. I was saying
this over at Tuscola last year and I got a letter from one ol' coot. He said
he'd tried my advice on his wife and the ol' gal thought he'd gone crazy,
so she give him a sounding smack on the face and run fer a broom to sweep
him out . . . but things is goin' all right now, he says, and he thanks me
for tellin' him . . ."

Jones was a temperance speaker, a man from a good southern family
who hit the sawdust trail after first getting considerable barroom sawdust
in his own shoes, and in towns like Bedford he put punch into his dry
argument with sharp, illogical figuring that left an impression on his audience.

"Look!" he would suddenly explode, waking up the sleepy men in the front row, "What do you all think a fellow is wuth in this here community . . . a human being, I mean, in dollars and cents? Well, I kin tell yo' mighty quick. How many people live in this there town?"

The answer might be: "Twenty-five hundred."

"How many saloons y'all got?"

"Ten."

"What license does each saloon pay?"

"Two hundred and fifty dollars."

"Brethern, what y'all gittin' fer hogs?"

"Five dollars."

"How many pounds average is a good fat hog?"

"About three hundred and fifty pounds."

Jones would pause, then begin again derisively: "Y'all gits two thousand five hundred dollars fer saloon licenses. That's jes a dollar a head fer each and every inhabitant of this here town, an' around eighteen dollars fer ever' hog. . . ." He would calculate again, then blurt, "Don't y'all wish yo' was a hog!"

Shouting Sam lived only two years after his Bedford appearance, but he packed them in at Chautauqua programs, winter Lyceums, church revivals all over the south and middle west right up to the end, with crowds of men and women shocked into attention either by his bluntness or the tobacco stains on his teeth; shamed, if they were backsliders, into going to church next Sunday, into voting dry next election. He was a fundamentalist of the old school who didn't approach the problem with any intellectual reasoning; he just "believed," and if the people he exhorted couldn't sing *The Brewer's Big Horses Won't Run Over Me* as if it were the national anthem, everything stopped right there while they learned it.

Long after Jones' death, an Ohio businessman went out on the road for a small Chautauqua circuit with what he called a *Transfiguration of Sam Jones,* offering committees a choice of four Sam Jones' sermons. The stunt did not last long, but the fact that it was attempted shows the power of the Sam Jones name in the early years of the century.

An additional representative of the clergy at Bedford who, like Joseph Crane Hartzell at Iowa Falls, stood out as man of action as well as orator, was Charles Henry Fowler. Like Hartzell he was a Methodist Episcopal bishop.

Bishop Fowler was seventy-six years old the summer that travelling Chautauqua was born, but his voice could still fill the tent, find its way through the thick canvas and reverberate across the hills. Less respectful members of his denomination affectionately referred to him as "Whirlwind Fowler," and one had only to listen to him once to understand the name. Canadian-born, brought up on an Illinois farm, president of Northwestern University while still a fairly young man, in 1871 he had fought the great Chicago fire. Thereafter he spent a year raising funds to rebuild the city's two hundred burned churches, telling the story so dramatically from coast to coast that his reputation as an orator was made. From then on he was in the Methodist mind for difficult jobs, and the harder they were and the farther they made him travel, the better he liked them, be it Russia, China, Japan, Korea or India. American audiences got one of their earliest pictures of Russia on a Chautauqua platform when Bishop Fowler related his experiences in organizing the first Methodist church in St. Petersburg.

I don't recall which of his famous speeches Bishop Fowler delivered at Bedford, except that somewhere in it, as always, the Chicago fire crackled, fanned to fury and then was extinguished by the power of his eloquence. He published many of his Chautauqua and Lyceum speeches in two volumes titled *Addresses for Notable Occasions* and *Patriotic Orations*. Bedford, in July, 1904, probably heard a patriotic oration, for the occasion was not particularly notable to any except Vawter and his new superintendent. Whatever Bishop Fowler called his speech, it was stimulating and full of humor, and very loud.

Congressman J. Adam Bede made all fourteen towns on the new circuit in 1904 in a series of debates. Part of the time, as at Iowa Falls, his opponent was Judge Martin J. Wade of Iowa, and the pair, both Congressmen, argued *The Political Issues of the Day*. Bede, a former newspaper editor, had been a United States marshal during the railroad strike in 1894, and his experience during that unhappy incident spiced both his speech and his thinking. He was a Republican, later a Teddy Roosevelt Progressive. Wade was a Democrat, whose favorite topic before Iowa fathers and mothers was that the Constitution should be taught to their children in the schools. Congressman Bede did not disagree with that idea; nor did Wade disagree with Bede's belief that Socialists were public enemies. So their debate was scholarly and not too exciting.

Most of the time, however, as at Bedford, Bede tangled less politely with Milwaukee Socialist Emil Seidel, a studious-looking firebrand who liked nothing better than a good platform encounter. Since Bede and Seidel had little political philosophy in common, they put on a spirited show over the question, *Is Socialism Desirable in the U.S.?* Seidel, a Wisconsin pattern-maker who perfected himself in his trade in Germany, went in slugging, just as he always had slugged at life. Somewhere in his speech he always told the crowd that back in 1892 his own poor little ballot had been one of the grand total of two Socialist votes in his Milwaukee precinct, but now, in 1904, he was alderman of the famous Twentieth ward. He could not foresee that in a few more years he would be Milwaukee's mayor and in the vigorous 1912 campaign would be honored with second place on his party's national ticket.

Bede, on the other hand, was the polished debater, a master of lively banter and sharp give and take. He knew better than most how to "make 'em laugh" and his funny remarks, on stage and off, went up and down the circuits. "This country ought to adopt Ireland," he once told a crowd near Boston, "and then raise its own policemen." Bede's habit of opening his debate with two amusing stories annoyed Seidel. It was all very well for Bede to be funny in Congress; his fellows there liked it, but Socialist Seidel did not. He was no storyteller and he saw no levity in the subject of Socialism. Bede usually started the debate and talked for thirty minutes, then the bespectacled Seidel took his thirty-minutes worth, after which they engaged in rebuttals. But at Bedford, Congressman Bede was delayed and he sent word for Seidel to open the program.

Seidel not only was willing but, surprisingly, he was delighted. To the consternation of the platform manager and other regulars in the tent, the Milwaukee alderman stood up, faced the waiting audience, and told the first of Bede's nightly stories. The people enjoyed it and laughed hard. Then Seidel told the second story. The crowd roared this time. After that Seidel went on with his regular speech and had just finished as Bede arrived.

Humorist Bede smoothed his hair, which he wore parted carefully in the middle, adjusted his flaming red tie, bowed, and launched into the same story the audience had just heard from Seidel. When it ended there was a puzzled silence. Bedford didn't intend to laugh at the same story twice in the same hour. Bede hurried into his second. The same silence greeted it. Bede turned to Seidel, confused.

"I've told them both already," the Socialist confessed.

The audience laughed hard, but Bede didn't. For once, like Seidel, he saw nothing funny in the situation. Thereafter he was careful to be on time and the pair slugged it out each night, giving the people a cracking good show. Ten years later they were still doing it.

The whole Bedford show came off without serious hitch. The tent did not blow down. No member of the enraptured audience fell off his high, hard seat. The naphtha lamps did not explode. I had no way of knowing that Vawter had lost his savings in the venture. Even had I guessed, it would not have dented my conviction that Chautauqua was on the road to stay. I read it in the people's eyes and faces. Here was a strange, new something that they wanted with all their plain country hearts. Here, in the midst of summer's hard labor, had been relaxation, inspiration come to rest briefly on the lonely back acres of the awakening nation.

Here for nine full days had been gaiety, music, mystery, adventure, good clean fun. Here, in a shabby old rented tent, under the flicker of sputtering white lights, were dreams come true. These people would ask for it again and again. Chautauqua had been born for them.

Chautauqua Takes Hold

9

Keith Vawter later admitted that he lost $7000 on his 1904 experiment, a shocking sum for those years, enough to buy many blocks of Chicago real estate. In addition, he had lost a hard summer's work. If he had been less stubborn, he would have abandoned his plan then and there. On paper it had seemed feasible, but out in country mud, weaknesses had bogged it down. He had every good reason to put aside the dream, concentrate on Lyceum, at which he made money without great risk, and his "folly," as rivals called his idea of tent Chautauqua, would soon be forgotten.

Many managers of permanent assemblies made no secret of their delight at Vawter's failure. They had refused to join his experiment and now they were vindicated. Chautauqua, they repeated, was the business of an individual community, nothing to be dragged out on the road like a carnival or a medicine show. Their towns wanted their own assemblies, they needed no packaged program from any slick booking agent. Hereafter, they predicted, this crazy man Vawter would stick to his own field as manager of a lecture bureau and let them run their assemblies as they saw fit. And how about trying to push him down next summer on lecture rates?

These individuals did not know Keith Vawter. A high-minded gentleman of superior intellect, he could be as obdurate as a Missouri mule. His sense of what midwest Americans wanted in good entertainment, and what they would pay for it, amounted almost to genius. Despite his first disaster, he was convinced that tent circuits not only could be profitable, but that they would bring pleasure to hundreds of thousands of people who could not afford money or time to travel any distance to a permanent assembly, but who would go eagerly if the show were brought to their home towns. To him this was a challenge.

So while managers of independents and rival bureaus smugly prepared to bury Vawter's "crazy idea," he went to work to prove that he had been right. He needed money, however, and partly for that reason he sent me to Ohio the next summer to establish in Columbus an outpost of the Redpath Lecture Bureau.

Until now the Redpath organization had treated this lecture-loving state as a no-man's land between Peffer's well-run Philadelphia office and Vawter's new Chicago area. They had abandoned it to the caprices of two other agencies, the Central Lyceum Bureau of Rochester, New York, and the John E. Brockway Bureau of Pittsburgh. Brockway had been in the business a long time. In the 1880's he had run a Lyceum course in his home town of Greenville, Pennsylvania. In recent years, in the east, he had represented the Slayton Bureau of Chicago, a group dating back to the days of James Redpath. Vawter believed that, of late, all of them had wasted golden opportunities. He proposed now to challenge Central in its own back yard.

I went to Columbus keen for battle but, alas, the Ohio agent for Central was not a fighting man. As soon as the famous Redpath name appeared, he capitulated and before long he even went to work for it. In two years the Redpath company bought the Slayton-Brockway groups. For my own part, instead of drawing a prosaic salary in Ohio, I was to pay both Vawter and the parent Central Bureau each three percent of gross receipts and pocket whatever net profit remained. We sold winter Lyceum courses to big and little towns all the way from smoky Youngstown to the busy port of Toledo, from the winding Ohio River to Lake Erie. When the year ended, my own share of the profits was an unbelievable $10,000.

Back in Chicago, in the interval, Vawter was slowly shaping plans for his next caravan. This time he would overcome all foreseeable obstacles before rushing people, equipment and tents over the hazardous road. He alone would make decisions. He would permit managers to buy his program only if they fitted their dates into his route and his calendar. When and where his talent would appear, how long it would remain in any town, would be his decision and his alone. Once dates were set, no one could change them.

He also would offer his program as a whole, take it or leave it. Nor would he haggle over prices. If anyone wanted to use his talent under that arrangement, he was welcome.

In the spring of 1907 he was ready again. It was a good year. Teddy Roosevelt was "feeling bully" in the White House. Down Panama-way Goethals was winning his fight with landslides in Culebra Cut. In New York City virtue had triumphed and *Salome* and all her seven veils had been banished from the "Met." Best of all, Iowa corn was up toward fifty cents and might go higher. Certainly this time it ought to be a good season.

Meanwhile a few other bold spirits, having eyed Vawter's trek across

Iowa and Nebraska three years before, had dared to try to do likewise. The gospel of temperance inspired the first of them. In 1905 Fred W. Bartell, of Baptist Arkansas, dismayed that in the Presidential election the year before the Prohibition party had failed to poll even a thousand votes in his state, put a reform circuit briefly on the road. C. Durant Jones, a one-time candidate for governor of Iowa on the Prohibition ticket, also piously called his first shows "Temperance Assemblies." Another temperance organization that called itself a Chautauqua was the National Lincoln, a particularly biased outfit fathered by the Illinois Prohibition Party. We bought its remains in 1922.

Many critics never forgot the melancholy atmosphere of the early anti-liquor zealots. One commentator, as far back as 1901, was George Cram Cook, who later, as a founder of the Provincetown Players, was to leave his mark on the artistic world, as did his wife, Playwright Susan Glaspell. Writing from Davenport, in his native Iowa, to a performer on an independent platform, Cook said: "You read with heart and art, and then a somewhat sour clerical person talked intemperately of 'Temperance.' You, I perceived, were the sugar in the Chautauqua lemonade."

One season in those early years, twenty-one [1] separate circuits were operating, some on shoestrings, others with fair financial backlogs. Several special pleaders besides the Prohibitionists borrowed the name. A farm machinery manufacturer used it for a traveling exhibit; Chicago labor unions presented their case in a "Chautauqua" named for Opera Star Mary Garden. Even the Ku Klux Klan got into the act with a "Klantauqua" dedicated to bigotry and hatred.

Vawter's own 1907 season had been a success. Aided by J. Roy Ellison, he pitched his tents in thirty-three Iowa, Wisconsin and Nebraska towns. That year he introduced the "guarantee system," under which a community, sold on the "new Chautauqua idea," put up $2000 to assure the show's return the following year. In 1907 and 1908, Vawter again offered J. Adam Bede, the prophetic Thomas E. Green and Juggler George Garretson. He also added several new personalities.

Among these was an undistinguished lieutenant-governor from Ohio, offering a lecture on Alexander Hamilton. His name was Warren Gamaliel Harding. Handsome, full of small-town urbanity, he was simple and warm-hearted and the talent, in particular, loved him.

Old Chautauqua folk remember Harding as a brilliant orator, but can't for the life of them recall exactly what he said. His words, one circuit manager reported, "marked him as a man of the people and a champion

---

[1] These included Travers-Wick and Midland from Iowa, Britt (later Standard) of Nebraska, Central Community and International from Indiana, Acme under W. S. Rupe, Radcliffe from Washington, D.C.; from Kansas J. Shannon White and the "Cadmean System," honoring the mythical hero of the alphabet; likewise, Alkahest, meaning the "liquid that could dissolve pure gold."

of their rights." They affected Critic H. L. Mencken differently. "A string of wet sponges," he called them.

Harding's friendliness was genuine. Back in Marion, Ohio, he had been a good first baseman, played alto horn in the Citizens Cornet Band and still owned a good small-town newspaper. In Chautauqua he was a good trouper. As lieutenant-governor, and later as senator, lecturing on *The Big Stick,* he stopped to chat on street corners in Chautauqua towns, often visited the local newspaper office, shook hands around the "back shop" and, to prove that he could do it, would set a stick of type.

Our people liked to tell of the season when at Nashville, Tennessee, Harding's train was late, and carrying his suitcase and gold-headed cane, he ran from the railroad station and asked which streetcar went to the Chautauqua grounds. Misdirected, he rode to the wrong end of the line. He was an hour late reaching the tent where the Beulah Buck Musical Company which "pre-luded" him had heroically gone twice through its whole repertoire, keeping the people in their seats. The point of the story was that this "distinguished senator" was, at heart, a man of the people who chose to ride a streetcar rather than in an elegant hack.

Chautauqua people did not like Harding's wife. She was demanding and most talent had heard her say—or at least had heard from somebody else who heard her say—that "the way to keep a husband is never to let him travel alone." Taking her own advice, she spent weeks each summer on the road with him. Disclosures of the scandals of Harding's administration, after his death, shocked Chautauqua people, some of whom tried to explain the sorry business by saying Harding was always too good to his friends. Another Chautauqua speaker and another President, Bishop Vincent's friend, Grant, had suffered from the same political malady.

For the 1907 tour Vawter also presented a Hungarian Orchestra, ten impressive Pueblo Indians, a Hesperian Quartette and a Negro group called the Sterling Jubilee Singers. This latter type of company was known in the trade as "Jubes." The Sterlings, four men and four women, sang well. Customers used to say that to hear them render *The Sun Do Move* was worth the price of a season ticket. The Sterlings also laughed a lot among themselves; however, it was a Sterling who, when a tent collapsed on him in an Ohio windstorm, cut his way through the canvas with a razor that he "just happened to have" in his pocket.

In spite of a program as good as the one in 1907, Vawter lost money again in 1908. At the close of the season several lecturers, including the future President of the United States, took promises-to-pay instead of pay checks. This time Vawter did not blame the loss on balky independent managers. He realized that his cycle of six-day programs, opening on Tuesday, closing on Sunday, was an awkward arrangement.

In 1910 he finally solved the problem, and all other managers henceforth copied his method.[1] That year Vawter worked out the true circuit plan, both as to program arrangement and delivery. First-day talent remained first-day all season, second-day remained second-day, and so on for the seven days. Thus all groups travelled the same routes for the first time, and railroading and programming became simplified. Working with Vawter in this development, and at least partially responsible for his belated financial success, was Charles Francis Horner, who eventually, under his own name, would become a power in the business.

Meanwhile, with Ohio-made riches burning holes in my pockets, I, too, had bought a share of the parent Redpath bureau. I became a fourth partner with Vawter, Peffer of Philadelphia and Hathaway of Boston, and leaving my brother, Vernon W. Harrison, to manage Ohio Lyceum, I moved back to Vawter's Chicago office.

This arrangement could not last long. Vawter worked better alone. So before the 1909 booking season, we split the Chicago territory. Under the name "Redpath-Vawter" and with Horner still his assistant, Vawter took the area west of the Mississippi. Under "Redpath-Chicago," I would concentrate on Illinois, Indiana, Ohio, Michigan, Kentucky, Tennessee and the Gulf states. Vawter's base was Cedar Rapids, Iowa.

In three more years Horner and Vawter likewise separated their territory and Horner established in Kansas City a system called "Western Redpath Chautauqua," later "Redpath-Horner." His enterprises swelled quickly into three great circuits, from Missouri and Colorado and the Arkansas and Texas cotton country, north into Wyoming and South Dakota. In programming, Horner, a man of enviable energy, encouraged amateurs. He enjoyed training his own talent and ultimately he opened a school of dramatic art, in conjunction with his booking office. The Horner Institute of Fine Arts, later the Kansas City Conservatory, is still a going concern.

Ellison, likewise, left the Vawter Company in booming 1912 and with Clarence H. White founded the Ellison-White system that, geographically, was to become the largest on the continent. With a "South Seas" company, Ellison even tried to crash the gates of Australia and New Zealand. A major contribution of this manager to the whole movement was in the field of transportation costs. In 1915, when his routes covered two and a quarter million miles, he persuaded a reluctant railroad to sell him one-trip excursion-rate tickets for his talent . . . not a mean achievement.

Also in 1912, Paul N. Pearson, professor of public speaking at Swarthmore College, Pennsylvania, and a popular Lyceum orator, launched his own system, known first as the "Pennsylvania Chautauqua Association," later simply as "Swarthmore." It has been said, perhaps with justification,

---

[1] In 1911 Vawter's tents appeared in sixty-eight towns. His average day's travel was down to forty-seven miles. He employed 227 persons that summer, used twelve freight and baggage cars.

that Pearson's programs were gauged to a higher intelligence quotient than others. Certainly there was less razzle-dazzle on Swarthmore.

Pearson, a devout Quaker, anxious to advance Christian education on all fronts, insisted that every speaker under the dignified Swarthmore banner actually have something to say on an important subject. He frowned on purely "inspirational" oratory. His two great eastern circuits operated in New York and New Jersey, through lecture-conscious New England, down into old Virginia and a few points south. Occasionally they met those of our smart-showman partner Peffer, whose Redpath circuit came to be called "Redpath-New England." Pearson's and Peffer's lines crossed, but never tangled.[1]

In 1912 programs from all these platforms drenched the nation with culture and good clean fun. Tents popped up in vacant lots and all America swarmed down the aisles. Chautauqua had taken hold. At times, among the smaller operators, it was a cutthroat business, but not among the Redpath bureau managers. In spite of occasional misunderstandings, we were all for one and one for all. There certainly were towns enough and crowds enough and money enough to go around. Or so we thought. To those of us embarked in 1912 on this exciting enterprise, it looked as if it could last a hundred years, thanks to Keith Vawter. To him went all credit from the trade. When managers honored him with a dinner a few years later, Louis J. Alber of the Coit-Alber Lyceum and Chautauqua Bureau, summed it up in a toast: "You builded better than you know, Mr. Vawter, when your idea gave such tremendous impetus to this experiment in democracy."

As for the Redpath-Chicago office, it was ready that season to put its own show on the road. With high hopes I had gone the preceding fall to Pulaski, in southern Tennessee, to sell the next summer's program. We opened there in June, 1912.

[1] Not until the First World War did any aggressive competition pitch its tents in Redpath territory. Then a pair of high-class showmen, Arthur C. Coit and Louis J. Alber, organized Coit-Alber Chautauqua with Cleveland as its base. Also in the field briefly before the first world conflict was C. Benjamin Franklin, who later returned from the war to organize the Associated Chautauquas of America.

Up Goes the Brown Tent

10

Pulaski, Tennessee, where Redpath-Chicago launched its first circuit, was a cotton center of about 2500 persons in 1912, a sleepy little county seat just north of the Alabama line. History made it a good Chautauqua town. On the credit side it had fostered one of the south's early centers of female learning, later Martin Junior College; before the turn of the century it boasted a second seminary. (To its discredit, the Ku Klux Klan in Reconstruction days had swept like a fire from Pulaski across the state.)

A statue of Sam Davis, the spy who died rather than talk, decorated its public square. It had a fine town hall and courthouse, its jail was empty and Giles County, though slipping a little in population, could produce a good-sized audience used to thinking for itself. In fact, one of the first boasts that Redpath's advance man heard, arriving in town, was that Democratic Giles County had one citizen stubborn enough to vote dry in the last Presidential election and three who admitted openly that they were Socialists.

Author Opie Read, a southerner, and therefore possibly speaking with prejudice, always claimed that the south was Chautauqua's happy hunting ground, that the southern audience, with its Anglo-Scotch-Irish inheritance, was so spontaneous and quick to understand that "instead of struggling to follow a lecturer, it ran in advance of him, helping him over difficult gorges." Be that as it may, we picked Pulaski for our tryout because of its geographical location. The north-bound circuit was to be Redpath-Chicago's first summer adventure, but we made no claim to being pioneers. Vawter had been that. We were simply ready to follow in his tracks.

The previous winter we had signed up sponsoring committees in thirty-nine communities in Tennessee, Kentucky, Indiana and Michigan, all virgin soil for tent Chautauqua, all willing to take a chance. We had gathered an array of talent and built a program that we hoped was varied enough to please all types of audiences, southern or northern. We had bought new tents and equipment, worked out railroad schedules, employed the most experienced superintendents to be found, hired nine energetic crews, each consisting of four college boys, to do the physical work. We had printed tons of promotional material, booklets, pamphlets, program folders, posters, blotters, stickers for envelopes, buttons, banners for Main Street, streamers for the noisy, canvas-topped cars lining the curbs now in the larger towns. Loaded down with this material, advance men had swarmed into the field to drum up enthusiasm and put up advertising. By June 1st we were on our toes.

The 1912 theatrical season was important all the way from Broadway to Pulaski. In New York a lovely young actress named Laurette Taylor opened in *Peg o' My Heart,* a sentimental confection whipped up by her husband, J. Hartley Manners. Jane Cowl, in Bayard Veiller's *Within the Law,* began a melodramatic run of 541 nights. Elsie Janis, a Columbus, Ohio, girl who in five more years would become the "Sweetheart of the A.E.F.," kicked up her pretty heels, with Montgomery and Stone, in the tuneful *Lady of the Slipper.*

Also, that Broadway season, a blond named Mae West joined the Dolly Sisters, Leon Errol and Frank Tinney in *A Winsome Widow.* George M. Cohan was singing *Forty-Five Minutes from Broadway* and Maud Adams was asking the audiences at *Peter Pan* whether they believed in fairies. They did.

That same stupendous year William Faversham was playing *Caesar,* Madame Nazimova was emoting violently in a play full of dark hidden meanings, Sothern and Marlowe were bringing dignity to the stage and John Drew was bringing it sartorial distinction—Broadway was a street of Thespian dreams! And so was Main Street, in Pulaski.

A fact never to be denied is that, from beginning to end, circuit Chautauqua was a series of earth-shaking crises and startling, sometimes agonizing surprises. Redpath-Chicago's opening in normally tranquil Pulaski was no exception to this devastating rule.

Unknown to us, a would-be competitor had shown up in the area during the winter. After we announced Pulaski as our jumping-off place, a manager of a small independent southern booking office had rushed into the town with shocking stories of what would happen to honest citizens reckless enough to sign up with Redpath. He hinted darkly that Redpath-Chicago was just a gang of tricky Yankee cutthroats and that the splendid people of Pulaski would rue the hour that they allowed their signatures to go on our dotted lines, or the money from their tannery, their cotton, flour and planing mills to disappear into our bottomless pockets.

"Yankee" was still a bad word along the borders of Alabama and Tennessee. All Pulaski waited to see what actually would happen. What did happen confirmed the darkest suspicions. The Redpath tent, the new, elegant, expensive brown canvas that was to establish on our circuit a new tent style, got lost . . . and in Chicago I was in bed with the mumps!

Vernon Harrison, pinch-hitting for Chicago from the Ohio office, reached Pulaski three or four days before opening date, to find our superintendent and crew ready and waiting, grass cut and raked on the tent site on the courthouse lawn, the advance sale of tickets respectably near the top. People on the street were talking hard about the coming show. A goodly number of them were wearing "I'll be there" buttons on their coat lapels. Our new posters splashed color in store windows and on billboards. Across Main Street fluttered the bright strings of pennants, all advertising the wonderful coming event, a device Keith Vawter had thought up the previous year which soon would become the gay symbol of all Chautauqua towns.

But somewhere in the five hundred single-track miles between Chicago and the southern boundary of Tennessee, in one of a hundred railroad yards or sidings, our canvas, tent poles, piano, stage backdrop and seats had been shunted into oblivion. Railroad officials, promising of course to look into the matter, added casually that such investigations might consume a week.

"No tent?" cried the hotheads in the population. This certainly proved Yankee chicanery.

Vernon Harrison, sensing the growing uneasiness of the committee, dared not wait for the railroads to act. He went to work swiftly on the unsubstantial long distance telephone line which in those days sometimes, but only sometimes, linked Pulaski with the outside world.

After frantic calls to Chicago and Columbus, he started hunting a substitute tent near at hand, close enough to reach Pulaski in twenty-four hours. He needed one that would seat a thousand persons, for if the committee had sold seven hundred and fifty of the two-dollar season tickets here in Giles County, then at least two hundred and fifty more single admissions must be counted on for the "name" programs.

Time was frighteningly short. At last, in Nashville, he found a tent of sorts. It was not what he needed, but an inadequate tent was better than no tent at all. In desperation he ordered it shipped by express on the next train. It proved to be old, dirty, battered. It leaked. It threatened to come apart at the seams in the slightest breeze. By crowding it might seat 500 persons.

The local committee naturally was indignant. Angrily, under the Redpath nose, the chairman waved his copy of the signed contract and shouted that signatures or no signatures, the people of Pulaski weren't going to pay

for what they didn't get. There were good lawyers in town who would see
to it that the rights of southern citizens were not trampled. There were
courts of justice in Tennessee, suh!

The Redpath representative, acting quickly, produced his own copy of
the contract, glanced at the signatures, then slowly and dramatically tore
it into small shreds. He dropped them into a wastebasket and dusted off
his hands.

"There, gentlemen," he said, "now there is no contract binding you to
anything. The Redpath bureau doesn't need the signatures of honorable
men and women. We know that you are honest, we want you to know that
we are, too. You are not obligated to pay us a single cent. But we will
present our program just the same. I'm sorry about the tent. But when
our own arrives, we'll put it up at once. Meanwhile we trust you. We hope
that you trust us."

Abashed committeemen let the rebel yell die in their throats. This handsome young Yankee fellow certainly had proven himself a gentleman after
all. But what about all those customers who wouldn't be able to get into
this small tent and would be left outside waving their two-dollar tickets?
What about the seats? What about a piano? The superintendent's assur-
ances were convincing: he would find temporary seats locally, he would
rent the best piano he could find. As for the people unable to get into the
tent, Redpath would cross that frightening bridge when it came to it.

Manager, superintendent, crew, everyone prayed for rain the first night
—not a cloudburst, of course, just enough to keep the crowd small, without miring the Chautauqua grounds. Providence answered. The rains came,
heavy enough to maroon at home country folk who knew better than to
drive on red clay roads immediately after a storm. Pulaski folk attended,
but not in such numbers as to create a problem. The shabby little tent
leaked in spots but it gave shelter enough.

Next morning, the southern sun rose full of bright promise and the train,
unexcitedly chugging down the Nashville-Decatur grade, brought Redpath's elegant new brown tent. The poles were up and the canvas taut in
two hours; before the afternoon ticket holders swarmed through the gate,
seats were in place and stage ready with its backdrop and big American
flag, its piano and the pitcher of water. Redpath honor had been vindicated.

The first day's program had opened with music, of course. Vawter in
his trial run eight years before had used the dignified Chicago Lady Entertainers as openers, but the world of entertainment had moved forward
in those eight years, so instead of 1904's formalized program of songs and
hymns, Chicago-Redpath led off with the Ladies Spanish Orchestra. If the
seven black-haired young women were not actually Spanish, they looked
and acted it and their first offering was the *Wilhelm Tell Overture*. Music

accelerated as the week went on, until on closing day it climaxed with what for the 1912 era was a lively musical show in costume.

The Anitas, a "singing orchestra" of five vivacious young girls under the management of Mrs. Ralph Dunbar, and sentimentally named for my home town of Anita in Iowa, not only sang but played a variety of instruments. The group included a violinist, cellist, pianist, cornetist, and, youngest and liveliest, a "flute virtuoso" with entrancing curls, who never had played a flute till she got her job, and now could play the numbers on the program and nothing else. Her snap and girlish voice made up, however, for any weakness in repertoire on the flute. She was a hit with her first song, that sentimental favorite *We Were Sailing Along on Moonlight Bay*. The audience thought it great, but her encore convulsed them, a pert rendering of a ditty called *Miss Gibbs,* which she sang and sang until audience and singer both had had enough.

> "Mar-y, people call me pretty Mar-y!
> "I don't believe them, for they often tell me fibs."
> ("Oh, do believe us!")
> "I'm a girl and not a fairy,
> "I don't see why you call me Mar-y,
> "When my name's Miss Gibbs!
> "Miss Gibbs, if you please. . . ."
> ("Let us call you Mar-y, dear")
> "Miss Gibbs, if you please, Miss Gibbs." [1]

It was a good catchy 1912 song and eighteen-year-old Miss Fay Pettit of Wellington, Kansas—she is now Mrs. Joseph C. Maddy, wife of the founder of the National Music Camp at Interlochen, Michigan—caught the crowd's fancy with both song and reading, though her training in elocution before she signed her contract had been as sketchy as her instruction on the flute. Mrs. Dunbar, in turn, "interpreted" *A Child's Dream of a Star* and as an encore read a sprightly piece about *The Perfect Man:* "Have you found him? No, not yet . . . he's the husband of the widows I have met. . . ," sad or humorous, whichever way you wanted to take it.

For one cycle of songs the Anitas dressed as Goose Girls, for another they were Japanese, and in bright kimonos told the story of the *Willow Pattern Plate,* keeping time with their paper fans and parasols and making a pretty picture indeed. There was also a Dutch number, for which the young ladies appeared in wooden shoes and lace caps and aprons over bulging skirts, while Mrs. Dunbar read Eugene Field's *Wynken, Blynken and Nod.*

Of course the girls did not dance as they sang. That would have been going too far in 1912. But they did clump-clump in a lively tempo.

Maybe they weren't the Rockettes, but neither were they Vawter's staid Lady Entertainers. Let us say they were good clean fun.

And like most other young people on the circuits the Anitas also had fun. When their own stint was over, that last night in Pulaski, they went off gaily to a moonlight picnic with the four dashing and handsome young men of the Strollers Quartette, who, next afternoon, dressed in magnificent Scotch kilts, were to entertain another appreciative southern audience, and with whom the lively Anitas met up after that in every town they could, even though one of the young men looked a little fat off stage and not so dashing. The Strollers' songs were most beguiling, the Anitas thought, their acts most amusing. In one sketch reverently called *The Shades of the Masters* the four young men impersonated the spirits of Wagner, Beethoven, Mendelssohn and Liszt returned to earth to discuss what the musical world was coming to.

With the new tent in place and the sun shining and the committee in chastened mood, the Redpath superintendent thought that certainly things were back on the right track; but no, there were to be other troubles.

Among the lighter numbers of the programs as built up in Chicago were "two lightning-change artists." One was Edward Ellsworth Plumstead, who did amusing character portrayals, changing costumes and wigs on the stage. The other was Walter Wilson, a big, long-legged, nimble impersonator with a deep bass voice, who pre-luded Bohumir Kryl's band with an act representing half a dozen characters, from "hayseed" to "soldier tramp."

Like Plumstead, Wilson diverted his audience by changing costumes in full view of the crowd; unlike Plumstead, he included his pants in the change. In preparation for this, Mr. Wilson wore a suit of white silk tights under his outer clothes. When he slipped out of his trousers that June night in Tennessee, the audience was not familiar with long silk tights, but it did know all about long winter underdrawers.

Underdrawers, when discussed at all in polite society, were referred to in those days as "unmentionables," and they certainly were nothing to parade before a mixed audience of God-fearing southern ladies and gentlemen. No Tennessee citizen stalked out of the tent, but there was a definite disapproving murmur that any platform manager could understand and did, and the rest of the season Wilson confined his costume changes to shirt and coat and left his controversial nether garments strictly alone. If the Baptist south did not like white silk tights, what would the Methodist people up in Indiana say?

Wilson played both the flute and saxophone as part of his act. He featured particularly a serious and somewhat loud saxophone rendition of *Rocked in the Cradle of the Deep,* with variations. As musician he appeared in proper formal evening clothes. All audiences, beginning with the Dakota homesteaders, approved of evening clothes.

The rest of the week was a success. People from all over the southern tier of Tennessee counties and from the northern fringe of Alabama flocked into town in Fords, horse-drawn buggies, farm wagons, on muleback and on foot. They were entranced by the music, mystified by the magic. They laughed at the jokes. The stirring talks uplifted their spirits. They approved when the committee signed the contract for the next year.

The program, as preserved by the *Pulaski Weekly Citizen,* was:

PULASKI CHAUTAUQUA
June 15 to 21, 1912.

Superintendent . . . . O. W. Thomas
Morning Hour Lecture . . . . C. E. Varney
Boy Scout Master . . . . R. G. Coonradt

Program Begins Promptly

Boy Scouts—9 A.M.
Afternoon Music—2:30
Night Music—7:30

Morning Lecture—10:00 A.M.
Afternoon Lecture—3:00
Night Entertainment—8:15

Saturday
Afternoon   Concert—Ladies Spanish Orchestra
             Lecture—"A Lesson to the Nation"—Judge A. Z. Blair
Night   Concert—Ladies Spanish Orchestra
             Character Studies—John B. Ratto

Sunday
Afternoon   Concert—Carroll Glee Club
             Lecture—"The Modern Mormon Kingdom"—Sen. F. J. Cannon
Night   Vesper Service
             Concert—Carroll Glee Club
             Reading—"The Dawn of Tomorrow"—Mary Agnes Doyle

Monday
Morning   Boy Scouts
             Lecture—"Man's Search for God"—C. E. Varney
Afternoon   Song Recital—Artists from LeBrun Grand Opera Co.
             Lecture—"The Man Against the Mass"—Frank Dixon
Night   Grand Opera—LeBrun Grand Opera Co.

Tuesday
Morning   Boy Scouts
             Lecture—"Sane and Safe Faith"—C. E. Varney
Afternoon   Concert—Musical Favorites
             Lecture—"A Message From Kansas"—Gov. E. W. Hoch
Night   Concert—Musical Favorites
             Indian Lecture in Costume—"Things I Saw and Did as a Savage"
             —Tahan

Wednesday
Morning   Boy Scouts
             Lecture—"Philosophy of Habit"—C. E. Varney
Afternoon   Concert—Bohumir Kryl and Band
             Entertainer—J. Walter Wilson
Night   Concert—Bohumir Kryl and Band
             Entertainer—J. Walter Wilson

Thursday

Morning   Boy Scouts
            Lecture—"The Value of Imagination"—C. E. Varney
Afternoon   Concert—Mendelssohn's Quartette
            Lecture—"Traitors to Justice"—Judge M. A. Kavanagh
Night   Concert—Mendelssohn's Quartette
            Magician—Reno

Friday

Morning   Boy Scouts
            Lecture—"The Use of The Will"—C. E. Varney
Afternoon   Concert—Anitas Ladies Orchestra
            Author and Humorist—Opie Read
Night   Concert—Anitas Ladies Orchestra
            Entertainer—Ellsworth Plumstead

And all of this for a two dollar season ticket!

The first-day contingent started northward as soon as its evening show ended and the second day's talent took over the creaking stage. Then they, too, packed up their equipment and boarded the night train and the third program moved into their places. Thus for seven days, orators, musical companies and entertainers tried out their shining wares on Pulaski, made what changes seemed necessary, pulled out the song or act that had won only meagre applause, substituted a better one and set forth in high spirits for the summer's road. The seventh night all seven groups were on the move.

Each outfit paused in four other Tennessee communities. Columbia, a larger town in the adjoining county, followed Pulaski. There, church-going southern matrons, banded together into the local King's Daughters, set up a "refreshment tent" on the Chautauqua grounds, so that perspiring performers could cool off with lemonade and home-made cakes, and incidentally shake the hands of the town's great, near-great and socially ambitious. They played Murfreesboro, where the Civil War's Battle of Stone River had been fought; farther west, the town of Paris; over toward the Mississippi River, Union City. Then, jumping the Kentucky line, they visited tobacco-raising Mayfield. It was here at the Mayfield Hotel, where a great banner across the front blazed the one word "Chautauqua," that the talent picked up the story, to become hoary on the circuits as the years went by, of the old Negro on his vegetable wagon who, seeing the sign, would not go into the building, and when the proprietor came out to discover why, demanded, "What disease you quarantined for, boss?"

In Kentucky the troupers made eleven stops. Hopkinsville and busy Bowling Green with its fine old houses, Danville and Cynthiana on the Licking River, and half a dozen other towns greeted entertainers and orators with southern hospitality. The trail left Dixie at Henderson and crossed the Ohio River into Indiana, where seventeen Hoosier communities in the next seventeen days watched the big brown tents pop up in pastures and village squares. The average distance between the towns was approximately fifty miles; absent were the long backtracking hops that once had bedeviled Vawter.

The Indiana localities for the most part were larger than those farther south: old Vincennes on the Wabash River; Brazil, where the strip coal miners crowded the tent; Muncie, the hard-knuckled heart of the booming "gas belt," with glass blowers' and gas-field workers' money eager to be spent—the town that, years later, under the pseudonym of "Middletown," was to be the subject of a penetrating social study of a midwestern industrial city by Robert and Helen Lynd. Unsuspicious in 1912 of this coming role, it achieved that summer, in Chautauqua minds at least, a different kind of glory. It had the largest committee ever to sponsor a Chautauqua program, seven hundred members of Muncie's Federation of Women's Clubs.

Westward, at Crawfordsville and Lafayette, the seven-day course broke the summer vacation solstice for faculty families at Wabash College and Purdue University; came Huntington next, just beginning to feel its industrial oats; and the interurban town of Bluffton, where the *Evening Banner* printed an excited special edition.

Everywhere communities covered the Victorian faces of their public buildings with bunting, home-town bands tooted as the troupes piled off the train, excited caravans rolled in from neighboring towns. After Indiana, the tents jumped into Michigan, with six stops in fairly large communities: Monroe on Lake Erie; Mt. Clemens with its mineral baths; Charlotte; Niles boasting of a history under four flags; the state capital at Lansing; and finally Flint, which in those days was famed as the world's largest producer of buggy whips. Next the trail dipped back to four more towns in Indiana, ending the season the first day of August at Rochester, seat of Fulton County.

Thus our initial Redpath-Chicago circuit covered every type of town. Proud, respectable old communities and new booming cities, north, south, rich, poor, industrial and farming, with audiences of strictly middle-class citizens with personalities and tastes of their own, but all with common desires. Like their parents in the days of Josh Billings, they wanted a chance to laugh; then to learn something they didn't know or had forgotten, or did know and believed in so much that they wanted to hear it again.

The full Redpath talent list in 1912 included forty-four lecturers, seventeen entertainers and thirty entertaining companies, but the headliners were Bohumir Kryl's Bohemian Band and William Jennings Bryan. We booked the bandmaster for the whole tour and Bryan for such dates as he could squeeze into the weeks before a Presidential election. The Democratic National convention was just about to open in Baltimore as the three-times defeated Presidential candidate took to the road in Tennessee. When its tumult finally ended in July, Bryan began campaigning hard; the Democrats needed his golden voice. In seven days he averaged ten

"Wilson speeches" a day, long and short; but in spite of this he managed to appear in thirty-four Chautauqua programs before fall, dropping politics for *The Prince of Peace*. At least half of the towns were on our circuit out of Chicago.

William Randolph Hearst's newspapers were attacking Bryan mercilessly that summer, chiefly for having given his support to Woodrow Wilson. In cartoons and editorials Hearst thundered, "Bryan is through!" But the campaign so overshot its mark, so enraged Bryan's admirers, that songs in his praise rose along our whole route in the south and middle west.

One mid-summer day when Bryan hoisted his big body off a train at South Bend, Indiana, hoping to find quick transportation over the state line for Chautauqua's "Bryan Day" in Niles, Michigan, a waiting crowd

with a convoy of fifty flag-draped automobiles paraded him through South Bend and in spite of Mr. Hearst, deposited him with cheers outside the brown tent in Niles. In Michigan's traditionally Republican territory of Charlotte and Lansing, a chorus of factory whistles and church bells announced the Democrat's arrival. Stores closed and offices hurried employees out to the street to wave flags as the Bryan caravan rolled past. At Charlotte the National Guard regimental band from the state capital was on hand to escort "the great Commoner" to the Chautauqua tent. We were indebted to Mr. Hearst for excellent free advertising that year and we cashed in on it.

Marcus A. Kavanagh, Judge of the Superior Court of Chicago, speaking on court reform, received similar welcomes from the Knights of Columbus. He was a national official of the organization in 1912, and in a dozen towns members in uniform walked briskly with him from the station to the Chautauqua grounds. At Henderson, Kentucky, half a hundred crowded onto our platform as a "guard of honor"; at Brazil, Indiana, a whooping crowd of 2200 turned out to hear him.

The judge had signed for this opening season with a speech called *Traitors to Justice,* because, he said, he was finally convinced that "reform in court procedure and law enforcemeent will never come through the legal profession, but through the sympathy and effort of the general public." He had been on the bench twenty years by then, a serious-minded, serious-looking man who believed in capital punishment, one of the few judges in the world who ever sentenced to death a man who had pleaded guilty. Kavanagh was gentle in his approach to law-abiding people, stern with lawbreakers. Few persons in the tents had ever heard in those days of a nonpartisan municipal government or a nonpartisan judiciary, but if they sat through Kavanagh's speech, and he made it an interesting speech, they went home well informed. And a bit ashamed, also, if they ever had dodged jury duty. He also disliked golf players, ". . . spending $50,000,000 a year on a game that requires neither courage or intellect."

The judge travelled frequently in later years with Edward Reno, the magician. Reno carried a famous little purse about the size of a dollar, and while he idled with Judge Kavanagh at a railway station, he used to get the purse into Kavanagh's pocket, then pull it out and extract a six-inch open knife from it; or quietly slip out the Kavanagh handkerchief and put an American flag in its place.

One speaker, neither fish nor fowl, who contributed nothing to either the political or moral scene our first season, but was good box office, was the Honorable Albion Zelophehad Blair, of Adams County, Ohio (not to be confused with lecturer Albert L. Blair, Brooklyn journalist). Albion Blair had been a country lawyer in the days when lawyers were not required to have legal training. Soon after neighbors had elected him county judge, a notorious murder trial came up in his court. He shocked learned counsel by his handling of the trial, since he based unorthodox decisions on what he called horse sense. His opinions, delivered in somewhat startling language, were caught up in the press and overnight he gained celebrity as "the hanging judge." He expanded at once into a cracker-barrel philosopher and his unconventional comments on the passing scene, made in ungrammatical but pithy sentences, began to be widely quoted. "We seen our duty and we done it," was one of the gems from his facile tongue. He made the crowds laugh. If any smart-aleck young lawyer tried to heckle him, a rare happening in Chautauqua tents, "Judge" Blair was ready. He lasted, I believe, two seasons.

The morning hour speaker for this trek was Charles E. Varney, an evangelist by profession from Paw Paw, Michigan, who talked to the club women on such intangible qualities as will power, imagination, habit. The most popular forenoon feature, however, was one we initiated that year. The idea of a "Junior Chautauqua" to keep the children busy had originated on the Horner circuits. Vawter had sent a "Squaw Lady" abroad in the land to sponsor groups of Campfire Girls; our "Story-Hour Lady" eventually was to follow her. But in 1912, with the cooperation of the national Boy Scout movement, we introduced Scouting. Attached to our staff for each town was a trained scoutmaster, who enlisted all willing boys into troops for drill, nature study and cross-country hikes. The south, with its taste for the military, took to the idea favorably.

Before we left Kentucky, attendance at single shows averaged well over the thousand we had set as a break-even point. To get all the crowds under canvas for special evenings would have required a tent at least half again as large as those we carried. So, going through Indiana, we started to roll up the side walls. Then, to keep small boys and older ones from watching the show from outside, we set up a circle of well-guyed wooden fence posts ten feet apart and fastened to them a brown canvas screen seven feet high. With enough posts and enough of this quickly unrolled fencing we could, if we wished, push back the outer walls as far as fifty feet and make room for an extra thousand or fifteen hundred paid admissions. Later, against the outside of this fence, we stretched our enormous Redpath Chautauqua signs with block letters four feet high, on white backgrounds. It took no spectacles to read them from almost a quarter mile away and eventually we carried flood lights to illuminate them at night.

Rolling up the sides of the tent had a second advantage. It gave the precious breeze a little play, for we had journeyed no farther than our second town down in Tennessee when we discovered the one problem above all others. This was the heat, the oppressive, almost suffocating heat under the big top on a blistering afternoon, and most afternoons on the south and midwest circuits seemed to be blistering. The old "Chautauqua salute" of waving handkerchiefs still popped up here and there, but topping it now was that perpetual motion I had faced first in Iowa Falls, the constant mopping of brows and the wigwag of the palm leaf fan. Fans never wagged in unison. If they had, it might have been even more disconcerting to the lecturer. We never escaped the heat. Wherever the tents stood in the sun, the audience fanned, the talent suffered and on the vaudeville stage comedians coined the joke, "Under the canvas the heat was in tents."

Of course, the open sides of the tent allowed outside noise to enter. A performer, and heaven help him if he possessed sensitive feelings, must compete with children playing at the rear of the grounds, with honking autos or whistling trains. This is why author Opie Read, asked one day by a stranger for directions to the Chautauqua tent, replied with the counter question, "You have two railroads in this town, mister?" And when the answer was "Yes," Read said, "Well, then, mister, wherever those railroads cross you'll find the Chautauqua."

Redpath-Chicago had bought nine of the new brown tents for its 1912 trek at a cost of $3500 each. Eight would have sufficed, if everything had moved smoothly, but life rarely moved smoothly. Seven were in use at one time, the eighth was rolling to a new location. The ninth was insurance in case floods washed out the railway tracks, as they did on the Gulf circuit in Louisiana in June, 1927; or in case a cyclone ripped a tent in two, as it did in South Dakota in 1922 with the Tull Players in the middle of *A Pair of Sixes*—they were all in costume except one actor who was caught (while changing) in garters and undershorts; or in case the stage caught fire, as once happened when Julia Claussen was singing the aria from *Samson and Delilah*. At such times that ninth tent paid off handsomely.

They were in reality square tents, with a forty-foot center section inserted to give length, so that each one had two center-poles thirty feet tall, eight quarter-poles, and many shorter ones supporting the sides. In our Tennessee opening and for a few years after that our center-poles were of wood, which meant constant trouble in getting them on and off railroad cars and in finding trucks big enough to haul them to the grounds. The metal poles we eventually used could be telescoped and presented no transportation problems, though they, too, were not immune to catastrophe.

In Bowling Green, Kentucky, one July afternoon in the later years, Pianist Magdalen Massman, then accompanying the Cathedral Choir, was on the third page of the first song, when, crack! came the warning of the storm. Musicians and audience fled into torrents of rain as the huge center-pole bent like a hairpin. The Choir gave its night program in the auditorium of Bowling Green's State Teacher's College, not too unhappy even if the scenery and clothes were ruined, for of course the acoustics to a musician's way of thinking were much better inside a building.

Our tents, all tents, seemed to have one idiosyncracy. They were so built that when it rained hard, water would gather in a great pocket, not at the sides or rear, but always, perversely, just in front of the stage. Crew boys would have to take a long pole with a cross board and push against the pocket. One other July day, again in Kentucky, this time in the town of Owensboro, the board came loose and the boy jammed his pole straight through the canvas. Barrels of water swept down across the stage, soaking an angry magician and his apparatus.

The crew boys were still green the night the first show finished in Pulaski. But they had guy ropes free before the last note of the *Star Spangled Banner* faded and they worked all night, stacking seats, dropping the tent, hauling the gear to the railroad, loading it aboard the first train. Our equipment that year filled half a baggage car, "Chautauqua pullman" the boys called it, and one of their jobs was to see that it was never sandwiched somewhere in the middle of a milk train. Because of the seven-day program and the nine tents, each crew and tent leapfrogged over eight towns and arrived in the new location with at least twenty-four hours to spare. Thus the crew which had worked seven days in Pulaski passed around the next eight towns and unloaded in Danville, Kentucky.

It was a successful season for everyone. In addition to Redpath-Chicago's thirty-nine towns, Redpath-Vawter played seventy-four and Horner from Kansas City one hundred and forty, making more than two hundred and fifty programs under Redpath management, one third of all the Chautauqua assemblies in the United States that summer. For our own part, we ended with a little money in the bank; not a great deal, but enough to pay off bills, repair the tents, print more advertising for the next year and go into the winter Lyceum business with something besides our hands in our pockets. Also, we had learned from experience, just as Vawter had learned in 1904, what things we had best leave undone and what others, heretofore undreamed of, we must do. We learned how to cut close financial corners, but chiefly that year we learned how to handle tents and crowds.

Redpath-Chicago's "lost" tent at Pulaski was the first of hundreds of the big canvas shelters which were to become a trademark of the circuits. From the day of Bishop Vincent on down, the words "tenting" or "going to Chautauqua" had been almost synonymous. Supplying a family with a tent for the week became a lively, money-making business for people in many communities, and up until the First World War advertisements for tents appeared in the newspapers near the announcement of the program. An eight-by-ten canvas could be rented for $2.25 for the week. A big fancy one, fourteen by twenty-four with six-foot walls, cost nine dollars; in Pawnee City, Oklahoma, I once happened to read an ad: "Tents with floors one dollar extra."

Eventually all bureaus from coast to coast adopted our color. For several reasons brown was advantageous. It did not grow dingy as white canvas would, or show the marks of travel and muddy fields. It made the tent seem cooler on a sunny day whether it actually was or not. Moreover, it put Chautauqua in a class by itself. That was no circus or medicine show looming up there in the middle of a field. The brown tent after 1912 meant Chautauqua and nothing but.

Music in the Air

11

It took all kinds of music to build a Chautauqua program and all kinds of musicians to provide it. There were brass bands and soprano soloists, sober-faced choirs and male quartets. They sang everything from Richard Wagner to Carrie Jacobs Bond, played everything from the harp to the xylophone.

The musicians were men and women, young and old, but especially women, lighthearted, pretty girls having fun and frolic on the road. There were orchestras, duos, sextets, Swiss yodelers in genuine *leder hosen* and Alpine caps, with whom Bryan cheerfully shared the platform. There was the drum and bugle corps that future President Harding did not find too noisy.

But always, and particularly, there were the bands.

Every self-respecting town in the year the Chicago circuit took to the road had its bandstand. It graced the park down by the river or the shady court-house yard, where grown men played their hearts out every Saturday night and used what leisure they had during the week for rehearsal. And small boys hung around as eagerly for the "practice" as for the Saturday concert and whistled the tunes all week. Man or woman, girl or boy, if you loved to sing and church rules didn't allow you to dance, why wouldn't Chautauqua, that too-short week in summer, be a "glorious thrill," a "musical experience"?

Most of the music that exciting week was "popular," though many brilliant artists travelled the circuits and offered the lighter works of great composers. From Maine to Texas, Dvořák's *Humoresque,* Mendelssohn's *Spring Song,* Franz von Suppé's *Poet and Peasant Overture,* Wagner's *Pilgrims' Chorus* were perennial favorites. Audiences flocked to hear Victor Herbert, Gilbert and Sullivan and Johann Strauss. They knew what they wanted. Big-city critics charged that directors offered only the frothiest fare to people famished for Beethoven. Examinations of old programs now and polls of opinion at the time disprove this.

In one such poll, a summer when going-to-Chautauqua was at its peak, Speaker Allen Albert and the musical group that pre-luded his lecture kept a diary of special requests, country-wide, from April to September. The top favorites, a formidable nineteen when the season ended, had no jazz at all and only four "popular" songs, if one puts *A Perfect Day, Love's Old Sweet Song, Aloha Oe* and *I Hear You Calling Me* into the "popular" category. The other choices ranged from Beethoven's *Minuet in G,* Rubinstein's *Melody in F,* to *Cujus Animan* from the *Stabat Mater* of Rossini. A majority of plain, ordinary Americans asked for, and got, *The Largo* from Handel's *Xerxes, Meditation* from *Thais, Thy Sweet Voice* aria from *Samson and Delilah, One Fine Day* from *Butterfly* and half a dozen other classical treasures.

There had to be balance, however. In nooks and corners of every program, *Bonnie Sweet Bessie* or *The Heart Bowed Down* had to have a place among grand opera arias. So there were bound to be extremes, not only within programs, but between types of programs, and it was in this connection that critics of Chautauqua used to say unkind words.

This was unrealistic. In contrast to grand opera, Chautauqua had no high-minded patrons in diamond chokers ready to make up annual deficits. It must pay its own way. Had every number on every program appealed only to the discriminating persons who asked for *Cujus Animan,* or only to those who wanted to hear the beautiful young ladies who sang *Oh, Promise Me* at the town's most important weddings—then in no time at all Chautauqua would have played to empty seats. Directors had to give variety, and to find an analogy, one need only consider radio and television today. No sweeping generalities about radio music could be anything but ridiculous. The broadcasters must widen the appeal of their medium and thus they offer good symphonies and operas and also a great deal of discordant frightfulness, knowing that both types of program will be appreciated by their particular devotees. Chautauqua, likewise, had to span a wide range of tastes, enlightenment and experience.

The gusto that certain performers gave to what otherwise would have been only routine programs offended serious musicians, even some managers, and of course left the local music teacher in confusion. More than one good teacher, the week after the Chautauqua tents left town, had to admit ruefully to her young pupils that she neither could juggle while playing *Dixie* on the piano nor render *Old Black Joe* on a trombone while standing on her head. Nor could she play a difficult sonata dexterously with one hand, and the left hand at that. Nor as another well-known pianist did, ask a delighted, uninhibited summer crowd to name its seven or eight favorite compositions, and then quickly and skillfully weave them into a medley. Such accomplishments never failed to titillate listeners of all ages.

For a critical manager to drop in unexpectedly to inspect a program often caused unhappiness among self-conscious talent. If they discovered the threatened visit in time, they would punish themselves with a special rehearsal. Managers did drop in, however, and on one of these occasions I chanced to hear a charming young woman named Mae Saltmarsh actually accomplish the impossible by playing the piano and the trombone at the same time. She enchanted a large audience. It was not Carnegie Hall but the customers had a good time; just as they did listening to Kate Mortimer, the "whistling artist."

The bands, tooting their melodious way up and down the circuits, always started a parade in their wake. No system ever lost money on a good band. Vawter once named Thaviu's International Band as his greatest musical drawing card over the years, a company of thirty, including a sextet of grand opera singers offering Verdi's *Il Trovatore.* Among bands on the Chicago circuit, Kryl's and Creatore's by all odds were the headliners, though trombone specialist Jaroslav Cimera easily held his own the seasons that he travelled.

March King John Philip Sousa, who, as conductor of the Marine Band in his early years, earned the title of "Bandmaster to Five Presidents," discovered Bohumir Kryl. Sousa's own great military band played occasional concerts at the "permanent" assemblies. The Redpath organization, however, never was able to tie him to a contract and he never took his aggregation on a circuit of touring tents.

But all Chautauqua bands played Sousa marches, as did all city bands, all village bands, and in lively big-top tempo, all circus bands. In our tents, Sousa's *Stars and Stripes Forever, Hands Across the Sea, Semper Fidelis* and *Washington Post* marches were staple fare.

Sousa's philosophy of music influenced not only other bandmasters but the discerning directors who made up Chautauqua programs. The popular song, Sousa believed, came with the dawn of history. He contended that among the first ever written was that which Moses and the Children of Israel sang, rejoicing over the destruction of Pharaoh's army. Also, Sousa believed that David the Psalmist was the first bandmaster, that he organized the first orchestra and that his troupe "numbered two hundred, four score and eight." Therefore, if Moses and his people, celebrating, sang, "The horse and his rider hath He thrown into the sea, the Lord is a man of war," Uncle Sam and his people, under similar emotions after military victories, shouted *There'll Be a Hot Time in the Old Town Tonight* or *Kelly and Burke and Shea,* Joseph I. C. Clarke's Spanish-American War song for which Sousa wrote the music.

Bohumir Kryl was working as a sculptor when Sousa chanced to hear him play *Inflammatus,* from Rossini's *Stabat Mater* on the cornet. He recruited him at once for his band. The sculptor-musician, who also had been a wrestler of some prowess, was graduated from Sousa's aggregation with the March King's best wishes and started a band of his own.

Kryl was a short, chunky, volatile genius with a wild mass of blond hair that made his big black hat seem to ride two inches above his head. He was an artist and, like many other such gifted individuals, was not the easiest of men with whom to get along on all occasions. He was extremely popular with Chautauqua crowds, but less so with the travelling talent who rubbed elbows with him all summer on the road.

Members of his band complained to superintendents and circuit managers that he took advantage of their unworldliness. No musician in any category was well paid and the story went that a first-chair player in Kryl's band, with a little more money in his pocket than the others, on arriving in some one-horse town would rent a big room for himself, so his impoverished mates could sleep on the floor.

Be that as it may, audiences gathering in the evening to hear Kryl's rendering of the *Anvil Chorus* from Verdi's *Il Trovatore* never forgot it. For this spectacular number Kryl carried four anvils with four husky tympanists in leather aprons who banged out the rhythms. As the hammers clanged down on the anvils, an electric device sent sparks cascading around the darkened stage.

Kryl made big money, and lost it, but in the end is said to have played the stock market so shrewdly that he amassed a considerable fortune. His daughters toured the Chautauqua circuits later, before going on the concert stage, Marie at the piano, Josephine on the violin.

It was a program by temperamental Bandmaster Kryl that wicked little boys once disrupted in Henderson, Kentucky. Rounding up all available dogs, they set them free outside the canvas fence, just as a cornet virtuoso began his triple-tongued solo. The dogs, having ears sensitive to horns, especially the upper register, naturally broke into wails and the audience, for one price, got not only a fine evening of music but also a dramatic demonstration of artistic frenzy.

Crew boys considered sad-faced Giusseppe Creatore with his handle-bar mustaches as much of a martinet as Kryl. They could not translate the angry foreign words that he yelled at his men when some poor fellow let slip a sour note, but from the scared looks on the Italian faces they could imagine.

In those years most bandleaders and their players were foreigners or first generation Americans—Bohemians and Italians chiefly, and how they went in for curled mustaches! And how folk from the farms with picnic lunch boxes admired the burnished buttons and gold braid, even the "foreign" look. It was to offset this appeal that a rival operator, having no "foreigners" to offer, one year advertised an "AMERICAN band with ALL-AMERICAN players." Redpath had an answer. It sent out The Old Colonials to depict *The Spirit of '76* in powdered white wigs and elaborate satin costumes under an Italian conductor. If Senor Carmeling had first tooted his trumpet in a Roman regiment, all to the good. His baton swung just that much livelier directing *The Heroes of Valley Forge*. Redpath actually used several "all-Americans." Harold Bachmann and his Million Dollar Band was "all-American," so also was Sand's Regimental. They packed the tents with single admissions.

Among other Italian conductors were Ferrule who even more than most led with waving arms and leaping body, and young Joseph Quintano in his white uniform with red buttons. The Victor Brothers' International Music Bureau furnished most of the Italian bands. Signor Calefaty Victor was its president, the snappy Royal Italian Guards its number-one and highest-priced attraction. It was the son of the Royal Guards conductor, on the seven-day circuit out of Chicago, who complained bitterly all one summer about American musical taste. His chief scorn was aimed at *By the Light of the Silvery Moon,* popular that season. Most bandleaders, it seemed, had been child prodigies. Quintano, for example, was playing cornet solos in Italy before he was twelve.

Sam Schildkret, director of the Hungarian Orchestra, had a theory that the people who needed music most were the ones who could never afford to pay for it, and whenever he had enough money in his own pocket, he rented an opera house and gave a free concert.

Every small town with a yearning to be a city had its "opera house." Sometimes it was a dowdy auditorium with a stage at one end, or it might be the second floor above the hardware store, or, more probably, it was part of the Masonic Temple. It was in the opera house that *Uncle Tom's Cabin* played or Lew Dockstader's *Minstrels.* An occasional Shakespearian troupe or a rag-tag company of *Midnight in Chinatown* made one-night stands at opera houses at a price range from ten to thirty cents, with rich folks filling the stage boxes at half a dollar each. In later years vaudeville took over most of these shabby temples and fastidious actors often complained that their dressing rooms still smelled of the bloodhounds that had chased Eliza across the stage in a long-gone "Tom show."

Sam Schildkret played to standing room only any night he rented a hall. A genius with the flute, he had been entertaining Americans since the Chicago World's Fair in 1893. He was another example of the versatile type of trouper. If the engineer of a fast train didn't plan to stop for the handful of show folk determined to make their next date, Schildkret stopped it. At a station in Indiana one night he built a fire on the tracks.

Boarding a train scheduled for "no-stop" always called for ingenuity. Fat Ralph Bingham once wired a division superintendent to stop the train "for a large party." He was the large party. Another group, stranded in Bristol, South Dakota, lighted a station lantern and set it in the middle of the track to flag down a fast night express; in the party was William Jen-

nings Bryan, and but for him the profane conductor who piled off while the crowd piled on would have allowed none of them to stay aboard.

Bands pulled the crowds into the tents, but Chautauqua was born to the accompaniment of a male quartet. These vocal ensembles went out by the dozens, from the days of the famous *Temples of Boston*—a group that came into being for the dedication of Boston's Masonic Temple and whose reader, Miss Fay Davis, dashed off the platform once in the college town of Wooster, Ohio, when a mouse appeared.

There were the Whitney Brothers; the Mendelssohns; the Dunbar Quartet and Bells; the handsome young Panama Singers, high-stepping along in white sailor suits with a tune called *Who Dug That Ditch? Uncle Sam!* The Chicago Glee Club disbanded in 1915 after sixteen years and 3901 engagements. The Music Makers introduced the African marimbaphone, a wind instrument that became as fancy a drawing card as the Russian balalaika.

But the aggregation most fondly remembered is probably the Weatherwax Brothers. This lively group roamed from the Atlantic seaboard to the Rockies from 1901 until the last tent came down—without missing a single curtain and with more dates for time on the road than any other attraction Redpath ever booked.

The four brothers, farm boys from Charles City, Iowa, came from a singing family. "The singin'est family you ever saw, us five brothers and Pa an' Ma, we'd sing for socials an' bazaars, July 4ths an' G.A.R.'s; in fact we'd go to anything an' nose in an' start to sing." The McKinley campaign was one of the first events they "nosed" into. In 1909, deciding they had wasted their sweetness too long on the desert air, four of them took to the rural road, and for small change sold their musical wares, plus personality, across Iowa and Minnesota. Then Keith Vawter happened to hear them, and their longtime ticket was written for Redpath.

In November, 1911, Vawter commented in a letter, "A good quartet, to keep in the limelight, must be a cracking good vaudeville show for an hour and a half." The Weatherwax Brothers, subscribing to the idea, early supplied themselves with silver trumpets, two B-flats and two E's, and with a fast-paced program of harmony and heart-throbs, melody and monkeyshines, they achieved the limelight and stayed there. Asa, the oldest, now dead, and William of Clarence, Iowa, sang first and second tenor; Lester, now of Wichita, Kansas, baritone; Tom, at present of Des Moines, Iowa, bass. The four brothers, departing from Chautauqua's customary white pants, wore light gray suits, all alike, to "pre-lude" a performance, but in the evening when they carried the whole show on their four pairs of broad shoulders, they dressed in what William still calls "claw-hammer coats."

Lester delivered the serious reading. Best audience reaction always went to *Man in the Shadow* by Richard Washburn Child, author and post-World

War I American ambassador to Italy. Novelties were left to William. If a new "original" was needed for the afternoon concert, Brother Bill simply dug up his pencil and sense of humor, down in Athens, Georgia or Zanesville, Ohio, or wherever the tent happened to be, and wrote it. His most famous number became his *Essay on Grass*. In it he started out glibly:

> "Oh, the gentle grass is growing
> "In the vale and on the hill:
> "We cannot hear it growing
> "Still it's growing very still. . . ."

and then he would stutter and forget.

A horrified brother would rush from the wings to prompt him: ". . . and in the spring it springs to life. . . ." More stumbling, more prompting, in whispers at first, but as the actor's pretended confusion grew, so did the prompting voice, until in the end it was sheer madness. The Marx Brothers didn't invent zany antics.

James Whitcomb Riley was the midwest's hero at the moment and night after night Bill recited *Little Orphant Annie* and *The Raggety Man*. The song repertoire covered a wide range, from Poe's *Annabelle Lee* to Gibney's *Song of the Vikings*. Rousingly, the four "warriors from the north land cold" boomed Gibney's lines:

> "The wind is blowing from off the shore
> "And our sail has felt its force,
> "For our bark bounds forth o'er the crested wave
> "As a wild and restive horse. . . ."

Gradually, however, as the years went on, the Weatherwax theme song became Dr. William Pitts' *The Little Brown Church in the Vale*.

It was Lester's task to introduce this number, with a brief speech explaining that a little brown Congregational church, "painted brown because brown paint was cheapest," actually did exist at Old Bradford, near Nashua, Iowa. The song caught. Before long, when the quartet bore down lustily in its:

> "Come, Come, Come, Come,
> "Come to the Church in the wildwood . . ."

the audience either cheered or joined in. In June, 1955, when the congregation of the Little Brown Church celebrated its one hundredth birthday, the surviving Weatherwax brothers of the quartet that had made it famous, sang again on the program, and at its end shook hands again with everybody in the audience, the way they always had done in Chautauqua.

Another quartet on the road as early as the Weatherwaxes were the good-natured, fastidiously dressed Whitneys—Alvin, William, Yale and Edwin, sons of Methodist temperance lecturer, E. J. Whitney. All four were of a positive nature. Naturally they sometimes argued a bit over how a song should be sung. One brother would think a phrase should be boomed out, another not. Words sometimes got bitter, till finally Alvin would shout, "We agree!" and the argument was over. After a few years "We agree!" became a catch phrase for other talent.

Their songs ranged from folk to classical, from *Rio Grande Rag* to *Danny Deever* and "I'm Captain Jinks of the Horse Marines, I give my horse good corn and beans." Eugene Field had died before the Whitneys achieved their top fame but his sentimental poems were still bittersweet gems to many American parents and the Whitneys' most popular encore was their barbershop rendering of Field's *Little Red Drum:* "I'm a beautiful red, red drum and I play with the soldierboys . . . there's Tom and Jim and Phil and Dick and Nat and Fred . . ."

This arrangement and one of Edwin Whitney's recitations, *The Darky and the Boys,* became wide-selling Victor records. Like Ralph Bingham's vernacular pieces, *The Darky and the Boys* typifies the mild humor that a large cross-section of the public listened to with relish in the 1910's. Graveyards, it seems, held a particular appeal. Whitney's story concerned a pair of boys gathering walnuts. After the two had stuffed pockets and blouses with nuts and even tied their trouser legs at the ankles and filled them, too, they started home. The first shade tree they came to, where they could sit down and divide the nuts, was inside a high wall around a graveyard. Climbing over the wall, one boy dropped two walnuts and left them outside on the ground; he would pick them up later.

Out of sight under the shade tree, they dumped all the nuts into a pile and started to share them equally, the first boy saying, "I'll take *this* one," his friend echoing, "I'll take *this* one."

An old colored man, happening along the road, heard the voices inside the graveyard . . . "I'll take *this* one . . ." "I'll take *this* one . . ."

"Oh, God," he cried, "this ain't no place for this here ol' man," and down the road he pelted as fast as he could run . . . "Pitty-pat, pitty-pat, pitty-pat . . ." till he met a white friend to whom he cried: "Massa, Massa, I just come past de graveyard and I hear de Lawd and de Debil in dar dividin' up the folks . . ."

"You're crazy," said the white man.

"I hear 'em, swear to God I do . . . Come, you'll hear it . . ."

Back the pair went and, sure enough, the voices still were going on . . . "I'll take *this* one . . ." "I'll take *this* one . . ."

"Does you hear, Massa?"

"Yes, I hear . . ."

"I'll take *this* one . . ." "I'll take *this* one . . ." "Well, that's all," one boy said, "except the two outside the fence . . ."

"And they tell me," Whitney continued, "that the white man beat the Negro running."

Dapper Edwin Whitney stayed on the road as a reader after his brothers ended their singing careers. As late as the 20's he was filling both summer and winter engagements.

From the day at Chautauqua Lake when the Fisk Jubilee Singers entertained President Garfield, down into the early 1920's when the public finally tired of plantation songs, singers from Dixie Land, "sometimes up, sometimes down," were easy, popular acts to sell. As interest finally waned, directors tried to keep the idea alive by expanding a program from a group of simple songs of the south into a pretentious epic. In one of these attempts the talented Dixie Chorus of eight men carried a thousand-dollars' worth of costumes and settings that ranged from an African jungle to a southern cotton field.

Male choruses in general became as popular as quartets and a Chicago producer named Ralph Dunbar, one of the brothers in the first Dunbar Quartet, was a genius at building and training these fairly complex organizations. The pretentious Dixie Chorus was his, and he sent out dozens of others, for it was a poor circuit indeed that did not boast at least one Dunbar company each season for some twenty years. These teams travelled under many names—the Dunbar Singing Orchestra, made up of six girls, and the Royal Dragoons, the Troubadours, the Imperial Grenadiers, the Russian Cathedral Choir, and of course, Dunbar's Original White Hussars. The Hussars were a hit wherever they appeared, so popular, in fact, that the adaptable Ralph Dunbar found it necessary on occasion to send out several "original" Hussar troupes, of course into widely separated parts of the nation.

The size of a Hussar, Dragoon or Grenadier chorus ranged from nine to twenty-five men, depending on the importance and financial condition of the circuit that booked them. They not only sang remarkably well, but Ralph Dunbar had instilled in them the fundamentals of smart show business. The evening program usually started with the singers in formal dress. Originally they had worn Russian costumes, but the audiences could take just so much Russian and no more, even in those days. So following an intermission, in which the soloists entertained, the troupe would reappear as a vested choir. After three or four solemn numbers in this costume it again was time for a change.

Then came the flashing white uniforms, white boots, white busbies with glorious pompoms. With military precision the smartly turned-out Hussars went through an intricate close-order drill with gymnastic overtones. Nearly all of the young troubadours played a brass or wind instrument and they made the canvas shake with *Smiles* and *The Rocky Road to Dublin,* in rich close harmony; or, for the more discerning in the tent, the *Soldiers' Chorus* from *Faust,* the *Pilgrims' Chorus* from *Tannhauser.* They often opened with *El Capitan*—in the south, with *Are You From Dixie*—to create a happy riot at the start. And always somewhere in the program

Civil War veterans wiped their eyes as the group swung into *The Boys of the Old Brigade,* with its rousing, accented chorus:

> *"Where* are the *boys* of the *Old Brigade*
> "Who *fought* with us *side* by *side?*
> *"Shoulder* to *shoulder* and *blade* to *blade,*
> "They *fought* till they *fell* and *died . . ."*

"And died," a booming bass voice would repeat.

Of course the final number was the national anthem, American not Russian, for most of the Hussars were midwest college boys earning their next year's tuition and keep.

El Capitan, the tuneful musical show which DeWolf Hopper took to the road in the 1890's, vied with Gilbert and Sullivan operas in the popularity of its revivals. When Admiral Dewey's squadron sailed up Mirs Bay to attack Manila in the Spanish-American War, the band on the Flagship *Olympia* played *El Capitan.* On the day of the Admiral's triumphant parade in New York City, the march that Sousa's band thundered as it passed the reviewing stand again was *El Capitan.*

Sousa had written the music and some of the lyrics for the libretto by Charles Klein. All through the Chautauqua years, choruses and bands delighted audiences not only with the name song, but with other lyrics from the book, such as *Sweetheart I'm Waiting* and *The Typical Tune of Zanzibar.*

One year the White Hussars became Black Hussars and once Dunbar shifted to White Hussar Girls, but they never were as popular as the stalwart young men. Dunbar in his youth had been in vaudeville. Later he chose as his musical director Al Sweet, a former bandmaster of the Ringling Brothers Circus, a stern drillmaster who, like Creatore and Kryl, put the fear of God into his men. Talent, crew and the shocked people of Richmond, Indiana, never forgot the way Showman Sweet publicly "cut down to size" the careless young man, a little on the fat side, who appeared on the platform one afternoon with disreputable brown shoes beneath his white flannel trousers and blue coat. White flannels might shrink in the local laundry till they burst their seams and tight shoes blister the feet, but a boy wore what was fundamentally correct if he worked for Sweet.

Chautauqua's mixed quartet swelled into companies of every contrasting type and size. A topnotch example was the Oratorio Artists to whose ranks at various times Elsie Baker, contralto, and Soprano Florence Hinkle both gave prestige. For years, Redpath-Chicago sent out impersonator Walter Eccles and his College Singing Girls, eight proper and personable young ladies in street skirts just an inch off the floor, and, in their shorter dresses, discreetly well-gaitered. Eccles' monologues, we emphasized, "always include one good story or poem that helps and uplifts."

There were many, many others. The sedate Cathedral Choir of four men and four women offered religious music for half of their concert. The Beulah Buck Quartet introduced Marjorie Paddock as a soprano. Mrs. Buck, who had been a country schoolteacher before she took to elocution, doubled as reader and soloist, a practice which kept costs down for the home office.

For years, too, there were the six laughing Killarney Girls, bewitching all the young men in the audience with Irish folk songs—crew boys, on most circuits, were asked not to "date" local girls, but no edicts could be laid down forbidding the dashing young blades of a community to wait after the performance for the prettiest girl entertainers.

It was the Killarneys' clever reader, Rita Rich, who popularized the old ditty:

> "Sing, Kate, sing!
> "You're thirty-five in the Spring.
> "Don't let him go
> "Till he buys you a ring.
> "Sing, Kate, sing!"

Hard-working Ada Roach served an apprenticeship with the Killarneys before she took out her own company. In her most popular program she featured Charles F. Horner's play-opera, *The Heart of the Immigrant,* taking the part of the Irish girl. She closed her show rousingly with *I'm a Citizen of the U.S.A.* and in between sang *Smiles* as often as a *Smiles*-crazy audience demanded. It was the girls of the Ada Roach Company in 1915, when their Ford bogged down in the mud near Bloomfield, Nebraska, who tramped six long miles carrying their own suitcases to make their curtain.

Williamstown, West Virginia, remembered for many years the Fourth of July in 1915 when the young ladies of one company went for a "quiet walk" and a bootlegger whom the sheriff was chasing sought safety close at their heels. Unaware of him, the young ladies walked on, until the posse started shooting. Then they found that they could run, too. Another story, concerning another sheriff and another troupe, went across the routes that same year. It was in Oklahoma and the Harold Tregillus Concert Company was putting on its musical act when hilarious cowboys began to shoot up the town. A deputy rushed into the tent for the sheriff, who was whooping it up with delight in the front row. "Get up and leave now?" he answered the deputy. "I should say not. Let 'em wait till the show's over."

Managers found the Smith-Spring-Holmes Orchestral Quintet easy to sell, possibly because the name of its reader-soprano was Coyla May Spring and that of her cello-playing sister Lotus Flower. Townsfolk reading such delectable names in the prospectus felt impelled to see their owners. Neither the girls' looks nor Lotus Flower's smile was disappointing. Nor their music.

Looks never mattered with the male singers. A boy in the Lyric Glee Club, going into his hotel one night, heard one woman ask another how she had liked the concert. The answer was, "They're a homely bunch, but oh, Lord, how they can sing!"

Romance blossomed in the Smith-Spring-Holmes company. Lotus Flower Spring married Guy Holmes, flute soloist; Coyla May Spring, Composer Clay Smith—but neither girl would give up the name Spring. Smith, who did his first trouping with Barnum and Bailey, used a trombone, we advertised, "of eighteen-karat gold."

The Kellogg-Haines Singing Party, a highly-trained group named originally for Soloist-teacher Stella Kellogg-Haines of St. Louis, advertised "vaudeville stunts avoided," and made a specialty of elaborate costumes to fit elaborate high-class acts. Costumes of some kind were almost a must for musicians of this period. Grandmothers, even some of the mothers, dreaming happily of other times, had brought native costumes with them from the old country, stored now tenderly in an attic trunk, and music of the homeland struck a deep note when rendered by singers arrayed in the dress of that beloved homeland. If the company were not actually "foreign," if it were just plain American, with no hint of far places, it still could be "colonial" or "early American" in its dress.

Redpath records show that by and large people never tired of foreign groups, though the songs themselves, preferably, were in English. Trailing the famous Hussars were the Imperial Russian Quartet, this one actually composed of Russians. There were the sprightly Alpine Singers and such specialized orchestras as the Ladies Spanish or the Yugoslav Tamburica. There was one choir of five African Kafir boys and another group called the Tyrolean Yodelers, with its startling switches from normal to falsetto register. Mrs. Potter Palmer had brought them to Chicago for the World's Fair and they kept their name until the mid-1920's. There were Scotch, Welsh, Gipsy, Hawaiian, Mexican, Filipino, Bohemian and Polish companies, the Mercedes Ladies Zither Quartet and many others as exotic, each emphasizing its own national folk dances and folk songs. The native land of the Musical Guardsmen never was made clear, but to judge from its resplendent uniforms it hailed from either Ruritania or Graustark.

Among these imported groups the jubilant Hawaiians with their steel guitars possibly were the worst trial a superintendent had to bear, perhaps because he tried to Americanize them too fast. At every stop, before leis, sashes, ukeleles or guitars emerged from the battered luggage, every Hawaiian searched the new town for a place to swim. They had been raised in water and they swam like eels, preferably without clothes. Their code of manners naturally was different from that of the troubled superintendent, and next to water, what they desired most was to sleep together under the platform of the Chautauqua tent. The management forbade it, not because it questioned the morality of this custom, but would the people of Sawbuck, Illinois, or Wheatfield, Kansas, understand such goings on? Occasionally, of course, the love of swimming had its values. En route to Watonga, Oklahoma, one rainy season, Lecturer E. L. Rogers and the Hawaiian Players came to a bridge several feet under water. The Hawaiians, holding their instruments and their clothes high on their heads, leaped in joyfully. History doesn't tell what happened to the marooned lecturer.

Of all companies of talented young women bouncing over muddy roads with baggage, instruments, property trunk and a lecturer or two, all usually crowded into two Ford touring cars, none had more fun or gave more concentrated pleasure than the six Military Girls. This was a Redpath-Horner musical company in which the sparkling Miss Fay Pettit of Redpath-Chicago's 1912 Anitas became a member. With her in the Military Girls were her twin sisters, Gladys, soprano and pianist, and Ailene, violinist. The latter, like Miss Fay, was still in her teens when she joined the first company, and with her twin became a happy example of that rampant Chautauqua custom, romance on the road. Both girls married Chautauqua superintendents. Not until after the tents folded did I know that among all the talent the summer trek was brightly called "the mating season."

Another one-time member of the Military group was Soprano Laura Townsley, a character singer who became a protégé of Mme. Schumann-Heink and, still later, the "Mary McCoy" of radio; in the 1930's she went on the road again as "Mitzi" in *Blossom Time*. In this as in all companies, personnel shifted from year to year. Girls got married or competitors hired them; young men, having tasted sweet applause, became bold and took out their own troupes.

The Military Girls played flutes, cornets, violins, piano and trap drums. In their first publicity picture their drums innocently faced the wrong way, because at the time none of the young women had yet learned how to play a drum. Such was youth and derring-do. Managers soon used these girls exclusively as "openers." They were Chautauqua personalities, collecting adventures wherever they went. Any conveyance would satisfy, even entertain them, horse and buggy or freight, or if rains had weakened a bridge, a hand car. One August day, crossing sun-baked Kansas, they joyfully peeled onions and potatoes in the caboose of the freight train and cooked a stew for the crew.

Invariably the Military Girls made their dates. If the 4:00 A.M. train whistle awakened them when the boardinghouse alarm clock failed, well, five minutes had to be enough; astonished brakemen helped them aboard the train in kimonos over their night clothes. Their costumes on the stage were of hot khaki with long, lined sleeves, their military caps were heavy and tight, boots and collars high, but if asked, they denied that they were hot. "Oh no, not at all, just comfortable"—even the afternoon when one of them dropped her drum and fainted on a stifling Texas platform.

The Pettits objected to nothing, except a possible breach of propriety. One sister, arriving for spring rehearsal with Redpath-Horner in Kansas City, discovered that the skirts of the new tailored uniforms were fifteen inches off the floor. To be sure, there were respectable thick woolen bloomers underneath the skirts and these bloomers were tucked into high leather puttees, but the sister protested to Manager Horner, "No decent girl would appear on the stage in so disgracefully short a skirt." She capitulated after Miss Fay modeled the uniform.

As a further distinction, this company was the first on the road to solve the perplexing problem of how girls could manage to get their hair washed. In those years nice women never patronized men's barber shops. The Military Girls made a deal: would the barber let them come in after he closed? He would.

A successful troupe had to be ingenious. The Dollie McDonnels, playing Findley, South Dakota, at about this same time, found as opening hour approached that their trunks had not arrived. They gave their concert in clothes loaned by their hotel landlady and next morning thanked the fate that had kept their trunks safe elsewhere, for the hotel burned down before their train left.

The Military Girls' acts, songs, and recitations all were advertised as purely "American." They featured such poems as Paul Laurence Dunbar's *Cushville Hop,* his *Cornstalk Fiddle,* and the Indian legend of the drowned girl who sprang back to glory and grace as a water lily. Their best remembered act, however, described in the programs as an "action song," was *Broomstick Cavalry,* in which with brooms for guns and Miss Fay as the Captain, they sang Carrie Jacob Bond's

> "Say, how would you like to be a soldier?
> "A soldier in a uniform of blue,
> "With a cap and cape so bright,
> "Buttons shined like stars at night,
> "And a pocket full of bullets,
>   Goodness me!"

Press notices of this act were universally good. Charm, vitality and grace had values.

Family teams, though successful in scattered instances, could be the bane of a director. A husband might be a true musician, his wife mediocre, or vice versa, but if a manager wanted one of them he must hire both. Also, regrettably, an "artist" who sounded wonderful at spring rehearsals occasionally turned out to be no genius in mid-summer heat, or could handle a few selections, but be unable to carry a whole program. When that happened we usually cancelled the contract and substituted another performer.

Child labor laws were still more talked about than existent in 1912 and since the Chautauqua season coincided with school vacations, it was not unusual for children to troupe with their parents and perform with them. It seemed to me, at times, that some families had no other home than the tent. The child who could play or sing need not necessarily play or sing well to win an audience; her tender years would do that for her.

Mr. and Mrs. George Lincoln McNemry of the Harmony Concert Company, for instance, presented their five-year-old daughter as a full-fledged member of their group. At New Haven, Michigan, one summer, seven bouquets went up to the platform for the child's skill—or daring—with tambourine, triangle and xylophone.

In the Townley Concert Company, son Gorham, aged twelve, did female impersonations for similar applause. In other groups ambitious boys, or perhaps just obedient ones, pounded at drums, and hair-ribboned small misses performed bit parts, if only with sleigh bells. There were dozens of companies made up altogether of children. Curly-haired Blatchford Kavanagh, in his black velvet suit with white lace collar and red bow tie, the "original" in Henry B. Roney's Boys, grew from childhood to manhood on the circuits. The Chicago Boy Choir originated in a Sunday School mission—four baby-faced youths in every kind of costume, from kilts to surplices, playing bagpipes or marimbaphone with equal facility.

Life for these children may have been exciting but it was not easy. The stranger who, late one night, asked a Chautauqua child sleepily waiting for her parents in a Chicago railway station, "Honey, what time do you go to bed?" undoubtedly got the true answer: "I go to bed when we get anywhere."

All of these versatile and gay performers, young or middle-aged, most of them serving as "pre-luders," lightened the customer's diet, but it was the Alice Nielsens and Tamaki Miuras, the Julia Claussens and Elsie Bakers and Florence Hinkles, who brought splendor and beauty into the tents and established Redpath's reputation for polished musical performances. Men and women sat silently for a long breathless moment after Irene Stolofsky finished Paganinni's *D Major Concerto* for the violin. Here was the stuff of dreams. Schooled or unschooled, farmer's wife or city clubwoman, who could fail to enjoy it? And how, before radio, would they ever have heard it if Chautauqua hadn't come their way?

On Main Street arrived such names as Augusta Lenska, Russian-born contralto; from the Chicago Operatic Company, Marjory Maxwell and Myrna Sharlow, baritone Arthur Middleton. Violinist Estelle Gray appeared many seasons with her Russian husband, Mischa Lhevinne. Miss Gray fitted into the nomad's life. She had given her first concert at the age of eight and from then on no emergency upset her. Even when she fell on the street and smashed her Cremona violin, she went on with a substitute fiddle until a wizard repaired the great instrument. She was on the road to provide music and not rain nor heat nor gloom of night kept her from it. Once in North Bend, Nebraska, on the Horner circuit, she played while rain leaked through the tent over her till the violin strings broke. It was while she was with Horner, too, that in the middle of Sherwin's *After the Lights Are Out,* the lights did go out. She played right on into the *Danse Macabre* of Saint-Saëns, with its portrayal of death and hobgoblins. Near the end of that composition, a cock crows, as a warning that the day approaches, and at this particular moment the lights came back on. Lights in the Chautauqua tents often seemed to be controlled by the devil. Once in Paris, Texas, they went out while Lawrence Lewis of the Chicago Artists was singing *Lead, Kindly Light*.

Marie Stoddard and Frederick Wheeler both got their start toward the concert stage with the Oratorio Artists. Louise Stallings, New York mezzo soprano, appeared with various groups, eventually with her own top-notch company. Metropolitan star, C. Pol Plancon, sang one season with the girls of the Aida Instrumental Quartette; smiling Baritone David Bispham recited Shakespeare to the music of Mendelssohn as beautifully in Tennessee as he had at Covent Garden.

Singer Charles Edward Clarke usually appeared with his Polish wife, Rachel Steinman, the violinist; their dog, Teddy, spent his time under the platform digging for bones. Clarke, a Canadian, almost invariably opened with a light air from the opera *Pagliacci,* then balanced his program with a musical reading of Longfellow's narrative poem about the once-proud King Robert of Sicily, "brother of Pope Urbane . . . in his foxtail coat . . . on a piebald steed. . . ." It supplied good music, good humor, good verse, a bit of "inspiration," and, as Clarke sensed, filled the old rule that people often like best the things with which they are most familiar. Most listeners in the tent, at some time or other, had sung, read or recited the lines in Longfellow's closing stanza:

> "The Angel smiled . . .
> "And through the open window, loud and clear
> "They heard the monks chant . . .
> " 'He has put down the mighty from their seat
> " 'And has exalted them of low degree!' "

It was a musical program, but some people, at least, went home thinking, "I, too, like King Robert of Sicily, shall strive to be a better man."

Our Bergen-Marx Company was made up of Baritone Alfred Hiles Bergen, Hans Dressel, a London cellist, and Leon Marx, who before he was twenty was playing first violin in Chicago's outstanding Theodore Thomas Orchestra. It was on Bergen, American-born composer of the pretentious Indian cycle, *Song of the Birch,* that the Redpath Lyceum bureau pioneered with a $120,000 insurance policy, the first ever taken by a booking agency on a voice. Until then only musicians' hands had been thought to deserve protection.

The really great men and women of both stage and concert hall, who came to spend frequent summers in Chautauqua, almost without exception were easier to get along with than the would-be greats and the almost-greats. They were secure, untroubled by petty jealousies, and most of those I knew were folk of simple tastes, with manners more than skin deep.

Among them was Mme. Ernestine Schumann-Heink, who shared her knowledge of "this business," as she called her world of music and entertainment, with any eager youngster at hand to listen.

When I was a young agent selling talent for Lyceum, Keith Vawter sent me one season on tour with Mme. Schumann-Heink and I discovered then, as I found later when she filled occasional Chautauqua engagements, that this big-hearted woman took her art seriously, but never herself. She could joke about herself and did frequently. Once in Chicago when she was appearing under Redpath direction, a small car was sent to her hotel to take her to the concert hall. The door of the car was narrow. She tried to get in, failed, tried again.

An attendant finally suggested: "Why doesn't Madame get in sidewise?"

Schumann-Heink, turning 'round, chuckled and demanded, "With Schumann-Heink, which way *is* sidewise?"

She was in her late, well-padded forties on that first tour, I in my early twenties, and in her hearty Teutonic accent she always called me "My boy." On the evening of her first concert at about 8:30, I went to her dressing room to report happily that the house was a sell-out. To my amazement I found her in a frightening condition.

"Oh, my boy!" she cried, rocking back and forth and holding her big arms around her ample middle. "I so sick! Schumann-Heink cannot go on. No, it is too bad! Schumann-Heink must disappoint all these people. Schumann-Heink very sick!"

To say that I was more distressed than she is to put it mildly. I thought of the thousand paid customers, waiting bright-eyed and eager to hear this tremendous voice. I thought of the local committee to whom I must break the devastating news. When I asked her just where and how she felt ill, she only motioned me away. And then came the knock at the door: "Time to go on!"

Mme. Schumann-Heink stood up immediately. She straightened her dress, touched her hair, gave me a ghost of a smile and sailed out in front of the footlights. Beaming over the ovation, she began to sing Mozart's *Sextus*. Poor woman, I thought, how she must be suffering! At the end of the concert I hurried toward her. How was she feeling now?

"*Ach, gut!*" She beamed at me. "Schumann-Heink feel fine. We go eat."

The next night in another town the same frightening incident occurred. Again she rocked and moaned. She would not be able to go on. Again she sang superbly and came off feeling fine. The third night again, as the moment of her appearance arrived, she was miraculously cured of whatever caused her anguish. This time I made bold to ask. How could anyone be so wretchedly ill up to the second of curtain time, then in a trice be completely cured?

"My boy," she said, patting my arm, "if you stay in this business, is one thing to remember. Every artist . . . *ja* . . . *every* artist feel sick before *every* performance. The one that does not feel sick, that one is no artist! Remember that."

I remembered, all the years I sent big tents up and down the land. The lecturer who did not meet each new audience with a hollow feeling in his stomach was not much of a lecturer. The actor or musician who saw the footlights turn on without a wave of uneasiness, sometimes amounting to nausea, was at best a second-rater. Art never takes anything for granted.

One of our towns on that first Schumann-Heink tour was Lima, Ohio, where relatives of mine lived, among them an elderly bedridden aunt who loved music.

"What street she live on?" the great lady asked.

I told her and she said nothing more, but after the concert the world's greatest contralto climbed into a taxi, located the house and in a bedroom, without accompaniment, sang *Auld Plaid Shawl* and *A Red, Red Rose.*

I recall another experience, also in Ohio on that same tour. A local impresario had brought Schumann-Heink to town. He had paid Keith Vawter his thousand dollars in advance, but at noon before the concert it began to rain and at curtain time the auditorium was only half-filled. The local manager, rapidly becoming frantic, counted his gate receipts and discovered that he was three hundred dollars in the hole. When I reported that fact to Schumann-Heink, she said, "My boy, tell this man Schumann-Heink, she do not want his money! She return whatever it is, the loss."

"But you can't do that," I protested.

"Ach, yes, my boy," she answered, "Schumann-Heink can. If you stay in this business, is one thing to learn. Never let them lose money on you. If Schumann-Heink go out now and sing like the angel, and that man, he lose money, then Schumann-Heink, she no good! Her voice, it is *kaput.* But if Schumann-Heink go out and sing off key and the management make money, then he tell everybody, 'Schumann-Heink, she sing like the angel.' Now, go tell the man."

Mme. Schumann-Heink never did a full season of concerts under canvas tents, but she did fill many special dates for the Redpath organization. I never knew a time when her simple, warm-hearted modest manner did not win her friends. At Springfield, Illinois, in 1914, the little eight-year-old girl who had just heard the great lady sing *Child's Prayer,* and who, as Schumann-Heink started for her car, was overheard singing it to her doll, got a hug from the great lady and the basket of roses that had just been sent up to the platform.

A few seasons after Redpath-Chicago began stringing its banners across Main Street, its management brought one pleasant old American custom into fine flower. It happened by accident. In Lansing, Michigan, a storm stopped the show. To keep people from getting too restless, a local clergyman jumped up and started them singing. It was such a success that the

Chicago office hired the man for the next season and from then on professional song leaders, known as "tune heisters" by disrespectful crew boys, became regulars in the organization.

The "tune heister" did not need to know a great deal about music, but plenty about mass psychology. Success also depended in large part on gymnastic ability, and it was advantageous to possess a fine set of teeth, for an appreciative smile, usually of the ear-to-ear variety, was a most effective tool. Summer audiences put their hearts into *I Want a Girl, Your Old Gray Bonnet, Juanita, Sweet Adeline, Down by the Old Mill Stream*. They made the tents quiver with *Love's Old Sweet Song* and *The Long, Long Trail*.

"Tune heisters" still are with us and occasionally, at some luncheon club, I see an old Redpath boy, balding and expanding in girth, leading his brothers in song. He was no artist, he never had been. But he gave the folks a good time. On any program, in any town, in any season, what more could one ask?

Ralph Bingham and John Bunny.

"Let's Face the Issue . . ."

12

It is a pleasant August evening in 1912. Charley Stover, clerk at the Hoosier Drug Store, leans forward in his third row seat to make sure that he hears all the well-dressed fellow on the platform has to say. Charley, just turned twenty-one, will cast his first vote come November and a voter must understand the issues. The *Muncie Star* said so just this morning.

The fellow on the platform this evening is talking about how senators should be nominated and elected by the people, rather than by politicians in the legislature. He isn't reading his speech. He doesn't even have any notes. But he certainly is full of his subject. What he says makes Postmaster Ep White so mad that Ep gets up and stomps out of the tent. But Charley Stover can't see why anybody should get mad at such a sensible idea. He'd like to have a hand in picking his own senator.

Programs on all Chautauqua circuits, Maine to California, reflected the excitement of political campaigns, but especially was this true of the rousing Presidential race of 1912. That was the Bull Moose year, when Teddy Roosevelt with his righteous anger at Wall Street, William Howard Taft coming out flat-footed for high tariffs, and Socialist Gene Debs, between jail terms, all lost to New Jersey's Governor, Woodrow Wilson. Both in the campaign itself, and in the fiercer nominating conventions that "preluded" it, speakers on all sides of all fences were Redpath headliners and many of them had been for years.

These men had not been introduced in Chautauqua as politicians. They had talked on "good government." But who could keep a fervent party man, billed for a nonpartisan speech, from emphasizing his side of the story? Or how many Charley Stovers would really want him to?

Some of the politicians who sought summer speaking dates did it simply

because they would be running for office again in another year. Some
were lame ducks, jobless and full of unuttered oratory, but many of them,
busy, tired men who took to the dirt, heat and noise of the road, piling
off the day coach at 7:27 P.M. for a 7:30 lecture, exhausting their voices
in big tents without microphone, did so because they were passionately interested in some particular piece of legislation.

So far as Charley Stover and many others were concerned, it was a one-
sided show; the fellow on the platform had his say and that was that. They
could go home and think over what he presented as immortal truth, but
rarely could they challenge him from the floor. The day of questions and
discussion periods had not arrived. The first Chautauqua forum was tried
out in the east in 1919; it never became a regular feature in the midwest.

When I first started out with my own circuit, the lecturers numbered
between fifty and sixty percent of our talent, in comparison with entertainers and musicians, a ratio reversed by the end of the decade. Some chron-
iclers of the story make the charge that too many of these lecturers
were "reactionary" or afraid of offending the "moneyed interests that signed
the guarantee." One objector, who tried unsuccessfully to get a job on my
circuit, claims baldly that "liberal speakers were not wanted." Apparently
he had not seen the cartoon in the Indianapolis *News* in the fall of 1908
labeled "A New Figure in the Political Arena." The "new figure" was a
husky Chautauqua gladiator holding a shield called "Facts" and a sword
of "Political Independence." Fleeing in terror were the "Standpatters,"
"Machine Politicians," "Yellow Dogs."

In denying the reactionary charge, one must immediately face the fact
that the words "liberal" and "reactionary" never have meant, and probably
never will mean, precisely the same thing on Manhattan Island as they do
in Manhattan, Kansas. Nor is the political climate the same in 1956 as
it was in 1904, or in 1912 or 1920. The proponent of lowered trade bar-
riers, for example, is not considered quite the dangerous fellow today that
large segments of the population once believed him to be. But at least
Charley Stover and his companions sitting in the Hoosier tent were not
afraid of listening to anyone's ideas. There was no shush-shush of public
issues those years in America, no undemocratic fear of speaking out. The
ten million people who crowded into the tents during Chautauqua's hey-day
wanted, and got, the pro and con of a problem.

In Congress and in many state legislatures, lecture managers had at their
disposal a steadier flow of real oratory than is available now, and undoubtedly the public listened more eagerly to it than it would today. For one
thing, the speaker did not have to compete with soap operas and no fifteen-
minute radio periods cramped his flow of words. There were gifted orators
by the dozens and Chautauqua grabbed them, and the orators grabbed
Chautauqua, to air all colors of opinion. They praised and condemned socialism, the protective tariff, Wall Street, rural cooperatives, votes for women,

the Yellow Menace, free verse. Political extremes reached from the bitterness of Jacob Riis in the days of my first expedition into South Dakota, down to the "normalcy" of Warren Gamaliel Harding.

Between these limits we offered every political and social hue. Even cigar-smoking Republican czar Uncle Joe Cannon had his day, beginning with the old independent assemblies. So did "Pitchfork Ben" Tillman of South Carolina, who earned his nom-de-barnyard by threatening, "I'll stick mah pitchfork into his fat ol' ribs," meaning the ribs of President Grover Cleveland.

People chuckled whenever they saw Tillman's name on a program because that generation never forgot the Tillman "cow" cartoon. It was drawn by Tom Fleming for Bryan's 1896 campaign, and used again in 1908 when Bryan ran on the anti-trust issue; but Tillman was responsible for the idea illustrated by the cartoon. In the drawing an elongated cow stood astraddle the Mississippi River, eating corn, with her front legs in St. Louis and her hind legs in New York, where a gentleman in a high hat, labelled "Wall Street," milked her. In other words, New York milked the cow while the west and south fed her.

Cannon, the hayseed personality from Illinois whose racy tongue worried every manager, kept at Chautauqua until one day in Kansas he collapsed on a platform—just a few weeks, as it happened, after another Redpath orator, quiet George W. Norris, of Nebraska, had stripped him of power as dictator of the House of Representatives. Norris, respected everywhere, lectured every summer, chiefly on the Horner circuit, while he fought "Cannonism."

Often in the same week's program in the same town, there were lecturers as dissimilar in both looks and ideas as silver-tongued Albert J. Beveridge of Indiana and Muckraker Lincoln Steffens, a shabbily dressed little man with heavy spectacles, rumpled hair and a small beard; or the blind Oklahoma liberal, Thomas P. Gore, on the heels of standpat Simeon D. Fess, of Ohio; or Democratic Boss Champ (for Beauchamp) Clark following Labor Leader Samuel Gompers, whose lecture, *Toilers Organized, What Are Their Aims,* was so long and heavy that sometimes even his best friends went to sleep in the middle of it; or hidebound Prohibitionists like J. Frank Hanly of Indiana at the other end of the pole from Progressive Robert Marion LaFollette of Wisconsin. These, and many others as diverse in viewpoint, all had had a fair hearing on some Chautauqua platform, or were still having it, when Redpath-Chicago tackled its first circuit in Tennessee.

My own experience with "Fighting Bob" LaFollette dated back to my booking-agent days when he was governor of Wisconsin. Later I managed his lectures for perhaps a dozen years. Short, handsome, with blue-gray eyes and six inches of hair sticking up on top of his head, he was a scholar-politician who believed every word he uttered, and couldn't be influenced

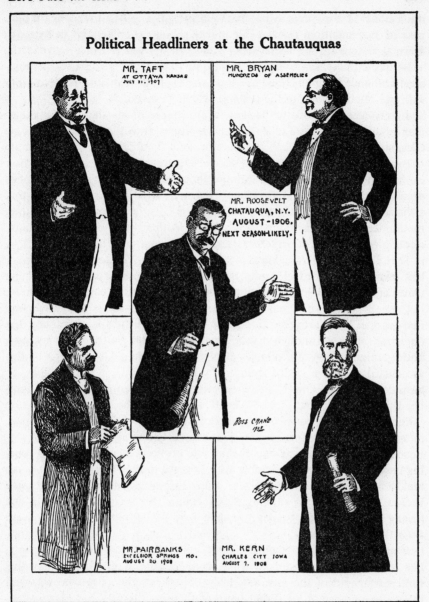

Political Headliners at the Chautauquas

with money, fame, security or social advantage. The first time I heard him, he did not mention politics. He talked about *Hamlet*. He delivered a learned lecture on the Melancholy Dane. In his superb voice he read the most quoted passages from that most quotable play, and then for his midwest audience he interpreted the lines, translating them into modern English and relating them to the times in which we lived.

Later, after LaFollette became a storm center in the United States Senate, his Chautauqua talks took a new turn. Into the crowded tents on August afternoons he carried the reformer's flaming zeal. No poetry, no dramatic climaxes lightened his political lectures. He just gave facts. After an hour he took off his coat. Another hour and off came his necktie. His target then was "Special Privilege," his theme the unfair advantage that politicians, dancing to the tune of Standard Oil, the railroads, Wall Street or the beef trust, were taking of the poor. With fighting eye, fighting chin, fighting voice he got down to brass tacks in the matter of high tariffs.

LaFollette had one weakness as a speaker. He talked too long. Aware of this, his wife supplied him one summer with a Swiss wrist watch with an alarm and occasionally even sent one of their two sons, Robert Jr. or Philip, out on the road with their father, to stand in the wings and wave him into silence. We discovered that if we billed LaFollette for afternoons, the audience, absorbed though it was, might get so tired that it failed to come back at night. If we put him on at night, people might stay home to rest the next day. So we settled it finally by presenting him, when possible, on Saturday evenings. One Redpath superintendent, when asked what "Fighting Bob" talked about, said, "About four hours. The first two hours the farmers wanted to rush to Washington and shoot Speaker Joe Cannon. After that they were for Cannon and wanted to shoot LaFollette."

Senator LaFollette was one of that able group of men and women touring under the Chautauqua banner who brought to the American people the realization that the United States was *their* government and that *they* should take a hand in running it. Of course, we were not being guided wholly by altruism in booking members of this group; it was also good show business.

If one goes back over the list of speakers and the record of gate receipts, one striking fact emerges. In what today is considered the conservative rural stronghold of the midwest, liberal speakers, the ones who attacked the status quo, who did verbal battle with the "interests," got larger fees and packed more customers into the tents, than did the more conservative thinkers. The "outs," of whatever party, then as now, could be counted on to be more dramatic than the "ins." They gave a better show pointing out errors than officeholders possibly could give in defending their records. Also, a man out of a job would suddenly remember that there was such a thing as a lecture platform. When the Republicans were in power in Washington, through the first years of tent Chautauqua, our speakers were

"Let's Face the Issue . . ." 121

Democratic three to one. After 1912 when the Democrats were in, more Republicans took to the platform.

Speaker Champ Clark's repeated appearances in midwest Chautauqua certainly contributed to his sweeping victory over Woodrow Wilson in the Illinois preferential primary in 1912, the first ever held in that state. Clark, who began lecturing for the Redpath bureau in the late 1890's, was neither reformer nor crusader, but simply a canny, ambitious officeholder, who signed up summer after summer with the frank admission, "I need your stage. It gets me votes."

In the fall of 1910 I went to see Clark at his home in Bowling Green, Missouri, to write the contract for his next lecture tour. For two or three days I travelled with him as he tramped through his district mending fences, speaking by kerosene lamps to a dozen voters here, a half dozen there. Redpath was paying congressmen $300 a week in that period, senators $500. He was a congressman, so I offered him $300. He refused.

"I'm going to be Speaker of the House," he said. "I want $500."

He was right; he became Speaker the following April, with the first Democratic majority since 1893. We settled for the $500. But when summer came Congress stayed in special session. Clark could make only ten of his scheduled sixty dates and it cost the circuit $7000.

"There's one great virtue in Chautauqua money," Clark told us once. "You don't need to explain where you got it. And Chautauqua never tells you what to say."

Even on the platform Clark was always frank about his ambition to be President. One hot summer night in Georgia I heard him begin his speech: "My title this evening, ladies and gentlemen, is *'Picturesque Public Men'* . . . in the Congress of the United States, where I propose to stay until I am dead, defeated or promoted." Within a few days after Woodrow Wilson defeated him for the Presidential nomination at the Baltimore convention, Clark was out on the road, filling his dates in Kentucky and Indiana on my 1912 circuit. He was a very disappointed man and for the first time his famous wit carried a sting of bitterness. Of course he blamed his defeat on Bryan. Nebraska had "instructed" for Clark, and Bryan had withdrawn that support in the belief that Clark had become indebted to the "interests."

Clark never forgave Bryan and it became important, in succeeding years, that we route the two men as far apart as we could. Bryan always regretted the rift, always tried to patch things up with Clark. Eight or ten years later, when friends were honoring Clark with a birthday party in Bowling Green, Bryan, who had a Chautauqua date elsewhere, was so determined to go that he "bought off the committee" and went to Bowling Green to the party. He was repaying a courtesy. In 1910, Clark, then his most loyal friend, had made one of the most complimentary speeches at Bryan's fiftieth birthday celebration.

Normally easy-going, Clark, like Bryan, got along famously with the rest of the talent. "A meetable man," they called him. He made himself one of them, but when a group walked down the street in some Chautauqua town, it was Clark at whom the people stared. His big, tall, erect figure, solid nose, long mouth, thin shining white hair, his gates-ajar collar, his coat with its satin-lined lapels didn't belong to any Mr. Nobody. To be sure, he was not always temperate. Try hard as he might, no manager could hide under a basket the story that the famous Speaker of the House alighted one morning from a train in Pennsylvania, carrying his shoes, unable to appear on the platform that day. But in a wave of honest contrition he sent Redpath headquarters what he thought its commission would have been if he had kept his engagement.

One of Clark's lectures, particularly popular with Bible-loving Chautauqua audiences, was called *Richer than Golconda,* a collection of stories proving the effect of the Bible on law and custom. Another dealt with Daniel Webster, another with Aaron Burr. A long time later Clark's son, Bennett Champ Clark, was also elected to the House and lectured for Redpath; political speakers were in the discard and the tents were down before the son became a senator.

Blind Senator Gore of Oklahoma sandwiched his lecture appearances on our 1912 circuit in between his speeches for the Wilson campaign, which he opened officially in Illinois for the Princeton professor. "The blind man eloquent," Bryan always called Senator Gore. Except for one speech linking Lincoln and Jefferson Davis, Gore's favorite platform topic always was "good government as against the grafter and his graft," so it was only to be expected that in tumultuous 1912 he would portray Woodrow Wilson as the hero of that doctrine.

Another Redpath-Chicago lecturer who managed to get in work on the side for Candidate Wilson was Harvey Wiley, the "pure food" man, who was filling his initial dates for us that year and who bolted the Republican party in this campaign. We liked to allude in print to Woodrow Wilson himself as a "one-time member of the Redpath family," but it had been in Lyceum, not on the tent circuits.

The most vociferous partisans, however, were on the Theodore Roosevelt bandwagon; not just the lecturers; even men from the entertainment lists sometimes cancelled good, money-paying dates so they could campaign for "T.R." Headliners like Governor Hiram Johnson of California who was Theodore Roosevelt's running mate, San Francisco's great graft prosecutor, Francis Heney, Judge Ben Lindsey of Colorado who had been a runner-up for the Vice-Presidential nomination, ex-Congressmen Victor Murdock and Adam Bede—these and others on our 1912 summer list stumped hard for Teddy Roosevelt between dates, and if any loophole appeared they stumped on the dates, too. Chautauqua paid for their bread and butter and clean shirts and they worked for the Progressive ticket for nothing. And all the tempestuous summer Bede continued to debate Socialism with Emil Seidel, the Socialist party's Vice-Presidential candidate, while Seidel campaigned between acts for Eugene V. Debs.

Governor Herbert S. Hadley of Missouri, with the Redpath bureau since the Redpath-Slayton days, and particularly popular with the farmers because he had fought the lumber and harvester trusts, was one of our regular lecturers who did not bolt the Taft organization to join the Bull Moose organization.

"The Progressive Party was born from a dozen Chautauqua speeches in Iowa and Kansas," Editor William Allen White once remarked. Certainly there was not an idea in T.R.'s "New Nationalism" of 1912 (F.D.R. was not the first Roosevelt with a "New" slogan)—nor in Wilson's "New Freedom," nor in Senator Bob LaFollette's "National Progressive" program which preceded both the other two—that had not been stressed repeatedly in some Chautauqua tent. Among them were tariff revision, the initiative, referendum and recall, woman suffrage, prohibition of child labor, a corrupt practice act and dozens of other social ideas.

The tent circuits were heavily indebted to the old independents for the part the states of Kansas, Nebraska, Missouri, Iowa and their neighbors played in supplying speakers in that period. This whole territory had given exceptionally strong support to the pioneer assemblies. Local enthusiasm for the Chautauqua movement had been such that, in the 1870's, an inspired Kansas legislator, after visiting Bishop Vincent's New York grove, had succeeded in giving the name "Chautauqua" not only to a whole Kansas county, but also to the principal street in its county seat and to a nearby whistle-stop, an example which half a dozen other states followed at one time or another. The assemblies were powerful. It was only natural that officeholders learned early to use these platforms as sounding boards.

Nebraska, in addition to Bryan and Norris, furnished our circuits with men like Republican Elmer Burkett and silver-haired Democrat Ashton Shallenberger. Burkett talked steadily for fifteen summers against government ownership of railroads. Shallenberger, the second Democratic governor in Nebraska's history, was a "T.R." type of orator, with a reputation among the talent for "getting the tent" with his first amusing story. The farmers liked him because he backed the first rural credits bill that gave the farmer a chance to get money on the same basis as a businessman.

Kansas ex-Congressman Victor Murdock, whom we advertised as "the original insurgent," was a Roosevelt follower who kept slapping savagely at reactionaries in all parties, long after he left office. In 1912, in a Kentucky town, he made newspaper headlines by telling an audience that if Congress really desired to do something popular, "it should suspend publication of the Congressional Record, take the money so saved and print daily for general distribution the record of the beef barons' trial in Chicago."

Murdock, a newspaper man by profession and a positive fellow who parted his hair straight down the middle, measured the content of every speech by a yardstick of timely news value. He was convinced, and the fees we paid him over a decade bore him out, that the "dominant characteristic of the public in this period is its desire for current news on public questions."

Another speaker from Kansas, not as fiery as Murdock but just as earnest, was self-made Joseph L. Bristow, the officeholder who later appointed Dwight D. Eisenhower to West Point. Bristow was already in the Senate when he joined Redpath. A talking point in our brochure was that, as a young lawyer, he once had to choose between buying an overcoat or a new Webster's dictionary and he chose the dictionary. Undoubtedly a more important reason why we hired him was the fact that he had come to public attention by fighting Mark Hanna.

The name of Hanna, the Ohio Republican "czar" who coined the word "standpat" for his party and elected William McKinley President over Bryan by "frying the fat"—meaning that he pulled campaign money out of Big Business—was a household word, hated or respected. The Hearst press had contributed to this by almost daily merciless cartoons catering to the habitual irreverence of Americans for public personages.

In the New York *Journal,* Homer C. Davenport had blithely caricatured Hanna as a comic fat figure in clothes adorned with dollar signs, reclining with his feet on a pile of money bags, the skull of Labor on the ground beside him. Frederick Opper, in the same newspaper, had shown the Trusts skinning both the Farmer and the Laborer, with Hanna and McKinley happily standing by. Hanna, in the public mind, was Wall Street and Big Business and Trusts. You were for him or against him. Bristow, Republican though he was, had tangled with him. As McKinley's assistant postmaster-general, the Kansan had been sent to Cuba to clean up its postal service and in so doing had dared get into a public argument with Hanna and the sugar interests. On the Chautauqua platform Bristow discussed Cuba, the oriental question, taxation, the American navy, army and American youth, all under the covering umbrella, *Responsibilities of the American Citizen.*

Bristow's fellow Kansan, Edward Wallis Hoch, began filling dates for Redpath while he was governor. He, too, had fought Standard Oil and the railroads, bringing Kansas a two-cent fare for one thing, and he, too, talked about the fight in fiery words that packed the Chautauqua tents.

In Minnesota and Iowa as well as in Kansas, so far as the overflowing crowds went, "Hoch Day" sometimes looked like "Bryan Day." Hoch had helped dry up Kansas. When his daughter Anna swung a bottle made by Tiffany to christen the battleship *Kansas,* instead of champagne the bottle held spring water from the Sunflower State. Platform superintendents found Hoch fussy about one thing: he wanted the lights in the tent so arranged that a speaker, in his words, "could pierce the audience with his eyes."

From Missouri came Joseph Folk, the reform governor whom a St. Louis boss described as "acting as if he'd written the Ten Commandments." The Democratic machine had first elected Folk, thinking him "safe," soon found him looking too closely at public utility franchises. Men went to jail, the St. Louis race-track syndicate went out of business, and saloons closed on Sunday. The people responded. So in the next election, when Teddy Roosevelt carried Missouri heavily for the Presidency, Folk, a Democrat, outstripped him by a big margin for governor. He then gave Missouri its first taste of reform—laws against lobbying and child labor, for compulsory education, statewide primary, initiative and referendum.

On our 1912 and 1913 circuits Folk gave the details of his battle in a lecture billed as *A Fight for a State*. In that second summer he made the speech one hundred and ten times, from Florida all the way to Michigan. "If the government anywhere neglects the people," he thundered, "it's because the people neglect the government. If corruption exists anywhere, the people are to blame." Publicity for Folk never was difficult. Governors of the states he visited invariably gave big receptions for him.

Iowa first supplied us with the oratorical talents of that white-haired, white-mustached Republican governor and senator, Albert B. Cummins, and his fellow senator, Jonathan P. Dolliver. The farmers in our audiences never forgot that, singlehanded and green as grass, Cummins as a young man had "licked the barbed wire trust," and in overalls and Sunday suits they flocked to hear him and then went home and voted for him for twenty years. Cummins never could speak without taking a jab at the railroads. No railroad official ever sat on a Chautauqua committee bringing Cummins, the railroad buster, into town. His speeches on tariff revision eventually became known nationally as "the Iowa idea"; in 1909 the two Iowa senators, Cummins and Dolliver, had been among the ten lonely Republicans who voted against the protective Payne-Aldrich tariff.

Dolliver, re-elected senator five times, was even more of an orator than Cummins, sometimes too much so for an audience that could take just so many grandiloquent phrases and no more. "He's too eloquent," superintendents reported, to the home office. "He makes the people get tired." This may have been true, but at least he had a better sense of public relations than many of our speakers. One summer while I was still working for Vawter, we booked Dolliver at Miami Chautauqua, a permanent assembly near Franklin, Ohio, with a tabernacle seating 5000 persons. The previous Sunday Walter Chandler of the New York Bar Association had delivered a lecture on the trial of Christ from a lawyer's viewpoint. The day was hot. A baby started to cry. Chandler became irritated and said, "Any mother with any sense would remove that baby."

He failed to say it with a laugh, the way good-humored J. Adam Bede of Minnesota did once on the stage. Congressman Bede, when a baby's crying became too persistent, said pleasantly, "What that baby needs is board, not room," and everybody laughed, including the mother, and with so much good nature in the air, even the baby stopped crying.

At Miami Chautauqua, however, after Lawyer Chandler's sharp remark, the embarrassed mother left, and with her went many of the sympathetic audience. The next Sunday Senator Dolliver arrived to speak before a crowd of about the same size. He was just under way when another baby cried. The audience stiffened and this mother, having heard of the incident the previous Sunday, got up quickly. But Senator Dolliver had heard the story, too, and now was ready to make Chautauqua amends.

"Madame," he said, "please return to your seat. I'd give a good deal of money to hear one of my babies cry this minute."

Dolliver was a great supporter of Gifford Pinchot. Before he became governor of Pennsylvania, Pinchot headed the United States Forest Service when he publicly accused Richard A. Ballinger, who was Secretary of the Interior for Taft, of turning over one hundred thousand acres of rich Alaskan forest and coal land to the Guggenheim interests of New York. Wall Street attorneys helped prepare Ballinger's defense while a liberal Boston lawyer named Louis Brandeis handled Pinchot's interests.

Siding with Wall Street and Ballinger, Taft fired Pinchot, then went off on vacation to play golf. Theodore Roosevelt quickly came to Pinchot's defense. A dozen western senators, headed by LaFollette, Borah and Indiana's Beveridge, took up the Pinchot cause. Ballinger at length resigned, but it was too late. The Bull Moose party was in the making; old standpat Republicanism was on the wane.

Dolliver carried his fight to Chautauqua tents, as did other senators and dedicated conservationists. Pinchot at last was vindicated and conservation of public lands and public power for forty years remained a government policy. The movement was a noble monument to the Iowa senator and Chautauqua speaker whom Senator Beveridge called, "Beyond any doubt the greatest orator of the contemporaneous English-speaking world."

Dolliver was succeeded in the Senate by Iowa's Walter S. Kenyon, who also took to the summer platform to discuss his bill forbidding the shipment of liquor into dry states.

Many other conspicuous political figures appeared on our lecture lists before the First World War. There was big, handsome, fluent Frank Willis, college professor, governor and senator from Ohio, who a few years later was to make the Presidential nominating speech for Warren Harding. There was controversial Caleb Powers of Kentucky, who had come out of prison with a pardon in 1908. A Republican, Powers had been convicted some years before—"railroaded," his friends charged—of complicity in the murder of Democratic Governor William Goebel. In prison Powers wrote *My Own Story,* discussed it in his lecture, re-established his career and served four terms in the House at Washington, meanwhile lecturing every summer.

Intermittently from McKinley through Harding, Assistant Attorney General James M. Beck, later Solicitor General, talked for the independents and in the tents on *The Constitution.* It was a serious speech. So was the one delivered by Senator Robert Owen, who lectured on currency a half dozen years before his name took on Owen-Glass Bill fame. Audiences remembered Owen's sharp black eyes longer than they did his complicated points about the Federal Reserve system which he helped to establish.

In quite another and more humorous class were the lively Hoosiers, Charles and Fred Landis, brothers of Federal Judge Kenesaw Mountain Landis, first commissioner for professional baseball. Charles and Fred both had served in the House of Representatives and they lectured on their experiences there, both satisfied just to "make 'em laugh," instead of going in heavily for political education. Fred, who originally was a newspaperman, wrote the short story that was the basis for *The Copperhead,* a movie and a play in which Lionel Barrymore had the leading role.

Charles Landis toured the cornlands once in a joint debate with Champ Clark. They were in Clinton, Illinois, guests of a fellow congressman, and in the evening in the public argument Clark made a blistering remark that offended a Republican in the audience and the man began to heckle. After a few minutes, Clark, pointing his finger at the heckler, burst out in a fury, "Say, you, when we get through here, you-all come out behind the tent and I'll cut yo' damn throat from y'ear to y'ear. I mean you feller with the gold teeth." The "feller with the gold teeth" happened to be the postmaster, appointed by Clark's host.

Landis, in his speech, often told a story dating back to the Spanish-American War when a committee of Indiana congressmen went to the White House to urge President McKinley to appoint General Lew Wallace, author of *Ben Hur,* to command a division on active duty. President McKinley listened to their arguments, probably having heard similar ones that day from rival committees, then turned politely to Congressman Landis' nine-year-old son who was with his father, and asked, "Well, sir, have you any suggestions to offer regarding the appointment of General Wallace?"

The boy answered, "Well, Mr. President, if it were me I'd send General Wallace to Cuba as a spy."

General Wallace himself never appeared on any tent circuit, but cuttings from *Ben Hur* by various readers were as popular stand-bys as selections from *Hamlet* and *Macbeth.*

Chautauqua took profitable advantage of the great Cook-Peary controversy. It gave both sides, even though its managers publicly supported Cook. Tough old Commodore Robert E. Peary, after several decades of polar exploration, came out of the Arctic in 1909 to announce that on April 6, with a servant, four Eskimos and forty dogs, he had reached the North Pole. To his violent annoyance he found that a soft-spoken medical man named Frederick A. Cook had just landed in Denmark from Greenland with a claim that he, Cook, had found the Pole—on April 21 the year before. Peary roared "liar." Cook answered more calmly but insistently. He had accompanied an expedition northward in 1907, had left his party, he said, and gone forward with Eskimos.

While scientists studied the data, lecture managers put the two explorers on the platform, each to tell his own story. Not on the same platform to be sure. Chautauqua audiences liked controversy, not mayhem. Cook already was a favorite. He had been a summer lecturer as early as 1904; in 1906 he had acquired fame by a claim that he had ascended Mount McKinley in Alaska, highest mountain in North America.

The affair raged for several years, with the public taking sides. But while monuments were being erected to Peary, Cook got involved in a Texas oil-field promotion and served time in prison. To the end of his life, however, he fought for recognition as conqueror of both the mountain and the North Pole. Copenhagen had welcomed him rapturously, but after a study of his documents, a committee from the University of Copenhagen declared that they contained no proofs. The scientific world found for Peary; now a segment leans toward Cook. Who was right? Discussion of the affair still would make lively listening.

In this, as in other controversies, managers aimed for a free platform. If in any field the approach to a problem was one-sided, it was national prohibition. Chautauqua speakers were definitely in the forefront of the fight for the Eighteenth Amendment. Chautauqua, as pointed out earlier, was born, lived and died in dry territory. The country and small towns where it found its audiences were the strongholds of the bone-dry sentiment. Many of the lecturers and practically all the bureau managers sprang from that territory. It is on record that in 1918 the International Lyceum and Chautauqua Association, representing both managers and talent, passed a resolution supporting prohibition.

Before the tents folded, managers on one circuit booked Alfred E. Smith for a few engagements. But the four-times governor of New York, who in 1928 in his unsuccessful race for the Presidency demanded repeal of the Eighteenth Amendment, though the Democratic platform supported its enforcement, was not the "Chautauqua type." It is doubtful whether even curiosity about this slangy, cigar-smoking man in a tilted brown derby could have lured crowds into the tent in certain sections of the west.

Al Smith represented everything that the majority of Chautauqua audiences abhorred and feared. He drank liquor, he was born in a New York slum and his voice, like a dull buzz saw with an East Side twang, was enough to damn him in Kansas and Tennessee. What he said in that voice, "for the record," was even worse. He fiercely attacked the W.C.T.U., fundamentalism, the Volstead Act, even William Jennings Bryan. No, the flashy New York governor, in spite of what he accomplished in his state for social welfare, was no man to pull folks into a Chautauqua tent. And except for one semirelated incident, to be discussed later, I can think of no other "wet" speakers hired before or during the Volstead era.

Stephen Leacock, the Canadian humorist and essayist, was not a "wet" speaker really, in spite of a report round-and-about that he criticized the Volstead Act on the platform and that his Chautauqua manager objected. Among clergymen we did book several who espoused temperance, as opposed to prohibition; one of these was the Right Reverend John Ireland, archbishop of the Roman Catholic diocese of St. Paul.

The confusion, particularly in the middle west in the first two decades of this century, as to the difference between "temperance" and "prohibition," needed to be cleared up if possible. Many people mistakenly used the words as meaning the same thing; so Bishop Ireland's loud denunciations of the liquor interests and saloons, but at the same time his disdain for prohibition and his advocacy of temperance, were difficult for some country audiences to understand.

Bryan and Evangelist Billy Sunday, of course, lead the "drys." Dozens of lesser men, not clergymen or evangelists by profession, echoed them perhaps less eloquently, but no less emphatically. J. Frank Hanly, a pious but not too distinguished governor of Indiana, elected as a Republican, crusaded on all circuits for two decades talking prohibition chiefly, until finally in 1916 he was nominated for President on the Prohibition ticket. John G. Wooley, a Prohibition-party candidate back in 1900, lectured whenever he could get a hearing up until the First World War. It was for one of Wooley's circulars that an inspired Redpath copy writer wrote, intemperately one must concede, "What Gladstone was to English liberty, what Bismark was to German Imperialism, what Phillips was to the cause of human freedom, John G. Wooley is to the doctrine of American citizenship."

Some years later, around 1920 probably, Mayor David Stewart Rose of Milwaukee approached the Redpath office in Chicago with the complaint, "You claim to represent all points of view but you never give the side of the liquor interests. The schools are supported by taxes from liquor. I will debate anyone on the wet-dry issue and the brewers will pay my expenses."

Redpath agreed and offered as adversaries Captain Richmond Pearson Hobson of Alabama, Governor Hanly and Canadian-born Samuel Dickie, at that time president of Albion College, Michigan. Mayor Rose accepted all three, Captain Hobson to be the first.

The series was announced, first for winter Lyceum courses, to be followed in summer Chautauqua, with Mayor Rose's services advertised as "the compliments of the brewers' association." The program sold like hot cakes. Three debates between Hobson and Rose took place during the winter. Then the brewers, discouraged both by the public's reaction and the decisions, abandoned the project and paid the local committees for what losses they might suffer as a result.

It was serious-minded Captain Hobson, representing Alabama in Congress, who first introduced a Prohibition amendment to the Constitution. Handsome, young, intrepid, Hobson in the Spanish-American War almost succeeded in bottling up Spanish Admiral Cervera's fleet in Santiago Harbor. With a crew of seven picked men, Hobson, then a "construction lieutenant," had eased the collier *Merrimac* into the narrow harbor entrance when fire from Spanish batteries disabled his steering gear and the collier sank at a point that did not completely block the harbor mouth. Hobson and his crew were captured by the Spaniards; a few days later they were exchanged. The young officer returned home, a hero overnight, to become the center of one of those hysterical phenomena that occasionally sweep the country.

One night in 1912, after a lecture in Chicago's Auditorium Hotel, while a crowd waited to shake his famous hand, a young woman came up and he kissed her. According to Redpath lecturer Wallace Bruce Amsbary who was standing nearby, the girl was Hobson's cousin. But an inventive reporter expanded the episode. In the headlines next day it was not one woman who kissed handsome Captain Hobson, it was several. Other newspapers copied the story. That was enough. Weak-minded females began kissing the hero whenever and wherever they could corner him.

Hobson, who more than anything in the world wanted to be judged seriously, did not take it like an officer and a gentleman. For a time he even refused speaking dates. Then his interest in "problems" got the better of him and he went on the road for Redpath with a lecture on *The Yellow Peril.* His next lecture advocated *American Naval Supremacy,* and he followed that with his plea for world-wide prohibition. Later he travelled with two other speeches, one urging American leadership in the international peace movement, the other discussing the link between narcotics and the white slave traffic. Entertainers travelling with Hobson found him a superstitious man. Even his best friends admitted that he would only get into a race for Congress "when the moon was right," and the story never dies down that once, commanding a ship, he made a detail of sailors drop all other duties until they found a lost black cat.

As controversial as Hobson, but for entirely different reasons, was the Roosevelt Progressive, Judge Ben Lindsey, famous founder of the juvenile court, for more than a quarter century its judge in Denver, and more than forty years a Redpath lecturer. George Creel in *Rebel at Large* says, "All of the reformers of that early day . . . Folk of Missouri, Tom Johnson and Brand Whitlock of Ohio, Francis Heney of California, LaFollette of Wisconsin . . . were made to run a gauntlet of abuse and defamation, but no

Bishop John H. Vincent,
founder of the Chautauqua
movement.

James Redpath, who created
the Boston Lyceum Bureau,
better known as the
Redpath Bureau.

*President Woodrow Wilson
and William Jennings Bryan
walking to a Cabinet meeting.*

*William Jennings Bryan arrives at a Chautauqua lecture stopover.
In the summer of 1912, Bryan filled 34 Redpath Chautauqua dates.*

*Edgar Bergen in his Chautauqua days, with
Charlie McCarthy and the later discarded Laura.*

*The White Hussars, famous singing band on
the Chautauqua circuit.*

Typical audience outside the tent.

Season-ticket holders at Marengo, Illinois.

A tent Chautauqua audience.

A tent on the circuit.

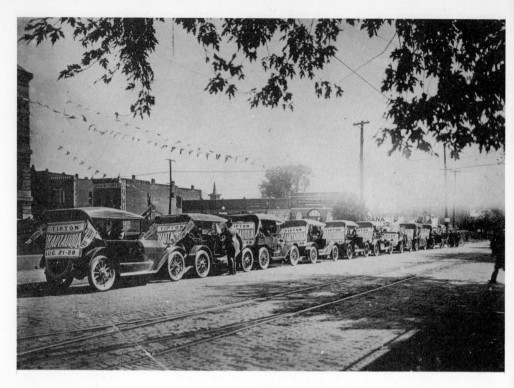

A Chautauqua boosters parade at Tipton, Indiana.

Ladies Harp Ensemble.

Dunbar's Handbell Ringers.

Daddy Groebecker's Swiss Yodelers.

Keith Vawter, initiator of Tent Chautauqua.

Opie Read as he appeared on Chautauqua.

Standing: 1. Prof. J. T. Marshmam of Penn. State College;
2. Wendell MacMahill, advance agent of the Redpath Circuit;
3. Percy Hunt, husband of Katharine Ridgeway; 4. Crawford A. Peffer.
Seated: right, Katharine Ridgeway; center, Judge Ben B. Lindsey;
left, Mrs. Crawford A. Peffer.

Princess Watahwaso.

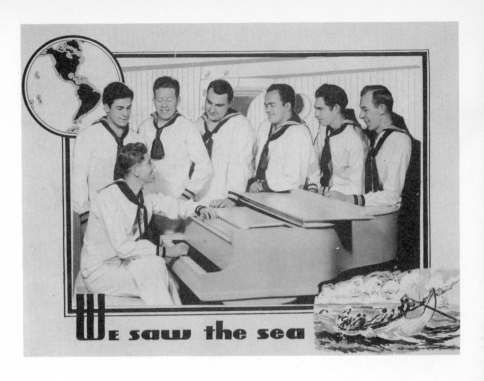

Phil Clark and his Marching Men of Song.

The DeLuxe Artist Singers in "Musical Memories."

Ben Greet, whose famous players toured the Chautauqua circuit.

Madame Ernestine Schumann-Heink, noted Metropolitan Opera contralto who was also a Chautauqua trouper.

*Alice Neilsen, opera star, on the steps of the private
car that took her over a Chautauqua circuit.*

Jessie Ray Taylor,
noted impersonator

*Julia Claussen, of the Chicago Opera Company, with
Harry P. Harrison, manager of the Redpath Chautauqua.*

one was ever called on to undergo greater persecution than Ben Lindsey."

A great humanitarian, with ideas of social justice far ahead of his time, Lindsey stirred up the wrath not only of the ordinary politician, but even of the ordinary old-fashioned policeman, with a speech dealing with the misfortunes of a mythical boy named Mickey. His program for juvenile probation and for an "honor system" were called "pampering" in the un-enlightened days before penology was recognized as a science. Local editors often threw verbal brickbats at Judge Lindsey before his appearance in a Chautauqua town; this naturally boosted the ticket sale. So did publication of his book, *The Beast and the Jungle,* in which he exposed Denver's political corruption.

Later more brickbats were to be hurled. The judge always had been interested in the problems of marriage and had been one of the first to ascribe juvenile delinquency to an unhappy home life due to ill-matched parents. So, striking at what he considered the root of youthful misbehavior, he suggested a system of trial marriage which drew immediate loud protests from both Catholic and Protestant clergy.

Persisting, Judge Lindsey wrote a book on the subject in 1927. *The Companionate Marriage,* it was called, and the Hearst press had a field day. He created another flurry of headlines when he arose in the Cathedral of St. John the Divine in New York and replied to Bishop Charles Francis Potter, who was officiating, for the latter's attack on him.

Asked once after a lecture in Youngstown, Ohio, how he could stay an optimist when he dealt all the time with bad boys, Judge Lindsey replied, "Bad boys? Not at all. No more than you or I were. The ones I deal with just got caught."

Aside from the "wet" point of view as against the "dry," only two other subjects that I know of were barred by common consent among Chautauqua managers. No lecturer dared to advocate violent overthrow of the government nor attack the Christian religion. Looking back on it now, the persistent and exceedingly popular campaign by ex-Senator Frank J. Cannon of Utah against the Mormon church, through half the life of the tent circuits, may have come close to sidestepping that second taboo, but managers did not recognize it at that time, perhaps because of the raging polygamy issue.

There was talk, too, that Granville Jones, an Arkansas judge who took to the tents in the 1920's with a speech called *Philosophy of a Hill-billy,* had an odor of the Ku Klux Klan about him, and that in some towns, acting as punch man for the new contract, he relied on Catholic-Protestant rivalries. I have also heard the charge that in the movement's last years a "free platform" was denied a pro-evolution speaker; that a man named C. D. Zerbe asked to lecture and was refused because "there were no openings." The incident is a little cloudy. Chautauqua was tottering in 1925, perhaps there *were* no openings. Bryan had died. So if intolerance did actually play a part in not accepting Zerbe, it was not for fear of hurting Headliner Bryan's feelings. Actually, Bryan's own adversary on the subject of fundamentalism, Attorney Clarence Darrow of Chicago, had lumbered out across many Redpath platforms, his thumbs hooked in his famous suspenders, had pushed back his forelock and said what he pleased, sharply and fluently, on evolution or any other topic. No one censored him —or Bryan. If Darrow, in Oshkosh, Wisconsin, wanted to say, "The earth is a speck of mud . . . I am aware that neither I nor anyone else has the slightest importance in time or space," no one tried to stop him.

It is difficult to know how to classify the afore-mentioned Frank Cannon, Utah's first senator after it became a state. Was he politician, reformer, agitator, or just a man out to earn a good living? At least he was another ex-senator with a Message; in his case, also an ex-Mormon. His speech, lashing out at polygamy, which he made sound like a threat to every American hearthside, was sensational. Whether the shocked crowds who flocked to the tents to hear him drank it in for that reason or because of his impassioned delivery, it is hard to judge now. Cannon took pains to explain that he did not advocate actual overthrow of the Mormon church. He was working, he said, "only against those phases of Mormonism that are crime and treason." The press, the sober as well as the sensational, gave him tremendous publicity, chiefly because of the Mormon elders from Salt Lake City who followed him in twos and threes into some towns, talking on street corners, occasionally entering the tent and mounting the platform at the close of Cannon's hour-and-a-half speech, asking to be heard.

On Redpath-Chicago's first trek, Cannon covered more than fifty percent of our towns—a short, squat, indefatigable figure with white panama hat, white tie, white palm leaf fan, and a proper-for-those-times senatorial forest of curly gray hair. The next summer, when he appeared in New Wilmington, Pennsylvania, on the same day as Laurant the magician, a lightning bolt struck the tent during his speech—a javelin from Jehovah his Mormon neighbors probably thought. Like Harvey Wiley, Cannon cancelled dates in 1912 to campaign for Woodrow Wilson.

Early in the winter of 1912, six hours after Harvey Washington Wiley resigned as chief of the Bureau of Chemistry in the Department of Agriculture—in order to say what he pleased about adulterated foods—the Chicago office of Redpath signed him for a tour. His first speech was called *Public Health, Our Greatest National Asset,* and it lasted seventy-five minutes. He was sixty-eight years old then and for nearly thirty years he had been the government's chief chemist. He lectured all the rest of that winter for Redpath Lyceum, gave twenty-four days to my first tent circuit and sixty the next summer; that was the beginning of a long connection between us.

Back in 1903 popular interest in Wiley had first been stirred by his "poison squad," volunteers that he organized in the Bureau of Chemistry to determine the effects of preservatives and coloring matter in food. The experiment led, eventually, to the enactment of the Federal pure food law and to better food inspection everywhere.

Wiley's ideas on social reform are still in the public mind. There was nothing lukewarm about him. He pioneered ardently on our platforms against patent medicines, for additional pure food laws, free school lunches for the poor, milk for babies.

"Give your child a tooth brush to chew on instead of a rattle," he told the mothers. His campaign in behalf of the health of school children never let up. "You give money for garbage removal," he thundered at embarrassed taxpayers, "but does your city do anything to furnish pure milk for needy children?"

In 1904 when I listened to James K. Vardaman deliver his one-sided speech in Iowa Falls, I had not yet had the privilege of hearing his fellow Mississippian, John Sharp Williams, but I was to listen to that honorable gentleman often, travel with him occasionally, before and during the Wilson years. Senators Vardaman and Williams had only two things in common. They came from the same state and both wore the label of Democrats. Williams, probably the most consistent Jeffersonian Democrat of his day, did not speak with Vardaman's grandiose oratory but with closer regard for the issues. When he walked out on a platform, pants bagging, black string tie dangling to one side, hair a little uncombed, and started off as he always did with a good story, the audience settled back for an enjoyable evening.

Senator Williams was deaf in his right ear and he had a way of holding his hand as an ear trumpet to catch the crowd's reaction to what he had said. His stories were inexhaustible. A typical one concerned another of our speakers, John Allen of Louisiana. Allen, emphasizing that he had been "Private John Allen" in the army, was running for Congress against a man with the rank of colonel.

"You get all the colonels to vote for you," he told his rival, "and I'll still win. All I need is the privates."

Williams went to Washington first as a congressman back in 1893. He supported Wilson passionately and the defeat of Wilson's post-war program grieved and angered him. He left the lecture platform about the same time that he left the government.

"I'd rather be a hound dog and bay at the moon from my Mississippi plantation," he said in 1923, "than remain in the United States Senate." So he took his pipe and went back to his plantation and did no more speaking for anyone. He had been one of the highest-paid lecturers in the business. As early as 1907, when popular Congressman Bede, for instance, was getting $125 a night for debating with Socialist Seidel, lecture managers were competing for John Sharp Williams at $200. They paid Judge

Lindsey the same. By the time Williams retired, his rates had skyrocketed
to $500 a night.

Probably the most colorful of the political orators of the south were
the Taylors of Tennessee. Old "Fiddlin' Bob" (Robert Love) Taylor
died in 1912, just a few weeks before Redpath-Chicago's opening in
Pulaski. He was a Democrat, three times governor of his state, senior senator when he died, and made his original spirited campaign in 1900 against
his brother Alfred who headed the Republican ticket, and his father,
Nathaniel Taylor, who was on the Prohibition ticket.

Tobacco-chewing "Bob" was the favorite in the always-Democratic west
and middle of Tennessee, "Alf" in the always-Republican east, and the
two brothers, both playing violins, made their speeches from platforms
banked, one with white roses, one with red, Tennessee's version of the
English War of the Roses. Farmers would drop work for two or three
days, drive twenty miles over the hills, hitch their teams to the courtyard
fence while they listened to Bob and Alf speechify.

The Weatherwax Brothers Quartet travelled with Bob Taylor for many
years to "pre-lude" his lectures. He was a poet at heart, with a happy knack
of dialect, a wealth of flowery words, a belief that a "hearty laugh is a
hallelujah." A reporter on the old New York *World,* after hearing Taylor
deliver his famous *Fiddle and the Bow,* called him "the Paganini among
politicians and the Patrick Henry among fiddlers." Like Opie Read, Fiddlin' Bob was a masterly storyteller and if their paths crossed on the road,
they often sat up all night swapping yarns. Governor Taylor's memory for
names was poor, in spite of his being a good politician, and for that reason his daughter often travelled with him. When someone came up to
greet him after a lecture, he would ask her hurriedly, "Who is this coming?"
and she might answer, "That is Jim Webster. The last time you met him he
had a sick horse."

"Jim, you old scoundrel," the governor would cry heartily, "how are
you? Did that sick horse ever get well?"

One winter before making summer schedules for Vawter, I was pressing
Taylor to know how to bill him and on what date he could start.

"Give me two more months to think," he said. "My old speech needs
a new title." His titles were catchy, so that people could remember them.
One he called *Birds and Bees,* another *Life and Love.* He fiddled, sang
plantation songs, jumped from the broadest humor to the highest eloquence, soothed his listeners with beautiful words "scattered like fireflies
over a clover field," charmed them with his courtly manner.

His eloquence and diction in *Life and Love* became a pattern for other
aspiring orators. After his death entertainers on all circuits read passages
from this speech again and again as part of their programs, but none could
deliver it as Fiddlin' Bob had delivered it. It ran:

"I saw the Morning with purple quiver and burnished bow, stand tip-toe on the horizon and shoot sunbeams at the vanishing darkness of night and then reach up and gather the stars and hide them in her bosom and then bend down and tickle the slumbering World with straws of light till it awoke with laughter and song. A thousand bugle-calls from the rosy fires of the East heralded her coming. A thousand smiling meadows kissed her garments as she passed. Ten thousand gardens unfurled their flower-flags to greet her. The heart of the deep forest throbbed a tribute of bird-song and the bright waters rippled a melody of 'welcome.' Young life and love, love radiant, radiant with hope and sparkling with the dew-drops of exultant joy came hand in hand tripping and dancing in her shining train and I wished that the Heaven of the Morning might last, forever.

"I saw the Evening hang her silver crescent in the sky and rival the splendor of the dawn with the glory of the twilight. I saw her drape the shadows around her, with a lullaby on her lips rock the weary World to rest. Then I saw her with her dipper full of dew-drops and her basket full of dreams slip back to the horizon of the morning and steal the stars again. The gardens furled their flower-flags and the meadows fell asleep. The songs of the deep forest melted into sighs and the melancholy waters whispered a pensive 'good night' to the drowsy birds and sleepy hollows.

"Life and love with a halo of parting days upon their brows and the star-light tangled in their hair, walked arm in arm among the gathering shadows and wove all the sweet memories of the morning into their happy evening song and I wished the Heaven of the evening might never end.

"So the mornings come, the evenings go, till raven locks turn white as snow. The mornings go, the evenings come, till hearts are still and lips are dumb. The morning steals the stars in vain, for evening steals them back again. Thus, life steals us from the dust; we wake to think and sleep to dream. We love and laugh and weep and sing and sigh; till death steals us back to dust again."

This was oratory, in the year Redpath-Chicago rolled down the long summer road with its first caravan.

Mother, Home and Heaven

13

To be sure, not all speakers fought dragons or windmills, socialism or civic apathy. Some were what managers called "mother, home and heaven" orators, the Chautauqua version of "God, home and mother." Speakers of this type rarely descended to the muddy level of crass partisanship. They left the earthy struggles of political forces to other men and from their cloudy eminences dispensed good cheer.

In this best of all possible worlds, even if it rained and the tent leaked, these merchants of perpetual sunshine stressed the satisfactions to be attained from lives of rugged honesty, frugality, chastity, forbearance, neighborliness, and mutual helpfulness. They wove verbal tapestries that depicted Pollyanna, Horatio Alger, Rebecca of Sunnybrook Farm and the little Dutch boy with his finger in the dike, all with beatific smiles and rainbows 'round their shoulders. In other words they "inspired," and culture-hungry rural America devoured their cheerful words. Wheat growers in the Dakotas, western cattle men, corn and hog farmers in Iowa, dairymen in Wisconsin, cotton planters in Tennessee, one or all might disagree violently with a political lecturer, or dispute business facts, but none was crass enough to object to "mother, home and heaven." None sold virtue and honesty short.

The political orator of the Bull Moose days reached his peak before America entered the First World War; by the time the last brown tent dropped, his name had almost disappeared from our programs. The inspirational lecturer and the educational speaker lasted longer. America was buying Gene Stratton Porter's books by the hundred thousands in 1904. Ten years later this Hoosier author was still a best-seller, as were Novelists Harold Bell Wright, John Fox, Jr., and Zane Grey. Their philosophy of sweetness and light and their heroes, unsullied by a single evil thought, found their counterparts on the lecture platform.

Russell Conwell, of course, was an inspirational lecturer. So was William Jennings Bryan with his *Prince of Peace,* and like these two box-office giants, lesser men used the same labor-saving device—one good lecture might suffice forever. If it had the right touch, the right emotional lift, if it started a tear down the face of the nice old lady in the third row, if a few brash young men stumbled out of the tent vowing to take a hand next day in making this a better world, its creator could stay in Chautauqua for years. Some of them did—for life. For an hour, often two hours, hundreds of men and women listened, laughed, wiped their eyes, applauded. An advertisement for this type of speaker might read, truthfully or not, "He makes you laugh, he laughs with you, when he stops you are thinking hard."

"Wasn't it wonderful?" women murmured to each other the day after the speech. "So inspiring!" Possibly by the third day they had forgotten most of what they had heard, but next season, if chance offered, they hurried again to the gate, with cousins, uncles and aunts, to hear the same man give the same speech. It was Vawter's opinion, after many years as a booking agent, that an inspirational speech was so full of generalities that little of it, including even Bryan's masterpiece, actually stayed in the listener's mind. Perhaps that is why folks flocked through the entrance gates a second and even a third time. The real reason probably is that America in those years simply liked speeches.

"Uplift" became a business for the mother, home and heaven orator and a hard and weary business it was. Its practitioners naturally liked to preach, or at least to talk, and those who repeated themselves, year after year, were skilled in tricks calculated to hold an audience which a one-season orator did not know. The one-season man on the circuits might be an author merely out to advertise his new book, or a dreamer with a bright idea to revolutionize a naughty world, for whom Chautauqua offered a brief sounding board. The real mother, home and heaveners had Messages. Their souls burned with them and they delivered them year after year in spite of heat, little sleep, poor food, a neglected home life. They dispensed cheer. They made people happy. They fortified ambition.

The true inspirationalist could deliver his speech with as much enthusiasm the hundredth time as he did the first. Or sometimes his bow had several strings and he played one, now another. Or, as today, a smart lecturer might have half a dozen different titles, but actually just one speech. In later years there was a well-known poet, best left unnamed, who offered the eager ladies on a certain Kentucky committee three titles: *Listen to America, Words and Music,* and *Songs and Singers.*

"Let 'em take their choice, whichever they think sounds best," he explained to his manager. "It's all the same speech."

The uplift theme naturally made its first appearance in the title and went on joyfully from there. Many of these titles sound hackneyed or sensational now. Undoubtedly some of them did at the time. But in 1908 and '10 and '12, spread lavishly in big red or black letters across the advertising posters, they challenged, they looked exciting. Catchy words did not make a speaker's reputation, but they helped, and a man with a well-established title made sure no one took off with it. It was his trademark. *Take the Sunny Side* belonged to Lou Beauchamp and no one else, *The Powder and the Match* to Judge George Alden. *Tallow Dips,* symbolic of the idea, "Let your light shine," was delivered 7000 times for millions of absorbed listeners by Robert Parker Miles, English-born newspaper columnist-preacher, who discovered when he was almost middle-aged that he could coin phrases people remembered. It was Miles who remarked of Henry Ward Beecher, "When he entered the room, his shoulders brushed the sides of the walls."

Lou Beauchamp's perennial *Sunny Side* was a grievous temptation to other ambitious lecturers. Its popularity arose so early in the Chautauqua era, and the words themselves were so happy a choice for an uplift theme, that solemn speakers could not resist reaching out for a share. There had been "Sunshine" Willits, Paul "Sunshine" Dietrick; happy "Sunshine" Bates with his *Silver Lining,* who, like Col. L. F. Copeland, former lawyer, died of fatigue on a Chautauqua trip.

Dozens of imitators carried similar hopeful messages. Their titles exalted the *Sunny Side of Life,* a *Sun-Crowned* this or that, *Sunshine and Tears,* or *Sunshine and Shadows.* Even sardonic humorist Strickland Gillilan cashed in on the sunlit glow when, tongue in cheek, he went out with *Sunshine and Awkwardness.*

These golden-voiced purveyors of uplift, in aligning themselves with "sunshine," were merely taking advantage of a people's longing for a happier world. They believed in their mission, which was to spread good cheer; their simple optimism was the nub of honest philosophy. It was not this type of title that eventually began to tire the more intelligent segment of the ticket-buying public. The ones that did, and caused acute pain to the more iconoclastic critics, were those that strained for variety by weird concoctions of words. Dietrich, for instance, advertised one speech called *Grasshoppers and Measuring Worms* and kept the meaning of this title a deep secret. H. W. "Taffy" Sears managed to contrive his nickname from his revolting phrase, *More Taffy and Less Epitaphy.*

C. C. Mitchell, a Baptist clergyman from Rhode Island, was built to be a humorist, but chose to be an uplifter instead. A genial fellow with so many double chins that one Chautauqua entertainer wrote back to Chicago, "If the railroads carried him by freight, they would lose money," he conjured up a name for himself that harked back to McNutt, the "Dinner Pail

Man." Mitchell jovially called himself "The Bombshell in a Nutshell Man," offering a speech called *The World's Ash Heap.*

Kansas newspaperman Ira David Mullinax, entering the scene a few years later, christened himself the "Pie Man," and for a title used what he thought was a catchy phrase, *Pie, People and Politics.* Sylvester Long, a perennial midwestern speaker, advertised that he had a "vital message dealing with first principles," which he mysteriously named *Lightning and Toothpicks.* It was built around the idea, " 'Tis not where you are standing, but which way are you going, up or down?" It epitomized "mother, home and heaven."

One public performer from Ohio modestly billed himself one summer as *The Peptomist . . . an Optimist in Action,* and on the White and Meyers circuit the same year Francis J. Gable spoke on *Laughilosophy,* explaining grandiloquently that it concerned "the doctrine of right living on the principle that it pays." Other examples of exaggerated titles are legion.

Alton Packard, the Redpath cartoonist, suggested one winter, not too seriously, that Redpath talent get up a debate among themselves "on the ethics of stealing literary material from fellow-lecturers." Thomas Brooks Fletcher, listening to the idea, didn't debate it, but just to prevent any misunderstanding he copyrighted his title for the coming season, *Tragedies of the Unprepared.*

Both in box-office appeal and speaking ability, Fletcher was one of the best "mother, home and heaven" headliners booked by Redpath-Chicago before the First World War. In his well-paid class, giving almost full time to the exhausting road, were William Rainey Bennett, Lee Francis Lybarger, Edward Amherst Ott, Ernest Wray Oneal, and Judge Alden.

Alden's title of judge had been earned on the Massachusetts bench over a period of ten years. He first appeared as a lecturer in 1906 for Peffer's Redpath in the east. In his Chautauqua lifetime he spoke in every state, hundreds of times in the more populous ones, and he was still filling platform dates in 1930, his close-cropped mustache just as trim but considerably whiter.

It was Alden's optimistic slant that the world was not going to the bow-wows, regardless of all rumors to the contrary that the political speakers might spread on the same platform. Trusts and wicked money barons were among us, Alden admitted, just as the pessimistic officeholder speaking in the tent yesterday had warned. But they were merely weeds in a system of which every one listening today was a responsible member. If a man would "know himself," "be a better man," the judge promised, he could knock the trusts into a cocked hat. Alden called this particular lecture *The Needs of the Hour* and its talk of trusts furnished copy for dozens of country editorial writers.

Snap Shots from the Chautauquas.

Other Chautauquas Headliners: Col. Copeland; Mrs. Booth appealing for the prisoners; Beauchamp; Fred Emerson Brooks; Robert M. LaFollette; Dr. Green in two poses.

Alden was a descendant of Poet Longfellow, as well as of John Alden and his wife Priscilla, and in his *Powder and the Match* he dared look out over his fancy rimless eye-glasses and capitalize on his ancestry by reciting his own verse. In *Ye Modern Maid* he took the "up-to-date girl" apart because she did "no darning, no cooking, no washing of dishes," ending on the refrain "the old-fashioned girl puts it over the new . . . Satan's still friendly with 'nothing-to-do,' " a sentiment with which most mothers in his audience were in pious accord.

In opening this speech Judge Alden used as a text a poem John Boyle O'Riley had written for the dedication of the Pilgrim monument. It began "Give praise to others, early come and late," and proceeded with the idea that as the Pilgrim Fathers laid stout ribs and keel, so also must their sons live and work. Like the sometimes irritable Strickland Gillilan, Judge Alden became easily annoyed at noise. So when people straggled down the aisles late, he showed this annoyance by backing up in his speech and repeating, "Give praise to others, early come or late." It did not take embarrassed late-comers long to get settled on the benches after that.

Alden was more sentimental than his contemporary, Thomas Brooks Fletcher. Fletcher could wring out the sad little tear, but his speeches, though classed as inspirational, usually had the overtones of the new social consciousness of the Theodore Roosevelt era, and there never was anything sensational about them. We advertised Fletcher's *Tragedies of the Unprepared* as "an effort to save the might-have-beens before it is too late"; his *Modern Judas* as a "protest against social, political and economic treason"; his *Martyrdom of Fools* as a "defense of the persecuted thinker," all extravagant words if used in this day and age.

Fletcher usually began his *Martyrdom of Fools* by announcing the title, and then adding quickly, "Glad to see so many of you here," which always brought a laugh. The day the *Lusitania* sank he was giving this speech in Brunswick, Georgia. He used his usual opener but that evening no one laughed.

Most small towns were drearily alike; the same Main Street with the same millinery shop, the same real estate signs, the same loafers in the barbershop, same fat cat sleeping in the same grocery store window. So talent, after covering the same circuit year after year, were always happy to find something, anything, that was new and different to break the monotony. With particular delight one summer the men in a musical company discovered in an audience in southwestern Illinois a woman they thought looked like a horse.

"Same long face, same mouth, same expression," a tenor reported. "Nice horse. But a horse, all right."

The word got around: "Look for 'Horse Face' in Blank-ville." The next company to arrive, coming out on the stage, looked quickly. There she

was, third row center, just as the others had said. A nice, very homely
horse, with a season ticket.

After that everyone appearing in Blank-ville looked for "Horse Face."
Finally Brooks Fletcher arrived. He started his speech, *The Tragedies of
the Unprepared*. Give the same speech a hundred times, and a man can
safely let his mind wander. In the middle of a sentence, Fletcher's glance
reached "Horse Face," and, completely unprepared for such a startling
sight, he faltered and forgot his lines. After frantic ad-libbing, he was able
to put a few sentences together and did not look again in the woman's
direction.

Like the Military Girls, Fletcher was jealous of his reputation for "always getting there"—he was one of the redoubtable ham-sandwich clan
who rode freight, handcar or bicycle to arrive where he should be on time
and who slept soundly on the baggage truck at a flag station if no other
bed was available. Once in southern Illinois, when he was trying to reach
a program before curtain, the only automobile available had no brakes.
He hired it anyway and the driver was half way down a steep hill when
he saw a bridge out ahead. Both men had to jump. Fletcher brushed himself off and appeared as usual that night. Unlike a lecturer whom we
shall call Mr. X, he did not mention the mishap.

Mr. X, in 1915, with a superintendent from the Redpath-Columbus
office, also was involved in an automobile accident. The superintendent
had minor injuries, Mr. X, none. But when he stepped on to the platform
for his afternoon engagement, he had an impressive limp and a bandage
on his head. With trembling voice and hands, he told of the "terrible accident," adding, "and as I leaned over our poor superintendent, who was
hurt so badly, he looked up at me and said in a weak voice, 'Mr. X, you
will have to carry on for both of us.' So, ladies and gentlemen, here I
am." The bandage and limp went over so well that he clung to them for
several days in succeeding towns.

Among Fletcher's many other lectures were *Community Deadheads* and
The Infamy of Intolerance. All his speeches were popular, all spotted with
humor, and we booked him season after season in the same towns. He went
to Congress later, at one time owned newspapers in Marion, Ohio, competing with Editor Warren G. Harding. For all one knows the future
President got the idea for his Chautauqua treks from his fellow towns-
man. Certain men, after getting the Chautauqua habit, became impassioned apostles of the idea. Fletcher would argue to the point of anger if
anyone legitimately pointed out a Chautauqua fault. In fact, some say that
Fletcher was responsible for the surprising remark, "Jesus Christ was the
first Chautauquan."

There was one great group of inspirational topics called, not the practical "How-to-Do's," which eventually became an important type of educational program, but the ambitious "How-to-Be's." The late Dale Car-

negie became the most famous exponent of this type of speech with his never-equalled homily, *How to Win Friends and Influence People.* An obituary in the New York *Times* at Mr. Carnegie's death made the point that, as a youth, "he became so impressed with the style of a speaker at a Chautauqua lecture that he decided to emulate him," practising "recitations on the horse he rode to and from college." Certainly there is a hint of the early Chautauqua Lake "Reading Courses" in the "Carnegie Courses" which are still being given. Over forty years nearly half a million persons have enrolled in them, to learn not only *How to Win Friends,* but *How to Stop Worrying* or *How to Start Living*—how, in short, to be the happy man or woman of whom the starry-eyed Chautauqua orator preached in Mr. Carnegie's youth.

The "How-to-Be" programs became rampant in Chautauqua. Earnest lecturers in frock coats told longing individuals *How to be Successful,* or merely *Content, How to Master One's Self, How to Make a Happy Home.* Even sober-sided Lee Lybarger travelled one season with a *How to Be Happy* title, which he delivered most seriously.

Another phrase, like the word "Sunshine," in which would-be Conwells saw profitable possibilities was *The Man.* Dozens of speakers dissected him. He might be *The Man Worth While,* or *Behind the Throne, Man of the Hour* or of *Tomorrow*—one determined lecturer probed relentlessly for *The Man Within the Man.* Philadelphia Baptist preacher Charles Seasholes, without so much as a nod to Edwin Markham's *Man With a Hoe,* crisscrossed the country, declaiming about *Man With a Pick.* For half a dozen years he gave the speech seventy times a summer. Many of the country people he was talking to lived "just to work" and it did not matter to them whether they used a pick or a hoe, if they could "be somebody" in the end, and they got Mr. Seasholes' point with no effort.

In all this onslaught, *The Man Who Can,* by William Rainey Bennett, was the most famous title and it belonged as conspicuously to him as *Tragedies of the Unprepared* did to Fletcher.

Long before the First World War we initiated a business practice of contracting lecturers to appear only for Redpath on a guaranteed annual wage, to cover both summer Chautauqua and winter Lyceum. Bennett, a Congregational clergyman who had ventured out independently with a few dates at $10 a night while preaching in Wisconsin, by 1911 was drawing $4000 a year from us. Later he changed his contract to $50 a day for independent Chautauqua dates and $225 a week on the circuits.

Black-haired Bennett and his Windsor tie made a tremendous impact on the average crowd. He "inspired" with a good hard push in the right direction, no gentle pat on the back. People a bit down at the mouth listened to his *Man Who Can* and decided that perhaps he was right; they, too, could do splendid things. One distressed individual in a Minnesota audience went home to write a letter to Redpath, admitting that he had decided life was no longer worth the effort, but he wandered into Bennett's lecture just to hear "one more rehash." It changed his mind.

Bennett, too, gradually began to emphasize social problems on the Chautauqua platform. In 1913 he went out with a speech called, far from tersely, *The Reign of the Common People* or *The World-Wide Foment Towards Democracy*. The phrase "One World" had not yet come into our vocabulary. So it is worth noting that even before the First War, Bennett, with his tendency toward big words, was talking to plain, ordinary people in small-town tents about "the self-assertion of the common man, a planetary, political movement which makes this age the most dramatic since the French Revolution." In its advance publicity Redpath-Chicago also took a bold fling at prophecy by saying, "This lecture shows the part America shall play in this world-drama. In fact, it might be called *The U.S. of the World*."

Lee Francis Lybarger, whom we modestly billed as "a new Patrick Henry," was a lawyer and teacher who talked fervently for the cause of labor, against socialism, frequently on the tariff, always with a philosophy of free trade from a Democratic viewpoint. "How many millionaires are there?" his voice thundered down the aisles. "How large are their fortunes? How were they acquired? Astors collect $500,000 a week. What equivalent service do they render?"

This outburst was entitled *Land, Labor, Wealth,* or *How They Got Rich,* an *Oration on the Dangers and Injustices of Our "Swollen" Fortunes.* The title of his chief tariff speech was just as verbose and the speech just as effective. He insisted on calling it, *The Get and Give of the Tariff, What Do You Give, What Do You Get?*

Lybarger experimented once with "serial lectures," in which one day's subject led into the next. Booked by Redpath to Miami Valley, Ohio, permanent Chautauqua for a morning hour lecture, usually only a moderate drawing card, he built up his curious audience from forty the first day to three thousand at the close of the third series, and for one morning session drew an unprecedented five thousand. He was tireless. When Emil Seidel and Adam Bede finally ended their long—and friendly—years of spirited debate on socialism, Bede took on Carl D. Thompson, an exponent of public ownership, a speaker whom the Missouri Public Utilities Commission tried, unsuccessfully, in the 1920's to force off Vawter's circuit. When the Bede-Thompson team also broke up, after a fairly short life, Lybarger took the negative against Thompson, in an hour-and-thirty-five-minute tussle.

Soon after joining Redpath, Lybarger wrote a creed for fellow lecturers that many of them respected, at least. He asked a mythical small-town committeeman, about to sign a Chautauqua contract: "What do you want from this lecturer? What you already know or what you do *not* know? What you believe or what you do *not* believe? Should he make you feel good by flattery, or feel bad by advocating things you oppose? The lecturer should take none of these things into consideration. It is not his mission to flatter or irritate, denounce the old or praise the new. He simply should proclaim the truth."

Vawter listed seven lecturers, including one woman, on his 1904 experimental tour. By 1912 the available supply had mushroomed into hundreds of good speakers, with hundreds of topics. Men like lame Frank Dixon, former North Carolina preacher and brother of Novelist Thomas Dixon, who appeared on my Pulaski "pre-meer," later filled one hundred and fifty engagements a year with his *Man Against the Mass;* in this, as with Lybarger, socialism lost again to individualism.

There were others like Byron Piatt of Indianapolis, who one season startled parents out of their wits with charges of immorality in high schools; or bald-as-an-egg Adrian Newens, an Iowan; or E. T. Hagerman from Milwaukee, who called himself "a man's preacher" and talked with no inhibition on "life, love, laughter; health, honor, humor." Occasionally, also, there were men with the erudition of William A. Colledge.

Colledge, born in Edinburgh, was a serious scholar and looked like one, in spite of the fact that he had fought in three wars against the Arabs and spent three rugged years with Stanley in Africa. Because he enjoyed coining maxims in language not above the heads of the people, the press began to call him Chautauqua's Ben Franklin. "Do not put the heaviest load on the weakest horse" . . . "When a man has no argument he usually wagers" . . . "The best of men often give the worst advice." These were typical morsels he offered as food for thought. Over a considerable period he directed Redpath-Chicago's educational department, lecturing in the tents in the summers on Scots Barrie, Stevenson and Burns.

Newens, a play reader originally, who later coached both our lecturers and entertainers, had one popular offering called *A Message from Mars,* a play in three acts built around the reform of a selfish man. One afternoon on Horner's circuit in Fredonia, in southeast Kansas, Newens was following the Killarney Girls with his *Message from Mars,* when there began a series of disturbances of the kind that made the life of a tent orator interesting and taught him patience. The tent stood near a barn with a mule. The mule began to bray just as Newens began to speak and was still braying when the fire alarm sounded. A hose cart rattled past and naturally a number of ticket holders, thinking it might be their own houses burning, got up and hurried out. Those who stayed had just resettled themselves and all the wakened babies had stopped crying, when a woman rushed back excitedly into the tent, and after searching up and down several aisles, found the friend she wanted and cried loudly, "My God, Mrs. B., it's your house has burned down!"

Mrs. B. ran out and patient Newens emptied his water pitcher and found the thread again in his *Message from Mars.* A noisy dray arrived next. It rattled all the way around the big tent to the "pup" shelter at the rear, to pick up the Killarney Girls' trunks for the railroad station. The babies cried again but Newens finished his show.

Back in the days of Bishop John Vincent, Chautauqua had rid itself of pure denominationalism. The influence never returned, even among the most fervent home-and-heaveners. Religious intolerance in every field—except possibly, as has already been noted, in Senator Cannon's attack on the Mormons—had its head knocked down as soon as it showed itself. Any representative of any faith had a welcome place on the platform, providing he possessed stage presence and had something to say.

I never heard of a preacher on Redpath or any other circuit who urged anyone to walk down the sawdust trail in a tent. Even the ebullient Sam Jones had not used this direct method, nor did fire-breathing, shirt-sleeved Billy Sunday.

Sunday's long evangelistic tours were made independently of any circuit, but if he had open dates he spoke willingly for us—for sixty percent of the gate receipts. He battled sin with vigor, eloquence and dramatic skill, and sinners and churchgoers both flocked to hear him. It has been estimated that at times in his skyrocket career Billy Sunday made one to five thousand converts a month, some of them undoubtedly from our platform, if only indirectly.

The Reverend Billy's public-relations sense never slept. One summer when his large frame house at Winona Lake, Indiana, burned to the ground, a reporter found him with his wife, "Ma" Sunday, surveying the still-smoking ruins. The reporter approached them from behind, unseen by either of them.

"What happened?" he asked.

Without hesitating, Billy Sunday propelled himself into a headline.

"The Lord gave," he said, "and the Lord hath taken away. Blessed be the name of the Lord."

The routine fire story became a story of Billy Sunday's Christian reaction and was carried by newspapers from coast to coast.

Everyone in Chautauqua got along with Billy more easily than with Ma, whom one beaten-down superintendent, after an encounter over a pay check, described as "tougher than whang leather." In this respect management found her a little like Mrs. Warren G. Harding.

There were many home-and-heaveners who were evangelists on Sunday and lecturers on temperance, honesty and frugality the remainder of the week. Few of them ever reached the stature of smiling Revivalist Benjamin Fay Mills, with his white temperance button on his black coat lapel and his philosophy, "All is well! Be of good cheer!" The platform career of Mills, who for a period abandoned orthodox church relationship because of his liberal ideas, was cut short before he was sixty, but for a quarter century many men imitated him.

One of these was the Kansas judge, Manford Schoonover, who like Beauchamp, advertised himself as a "reformed drunkard." Schoonover, without once slowing down, could spend a long, full summer talking about "the good time I have had loving my fellow man."

Another highly vocal member of the Redpath family whose message on drunkenness came from his own experience was Lincoln McConnell. He had been lawyer, cowboy, police detective, eventually an evangelist in Atlanta. He provided our program-makers with a dozen pleasant-sounding topics—*Blue Coat and Red Flag* was typical. But mostly he breathed fire and brimstone. He was another lecturer who offered special subjects for the Lord's Day. Shocked boys and girls in their best Sunday clothes did not squirm or make eyes in the back rows the evening McConnell declaimed on *Down Hill, The Psychology of Sin.*

Redpath talent scouts were not infallible. Occasional misfits and frauds were bound to creep into the lists. Discovered, they departed, sometimes before the connection had done the bureau any harm. The well-known clergyman who walked unsteadily into the Chicago office to ask for a little advance on pay (the day before he was to start out on the circuit with a speech expected to reform whole platoons of drunkards in a single night) left precipitately that same day for a home for alcoholics. There were other close calls, other individuals with feet of clay. We even had a sad experience once with a lady kleptomaniac who lectured her way up and down a circuit staying in the "best" homes—until the owners concerned began to report the loss of silver candlesticks.

Luck in catching all mistakes could not be expected. Oklahoma historians still dispute whether Joseph W. Griffis, a Presbyterian minister from Buffalo who appeared for many seasons as Tahan, a white boy brought up by the Kiowa Indians, actually was Tahan. At the time, his *Up from Savagery* was a lively horror story that fascinated its listeners. Not until years later did anyone challenge its authenticity.

Horror stories were usually resounding hits. One of the most startling, *Mantraps of the City,* was offered by the same Reverend Mr. Green whose unprophetic *Key to Peace* I first heard in 1904. *Mantraps,* an expert piece of its kind, was packed with examples of poor, honest country boys getting done in, either physically or morally, when they took up with evil companions.

One character whose name appeared at about this time might be classed as a shouting-evangelist, home-and-heavener, or as just plain headline hunter. This was Clinton N. Howard, who modestly described his lectures as "inspirational and radical," aimed "to get the world back to Eden." The "radical" undoubtedly referred to his titles, *Adam and Eve and the Baby, Why God Made a Woman,* or if anyone preferred, *Why God Made a Man.* Howard was a distinguished looking man. The Fort Worth *Star-Telegram,* after he had talked in Texas, remarked that he wore Stephen A. Douglas' collar and tie, Elbert Hubbard's hair and a Quaker hat and coat. I heard free-speaking Sam Jones introduce him once with the words: "You people don't know what I'm snickering at, but you'll pretty soon see when I introduce the next speaker. It's that little runt over there. He weighs 111 pounds in that frock coat, big hat and accessories. Ten pounds of that is hair, the rest is clothes, hide and backbone."

Howard claimed in his advertisements to have delivered his *Execution of John Barleycorn* to "acres of men." Perhaps he did, for in Canada his efforts were credited for Alberta's dry vote in 1915. Howard's sensational appeals were somewhat similar to those of James Keeley, who came out of Washington, D.C. one summer with an all-inclusive lecture on "reform, temperance, politics and economy" that he unveiled under the title, *Is It Family Life or Free Love?* Men of this type classed themselves as realists. They aimed to "shock" the public. How much lasting good they actually accomplished will always be a question.

Edward Amherst Ott also shocked his audiences thoroughly, but with no aim to achieve front-page notoriety. A speech that packed the grounds, from Crawford Peffer's eastern territory to the western Ellison-White circuit, was Ott's loud and challenging discussion of heredity. He corrupted the word into "Hittery-dittery," thereby coining a catch-word that helped people remember his speech.

Many learned voices those years were already arguing heredity versus environment. As a speech professor at Drake University in Iowa, Ott not only knew how to argue, but he had definite opinions on this particular subject. He was convinced that heredity alone controlled man's moral character. So he developed the idea in a frank piece of writing called *Sour Grapes*.

Ott's first intention was merely to deliver the speech on the Drake campus. But conservative university authorities said "No." So Ott took to the tents. A middle-sized man in white pants and blue serge coat, he marched out belligerently the first night, arched his bushy eyebrows, squared his jaw, and let go with the facts as he saw them, first about heredity and then on to marriage and divorce laws.

"I bring you tonight, good friends," he began, "no new fad of the hour." This was a fine and reasonable start, folks out in front thought. Most of them were weary of fads and both self-conscious and averse to any discussion of sex. "I deal in heredity," Ott went on. "If you don't like your environment, you can change it. But it's pretty hard to pick out your own father and mother."

The "Ott plan" provided for medical examinations and a ninety-day announcement previous to a marriage, and a proper education in the marriage relation. By 1912 the ex-college professor had repeated the speech a dizzy two thousand times in thirty-five states, Lyceum and Chautauqua together. His average audience numbered only seven hundred. But it counted up to a million and a half persons, who sat so amazed and impressed by his blunt words that half a dozen state legislatures rushed to amend their marriage laws.

Ott was a sell-out in every Chautauqua town. Hospitable women rose at dawn to prepare special breakfasts for him, or served big community banquets the night he tossed his bags down from the local train. He left the platform in 1917 after twenty-five years of hard, earnest crusading for what he believed to be the most necessary reform in the American scene. He commented once that in a single summer "men like Fletcher and Hobson address more people than Demosthenes and Cicero addressed in all their lives." The remark certainly was true of Ott himself. Unlike many of his fellows, he never had been a clergyman. He started his career on the New York stage.

The gems Ott dropped on hot afternoons in Florida-to-Michigan-to-California tents were strange talk to the intent farmers and schoolteachers, the merchants who had closed their stores for the session, the country bankers, the small employers not too familiar with the word "labor union." He warned them, forty years ago: "We need a labor reservoir for surplus men. Organize your industries on a year 'round basis. Stability in the labor market is the need of trade. Is it good social economy to lay off men with families to support, without cutting the pay of a corporation president?" And then, getting closer home with his hatred of "waste," he would demand: "How many churches is this town supporting? Are they all necessary?"

Reform in marriage laws was also a theme for serious Chautauqua lectures by Walter Taylor Sumner, dean of Chicago's Episcopal Cathedral of SS Peter and Paul, who later became Bishop of Oregon. Dean Sumner's name in the midwest stood for the fight against vice. Our superintendents often complained that he lacked brevity. The title of his address the second summer I had my own circuit was somewhat less than lucid. He called it, *Dawning Consciousness of Woman's Sex Loyalty.*

A broad line separated the run-of-the-mill reformer from a "name" clergyman who had achieved particular fame in a particular pulpit, who drew great crowds with great sermons and who took a spiritual message into the tents. The native interest of the Chautauqua audience in oratory supported men like Samuel Parkes Cadman of Brooklyn's Central Congregational Church, or Dr. Frank W. Gunsaulus and Rabbi Emil Hirsch of Chicago. And so Redpath continued to book Newell Dwight Hillis, whom I had first encountered as a young agent in Actor Joe Jefferson's dressing-room in Boston. Venerable Plymouth Church still drew crowds, as it had in the days of Beecher and Lyman Abbott, and Hillis, its incumbent orator, always reached the people on the benches, no matter where the benches were.

Hillis was high-priced. In spite of that, the reputation of his pulpit was such that managers competed for him. In addition to his church duties, by some miracle of transportation or endurance he filled at least one hundred and twenty-five Chautauqua and Lyceum dates a year.

Cadman, Hillis' fellow Brooklynite, was one of the first preachers in the nation to speak regularly on the air. He was English-born, of a race of Scotch preachers, English-educated, married to an Englishwoman; an immigrant, one might say, with an affinity for the New England tradition of eloquence which he carried into the pulpit. Cadman had two hobbies. He collected English china and antique furniture and he liked to chat about both to any or all who would listen, including an audience. He reached into his British background for his lectures on Gladstone and Lord Macaulay.

The south, which could supply fluent political orators of the Fiddlin' Bob Taylor quality, and garrulous evangelists by the dozen, still sent forth almost no lecturing clergymen. Midwest pulpits made up for it. Iowa's capital, Des Moines, a strong seat of the Disciples of Christ, had dispatched gallant soldiers and the Reverend Charles Medbury to the Spanish-American War. Like so many clergymen of his period, shocked by what they saw as chaplains in that ugly conflict, Medbury left his congregation frequently to talk about his war experiences.

Methodist bishops, in particular, were plentiful and long-lived. William Fraser McDowell, who had gone east from Ohio for a period as Lyman Beecher lecturer at Yale, seldom could desert the subject of foreign missions; but this was a time when that subject absorbed a good many fervent souls, so in the main it was all right. Bishop William A. Quayle was livelier. He preached sermons. He conformed to that extent. But he was more likely to drop his prepared speech and recite a play by Shakespeare or Victor Hugo, or, if the spirit moved him, talk dramatically about "God's Out of Doors." People smiled at his long, tousled red hair, his inelegant but never shabby dress, and loved him.

Bishop Quayle practically never had an open date. This was true, too, of solid, handsome, middle-aged George Bradford, chancellor of Oklahoma's Methodist University. People thought Bradford "looked like Bryan" and therefore must be a good speaker, and, moreover, they liked his plain talk. One day in Ohio Bradford angrily cried that if only he had his way, he would "adjourn Congress and all the state legislatures right this minute and not let them meet again for ten years. We don't need more laws, just more men willing to obey the laws we do have."

Like Lew Wallace's Ben Hur, Victor Hugo's character, Jean Valjean, over the years, was top source material. The Reverend Preston Bradley was one of dozens of lecturers, readers and actors who utilized the dramatic qualities of the immortal Valjean. *Night with a Conscience* was a good selling title. Bradley had started out in life to be a lawyer; he withdrew first from the law, then from the Presbyterian ministry, to establish in Chicago the independent Peoples' Church, meeting in theatres until the congregation finally could afford its own building.

Like Rabbi Harrison of St. Louis in Vawter's pioneering days, the fame of Rabbi Emil Hirsch of Chicago spread quickly across the country. Brilliant, independent, born in Luxemburg where his father had been chief rabbi of the Grand Duchy, Rabbi Hirsch was a liberal who brushed aside any religious forms that he thought no longer useful. He vigorously opposed Zionism, which was just beginning to be a lecture subject. Orphanages also stirred his righteous indignation; he wanted "orphans in *homes*," not "orphan homes."

Chiefly Rabbi Hirsch liked to consider himself "the Jew's ambassador to the Gentiles." The overwhelming majority of listeners in his occasional summer audiences were non-Jewish. His aim was to give them an appreciation of Judaism, just as in his pulpit he tried to teach his own congregation to understand Christianity. There were many others of his faith on the circuits.[1]

Rabbi Hirsch taught at the University of Chicago, as did another early Redpather, the Reverend Herbert L. Willett. When the Redpath organization bought the Slayton Bureau, back in the early 1900's, a few bold souls who had already ventured into the lecture field transferred with it. One was the Reverend Ernest Wray Oneal; another was Herbert Willett. There had been another Redpath personality with a similar name which sometimes caused confusion. This was doughty old "Sunshine" (Dr. A. A.) Willits of New Jersey. I say "doughty" and "old" justly, for "Sunshine" Willits in 1911, in his eighty-ninth summer, filled one hundred and twenty-seven Chautauqua dates in twenty states. It was his last safari; he died two years later.

Herbert Willett, the rather sedate pastor of Chicago's Memorial Church of Christ, confined himself to straight Biblical interpretations. For two decades, while the world swirled around him, he offered portraits of Moses, David, Job and Isaiah. Curiously enough, since the days of the old independents, when redoubtable George Wendling went up and down the land reciting *Man of Galilee* and *Saul of Tarsus,* there actually were very few speeches on Chautauqua platforms confined purely to Biblical characters, even on the restricted Sunday programs. Possibly this was because a lesser man dared not follow too closely in Wendling's steps.

Wendling's debates with godless Robert Ingersoll, whom James Redpath had dared to sponsor, put Wendling in a class by himself. I was with him one night in the Auditorium Theatre in Chicago at a lecture on atheism by bushy-haired Elbert Hubbard. "That's the best speech I ever heard," Wendling told Hubbard afterward, "only there's not a word of truth in it." Wendling lived until war-torn 1915. He had taken to the platform in 1880, the year James A. Garfield was the "dark horse" candidate for the Presidency.

[1] Among other Chautauqua lecturers of Emil Hirsch' faith were Rabbi Louis Wilsey of Cleveland's Euclid Avenue Temple, Rabbi Joseph Korn of Columbus, and Rabbi A. J. Messing of Chicago's west-side Reformed Temple Judea, to name only a few.

Hubbard, who began his career as a radical iconoclast but before it ended was defending the meat packers against Upton Sinclair's exposures in *The Jungle,* spoke chiefly in Lyceum. His topics there did not concern horrid agnosticism. Sweet titles, like *Beauty in the Home,* grew out of his work at Roycroft, his arts and crafts workshop outside East Aurora, New York. Some of our program headliners would occasionally hide away for a day or two of rest at Hubbard's Roycroft Inn. It was both quiet and diverting. Instead of prosaic numbers, guest-room doors bore the names of artists or authors. You slept not in plain "room ten," but in the "Robert and Elizabeth Browning Suite."

Any picture of clergymen plodding over territory where old camp-meeting sites were hallowed ground, leads naturally to the subject of "temperance." Some responsible churchmen were as smart as any politician: they made a distinction between "prohibition" and the more flexible conception of "temperance." The Catholic church furnished us a goodly share of temperance crusaders. Father P. J. McCorry, of St. Mary's Cathedral, Wichita, Kansas, who started for Redpath-Horner with an illustrated story on the life of Christ, switched to *Intemperance, a National Calamity.* Likewise, in the dry Kansas-Nebraska area, D. J. Cronin, a twinkly-eyed priest from Harvard, Nebraska, offered one title, *As a Man Thinks, So Is He,* that he described as being "by no means a 'dry' lecture"—a statement which might have been Irish humor, or not.

The real fighter, of course, who barred no holds, was Bishop Ireland of Minnesota. No one had more talent for making headlines—or probably enjoyed them more himself. Already seventy-four years old when Redpath-Chicago sent out its first tents, Ireland was a hearty campaigner who could out-argue and out-shout many an orator a third his age. A Kilkenny Irishman by birth, he had grown up on hard work on an Illinois farm, and in the Civil War had earned the title of "Fighting Chaplain" with Illinois volunteers. He carried all his life an edge of brogue on his tongue; therefore, in order to leave no one in doubt as to his nationality, he opened each speech with the blunt statement, "I am an American citizen."

From his earliest priesthood Ireland had been a thorn in the side of the liquor trade in the northwest. From Lake Superior to the then far Dakotas, he organized abstinence societies among both Catholics and Protestants. He believed that the liquor problem could best be solved by each individual for himself, that the law should not supplant individual conscience; but when liquor dealers disobeyed the statutes, he went out into the streets and alleys collecting evidence and then fought in the courts for its admission. Newspapers called his speeches "startlingly frank." Around 1900, because of his distaste for legislated prohibition, he had attacked that other headliner, William Jennings Bryan, and he continued to slug away at Bryan for years. Later, when certain members of his church attempted to halt his militancy in his fight for temperance, he appealed to Rome, and was rewarded by a Papal brief indirectly giving him approbation. All of this helped enormously with advance publicity on a summer circuit.[1]

A hard-pressed clergyman, whose frugal church board failed to pay him enough salary to live on, found fees from lectures very helpful. Others labored for the extra money, just to give it away. Rugged, independent Frank Wakely Gunsaulus, like Russell Conwell with his profits from *Acres of Diamonds,* is an example of the orator who took to the platform, month after weary month, to support a particular charity. With financial help from Philip D. Armour of Chicago, Gunsaulus, before the turn of the century, founded the Armour Institute of Technology, became its president and all his life thereafter worked doggedly to help support it. Any night that this shaggy man walked with his slight limp out across the stage, there were sure to be hundreds of paid single admissions.

Gunsaulus had started lecturing for the independent Chautauqua assemblies. He switched to the tent circuits, at first unhappily, in order to reach a larger audience. Aside from his pulpit in Chicago's Central Church, his interest centered always in his Institute, where he claimed that ten percent of the students owed their presence in classes to the "Chautauqua influence." His lectures, of which *Gates of the Soul* was among the best, were actually sermons.

Gunsaulus possessed a rare sense of humor. He also was kindly enough to show neither boredom nor offense when an inept platform chairman tried to be funny at his expense. Unfortunately this happened often in Chautauqua. The head of a local committee was chosen, not because he had inherited "Josh" Billings' or Mark Twain's platform skill, but because he could be counted on to sell two thousand season tickets. Frequently he insisted that he be allowed to introduce the evening's headliner.

Once, at a Gunsaulus program in his native Ohio, a chairman who fancied himself a comedian, began his introduction with this:

"Ladies and Gentlemen, we have a great *Gun* aimed at us tonight. A man built like *Saul.* Who will now fire at *Us. Dr. Gun-Saul-Us!*" The distinguished preacher, as he arose to speak, smiled wanly.

An example of Gunsaulus' humor at his own expense is furnished by a story he used to tell, of his first pastorate in Columbus, Ohio. He was very young and success apparently had made him brash. To teach him how to be humble, a presiding elder sent him out to ride a circuit. Gunsaulus went reluctantly. His route took him to Circleville, Ohio, and there at a prayer meeting, he asked a stern-faced deacon to pray.

The prayer, which Gunsaulus often quoted, was:

> "Almighty God, who does from Thy
> throne behold all dwellers of earth,

[1] Among other Roman Catholic clergymen in Redpath tents were Bishop John Henry Tihen of Nebraska, later the Bishop of Denver, and Canadian-born Bishop Francis Clement Kelley, founder of *Extension Magazine.*

make us to feel our littlenesses,
and do, we pray, take away from us
all pride and vanity. Inspire this
young man of God, Thy delegate, with
all the graces of Thy Kingdom. And
if the Divine spark with which You
have him endowed should grow dim, O
Gracious God, water Thou that spark!"

Gunsaulus' heavily lined face was an actor's face. He seemed to gesticulate not only with arms, eyes, eyebrows, but even with his heavy mustache. His enthusiasm bounced off the canvas walls. If he saw many young persons in the tent, he usually ended with Edmund Vance Cooke's lines:

"The harder you're thrown, the higher you bounce,
"Be proud of your blackened eye.
"It isn't the fact that you're licked that counts,
"But how did you fight, and why?"

It was the chronic bad dream of every Chautauqua circuit superintendent out on the road that some day his talent would fail to arrive. The expectant audience would assemble, wait, get restless, impatient, shuffle its feet. And no speaker. No one to take the lecturer's place. So finally no program.

In 1912 this happened to a Lyceum manager who had scheduled Dr. Gunsaulus to speak. He was to be in the little town of Jeffersonville, Ohio, on April 24th, but as the date approached, he was ill. So he asked Ernest Wray Oneal to take his place. Oneal, pastor at the time of Chicago's First Methodist Church, accepted, then absent-mindedly mislaid his note as to the date. It was the 25th, he thought.

On the night of the 24th, lecture-loving Ohioans gathered in Jeffersonville's hall, waited impatiently till 8:30, then went home, a little hot under their collars at both Dr. Gunsaulus and his substitute. The next day on the midafternoon train the genial Mr. Oneal arrived and to his chagrin learned that he was twenty-four hours late. What could he do, except apologize and go back to Chicago?

The committee was gracious. They voted next day to invite Mr. Oneal to return in a week. He managed it this time and his own and Dr. Gunsaulus' reputation were saved. I never learned whether the substitute gave his fee to the Institute of Technology. Perhaps he had some pet charity of his own or his church needed a new carpet.

There were many instances of generosity of the Gunsaulus and Conwell type. The lusty Jubilee Singers helped support Fisk University at Nashville. Reformer Maude Ballington Booth spent almost every penny she earned for over a quarter century to aid ex-convicts. Judge Lindsey shared his income with hapless boys. Sir Wilfred Grenfell, surgeon and great social worker, lectured in the United States for the sole purpose of raising money for his schools and hospitals in Labrador and Newfoundland.

Vilhjalmur Stefansson, booked chiefly in the west, and one of the highest-paid lecturers in the business, plowed back a heavy share of his profits into Arctic exploration. In 1921, the year his *Friendly Arctic* was published, he offered to work for Redpath-Chicago for one thousand dollars a week and expenses.

Booker T. Washington, the story goes, once contributed a lone dime. This great Negro educator spoke on a program at Fairfield, Iowa, one summer afternoon in the early days, and in the evening he was sitting in the lobby of the town's little hotel with other talent, when a travelling man—"drummer" was the word then—bustled in with his baggage. Seeing Washington, he ordered, "You, George, go get me a pitcher of ice water! Quick!"

"Yes, sir," Washington said without any other comment.

Washington fetched a pitcher with ice and water from the wash room and picking up the newcomer's grips, followed him up the stairs. When he returned to the lobby, he said to the others, sitting aghast, waiting for him, "The gentleman gave me a tip. I took it, so as not to embarrass him." He held up a dime. "It's fine. Ten cents will help one of my boys toward an education."

The Voice of the People

14

The career of William Jennings Bryan in Chautauqua probably never will be explained to the satisfaction of everyone. His popularity, which amounted to adoration in some quarters, is a phenomenon to be considered thoughtfully by historians seeking to throw light on the social forces which moved the nation in the first two decades of this century.

Theories by the dozen have been advanced, none in itself adequate, as to why, summer after summer, in heat, rain, wind or dust, immense crowds clogged the roads and nearly tore down the tents to listen to Bryan.

During the whole life of circuit Chautauqua, Bryan was its greatest name, but curiously enough, not as a political orator. He chose to be an inspirationalist. He set the mold for this type of speech and other speakers tried to fit their own words and personalities into it. From that day, in Chicago in 1896, when as "the boy orator of the Platte" he stampeded the Democratic national convention, until shortly before his death in 1925, his golden voice earned his bread and butter and bewitched America's citizens.

Bryan was a lawyer who rarely practised law, an editor who wrote only occasional editorials, a politician three times defeated for the Presidency, but an orator without peer so far in this century. He favored broad social legislation, low tariffs, woman suffrage, a federal income tax, popular election of United States Senators and free silver and he battled vigorously for them in political campaigns, but he practically never alluded to these earthy matters from a Chautauqua stage. He had bitter political enemies but he never mentioned them in Chautauqua. He never lashed out at them nor used his great summer audiences to pay back a politician in kind. He never changed the style of his clothes nor his outlook on life from young manhood to old age. He was not a deep thinker and he espoused causes many of which time has proved of doubtful value. But oh, how he could talk! An Iowa editor, after listening to him one summer afternoon, fled back to his desk and wrote: "Words flow from Bryan's lips like water over Niagara!"

The speech with which Bryan bounced to fame and the Presidential nomination at the Democratic convention in 1896 was one of the most skillfully constructed oratorical springboards in political history. The subject of bimetalism certainly was not in itself a cause to make men's hearts rise up. But he wove into his address both religious imagery and a revolutionary plea to the masses to cast off the shackles of party bossism and Wall Street domination and to join his crusade. With deft words and ingenious phrases, he aligned himself with the plain people and the plain people with God, armed them with justice and made himself their protector.

When Bryan declaimed, on that hot Chicago day, that his opponents should "not press down upon the brow of labor this crown of thorns," should "not crucify mankind upon a cross of gold," he not only was indulging in superb oratory, he was calling God-fearing, hard-working masses to the fray. They recognized the challenge when he cried, "The humblest citizen of all the land, when clad in the armor of a righteous cause is stronger than all the hosts of Error." He was a fairly young man and he was to speak day after day the remainder of his life. But no later oration was to equal *The Cross of Gold,* not even his Chautauqua masterpiece, *The Prince of Peace.*

Bryan talked religion in politics; he talked it in Chautauqua. The only other subjects that he presented in both forums were prohibition and peace, and occasionally woman suffrage. He clearly was more interested in religion than he was in government. In *The Prince of Peace* he declared bluntly, "The most important things in life lie outside the realm of government." Later he added, "I commenced speaking on the stump when I was only twenty, but I commenced speaking in the church six years earlier and I shall be in the church even after I am out of politics." The remark was prophetic. His last public words were in a church.

His detractors have claimed that even being Secretary of State was a side issue in his mind to his public lecturing. This is an exaggeration, undoubtedly. But in 1912, while the newspapers were taking Presidential polls that listed Bryan again as a possible contender for the White House, he was elected president of the board of trustees of the little Winona Lake, Indiana, Chautauqua assembly. I happened to meet him that day. Undoubtedly his political future interested him deeply, but he failed to mention it. His pleasure was over the Winona Lake appointment.

Such a post was trivial for a man soon to be one of the nation's highest officials, but trivial things touching everyday life were important to him. Once at a railroad station in a small Michigan town, getting out of a horse-drawn hack, he discovered that he had no money in his pocket. Turning to me, he asked to borrow a quarter. He paid off the hackie. We did not meet again until the next Chautauqua season. The minute he saw me approach, his hand went to his pocket and his first words were, "Here's the quarter. Many thanks."

Even before the *Cross of Gold* speech, Bryan was appearing at the permanent Chautauqua assemblies. He had already represented Nebraska twice in Congress and, joining the silver bloc there, he had demonstrated his ability as an orator. A speech on tariff in that period is particularly well remembered. But back in Nebraska he had failed for the Senate, in the days when the legislature chose senators. So in 1894, while editing the *Omaha World Herald,* he began speaking here and there, often for no fee. The Slayton lecture bureau was handling him at the time Redpath bought it.

When Vawter booked this Nebraska orator for the experimental 1904 tour, Bryan was already the undisputed leader of the Democratic party, twice by then had been its candidate for President. The first time, in 1896, if he had gathered only 50,000 more votes, out of a total of more than thirteen and a half million ballots cast, and if these votes had been scattered in the right states, Bryan, not William McKinley, would have been President.

Bryan travelled around the world in 1906. Crowds in Manila, Tokyo, Bombay, Cairo, Jerusalem, everywhere he appeared, demanded to hear *The Prince of Peace.* He returned home, probably weary with giving it, and in the course of time prepared a sheaf of other lectures: *The Price of a Soul, Brute or Brother, The Ideal Republic, The Making of a Man, A Conquering Nation.* In content they might have belonged to any mother, home and heaven orator. The people listened to them, then asked again for *The Prince of Peace.* He delivered it in three thousand Chautauqua tents after 1904. Conwell's *Acres of Diamonds* was heard by more audiences, twice as many by some estimates. But Conwell's speaking career covered forty years and perhaps half of his appearances were in churches and schools, not on travelling tent circuits.

All over the nation solid citizens put everything aside to hear *The Prince of Peace* on Chautauqua week's "Bryan Day." Did its content hypnotize them or was it the voice, big and easy and golden? They sat dead still in their seats as long as it sounded. If Bryan smiled, they smiled. If he frowned, they frowned. Babies could cry, trains roar by, thunder and rain shake the tent, but absorbed men and women still just sat and listened. The soothing voice comforted them. This simple, kindly man spoke to their hearts, never over their heads. Like themselves, they knew he had experienced bitter disappointment; never poverty or hard labor as many of them had, but if Providence had so ordered, he would have endured these, too, they were convinced. If he had never shared their muddy struggles, he could imagine them, and he did share with them their old-fashioned belief in God. Like these plain people of the broad, flat midlands, the far-west cattle ranges, the poor southern cotton fields, he had been scorned by the sophisticated east. Like these farmers and villagers who after years of weary effort were beginning to make their mass aspirations felt, he, too, had used his own sheer will power to become a driving force in America.

If this great man spoke in choice words and golden accent, so much the better. The truths he proclaimed were only those the people themselves would have proclaimed, if they only had known how. He belonged to them; he knew it and they knew it. He was "the Great Commoner," a man with a mission. They thought of him not as a politician, not as a Democrat or Republican, not as a paid attraction they had just spent thirty-five or fifty cents to hear, but as the echo of their own inner voices refined to purest gold. So they sat, in sweating ecstasy. When the golden voice ceased, they swarmed down the aisles toward him. He shook their hands willingly. The fame he most wanted, it has often been said, was their adoration.

There probably still are many million Americans who remember Bryan, a tall, bald man with bulging bay window, wearing an oversized alpaca coat, baggy black trousers, a soft white shirt with spreading collar and narrow black bow tie, slowly waving his five-cent palm-leaf fan as he marched out with majesty across the Chautauqua stage. They remember the slow way he smiled, with crinkles in the corners of his kindly eyes, or if he mentioned injustice the way he angrily snapped shut his thin lips.

There was nothing profound about *The Prince of Peace*. Most of its words were glorious, but its allusions were plain, about things close at hand, simple things that every man, woman and child could understand. Bryan started almost in a conversational tone but in a clear voice readily understood, not only in the far corners of the tent, but out in the fields beyond the rolled-up side walls.

"I offer no apology for speaking on a religious theme," he usually began, "for it is the most universal of all themes. I am interested in government, as you know. While to me, the science of government is intensely absorbing, I realize that the most important things in life lie outside its realm, and that more depends on what the individual does for himself than on what government does, or can do, for him. Men can be miserable under the best government and happy under the worst government."

So far, no eloquence. That would come later. In the beginning, he made himself one with the audience, as he addressed simple words, stating a simple faith, to simple people. His opening was a declaration of religious conviction. He was praising faith, not free enterprise, pointing out that religion can help, where government fails.

"Can God perform miracles?" he asked, and then he provided a homely anecdote to prove that He could.

He talked about a watermelon. He didn't need to translate the allusion in order to make everyone understand. The people out in front knew about watermelons, firsthand. But this was a very special watermelon, one weighing forty pounds, and that was big, even for Indiana and Illinois. He had been eating this melon one day "several months ago" when he happened to realize its exquisite beauty.

On the outside it was brilliant green. Under the green was a layer of pure white. And within that layer was the meat, a glorious red. And scattered through the red meat were hundreds of black seeds. The audience, listening to this description of a familiar object, found themselves sharing with the great man his sense of beauty, his feeling of awe. He paused, thumb and forefinger lifted, to indicate the size of the watermelon seed. "So big," he said. "Plant it, and another great watermelon full of beauty and luscious flavor, will grow."

One little seed, he repeated, would produce another great and gorgeous watermelon! How did that happen? Where did the seed get its reproductive power? Had the scientists in their laboratories, who were positive of so many things, ever been able to explain the miracle of growth? Could they, who so often scorned God, create a watermelon, or even a single seed, without God's help? Who drew the plan for this magnificent example of things outside the human range of accomplishment? Who was the Artist, the Master Craftsman, who could contrive anything as beautiful as that forty-pound watermelon?

"The scientists" were his whipping boys. He turned his scorn on doubters who insisted on a physical explanation for everything and challenged them to answer not only the Biblical stories of miracles, but of miracles encountered at that very moment, in everyday life. The men of science had no answers, he told them.

It was God who, touching "with divine power the cold and pulseless acorn," caused it to grow into a mighty oak. Could the scientists, so sure of themselves, accomplish that? Could they create an egg? What right had they to doubt the miracle of Jesus Christ, sent from Heaven to redeem mankind?

So there he was, talking reverently about God and the mysteries of life, in language that everyone in every audience could understand. He went on to discuss self-sacrifice and thus approached the title of his speech, *The Prince of Peace*. Christ had sacrificed, and only Christ could bring peace to troubled men.

And if the watermelon seed typified the miracle of reproduction, another seed familiar to all, a grain of wheat, could illustrate mortality.

The people listened and believed. There the mighty man stood, sweating even as the humblest of them sweat in Georgia or Illinois heat, common as the commonest laborer in the far back rows. He suffered from the weather just as they all suffered; unlike them, he always had a pitcher of ice water at his hand and drank great draughts as his speech rolled on.

Sometimes, in August, there also was a tin basin with a chunk of ice. He would cool his hand against the chunk and then mop his sweating brow. And always he held on to his five-cent palm-leaf fan.

Mrs. Bryan, describing the scene, once wrote: "When Mr. Bryan stood in the Chautauqua tent at night under the electric lights and the starlight, with practically every adult and most of the children from miles around within sound of his voice, he could forget the hardships and weariness of travel. His voice would grow deep and solemn, for he knew he was speaking to the heart of America." On one clear, still night, she added, when the sides of the tent were up, she understood him distinctly while she sat in a room three blocks away.

In *Value of an Ideal,* antedating *The Prince of Peace* by several years, Bryan had used a radish instead of a watermelon as an example, and thereafter when he came to town women began bringing him gifts of bunches of radishes. He accepted them with pleasure. He liked radishes, particularly white ones. They were good for diabetes, he thought. He put them in his hip pocket and munched on them when he chose. Supplying a forty-pound watermelon the women would have found more difficult.

Bryan was a middle-aged man when he gave his first lecture for Redpath-Chicago on the route north from Pulaski, Tennessee. From that day on, whenever he was scheduled, our superintendents knew that they had better get a little rest ahead of time in order to keep up with him. No one ever heard Bryan say that he was tired. Travel schedules might be long, hard, close; if there was a chance for an extra speech somewhere, he inserted it. He was unhappy, either in political campaigns or on lecture tours, unless he could expend to the full his enormous energy.

Bryan's son, Attorney William Jennings Bryan, Jr., of Los Angeles, recently discovered in one of his father's notebooks a schedule showing eleven speeches in six days, in the heat of a summer from July 29 through August 3. Nine were in Ohio, two in Indiana. "I can do one at Peebles August 4," he wrote, "if I do not go to Baton Rouge"; then continued: "After September 18 I expect to go from Missouri west to Wyoming and Nevada, then to Miami. From October 4 to 18 I am attending WCTU conventions in Missouri, Indiana, Ohio, Pennsylvania, New York, New Jersey, Connecticut, Maine and West Virginia, with other meetings in the east. Will then give some more time to Ohio."

In Chautauqua one season, not a campaign year, Bryan gave two lectures a day for a week and repeated it the next week, skipped two days and did another full week. If he spoke in Terre Haute, Indiana, on Monday night and his car next morning took him through the town of Brazil, on the way to Indianapolis, why not, he reasoned—and no one ever argued with him —pause in Brazil and look in for a minute on the morning lecture hour?

There was no airplane to take a lecturer swiftly and comfortably from place to place and Bryan might not have used it if there had been. He made the hops by day coach, by Model-T Ford or horse and buggy, and at least half a dozen times on my own circuits in a freight caboose. Only when the engagements were a full night apart would he use a Pullman car. Repeatedly, when trains were late or weather ripped a schedule to pieces, I have known him to combine train, car and buggy and arrive calm, still full of energy, in time for the opening.

If, in spite of all his efforts Bryan did arrive late, his faithful audience knew that the fault was not his. They waited patiently till he got there. Hours sometimes. On his way to the program at Hampton, Iowa, one night, the engine on his train broke down at Mason City. "I'll be there pretty soon," he sent word to the waiting crowd. No one left. At 12:20 A.M. he arrived and started *The Prince of Peace*. Old hands liked to say that if he did miss a train and had to hire a buggy, he always asked the livery man which horse was fast enough to catch up with the train, and he wasn't being humorous. He intended to board it at its next stop.

And no matter what happened on the road, Bryan never took offense. He was courteous, uncomplaining; his temper never short. If things went wrong, he pretended not to see or hear. At Attica, Indiana, one evening, I was standing in the lobby of the hotel talking to Prohibitionist Bryan and an admiring delegation from the W.C.T.U., when hilarity from the adjoining bar drowned out our words.

The door was open. I saw Author Opie Read, the star attraction of our afternoon program, lounging with glass in hand, nonchalantly "telling the boys a story." Bryan saw him, too. Without question it was distasteful to him. Read was breaking a rule. Talent were not supposed to drink liquor on tour; in Bryan's opinion they should drink none anywhere. But he said nothing; instead, he moved just enough to cut off the view, so the ladies would not be shocked at the sight of their other lecture-hero, and the next morning, affable as ever, Bryan joined Read and me at breakfast.

Entertainer Jess Pugh tells of a night in 1917 in Santa Fe, when he was working briefly for Horner as a platform manager, and because of a storm it was arranged for Bryan to speak in the Masonic Temple instead of the tent. The makeshift stage was so high that to reach their places of honor on the platform the local committee, including an overweight state senator, had to step first on a tool chest. Pugh lowered the curtain on the stage and Bryan mounted first. The fat senator started up next, but his toe caught and he fell. Bryan grabbed him by a pants' leg. Surprisingly the man became angry and kicked, yelling, "Let go my leg."

"I'm only trying to help," Bryan retorted. There was a scuffle, to the astonishment of the listening audience. When the curtain went up, Bryan's tie was untied but he was still smiling.

The crew boys, in particular, admired Bryan, possibly because like themselves he nearly always was ready for food, in spite of the bologna he sometimes carried in his pocket. Possibly it was for this mundane reason; more probably they liked him because he went back to their "pup tent" if he had a free minute, and talked to them. He knew every boy's life history after the first ten minutes and he remembered it the next time he saw the boy. When the big man needed sleep, he stretched out, just as the crew did, on a roll of extra canvas, though the boys knew well enough that if the next day's hop proved hard, "Old Dependable" to all appearances would stand it better than anybody else. Crews were critical. They might think some other lecturer too standoffish, pompous or demanding. To a man they cheered Bryan.

We used the phrase "The Great Commoner" in our advertising but it did not arise in Chautauqua. The story is that after Bryan made his *Cross of Gold* speech in 1896, a railroad president was offering him the use of a private car for campaigning when a friend objected. "No, you can't use a private car, you're the Great Commoner." The same philosophy influenced William Howard Taft in later years when, as a train stopped for him to alight, he walked forward from a rear Pullman car to a more plebeian coach. Two Bryan titles that actually did arise in Chautauqua, both of them affectionately, were the "Big Number" and the crew boys' "Old Dependable."

It is hard to imagine that the great Bryan, he of the silver tongue, ever suffered from stage fright, but members of his family and talent close to him confirm this. Like Madame Schumann-Heink, they say, he never stepped out on a platform without "butterflies in his stomach." He could not eat before speaking, a partial explanation for his prodigious appetite at other times.

Talent, made self-conscious by Mr. Bryan's extreme temperance as to liquor and tobacco, found it hard to explain what they considered his intemperance in food. Hilton Ira Jones, who traveled with the great man for three seasons, used to tell of arriving with him in Aberdeen, South Dakota. Relates Mr. Jones, "He walked up and down behind the tent before time for his speech, literally wringing his hands, so afraid he wouldn't 'get going.' Then as soon as it was over, he said, 'Let's go eat a bite now.' " The bite, in Mr. Bryan's case, was a planked steak, an inch and a half thick, covering the Sherman Hotel's largest platter, "enough for six men," which the shocked Mr. Jones sat and watched him consume without help.

Bryan wanted the children to hear him free, if only outside the tent with the sides rolled up. He insisted that adult admissions be kept low, from twenty-five to fifty cents, and any reserved seats not more than one dollar. Although many managers, vieing for the war horse's dates, offered him a guaranteed minimum of $500 an appearance, he refused that kind of arrangement. He was paid on a sliding scale, dependent first on advance season tickets, and second on single admissions to his particular program which at times exceeded $1000.

On Redpath circuits, Bryan's share of each season ticket, no matter what its price, was ten cents. The average sale of such tickets was one thousand, so his average income from this source was $100 a day. In addition to this, he took the first $250 in single admissions for the program on which he appeared, and Redpath took the second $250. Beyond that, we split with him, half and half.

Thus Bryan was assured of approximately $100. If we sold anywhere from $250 to $500 worth of extra tickets at the gate, he made $250 more. But if a rainstorm threatened to wash out the tent and kept crowds away, he smilingly accepted whatever did come in. For instance, at Independence, Iowa, on July 4, 1911, the weather was so foul that, even with Bryan on the platform, the gate receipts were only $116. He pocketed the sum, plus his original $100, and Redpath-Vawter took a thumping loss.

At Chautauqua's height, "Bryan Day" would bring five thousand persons into town, a sizeable audience before the era of loud-speakers, before automobiles were common, when crowds collected by slow train, horse and buggy or afoot. Amusement vendors of every kind naturally tried to profit by it. Souvenir sellers set up stands as close to the tent as they could. It was the little daughter of Lecturer Wallace Bruce Amsbary who, seeing Mr. Bryan climb off the morning Pullman car, clapped her hands and cried, "Oh, goody, goody, it's Bryan's Day," and when asked what was so good, she answered, "On Bryan Day the merry-go-round runs."

Like all Chautauqua lecturers, Bryan shared his programs with other acts. In 1913, when he was Secretary of State, he followed The Seven Swiss Girls, a team of yodelers and singers who practised their lively and somewhat raucous art for thirty minutes before he began to talk. Republican congressmen complained bitterly that summer about his brief absence from Washington. They accused him of neglecting State Department business, when international relations were growing more complex. They charged that in order to catch a train for his Chautauqua opening date, he had cut an ambassador off short in an important discussion.

A House committee heard Republican Jim Watson, himself a rafter-ringing orator who never turned down a chance to speak, demand that "There ought to be a law to stop him." "For one reason," the Hoosier added, "because he goes about abusing people who make money."

In Great Britain the press took an unhappy view of the whole business and one journal, the *Saturday Review,* after eyeing the American scene and particularly the Secretary of State through its critical lorgnette, called attention to the fact that several British soldiers had been disciplined that week for working as extras in a motion picture for pay, whereas in America a "cabinet minister" appeared with The Seven Swiss Girls "unchided and unabashed." It concluded: "In England a private in our forces is expected to be more discreet."

Bryan was forced finally to answer the criticisms, remarking first, "I regard lecturing as an entirely legitimate field," and later, "I need the money. I cannot live on my salary of $12,000 a year." As late as 1924 he felt compelled to refer to the Swiss Girls episode, saying, "President Wilson approved of my Chautauqua work, which, by the way, occupied fifteen days in the two years. I lectured at Chautauqua before I was nominated for President and after. President Taft lectured at Chautauqua after he was elected; Vice-President Marshall and Speaker Clark while they were in office. Nobody criticized them."

Bryan resigned from Woodrow Wilson's cabinet on June 7, 1915, exactly one month after German U-boats had sunk the British liner *Lusitania* with the loss of 1108 lives, 124 of them American. Wilson had been writing notes to the belligerents—notes which Bryan signed—warning them not to interfere with American ships or passengers.

Pacifist Bryan objected to the notes. He called them too bellicose, insisted that they might lead to war. When the German ambassador, Count von Bernsdorff, warned Americans to stay off vessels in the war zone or suffer the consequences, Bryan believed that they should stay off.

The *Lusitania* sinking shocked America. Germany charged that the ship was armed, which it was not, that it carried ammunition, which it did. Headlines and flaming editorials denied both charges. The nation bristled with patriotic indignation. Wilson wrote and Bryan, under protest, signed, another note. Dissatisfied with the reply, Wilson wrote again, in firmer language, to the Imperial German Government. This time Bryan refused to sign. He would not be a party to anything that might involve America in the war. Wilson argued with him and he resigned.

"I have to take the course I have chosen," he told fellow cabinet members at a final meeting. "The President has one view, I have a different one. I can do more on the outside to prevent war . . . I go out into the dark. . . ."

He went not to the "dark," but to the bright footlights of the lecture platform with a speech entitled *The Causeless War*. Ridiculed by leaders of both parties, lampooned by cartoonists, villified by the press, he stood firmly on his own feet and faced hostile, patriotic crowds day after day, night after night. His private feud with doubting scientists and liberal interpreters of the Bible forgotten, he turned his back on the screaming American Eagle and embraced the Dove of Peace. Not only pacifists flocked to hear him, but "hyphenates," as Americans of German extraction and sympathy were called.

Bryan's immediate target was increased military and naval appropriations. Crowds still bulged the tents and auditoriums, but many listeners were troubled. A cartoon by Rollin Kirby in the New York *World* had been reprinted all over the nation. It showed Bryan on a platform, with the audience fleeing, except for Kaiser Wilhelm in battle helmet, applauding from a front seat. Even in Iowa, the stout heart of Chautauqua, the Des Moines *Register and Leader* called the *Lusitania* sinking "deliberate murder" and demanded that the United States take "immediate action." Bryan and the nation knew that "action" should read "war."

On July Fourth in San Francisco, Bryan faced a crowd of 100,000 with his plea for peace. In August he spent three weeks on various Chautauqua circuits; sixteen of the speeches were for Horner in Nebraska. Then, as the imminence of war temporarily declined, he halted his peace campaign long enough to make sixty speeches in forty Ohio counties in a single week, plugging for prohibition.

In 1916, Bryan heard delegates at the St. Louis Democratic convention chant his name, demanding that he lead them. He remained silent; he was a good party man and that summer, too, his Chautauqua receipts were thin while he stumped for Wilson's re-election. In fact, at no time did a Presidential convention fail to take precedence over any lecture date. He liked to tell that in 1876, when he was twelve years old, he sold enough of his father's corn to get railroad fare and expenses to attend the Democratic convention in St. Louis, ". . . my initiation into national politics." The next one, because he was in school, was the only other convention he ever missed.

So again in 1920 Bryan cancelled his dates with Redpath. In early June, at the Republican convention in Chicago, he sat at the press table, a big, bulky, aging figure among younger men, reporting for a press syndicate the nomination of another Chautauquan, Warren Harding. Later in the month at the "wet" convention in San Francisco, after his planks for the Democratic platform were defeated decisively, he was disturbed; but, not showing it, he took to the road at once on a stiff three-weeks schedule for the Ellison-White circuit in the west.

Curiously enough, in the light of his later battle over fundamentalism, he never made a speech in Chautauqua dealing exclusively with the subject. References to Darwinism, to scientists with no faith, appeared time and again, but only lightly, usually with more scorn than positive argument. In *The Prince of Peace* he had said, "I do not accept the Darwinian theory but I shall not quarrel with you about it," adding in explanation, "All I mean to say is, that while you may trace your ancestry back to the monkey, if you find pleasure in doing so, you shall not connect me with your family tree without more evidence than has yet been produced." He had drafted state legislation forbidding the teaching of evolution in the public schools, but only toward the end of his career was he stabbing at the subject on the platform, in passages that he included in 1921 in a full length book, *The Menace of Darwinism.*

Bryan delivered his last Chautauqua lecture in 1924. The next year came his fateful joust with Clarence Darrow.

Bryan was an old man when he went north from Florida, where he had taken up residence, to defend religious fundamentalism in the little court-house at Dayton, Tennessee.

Tennessee's wool-hat legislature, in March, 1925, had passed a law making it a crime for any instructor in a university or public school to teach "that man has descended from the lower order of animals." John Thomas Scopes taught biology in the Dayton high school. Urged on by half a dozen "free-thinking" friends, he decided to test the law. He did, and was promptly arrested.

An enterprising Knoxville correspondent put the story on the press wire and the nation came to fascinated attention. The American Civil Liberties Union took up the challenge and brilliant, agnostic, liberal lawyer Clarence Darrow of Chicago was employed to defend the country schoolteacher.

"A man with an old face, always old," Poet Edgar Lee Masters had said of Darrow. "I make it a rule to expect the worst," Darrow once had said of himself.

Bryan, thrice candidate for President, the greatest orator of his era, went into the Tennessee hills, not to defend fundamentalism in itself, but the right of a state to be fundamentalist, if it so wished. The legal battle was unequal. Bryan was sixty-five and had not practised law for years. Darrow, three years older, came from a series of courtroom victories. Recently he had kept the two young Chicago "thrill-killers," Leopold and Loeb, from the electric chair. Champion of lost causes and lost souls, he had been the defender in the courtroom of Radical Big Bill Haywood. As attorney for the McNamara brothers, indicted for the dynamiting of the Los Angeles *Times* building, he, together with Lincoln Steffens, persuaded the brothers to change their plea from "not guilty" to "guilty" on the understanding that they would escape a capital sentence. One brother got a life sentence, the other fifteen years.

The paths of Bryan and Darrow often had crossed. They had differed but sometimes they had agreed. On many a moral issue they could see eye to eye. Darrow it was who said, "The truth is, no man is white and no man is black. We all are freckled." Bryan might have said that.

The Scopes trial rose to a crescendo. Darrow, witty, sharp, merciless, mocked Bryan's fundamentalism. Reporters wrote millions of words and those Americans who were too young to have heard *The Cross of Gold,* read what Bryan was maneuvered into saying and thought him out of his mind. But Evangelist Amie Semple McPherson at her Four Square Gospel Shrine in Los Angeles, without Bryan's knowledge, offered public prayers for his success. So did the Reverend Billy Sunday, Bryan's fellow worker at Winona Lake Assembly.

The judge, taking the matter out of the jury's hands, found Scopes guilty and fined him one hundred dollars; the defendant's case was being prepared for an appeal to the state supreme court.

Ill and bewildered, Bryan was not satisfied. He had won the verdict.

But it was not a victory. Before the trial ended, he had prepared a new speech, which concluded with the line, "Faith of our Fathers, Living Still." A court ruling prevented him from delivering it, and he had said:

"I will take it to the people on the road." Of course, he meant the Chautauqua road. But he did not. His last public utterance was a prayer, next day, at church services in Dayton and his last trip on the road was in a funeral coach back to Washington, D.C., in a dramatic journey reminiscent of Lincoln's last journey back to Springfield.

It has been said that Bryan was a mere shell of his old self by the time he reached Tennessee, that Chautauqua had drained him, that adulation from a noncritical audience had sapped his intellect, that he was happier in Chautauqua tents than in Washington because he wanted to escape reality. Who knows?

"Eloquence," he said once in a speech, "is heart speaking to heart." If that is its definition, he had demonstrated it on the Chautauqua circuits. The ingredients of his success there had been simplicity, the devout religious turn of his thinking, a oneness with his audience, his championship of the toilers, the sweating masses, the little people, the poor, the exploited —these plus the Voice, the clear, flowing, golden quality of his voice that Mrs. Bryan, after his death, said she missed more than anything else.

Bryan was aware of the strength of that voice. He knew that he possessed the power, whenever he chose, to stampede an audience. I heard once on the circuits a story that Mrs. Bryan related later in their joint *Memoirs,* a book which he began and she completed. It was to the effect that in 1887, when he was twenty-seven years old, he had spoken at a political meeting in western Nebraska and, arriving home at daybreak, he came into her room and wakened her and told her uneasily:

"I have had a strange experience. Last night I found I had power over an audience. I could move them as I chose. I have more than usual power. God grant that I may use it wisely."

It Takes All Kinds . . .

15

As I look back across the long list of lecturers and entertainers, brilliant preachers, dedicated reformers, intrepid travellers, lame ducks, cranks, self-seekers, artists and first-class actors who hopped onto the Chautauqua band wagon, I can think of no one who gave the people more for their money than big, stogie-smoking, six-feet-four-inches-tall Opie Read.

The audience loved Read for his casual, lazy air, his humor, his homey philosophy, the charm of his manner, his shabby, baggy-pants simplicity. To begin with, he was a "personality," the famous author of several books, out of the public mind now, but in demand when Chautauqua flourished. His novel, *The Jucklins,* had led the bestseller list back in 1895, ranking even Stephen Crane's *The Red Badge of Courage. Old Lim Lucklin* followed ten years later, and on the platform Read told his own stories about that fictional philosopher. In 1902 his novel *Starbucks* had appeared. When I ventured out in 1912 with the gay Anita Company "pre-luding" Read, a pioneer Hollywood film company had just made a movie out of *Starbucks,* with Read himself playing the part of Jasper.

The Hollywood publicity added mightily to Read's prestige. Here was an honest-to-goodness movie actor on a lecture platform and he drew heavy single admissions. He had been born in Nashville, Tennessee, of Scotch-English descent—his father's aunt was Mrs. Benjamin Franklin—so in the south we billed him as "a true southern type," in the north as "America's favorite author." The name Opie intrigued many copy writers. It actually came from a distant ancestor, John Opie, the painter at the Court of George II, who when the King asked him, "With what do you mix your paints?" answered, "Sire, with brains." For that John Opie was knighted.

One reason the plain people liked Opie Read was that no one ever was plainer than Opie himself. He was home folks personified. When he walked down a half-empty street in run-over shoes, stogie in hand, wrinkled coat over an arm, an old cap on his head, he reminded town after town of its own country editor, who as a rule was a shabby iconoclast with a heart of gold, able to speak with authority on everything from Elizabethan prose to the condition of the local jail, everything from the Darwinian theory to what that gang of highbinders was doing at the moment in Washington.

Fresh from college, Read went to work for Dana of the New York *Sun* for the fabulous, for those days, wage of fifty dollars a week. He started with Redpath at the same fee; at the end he was drawing five hundred a week. He was on the lists of Central Lyceum Bureau in 1892 when I entered high school in Anita, Iowa. He still was climbing off local trains when the last Redpath Chautauqua tent went to the warehouse to stay. His forty years on the platform gave him a supreme nonchalance and the fact that he attacked important problems obliquely, lending humor even to serious subjects, endeared him to people who liked to laugh.

Small boys, admiring the baseball bats in a store window, might suddenly discover, the day after the Chautauqua folks left town, that a big, easy-going stranger, they never were sure of his name, had bought them a whole bunch of wonderful new bats. Naturally some performers picked him for an easy mark. "I never forget when *I* borrow," he would tell his friends, "but I never can remember who borrows from me."

In spite of hidden generosities, there was one field, however, where Read never tossed dollars or dimes over his shoulder, and that was clothes. His home was in Chicago in later years and between Chautauqua and Lyceum seasons one could find him taking solid ease at the Press Club, glass in hand, in the same shabby attire, often the same suit, that he had worn all the previous season in the day coaches and on the platform, and probably would wear all next season again. He thought luggage a bother and year after year he managed to get along with very little or none at all. His pockets were large enough to carry his razor and shaving soap, and a man of frugal bent could wash out his underwear and socks in the basin of his hotel room. There remained the matter of his shirt.

Stories of Read's shirts took the same earmarks of folklore as those about the crowds on "Bryan Day." In that era a good nifty white shirt could be bought for fifty cents and celluloid collar and cuffs lasted almost forever. So when Read had worn one shirt to the point of exhaustion, he simply bought a new one. The story goes that in one South Dakota town, arriving at noon for an afternoon performance, he looked at himself in a window on his walk from the station, and as a result he bought a new shirt, sought out a hotel and asked the clerk for a room, for five minutes, in which to change. Five minutes later he had dropped the soiled garment in a waste basket and, wearing the new, he went back to the desk with the room key.

Jingling a handful of coins, he asked how much he owed, half expecting to be told he owed nothing.

"One dollar," the clerk said without batting an eye. Opie batted his. He demanded to know the price again. "One dollar," the clerk repeated.

Opie slowly counted out the amount in nickels and dimes. "Thank God I didn't change my underwear, too," he said.

Science lecturer Hilton Ira Jones, who travelled frequently with Read, reported that the author carried a little black book with his Chautauqua dates in it, and one day Jones, looking over his shoulder, read the letters "CS" opposite certain dates.

"What does 'CS' mean?" Jones asked.

Read answered, "Oh, my wife's fussy. 'CS' means 'clean shirt.' She's reminding me those are the days to put one on."

Even so, Read often forgot, and now and again an embarrassed superintendent, conscious of the niceties of life, might feel the need of mentioning it to him. Sam Blackwood, managing the Redpath show once at Battle Creek, Michigan, felt so compelled one day and began, reluctantly, "Mr. Read, your . . . ah . . . shirt . . ."

"What's the matter with it?" Read demanded, unabashed.

"Well, it's just plain dirty," Blackwood said.

Read looked down his expansive front. "It's all right," he said. "I come clean from Chicago."

If laundry was never a serious problem to Read, it was to most talent. Once a bundle got behind, it never caught up. William Weatherwax, of the Weatherwax Quartet, tells how his brothers and he, finding themselves with spare time once in Wilkes-Barre, Pennsylvania, rushed their stiff-bosomed dress shirts to a laundry, after a promise of one-day delivery. But the shirts were not ready at departure time. Next season the quartet registered at the same hotel in Wilkes-Barre. Looking at the famous Weatherwax name, the clerk turned to the rack and pulled out a dusty bundle. It was the shirts, waiting a year.

In the Chautauqua tents Read's most popular lecture probably was his *Human Nature and Politics.* We could book him anywhere in the United States and be sure of a warm welcome except in Arkansas. He had edited a newspaper in that state as a younger man, later a humorous weekly called the *Arkansas Traveler.* Arkansas did not object to the *Traveler,* but it believed that Read also was the wicked author of *A Slow Train Through Arkansas,* a "comic" book with a wide sale in cigar stores, full of earthy humor not at all complimentary toward the "Wonder State." The book was signed by Sam T. Jackson but that made no difference to the people of Arkansas. They blamed it on Opie Read. Read lived to be eighty-six. When he died, his old travelling companion, the Reverend Preston Bradley of Chicago, respecting Opie's jocular attitude when dealing with serious subjects, preached a humorous funeral sermon.

We billed Read as a "lecturer." If one left the mother, home and heaveners in a class by themselves, only a narrow, sometimes imperceptible, line separated the "lecturer" from the "entertainer."

John T. McCutcheon, brother of Novelist George Barr McCutcheon and friend of George Ade and Booth Tarkington, had been sharing his genial humor with Chautauqua audiences since the days of the Slayton Bureau. His amusing cartoons on the foibles of bespectacled, loquacious "Congressman Pumphrey, the People's Friend," laying down the law in ankle-length coat and jack boots, had come out in book form, and in 1912 he used it as program material. He chose, as usual, to be a "lecturer," although George E. Colby, then of Victor Lawson's Chicago *Daily News,* was booked as a cartoonist. I always had a suspicion that the humorist thought the word "lecturer" was more dignified. After all, the humorous clan once had been relegated to the razzle-dazzle "opera house," while the lecturer was honored in the formal auditorium.

Cartoonist Colby for a long period was our staff artist in Chicago. It was he who drew the "inspiring" cartoons that the alert publicity department flooded out to country editors in Chautauqua towns as the season approached. His stalwart "Redpath sower" dropped precious seeds across the land, to sprout miraculously into haystacks of "charity," "high ideals," "morality," "patriotism," "civic consciousness," "honesty."

On the platform Colby was a lively entertainer. In one program, entitled *Curiosity Shop,* he would ask "the prettiest girl in town" to come up to the stage and have her picture drawn. When none was so bold, he invited "the handsomest man." A man did pose always, undoubtedly by prearrangement, and Colby drew him carefully, but when he whisked the sketch upside down, it was a picture of a beautiful young lady. This stunt of drawing upside down was old but always popular; back in 1904 in Iowa Falls, Ash Davis had brought down the house with his similar portrayal of *The Statue of Liberty*. Even the great Richard F. Outcault, unsuspecting parent of the modern comic strip, who appeared with Buster Brown and Tige and the Yellow Kid in the early 1900's for $200 a night, now and again had used the same device.

Tall, lanky Alton Packard was our top cartoonist. The less elegant word "chalk-talker" had long since gone into the dust pan. Packard had joined the parent Redpath bureau in 1895, and he, too, stayed with it the rest of his busy life, a good cartoonist because he was primarily a humorist. It was Packard who spotted the brewery near Jamestown, on Lake Chautauqua, New York, with its sign, "Drink Chautauqua Beer." Alert for similar travesties, he discovered the "Redpath Saloon" in Chicago. He was so popular that some seasons, in 1915 for instance, on Redpath-Ohio, ninety percent of his towns were "repeats," a few of them for the fifth or sixth time.

For sketching, Packard used a board eight feet square that the most nearsighted fellow in the farthest corner of the tent could see. On it he swiftly created *Funny People,* one of whom might turn out to be the red-headed village drayman who had hauled his trunk that morning or the pompous local banker, so lifelike that everyone in the crowd could recognize him and laugh. Or, with the world approaching the First War, he might close with a discomfited little Mars, impaled on the point of an over-sized pen, with the words hopefully chalked, "The pen is really mightier than the sword." Or if it were Sunday, he might give his conception of Jonah in the whale, Noah on the ark. He had many imitators. One ambidextrous fellow from Illinois went out for a small company one summer claiming in his advertisement that he could "draw with both hands."

Lorado Taft, sculptor on the staff of the Chicago Art Institute, presented a lecture on art over all Redpath circuits intermittently for twenty-five years. Not a "popular" performer in any sense, he attracted consistently good crowds. By 1925, at the peak of his career, when his statue of Black-hawk was standing at Oregon, Illinois, and his Columbus Memorial Fountain in Washington, D.C., we were paying him $250 an engagement, which was above average for that type of program. Taft carried half a ton of paraphernalia and with the help of one assistant, demonstrated the "how" of sculpturing, first on paper on his easel, then with a chunk of damp clay. Asked once why he abandoned the comfort of his studio for the exertion of the hot tents, Taft is quoted as saying, "Ah, but in the hinterlands I might discover a great sculptor." Musicians on the circuits had similar hopes, and sometimes realized them.

Another craftsman laden with heavy luggage, not of the Taft calibre but a strong box-office attraction, was J. Smith Damron. In a muddy apron, Damron brought his potter's wheel and clay to the stage in a "demonstrated lecture" of moralistic tone, called *The Potter and the Clay.* Ross (short for Charles Edgar Rosecrans) Crane, who later travelled with a successful lecture on house decoration, also started out as a humorist and cartoonist. We supplied for Crane's act a piano, a kitchen table, an easel, crayons, clay and strong lights on the stage, and with this assortment he devised a satire on mankind that he mysteriously called *Strawberries and Prunes,* another extravagant title which seemed to sell tickets. Another artist, dating back to Slayton-Redpath days, was Miss Evelyn Bargelt, who combined cartooning with reading and music in the Bargelt Concert Company. It was Miss Bargelt's discarded sheets of drawing paper that a skeptic in one audience insisted on being allowed to examine. He explained that since he knew nobody could draw like that "off-hand," he suspected it was some kind of magic paper "that when you rubbed it, a picture came out."

All too frequently from companies on the road a superintendent would write the home office wearily reporting that this or that musician had shown "temperament": the piano had been at the wrong angle, the lights too bright or too dim, a train had whistled at the wrong moment, the tent was pitched, certainly by design, right next to a boiler factory, and if annoyances like this did not stop, Miss Blank would quit and return to the peace of Chicago. She seldom did, and one did not need to show too much concern about it—except on one occasion when, to prevent a famous star from quitting on the spot, we hurriedly amended a contract to include a clause about a cow.

In Chautauqua's earlier days a friendly red and white bossy might frequently turn up at the door of a tent, curious about all the commotion in her pasture, and no one thought much about it. But circuits were already in their prime when a frantic telegram came from Soprano Alice Nielson, who had performed the night before in LaFollette, Tennessee.

She wanted it thoroughly understood that she never—repeat, never—would sing another note unless Redpath guaranteed to protect her everywhere from what she chose to call "those creatures." Startled, we seized a telephone.

The superintendent, when we reached him, still was badly shaken. He explained that, arriving in the Tennessee town, he had found a pleasant, grassy meadow for the Chautauqua grounds, set up his tent conveniently only a step from a brick sidewalk. The weather was fair, the local committee reasonably cooperative, the audience seemed to enjoy the programs. Then, on the seventh and last morning, great activity began in the field behind the tent. Investigating, the superintendent discovered that the committee had forgotten to tell him that the Russell Brothers Stock Company, scheduled to open in the same field the day after Chautauqua left, dealt not in actors but in livestock, and that fine, high-priced, blooded cattle would begin to arrive twenty-four hours early and would be stabled only fifty yards from the stage.

Even so, all went well during the afternoon performance. All started well in the evening, until Miss Nielson, full of rich harmony, struck her first high note. Then, as with the dogs and Kryl's band, all went wrong. Over in the cattle pens the soprano's voice did something to the cows' ears. They protested in a mighty bellow. The second high note brought an even louder complaint, followed by long unhappy moo-oos. The quiet evening turned into bedlam and the soprano into a wildcat. Only the disrespectful younger generation got any real pleasure out of the bovine chorus.

Such was temperament, and unfortunately it did not always belong to a musician. Frequently the complaints to the home office came from Headliner Strickland Gillilan, whose serious, almost scowling face gave no hint to the world of his profession as a humorist. To all appearances, Gillilan was the unhappiest man in the world. On the platform he made a pretense at awkwardness, a device common at the time. He built his title, *Sunshine and Awkwardness,* around this pretense. But he added an ingredient all his own. He had a firm conviction, unique to himself, that insulting an audience also paid off. So he added insult to awkwardness. Perhaps he was right, for some charmed reason in his case, since he was a steady drawing card until his retirement from the platform. He died in Washington, D.C. in 1954.

Gillilan, shuffling out gawkily with his hands in his pockets, would open with the statement, "Don't expect oratory from me, ladies and gentlemen," and then as likely as not he might add, "I spent a week in this town one night last year."

The remark had no good humor in it, at least none that an anxious superintendent could see—unlike the famous one by Bill Nye years before: Nye peeped out from backstage before the performance began in an auditorium in Toledo and whispered to his companions, southern Novelist George Washington Cable and Poet Eugene Field, "You sure we've never been here before? We must have been. There's no one in the audience."

Bill (Edgar Wilson) Nye, lawyer-turned-humorist, had been one of the early attractions on the Redpath Lyceum lists. As a young man in Laramie, Wyoming, he had served simultaneously as justice of the peace, postmaster, city councilman and school superintendent, with time to spare for a sketchy practice of law. His letter of resignation as postmaster in Laramie is still a classic of this type of humor. Mark Twain could not have bettered it:

> Post Office Divan
> Laramie City, W.T.
> Oct. 1, 1883

To the President of the United States:

Sir: I beg leave at this time to officially tender my resignation as postmaster of this place, and in due form to deliver the great seal and key to the front door of this office. The safe combination is set on the numbers 33, 66, and 99, though I do not remember at this moment which comes first, or how many times you revolve the knob, or which direction you turn it at first in order to make it operate . . .

You will find the postal cards that have not been used under the distributing table, and the coal down in the cellar. If the stove draws too hard, close the damper in the pipe and shut the general delivery window . . .

Acting under the advice of General Hatton, a year ago, I removed the featherbed with which my predecessor, Deacon Hayford, had bolstered up his administration by stuffing the window, and substituted glass. Finding nothing in the book of instructions which made the featherbed a part of my official duties, I filed it away in an obscure place and burned it in effigy, also in the gloaming . . .

I need not say that I herewith transmit my resignation with great sorrow and genuine regret. We have toiled together month after month, asking no reward except the innate consciousness of rectitude and the salary fixed by law. Now we are to separate. Here the roads seem to fork, as it were, and you and I, and the cabinet, must leave each other . . .

You will find the key under the door-mat and you had better turn the cat out at night when you close the office. If she does not go readily, you can make it clearer to her mind by throwing the canceling stamp at her. If Deacon Hayford does not pay his box rent, you might as well put his mail in the general delivery, and when Bob Head gets drunk and insists on a letter from one of his wives every day in the week, you can salute him through the box delivery with an Old Queen Anne tomahawk, which you will find near the Etruscan water pail . . .

Mr. President, as an official of this government, I now retire . . .

Bill Nye

The characters Nye met in his varied capacities and the ridiculous situations he encountered, served as a reservoir for later platform talks. He was a cracker-barrel philosopher, a pioneer in the Will Rogers tradition, his humor as dry as Wyoming's arid plains. The permanent Chautauqua assemblies could count on him for a gay afternoon or evening of down-to-earth, clean fun. He ad-libbed as the spirit moved him or read from his amusing *Forty Liars and Other Lies,* or from his comic histories, published under the heroic titles, *Bill Nye's History of England from the Druids to the Reign of Henry the Eighth,* and *Bill Nye's History of the United States.*

In 1885 Nye teamed up with James Whitcomb Riley and they toured the nation in a happy alcoholic haze, taking turns reading from their works on the same program. This gave each of them a splendid opportunity, when the other was in public view, to slip into the dressing room for an inspirational nip. As the pair grew louder and funnier, everyone was delighted except the platform manager, who was frantically attempting to reach the end of the program without the audience suspecting the awful truth. Nye's more sober companion was onetime Chicago schoolteacher A. P. Burbank, who supplied pathos and restraint to balance Nye's absurdities.

Following this rollicking trip, Riley and Nye collaborated on the *Nye and Riley Railroad Guide,* a humorous travel book that had a fine sale. However, the pair was not teamed for a second season. The risk was too great.

In manners on the stage, Nye and Strickland Gillilan were miles apart. Temperamental Gillilan wanted short introductions, for which no one could blame him. He also wanted no musical prelude to detract from his own

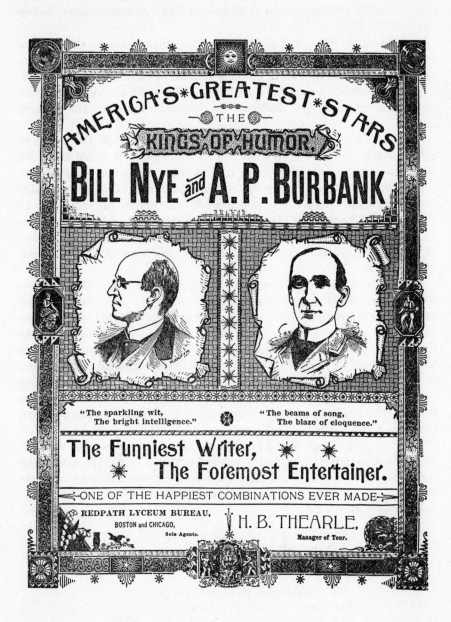

appearance, and by no means any interruption after he once started talking. A small-town preacher, who waxed eloquent in introducing the day's speaker, and went on and on while the irritated Gillilan waited, came down to earth abruptly, when Gillilan broke in, "Just a moment, before you go."

Women often brought their knitting when they came to Chautauqua tents. Gillilan considered it a rude habit and twice in the 1912 season he vented his irritation over it. In Sterling, Illinois, in the midst of his lecture, he paused, looked around at the clicking needles and remarked sourly that all good alienists agreed that knitting prevented insanity. The clicking stopped.

"So while it is highly discourteous of you to knit while I'm trying to entertain you," he added, "it's not half so annoying as it would be if you all went suddenly insane here in the tent. Go right on knitting! Knit!"

His second outburst came on the "mother" platform at Chautauqua Lake. A type of embroidery called punch work was abroad in the land. As Gillilan stepped out on the big stage he caught sight of the workaday needles and paused, frowning, while he tried to count them. Then he said acidly, "Ladies and gentlemen, and those others of you who have your punch work with you . . ."

Gillilan's recitation of his own poem, *Off Agin, On Agin, Gone Agin—Finnigin,* was a high point in a program. In 1897, a free and easy time when obscure reporters wrote, and their newspapers printed, wit and humor and anything else that came into their daffy heads, Gillilan was working for the Richmond, Indiana, *Palladium*. One dull spring morning when he needed copy, he heard that a freight car had been derailed on the Grand Rapids and Indiana Railroad, north of town. There had been an amusing exchange of messages between a section boss and the division superintendent. The latter, it seemed, thought that the garrulous section boss sent too long reports.

Gillilan had space to fill and he filled it with a bright piece of journalistic embroidery of a type that had a vogue for many years. He named the superintendent Flannigan and the section boss Finnigin and told in rhyme how Flannigan ordered Finnigin to "keep 'em brief."

Finnigin replied:

> "From Finnigin to Flannigan
> "Reports wont be long agin."

Then came the narrative of the derailment, with this conclusion:

> "He wuz shantyin' thin, wuz Finnigin,
> "As minny a railroader's been agin,
> "An' the shmoky ol' lamp wuz burnin' bright
> "In Finnigin's shanty all that night.
> "Bilin' down his report, wuz Finnigin!
> "An' he writed this here: 'Muster Flannigan:
> " 'Off agin, on agin,
> " 'Gone agin.—Finnigin.' "

After Gillilan's verse on *The Antiquity of Microbes* appeared in the *Palladium,* with its two lines:

> "Adam
> "Had 'em,"

an Indiana editor called him a "successor to Mark Twain" and Redpath quickly adopted the phrase in its advertising. Congressman Adam Bede, incidentally, wrote a second verse to Gillilan's poem:

> "Modern Adam
> "Had 'em, too."

Gillilan's own line in the Lyceum trade journal simply said, "Voice enough for anywhere. Talks Sunday." His contracts were never easy to handle. Vawter, asking Gillilan once what he would be worth the next year, was told in reply: "I can't afford to work for what I'm worth. If I can't get two or three times what I'm worth, I'll stay home."

In *Sunshine and Awkwardness,* Gillilan traced the history of humor, sorting it into "stupid" with sardonic examples, "rustic," "affectionate," "feminine" and "the humor of surprise." One of his stories in verse that people still remember he called *The Bicycle Race with the Train.* A boy kissed his girl good-bye as the train pulled out, then raced on his bicycle to the next stop and "got two kisses instead of one." Sometimes the people at Fencepost Corners didn't think this story very funny, but one man at least was sure to applaud. Gillilan would then step forward, bow awkwardly to that particular man, and say soberly, "Thank you, thank you,"—pause— "and thank the lady with you." For some mysterious reason this always brought a laugh, whether the original remarks had or not. People laughed, too, at his story about his little dog August, that got run over by a dray. The next day was the first of September, because that was the last of August.

Undoubtedly the brand of fun these humorists dispensed would not seem very funny today. What one now calls "sophistication" was not their forte. Their humor was whimsical or droll, never cynical. Satire would have withered and died quickly on the soil in which we planted our tents. Nor were most audiences of the period amused at slapstick, though that form of humor, as old as the Italian harlequins, was waiting at the entertainment door ready to re-enter. Only a year after Gillilan's outburst at knitting, Mack Sennett was to introduce burlesque satire in his Keystone comedies.

Chautauqua speakers with any ambition to achieve a reputation for wit cast their eyes enviously on Jehu DeWitt Miller. Miller was a walking encyclopedia, an enthusiast who spent every spare moment buying, devouring and digesting books. The big roll in which he presumably carried his clothes was actually filled with books, magazines, books and more books, treasures he had discovered on the current trip and would store somewhere before

his next. From his Philadelphia post-office box a friend sent the week's
newspapers and magazines regularly by express to whatever town Miller
happened to be hanging his hat in at the moment. Another lecturer, running
into him one Sunday at Enid, Oklahoma, found in the week's consignment
of mail a literary miscellany: the *Boston Transcript,* the *London Times,*
and from France the *Paris Figaro* and *Le Temps.*

Miller was unwed, a state of bliss that induced him to deliver with
breezy assurance his *Reveries of a Bachelor,* or to talk authoritatively on
Love, Courtship and Matrimony. He usually scheduled thirty Chautauqua
addresses each summer; tight Lyceum dates packed his winters. He was an
entertainer of the highest order, dispensing epigram and delicate wit with
a spontaneity that caused run-of-the-mill lecturers to groan with envy. He
reached fame as a fairly young man. His mates, admiring his great handsome head, his whitish sideburns, used to call him with great affection "old
Jehu Miller." He died en route to the west coast for three weeks' Chautauqua dates in the summer of 1913. He was a little like Opie Read. Leon
Vincent, a relative of Bishop Vincent, writing of Jehu once in the *Atlantic
Monthly,* described his clothes as being always of "the best cloth and the
finest tailoring, but within a few weeks he had lived in them so violently
that they were shapeless as a sack of coal. He did not wear clothes: he dwelt
at large in them."

A man who, like Miller, entertained with a gentler touch than Strickland
Gillilan, and who rivalled Ralph Bingham as a master of ceremonies, was
good-natured Jess Pugh. Here you had an example of that gifted race of
men whose love of acting will let them tolerate no other gods. Pugh, who
still lives in Chicago, was thirty years old, married, with one child, and for
thirteen years had worked in a Rushville, Indiana, bank when his urge to
go on the stage caused him to toss security overboard, and in 1910 sign
with Redpath-Vawter as a baritone and dramatic reader. He travelled first
with other companies, the Riner Sisters originally, but his personal success was so pronounced that he soon carried a program alone.

As a reader Pugh went out first with Scotch stories and cuttings from
Kipling, using members of his company for diverting stunts. In one Jess
Pugh Novelty Company act, for instance, an actor-musician used the
bow of the violin, another did the fingering, while both played the con-
certina. Just before World War I his assistant was Pietro Verdo, an agile
fellow who could play the accordion with his hands and with one foot
accompany it on the drum.

Being Indiana-born, Pugh's "hawg-calling act" in the *Homecoming of
Elmer Warts, Champion Indiana Hog Caller,* was a natural for him. The
piece, a satire on a home-town welcome for an athlete, was his first great
success. Another famous offering was his "sneeze piece," in which as Ralph
Bingham did earlier in *Brother Jones' Sermon,* Pugh figured that an un-
timely sneeze, like a man slipping on a banana peel, for some reason can

be very funny; at least lighthearted people at the start of the twentieth century so considered it.

Pugh built this sneezing act around a recitation about a horse race by a young elocutionist who had the habit of playing with a handkerchief while speaking. On this occasion the handkerchief held snuff and as the race began, so did the sneezing, until on the home stretch the disturbing convulsions were so continuous and the race so close that the shouting audience could only hope that both sneezer and horse would survive.

Once in Kansas, when Pugh let out the first sneeze, a boy's dog in the front row barked, at the second sneeze it barked again; at the third, it leaped up over the footlights and Pugh, not wanting his good white pants sacrificed, warily called off the contest while crew boys called off the dog. A dog, wandering into a tent, could be as great a menace as a herd of cows outside. Gillilan, after trying one day to go on with his speech while a dog sniffed at his legs, finally said to the audience:

"He seems a nice dog, probably comes from one of your best families, but he and I have had no rehearsals together. He doesn't know what I'm going to do next, and it keeps us both a little nervous. One of us is likely to do something any moment to offend the other."

An entertainer with a successful act, like the lecturer with one speech, always had the problem of knowing how many summers to persist with it before the audience lost interest. Once on Redpath-Vawter, when Jess Pugh decided that he needed new material for "closing the show" on a high note, he burlesqued the performers of the preceding week. Juggler, ventriloquist, banjo player, home-and-heavener, opera singer, all came in for clever but not barbed spoofing.

Pugh was a successful trouper because, like the Military Girls, he was adaptable. His first dress suit was second hand. It fitted him poorly, its tails were too long, people smiled, but Pugh wore it until he could afford another. When the mountaineers in Milton, West Virginia, laughed hard at the high-toned knickerbockers this city guy wore on the street, he retreated to his hotel and took them off and wisely refrained from wearing knickers again on the road. When the bugs around the sputtering flares in a windy tent at Middleboro, Ohio, got so thick that he couldn't keep them out of his mouth, he just swallowed them and continued his act. After the tents were down, Pugh turned to radio and for many years successfully played the title role in Clarence Buddington Kelland's *Scattergood Bains*.

Even the humorists managed to insert "new" facts and "know-how" into their material. Audiences of those years expected it. This curiosity was almost as deep a characteristic as the desire to laugh. It harked back again to the circumstance that a footloose generation, having moved west to the Mississippi river and beyond, felt with considerable mortification that they had left culture with their relatives in the east. They liked to be entertained but they also welcomed "instructive" programs. Doctors, scientists, inventors began gradually to draw as responsive an audience as did the Reads and Gillilans, and their lectures became more and more frequent on the circuits, particularly for afternoon programs.

Glenn Frank, while he was editor of *Century Magazine,* wrote, "The four most interesting men I know are H. G. Wells, Lincoln Steffens, James Harvey Robinson and Albert Edward Wiggam. Wells writes sentences that suggest a hundred times more than they say . . . Steffens is blessed with an almost divine sympathy . . . Robinson is that rarest of persons, a radiant cynic . . . Wiggam's peculiar value to American life is that he knows how to come out on the steps of the laboratory and tell us, who are waiting in the crowd outside, just what the scientists are doing inside."

Wiggam, another Hoosier with a gifted tongue, first discovered that he could speak in 1896 when, aroused against free silver, he campaigned as a "gold democrat." He was already lecturing on heredity and eugenics when I booked Jacob Riis in South Dakota. "He had a happy way of talking science, a sort of cross between Einstein and Billy Sunday," Frank described him further. All audiences found Wiggam's laboratory tales exciting, scholars found his *Decalogue of Science* important. It and *The Fruit of the Family Tree* were published in the early 1920's, two best-selling books full of the kind of wit and knowledge that made communities ask over and over for us to send Wiggam again.

Among the first professional men who took to the road for the Redpath-Chicago circuit was Dr. Woods Hutchinson, a serious-minded, serious-looking physician, who like "Dinner Pail" McNutt lectured on food. In the same period were the two Doctors Sadler, apostles in new dress of the old theme of individual improvement. Dr. William Sadler was a psychiatrist. Fortunately for Chautauqua, he respected the germ theory as much as he did Freud; it was he who, after one startling experience with the "Chautauqua salute," drove it out of business. His wife, Dr. Lena, was a Chicago gynecologist who had successfully beaten down the prejudice against women doctors. She was an active clubwoman, too, and the pair made a very presentable team.[1]

Taking a registered nurse with them, the couple offered a choice of one-to three-day programs, with the further innovation of a medical round table. Dr. William discussed worry and self-mastery, which to the folks in front meant the old, inspiring refrain, "How to Be Happy." Dr. Lena talked about the care of children and mothers.

This theme of individual improvement, played with a loud pedal for so many years, led naturally into the idea of community improvement. Almost overnight "Be a better man" yielded to "Make a better city." A young

[1] Other women doctors appearing at about this time included Katherine B. Davis, New York's Commissioner of Corrections, Dr. Lydia De Vilbiss of the Kansas Board of Health, and Dr. Carolyn Geisel, whom the Coit-Alber circuit billed in 1916 as "the apostle of health."

Des Moines, Iowa, advertising man, Ben R. Vardaman, was responsible for "Business and Community Betterment Day," which took its place among Chautauqua's special "days." Its purpose was to keep boys "down on the farm" or in the home town, and farming states were bound to appreciate such an idea. In Valley City, North Dakota, one July, eleven bands met Vardaman as he stepped off the train.

Schools, parks, jails, sewers, all came in for censure from a host of civic reformers like Allen Albert, Henry M. Hyde, or Frank Dixon still limping across the platform.

"If a fly comes to town," Dixon thundered, "close the schools, sound the fire alarm and do nothing else till you kill it!"

Hyde, of the Chicago *Tribune* staff, talking in 1916 on *Wholesale Manufacture of Criminals,* charged that the animals in his city's Lincoln Park Zoo "have better cells, better air, light and food, than the prisoners in your police station." To prove it he produced pictures of contented lions sleeping in the zoo and a dozen unhappy, dishevelled men, piled together in one cell, *not* sleeping.

Allen Albert, a sociologist and lawyer, once the head of Rotary International, usually created a local furor that eventually resulted in reform. He called his speech *The Forces that Make Cities.* Getting to a town ahead of time, he would nose about until he discovered a situation needing correction. It must have dramatic possibilities, of course, as in the city where he told an overflow crowd that he had examined their public school buildings "and all but seven of them are fireproof." Then he added, "And you have only seven schools." Every one was a firetrap. Who knew which would burst into flames tomorrow and snuff out precious young lives?

Reform groups everywhere were happy to pay Albert's price, confident that after his shocking disclosures outraged citizens would storm their town halls. In one South Carolina city, where Albert had discussed sewers and water supply, the talk had a realistic aftermath. He had predicted an outbreak of typhoid fever. City officials pooh-poohed the idea. So when three weeks after Allen's visit, an epidemic did break out, residents charged that he had polluted the water just to make his predictions come true.

An even livelier speech that swelled to sensational proportions was Ralph Parlette's *University of Hard Knocks,* with its jar of beans. Parlette, a striking fellow with big white teeth and a broad smile, who solved the laundry problem by wearing a black silk shirt which he washed out at night, used Gillilan's trick of feigning awkwardness. He also succumbed to long, alliterative titles: *Dollars and Destiny, Pockets and Paradises, Hurrahs and Heroes, Swat the Snake and Cooperate,* "all adapted for Sunday or weekday, pulpit or stage." But his masterpiece was *The University of Hard Knocks.*

Parlette offered it first as a story with a moral for children. He ended it four thousand times later for business executives, who had hired him, beans, black shirt and all, away from Chautauqua. His theme was not startlingly original: "It's all up to the man. He comes to the top or lands at the bottom, depending only on himself." But to illustrate it, Parlette produced a big jar of navy beans and unshelled walnuts, "the jar of life," with the beans and nuts representing the people. When, grinning, he shook the jar, the little beans naturally sank to the bottom, the big walnuts stayed at the top and children laughed and youths pondered.

This business of demonstrating on the stage grew phenomenally. Sometimes the showman brought a trunkful of gadgets so wildly impractical that they could fascinate as well as amuse. Or other times, as T. Baird Collins did with his airplane on a wire back in 1904, a smart exhibitor turned up with some daring prevue of the future.

About 1911 the newly formed airmail division of the United States Post Office authorized "aerial postmasters." These were local pilots hired to carry mail on a volunteer basis between nearby towns. Appointed in Chicago was a handsome, white-haired electrical engineer named Montraville Wood who had a gyroscope on his mail plane. It was only to be expected that, since any innovation paid off on the stage, before long Wood should bring his gyroscope to Chautauqua.

The apparatus measured about two feet wide, weighed twenty-eight pounds, revolved like a maniac on the loose and could quickly get the best of any bold spirit who accepted Wood's challenge to mount the stage and wrestle with it. Watching the contraption rise bodily, get up on its feet and turn around, many people thought it not only spectacular but perhaps a bit supernatural. They also believed that Wood's prophecy, made in 1912, that "some time in the future mail will be carried by air over certain routes" was undoubtedly very much exaggerated and ducked in their seats when he ran a monorail car on a slack wire out over their heads, with the car kept in balance by the gyroscope.

With his daughter, Allene, as his assistant, Wood also demonstrated the new ultra-violet ray. Using the ray of light as a crayon, he wrote on the wall in letters that remained visible for twenty minutes for all unbelievers to see. Wood was not just a "freak" lecturer. He was a serious inventor of hundreds of devices, among them the torpedo with ears. The so-called "electrical" lecturer who followed him, forecasting "what miracles electricity will work for future generations," also had a long run in the tents, some of whose patrons still lighted kerosene lamps every night and washed smoky chimneys next morning. A few of these pseudo-scientists even set up generators on the stage.

As in the case of musicians, lecturers who wore a special garb appealed strongly to those stay-at-homes who did their travelling vicariously during Chautauqua week. Among these performers were the Raweis, a father-mother-son team from the Maori tribe of New Zealand, who offered ballads and stories in native dress. The elder Rawei found Americans a little disconcerting. He never could understand why women in half a dozen Kentucky towns objected violently to re-booking him. All he had done was to suggest that many social problems might be solved if all married women wore tattoos on their chins.

The handsome young Greek, Julius Caesar Nayphe, whom we had no trouble booking in this period, always wore costume. In fact, in one section of his program Nayphe appeared dressed in three sets of garments, one over the other, two of which—not three—he removed piece by piece, talking all the while.

"Audience participation" had not become an entertainment catchword, but by some means Nayphe had stumbled onto the idea that it would pay off. So he contrived a scene in which five young women of the town assisted in demonstrating an "Oriental betrothal." They had to be the town's beauties, of course, and rivalry for the parts stirred up good local interest. Platform superintendents had a hard time with Nayphe's name. No matter how long some of them practised, it might come out anywhere from "Navy" to "Nephew." They had a little excuse for thus garbling the name since it was Greek. The superintendent who introduced the Cheney Concert Company once as the Shyann Sisters had no such alibi.

As study of God's out-of-doors developed as a feature, birds became especially popular material. Charles G. Gorst, the "Boston Bird Man," who brought the Junior Audubon clubs into being partly as an attendance-luring device, not only could draw his feathered friends—he even whistled Mendelssohn's *Spring Song* "as a mockingbird would sing it if he had a musical education." His friend, Naturalist Ernest Harold Baynes, also twitted and chirped a bit in *My Wild Bird Guests,* but for the most part he talked, excitingly, about animals.

Baynes had captured and photographed and hand-fed all sorts. He thought skunks particularly amusing, and one of the stories he liked to tell concerned the day he was in a hurry to get a chair in his neighborhood barbershop and so he took a skunk in with him in his pocket. The startled customers fled as he anticipated, but to his surprise the barber did also. Baynes' sense of humor, peculiarly, did not extend to the time during a later season when he was directing *The Bird Masque* by Percy MacKaye. We carried some two hundred costumes of birds for local children of various ages to wear while participating in this fantasy, in which Percival Vivian, from the original Ben Greet Players, took the part of the fawn. Vivian recently had appeared as a cat in a New York play and for one performance, to the children's delight, he danced out in *The Bird Masque* wearing the cat costume instead of the fawn's. Only Baynes was not delighted.

Chautauqua had no elephants, to the regret of all small boys. But it did have magicians and the small boys were willing in every part of the country to tack quantities of posters on telephone poles in order to earn a free season ticket. They waved that ticket excitedly at the gate the day the handsome "practitioner of the art of mystery" appeared in his tall silk hat.

All magicians were the small boys' friends, even the baffling man at the morning show in Paducah, Kentucky, who disappointed his young admirers by whispering as he opened his program. He was sorry, he told them, but he really couldn't talk. He had "one lung congested." Next minute he changed near-tears to shouts of laughter, by demonstrating that he could bellow with "the other lung."

The pattern for the magician's trade had been established in Lyceum long before anyone dreamed of Chautauqua in tents. A proper magician must appear in full court dress, including short buckled pants and long silk hose, must wear a waxed, upturned mustache, know how to bow from the waist and adopt, for platform purposes, an outlandish accent that might possibly be Roumanian or Hindustani. Even with the accent, he must be able to rattle off at a mile a minute that fascinating phrase, "master of prestidigitation and legerdemain," even though everybody knew that in plain English it meant that he could pull a bunny out of a hat.

From the time of Maro, "Prince of Magic," both the permanent assemblies and the circuit tents had depended on versatile magicians. When "musical glasses" were new there had been "Professor" F. O. Harrell, and Hal Merton, who was also a ventriloquist. There was an adroit pair named Hendrickson and Rosani, "magicians and shadowgraphists," "whose program," we advertised, "can be presented before the most critical lady audience without offending the fastidious." There were Illusionist Loring Campbell, later of Burbank, California, and McDonald Birch, a lone wolf of good personality with a "variety show of magic."

Dr. Harlan Tarbell, a long-time Chicagoan, was so respected by his mates that his six-volume opus on the practice and history of magic became their Bible. A tense, nervous man on the platform, an artist of sorts, who sometimes drew his own illustrations, Tarbell was one of the first to elevate his magic show into a lecture. Among them all, their sleight of hand tricks and their illusions were practically identical. It was the personality of the talented wizard himself that made them seem different.

The two magicians booked by Redpath-Chicago for a considerable period from 1912 on were Edward Reno and suave, courteous Eugene Laurant, "the man of mysteries." Laurant, whose Lyceum engagements dated back to the horse-and-buggy McKinley days, by 1918 was setting a pace for breathless talent by going and coming, if the occasion demanded, in a chartered plane. His travelling van, decorated in large letters with the words, "Laurant and His Show of Wonders, Redpath Chautauqua," was good publicity for everybody.

So far as personal characteristics and type of show went, Laurant and Reno were so dissimilar that both could appear on the same circuit, the same season, without any dissatisfied customer wanting his money back.

Fastidious Laurant carried elaborate stage equipment and sometimes as many as five assistants, of whom oldster Gradolph was the best known. Laurant, surprisingly, appealed to the elders more than to children.

Incredulous ears heard the battered old human skull that Laurant had just put down carefully on the table answer his questions smartly. Unbelieving eyes watched his phantom bride, one minute asleep on the couch, float away with the next breath into space, leaving only a glamorous veil as evidence that she ever had been there. Laurant opened his program often with a flower trick, not the one flower that other magicians used, but thirty-five of them. Another of his acts, an impersonation not a trick, he called *The Mystic Hat,* in which, by folding and refolding a felt hat brim into a dozen shapes, he presented as many different characters. He was a made-to-order personality for show business, as susceptible as others, incidentally, to romance on the road. Before the tents came down he too married a girl from his company.

Reno, whose wife, "Madame Reno," often appeared with him, was known in the profession as a "knockabout magician." Born in New York state, by the time he was thirteen he was in Africa performing tricks for the French soldiers. On our circuits, in contrast with Laurant, he carried very light paraphernalia. Friends among the talent used to say that all the equipment Reno actually needed was his fingertips, and unlike most magicians he did not take pains to protect them. If the tent were not up when Reno arrived at the Chautauqua grounds, he seized a sledge and helped the crew boys.

Reno carried a duck that waddled across the stage. "Call him 'Mister,' " he told the crowd, "he's very sensitive." The duck emerged, instead of a bunny, from Reno's hat. The hat, likewise contrary to custom, was not a silk stovepipe but a hard bowler or any old piece of headgear, loaned by a skeptic down in the audience. "Mister" Duck could also jump from a stew pan filled with fire; and to put out the fire, Reno drew bowls of water from a handkerchief that he had just shaken out from his pocket. His talented goose, "Jim," stepped as nimbly from the chafing dish in which Reno was cooking an omelet; flying about also on the stage, to take part in all the shenanigans, was a white cockatoo with a bad disposition.

After Reno left town, small boys tried for weeks to burn a feather in a piece of paper, rub the ashes and produce a dove. In Reno's clever hands the white dove, having emerged from the ashes, had swelled immediately into two doves that sailed into the top of the tent and lighted on the cross poles. Like Opie Read, Reno always made friends with the children in the towns, buying them new clothes and toys. One little girl, whom he called "Millie," he finally adopted. In starched white dress and big white hair ribbon, she later stood at his right hand on the platform, a clever and attractive assistant.

Reno did not insist on a paid audience. He carried a bag of tricks up Main Street in a hundred towns; the only pay he asked was the astonishment of a single citizen. Companies travelling with him tell how, in a dining car, when the waiter offered the biscuits, Reno would pull a fifty cent piece from the first one he opened. To the bug-eyed waiter's confusion, Reno demanded a fresh supply and from the first of these, pulled another coin. He next would ask for an extra knife. It turned immediately into a spoon and, reproachfully, Reno would reach into the fellow's white jacket and pull out the knife. After that he got a new waiter; the first always refused to return to the magician's table.

Before the days of the travelling tents, Reno crisscrossed the country as an itinerant performer. On one of these jaunts through Utah he stumbled into a fracas among the Utes. He was journeying with a pack burro north of Provo, along the northeast shore of Utah Lake, when, between the hamlets of American Fork and Pleasant Grove, he walked unexpectedly into a war council. Both sides were surprised, Indians and magician, but Reno, thinking quickly, went into his act. Rocks disappeared. He swallowed a knife that turned up immediately in an Indian's clothing. He tossed eggs into the air and found them, unbroken, in the braves' blankets. Finally, in a pistol shooting orgie, he caught a bullet in his teeth, and swallowing his pistol, discovered it in the chief's moccasin. The impressed Indians gave him safe escort.

In his days with Redpath-Chicago, Reno frequently displayed the same ingenuity. Once, late in the 1914 season, on the five-day circuit, to get to a town in time for an afternoon performance, he found it necessary to take an electric train that had a baggage compartment, but also a regulation against transporting trunks. Reno naturally had to take his trunk; if no trunk, no show. Investigating, he discovered that the interurban line did accept coffins, so he rented a coffin, packed his equipment in it, presented himself as a relative of the deceased and accompanied the coffin to the door of the tent.

The story reminds me of the time Impersonator Gay MacLaren, missing the only train for a date in Kansas, rode the intervening ten miles in a hearse. An undertaker had brought a coffin to the train she missed. The hearse would be empty going back. So she asked for a ride. After the Reno incident, I had a letter from a fellow manager. He thought Reno had disgraced the profession. I disagreed. I thought that Miss MacLaren and Reno each deserved a bonus for getting to their programs on time.

The Play's the Thing

16

The Chautauqua business like the human race was a welter of inconsistencies. But it was always consistent in one respect. It stayed decent. Those responsible managed to keep its humor clean, no matter how soiled the costumes or tents at the end of a muddy season. But decency and cleanliness were not enough to satisfy some strait-laced citizens in many towns around the circuits. People there were, in numbers, who had built-in prejudices against certain forms and methods of entertainment, against certain types of performer, which had nothing to do with delicacy, modesty, honesty, decorum or virtue. The more hidebound their concepts of morality, the more vehemently these censors tried to force them on their neighbors.

So the architects who built a summer Chautauqua program with a proper balance of humor and pathos, adventure and inspiration, music and the spoken word, steered a difficult course among the shoals of prejudice. The people wanted a good show, a fresh approach, but their delicate sensibilities must not be offended, no matter how unreasonable those sensibilities were.

Nowhere was this inconsistency more evident than in the attitude toward the theatre and all its works. Many people wanted the thrill of drama, the fun of make-believe, but none of the trappings of the play. They wanted performers who for a rapturous hour could transport them out of a drab, mud-bound world into fictional far places and other, better times, but they did not want actors. They had seen what they called "actors" in that disreputable free medicine show last year and all the other tawdry outfits that straggled into town to corrupt impressionable youth.

The long-faced morality of the Puritans had transported its seed in the covered wagons and that seed had taken firm root in fertile prairie soil. In Springfield, Illinois, when the great acting family of Joseph Jefferson was

189

barnstorming its hard way west, a religious sect had even tried to enjoin it from giving its play, and the name of the lawyer volunteering to defend the family had been Abraham Lincoln.

Bigots, shutting their ears to Lincoln's plea for justice and tolerance for the Jeffersons, had written their own eleventh commandment: "Thou shalt not tolerate grease paint," and Chautauqua in turn had to heed its doctrine: make-up and costumes were Satan's tools and all players were his servants, man or woman, but particularly woman. Any actress, no matter how talented or how pure of spirit, was referred to, by the more self-righteous as "that stage woman," which was a tidy euphemism for "harlot," and if she were not actually that bad, then certainly she was "no better than she should be."

The roots of this philosophy can be traced clearly to the gay nineties conviction in rural areas that all big cities and all their works were beyond the pale. The stage was a city phenomenon. Communications between city and country were meager and tales of metropolitan high jinks filtering into the more remote reaches of the land naturally were embroidered on the way. Nearly every family had its dissolute Great-uncle Jim, who in his rum-bibbing youth had ventured into Chicago or Philadelphia and enjoyed a delirious evening watching a road company of Niblo's *Black Crook,* in which "the women didn't wear petticoats," or at least not very long ones. If Uncle Jim had kept his diversions to himself when he reached home, drama would not have had such a hard time later on, but he told his cronies at the livery barn a fantastic story. For several generations isolated areas remembered it, and professional entertainers, like Bingham in the 1890's and the Chicago Lady Entertainers in 1904, stayed wisely away from the dangerous odor of a "New York hit."

So although Chautauqua played in a tent, set up a stage, sold tickets from an improvised box office, it had to avoid at the start the words "show business." It employed actors and actresses by the hundreds; it identified them as "entertainers," "readers," "elocutionists," "impersonators," "lightning change artists." Acting was iniquitous, "elocution" was not. The actor or actress who stood on a platform without make-up noticeable to the customers, dressed in respectable every-day clothes and declaimed a "piece" accompanied by suitable gestures, had every prospect of entering into heaven and mingling happily with the saints.

As far back as Civil War days, McGuffey's Juvenile Speaker, a beginner's textbook on the gentle and highly moral art of elocution, had found its way into thousands of American parlors. Compiler of the *Speaker* was William Holmes McGuffey. Born in southwestern Pennyslvania when the nineteenth century was only nine months old, he was a powerful influence on American manners and morals for a hundred years. A schoolmaster who became a college professor, then a college president, he also found time as a Presbyterian preacher to deliver three thousand sermons and to produce six *Eclectic Readers* that sold more than 122,000,000 copies.

The *Readers,* for children from first to sixth grades, were the backbone of all school curricula, except those in New England which clung to its own compilers. Revised occasionally, the "McGuffeys," as they were called, kept pace with literature and taste, and helped taste develop. Until the 1880's they were utterly humorless; they then began to use lighter material, including bits from Mark Twain.

It was the *Readers* that offended several generations of youth with: "Birds in their little nests agree . . . why can't we?" as an antidote to the juvenile propensity to kick shins and pull hair. McGuffey also included Shakespeare and Milton, Gray's *Elegy,* Lowell's *First Snowfall,* and Mrs. Hemans' *Landing of the Pilgrims.* Tennyson, Dickens, Macaulay, Longfellow and Miss Larcom all were there.

In 1860 McGuffey added a *Speaker* to his shelf of *Readers,* and it became an immediate and long-lived best seller. The "pieces for suitable occasions" ranged from "Friends, Romans, Countrymen," to Knox's "Why should the spirit of mortal be proud?" Naturally many a lesser compiler followed McGuffey's highly profitable footsteps into the field of elocution.

Dozens of minor works on the art of "speaking pieces" had already found ready buyers when, in 1896, there appeared a volume that resulted in more frightful public declamation than has ever before, or since, been visited on a helpless people. This book, an importation from naughty Paris, instructed in the "Delsarté method" of recitation, with line drawings of wasp-waisted ladies and high-collared gentlemen displaying by gestures and facial expressions every emotion from compassion to malediction.

Elocution became a plague. No community was immune, but it was the small town that succumbed most quickly. Nightly in Odd Fellows' halls all over America the boy stood on the burning deck and women wept, unashamed, over the death of little Nell. Elocutionists wrecked the *Hesperus,* spared every gray hair on Barbara Frietchie's head, charged with the Light Brigade, rode with Paul Revere, came down like the wolf on the fold and glowered at the Turk, who in his guarded tent dreamed darkly of the hour. *Thanatopsis* reached epidemic proportions. The ghostly hoofbeats of "a mousegray mustang" echoed through ten thousand halls as *Lasca* rode to death with appropriate gestures in Frank Desprez' sure-fire melodrama of life as lived "down on the Rio Grande."

With melancholy voice and face, interpreters of the poem asked:

> "And I wonder why I do not care
> "For the things that are, like the things that were.
> "Does half my heart lie buried there,
> "In Texas, down by the Rio Grande?"

Of course Chautauqua went in early for elocution. Circuit managers employed the finest readers they could find, and if some of these readers happened to be Broadway actors and actresses, out to make an honest summer dollar, so much the better, provided the folks out in front could learn the horrid truth gradually. Instead of hackneyed recitations from elocution books, these artists brought fresh material and methods into the tent. Their "stage" was an empty platform; scenery they manufactured out of the air.

There were dozens of them, ranging from veterans like Leland Powers and Katherine Ridgeway, and Frederick Warde concentrating on Shakespeare, to Powers' own pupil, handsome Phidelia Rice, reading Robertson's *David Garrick*. One of the last handkerchief "salutes" at Chautauqua Lake was for Rice, when he read *Garrick,* with Bishop Vincent, full of years, presiding. The good Bishop was powerless to halt the demonstration.

Wallace Bruce Amsbary filled his first Chautauqua engagement at an "independent" in Danville, Illinois, in 1897 with seventy-five readings in his repertoire. In 1905, with his wife, soprano Louise Amsbary, he signed with Slayton for six summer weeks in Iowa and from then on he appeared on both independent platforms and in the tents until they folded. On special "Joy Nights," beaming Ralph Bingham used to refer to Amsbary as "Wallace Juice Raspberry" and so familiar the people had become with him that no explanation was needed.

Among the Amsbary lectures were the lives of James Whitcomb Riley, Paul Lawrence Dunbar, good gray poet Whitman, Tolstoi, Kipling with his dream of empire. Like several contemporaries, fastidious Amsbary leaned heavily on French Canadian material. A collection of his own verse in that dialect was published under the title *Ballades of Bourbonnais.* Some of them with quotable lines became very popular. In fact Amsbary seldom appeared without a deep voice from the rear of the tent demanding, *Waitin' Fer the Cork to Bob.*

> "With poles an' tackle, bobs an' lines
> "Fur away from earthly whines,
> "Jes' take er beg er steel er rob
> "A few hours of spare time, waitin'
> "Fer the cork to bob!" [1]

Another of the better-known readers of this period was Charles Rose Taggart, the droll "man from Vermont," who twanged a lively fiddle and a salty New England philosophy. Taggart wore country bumpkin clothes with the pants too tight, but for some reason no one thought of them as costume. His old felt hat was his trademark; with it and his famous spectacles, low on his nose or high on his head, he portrayed the people of "down-east Pineville," their shoemaker, garrulous storekeeper, travelling book agent, characters in a debating society or at the county fair. He poked fun at the new-fangled phonograph, and at the same time made country-fiddler records; his recorded comments on woman suffrage and on Billy Sunday are now collectors' items. Taggart, on the stage before all eyes, slapped on a wig and choker collar, false eyebrows and beard, but this was

---

[1] Published in the New York *Dramatic Mirror,* Christmas Number, 1901.

not acting. This was being a "quick change artist," and there was no eleventh commandment against that.

Nor did any commandment keep Taggart from hiring a handcar, with two section hands, one Sunday when no passenger trains were running to get him to the next town. A cheerful trouper, he could be amused at any trouble that beset him. Girls in the companies came to recognize and treat accordingly the pompous lecturers who walked in ahead of them to a hotel desk and demanded the best rooms. Taggart took whatever came, rain, poor hotel, poor bed, poor food. This philosophy of patience he incorporated once into a set of verses that made the rounds of the talent. One stanza went:

> "If you strike a bum hotel,
>   "Take a walk.
> "If your room contains a smell,
>   "Take a walk.
> ·"Grab your grips and exit quick,
> "A five-mile hike will do the trick,
>   "Take a walk."

Montaville Flowers was an opposite type. Taggart's country bumpkin costume would ill have fitted Flowers. His manner was sophisticated; his "lightning changes" were of voice and facial expression, never of costume. He wore white tie and tails, whether he was impersonating the melancholy Hamlet or Barbara Frietchie. When Stonewall Jackson, riding into John Greenleaf Whittier's "Frederick town," shot Dame Frietchie's flag in two, Flowers did not whip a flag from his own pocket—what elocutionist worthy of his salt would need to? Jackson and the Dame were both on the platform with him as he declaimed:

> "Quick, as it fell from the broken staff
> "Dame Barbara snatched the silken scarf;
>
> "She leaned far out on the window sill,
> "And shook it forth with a royal will.
>
> " 'Shoot if you must this old gray head,
> "But spare your country's flag,' she said."

And to his men the rebel general cried:

> " 'Who touches a hair of yon gray head
> "Dies like a dog! March on!' he said."

John Greenleaf Whittier smiled happily through his whiskers in his grave and the audience applauded.

The skilled elocutionist read all the parts in any play, or made a cut and, ignoring minor characters, bore down heavily on the meatiest lines. Flowers, when he presented Dickens' *Christmas Carol,* skipped nimbly from Tiny Tim to Marley's ghost, which he played in a sepulchral tone that raised goose pimples on the children in the front row.

Flowers' masterpiece was a full evening of General Lew Wallace's *Ben Hur,* in which the actor again took all the parts, except the horses. *Ben Hur* was made for Chautauqua. General Wallace, hero of "bloody Shiloh," was basically a midwest, small-town American. He wrote the long novel, based on the coming of Christ, at his home in Crawfordsville, Indiana, which later would become "a good Chautauqua town." In 1880, when the book was published, the community boasted nine well-attended churches, four newspapers, Wabash College with thirteen professors, a busy coffin factory, and a population of 5251 sturdy souls. Wallace wrote into *Ben Hur* everything that his own and a thousand other Chautauqua towns wanted most, the flavor of far places and heroic times, deeply religious overtones, a classical atmosphere and lots of action.

At Lincoln, Nebraska, one fall, Flowers arrived by train for his *Ben Hur* program to find the station platform abustle with camels, horses, chariots and stage sets which were being loaded into five cars.

"And what is this?" he asked.

A bystander explained that a *Ben Hur* road company, with a cast of one hundred, was leaving after three successful nights.

"Three nights of *Ben Hur?*" Flowers exclaimed. "I'll make it four, then," and that evening, in an auditorium that still echoed to the frightening clatter of the treadmill on which the chariots had raced, he presented his one-man show.

The town of Lincoln, that had liked the first three performances, also liked the fourth. In other words, people liked *Ben Hur.*

There were four "impersonators" for whom local committees usually could sell standing room. These were Gilbert Eldredge, Halwood Robert Manlove, John Ratto and Everett Kemp. Eldredge, flouting the notion that men should not dress like women, added *Mrs. Wiggs* and that other homespun character, *Samantha Allen,* to his list. Similarly independent, he attacked the grease paint problem. In one lecture he traced it to the church; monks in the Middle Ages, he reminded, gave realism to a miracle play by artistically staining their faces with plant dye and tying on horses' tails for wigs.

Manlove, "the man of many faces," had a smiling personality very popular in the south. Once, from the Blue Ridge Mountains, he wrote to the Chicago office, "I made the date! Went through twelve tunnels in fifty miles, four miles on horseback, three hours in a hack. Good crowd."

These men all "read" the usual fictional characters popular in their day— Enoch Arden, David Harum, Charles Klein's pathetic little "Music Master," and many others. But what old Chautauqua-goers recall today is their humor, in their lighter encores and their "originals." They associate with each man some particularly amusing character.

Everett Kemp, to be known later to Kansas City radio fans as "Uncle Ezra," gave as his main reading in Chautauqua Harold Bell Wright's *That*

Printer of Udell's. But what people remember him for is a ridiculous encore, *The Man with the Bone-Colored Whiskers,* in which the whiskers played a smaller part than Kemp's infectious laugh.

Wandering the streets of Detroit one slippery morning, Kemp is supposed to have seen a "slim man with bone-colored whiskers" and a "fat man with big feet," who fell on the ice. A few nights later on the platform, for an encore, Kemp improvised an absurd tale about the two, calling it originally *The Man Who Apologized.* In the sketch, only two typewritten pages when set down on paper, he used two ancient sure-fire devices, the old banana-peel theme and the theory that if the storyteller laughs hard enough, his audience will laugh just as hard.

A man "with bone-colored whiskers, leaning against a building, laughed as if his heart would break, ha-ha-ha," at a man who slipped and fell. Later in the day he searched the other out, "ha-ha-ha," to apologize, but could not finish his apology because the memory of the incident set him to laughing again, "ha-ha, ha-ha-ha." Next day he tried once more to make amends, with the same results, "ha-ha, ha-ha-ha, ha-ha."

The third time he said, "Mister, I wish you would forgive me for laughing, but, ha-ha-ha, when you struck the icy spot and I saw your foot, ha-ha-ha-ha, ha-ha, I couldn't help ha-ha-ha-ha-ha-ha-ha. . . ."

By this time the audience was shouting, too, and Kemp's reputation as "the man with the laugh" was fixed on the circuits. It stayed with him until 1929 when he left Chautauqua for radio. Settling in Kansas City, he created "Uncle Ezra" on a KMBC program known as *Happy Hollow.* Today, in his mid-80's, Kemp, still with his laugh, is entertaining on KCMO's television station.

Ratto was the "funny Swede," the "funny Scot," but chiefly the "funny Irishman," who remarked, "Music is a g-r-r-an' t'ing, but Oi bet thir-r-ty foive cents wherever this mon Wagner is, they got 'im in a cage." Another of Ratto's characters was a somber Presbyterian preacher whose boy, Eliakim, was in college. The stern father had always advised his flock to shun football ". . . but now it's different, with my son Eliakim playing . . . ooh, that boy . . . tr-r-ee years in college and the most of it in the books yet."

Elias Day, a "characterist," and a really accomplished actor, still is remembered for his burlesque of Poe's *The Raven.* Rumpling his hair, pulling his cravat askew and assuming an expression of genial tipsiness, Day recited the poem; then he tried to explain it, intimating that Mr. Poe lacked a sense of spacial relations. He recounted, in Poe's own rhyme, how the raven entered and

> "Perched upon the bust of Pallas
> "Just above my chamber door. . . .
> "With the lamplight o'er him streaming. . . .
> "Cast his shadow on the floor."

Day then traced the route taken by the shadow on its way from the top of the door to the floor and decided at last, in a state of alcoholic confusion, that it was "a cross-eyed, hump-backed shadow, to get cast upon the floor." Even zealous temperance workers forgot their white ribbons enough to laugh aloud.

Day wrote most of his own material and the recitations of his wife, dark-eyed Oranne Truitt. His hand-to-bosom portrayal of "Colonel Fayerweather of Frankfort, Kentucky, suh," and *Cohen on the Telephone* were long time favorites. Mr. Cohen, trying to order a board to mend a broken shutter, was asked how long a board, and put down the receiver to hold up his hands and say, "About this long." The audience screamed. Who wanted to be subtle in a meadow outside a country town in 1910?

Women readers, mindful of the prejudice against the "stage woman," depended even less than the men on costume. Jessie Rae Taylor, a dramatic entertainer who appeared as late as 1955 in the Fountain Park, Indiana, Assembly, was billed in early advertisements as the only woman on the platform using grease paint and wigs in character work. Another "dramatic reader" was Isabel Garghill Beecher. The fact that we advertised her as a niece of Henry Ward Beecher did not hurt her with the ticket buyers.

"The Girl with the Camera Mind" was Gay Zenola MacLaren. Another of those dedicated spirits who set their hearts from youth on the rewards of the stage, she needed to listen to a Broadway hit only five or six times, without ever having seen the script, before she took it on the road. She recreated each character, imitating the styles and voices of the stars who played the New York leads. Thus she gave Chautauqua audiences David Warfield in *The Music Master,* Laurette Taylor in *Peg o' My Heart,* Frank Craven in *Bought and Paid For,* John Barrymore in *The Fortune Hunter.* In all, she presented thirty-seven different plays; in the Panama Canal Zone, where she gave a hundred-odd performances, Generals Smedley Butler and George M. Goethals called her their "One Girl Show Company."

As with the men impersonators, the women's acts that made people laugh were the ones remembered. Everyone had heard a child cry; so Rita Rich's trademark became her imitation of a crying baby. Similarly, Emily Waterman, a tall, angular woman who could lisp like a four-year-old, won her accolade for a short encore. Her sick doll's lament, "I dot a pain in my sawdust," became a catch phrase.

Meanwhile half the people in America had seen at least one movie and thousands were dedicated fans. The year 1896 brought the first, fuzzy, jerky motion picture to a New York music hall. The *Great Train Robbery* followed in 1903. It was the star of this melodrama, Broncho Billy Anderson, who introduced "they-went-thata-way" acting to a people who were never to tire of it. By the time Keith Vawter had forged his idea of tent Chautauqua into a workable product, big-city nickelodeons were flourishing. To an airless converted store building, city sophisticates liked to take their country cousins, there to witness breathlessly the cliff-hanging *Adventures of Kathleen,* the hair-breadth *Perils of Pauline.*

The "picture play," which a performer named Albert Armstrong took to the permanent assemblies about the time of the first nickelodeon, was not a motion picture but it pointed in that direction. On a muslin bed sheet, stretched across the narrow platform of a dark hall, Armstrong used a magic lantern to show hand-colored slides that told in continuity a complete story, and, as each photograph appeared, he read the accompanying lines. *Lorna Doone, The Sky Pilot, The Little Minister* were among his highly respected offerings.

Armstrong, standing unseen in the dark, did not claim to be an actor. But Chautauqua drama was on the march and another performer who helped it turn the corner from elocution to conventional play-acting was William Sterling Battis, the "Dickens Man." Battis *was* an actor and an English gentleman; not an elocutionist, not a reader, but an actor, body and soul. As a boy he had understudied Joe Jefferson, and for ten years he had played character parts on the legitimate stage. In Chautauqua, he used chalk and charcoal instead of grease paint, but, like Eldredge and Ratto, he daubed them on in full view of his curious audience, wiped them off while it watched. This was not the same as painting one's face in a dressing room and coming out under false colors.

Battis brought out his Dickens props and bag of tricks and laid them on a table for all to see—a walking stick, a large gray shawl, a little white bonnet and a linen duster. He wore the shawl to give the illusion of costume changes, over his head for Little Nell, high around his ears for Bob Cratchit, tight over his shoulders for Fagin. In the role of Sydney Carton, he slipped into the duster, letting it hang loosely about his upright figure as he lifted his left foot to a small box, presumably to mount the guillotine, while his clear, trained voice declaimed the "far, far better thing." Like Shakespeare, Dickens was "educational" and nobody was against education.

Battis wore his hair in long, expressive locks. For each new character his slender fingers pushed them this way or that, smoothing or tossing them into wild disorder. Then with a deft hand he put a line of black or a patch of white on cheeks or chin and a character emerged. The people cheered, laughed; if he wanted them to, they cried. Here, they were sure, was a genius. But if one lone man could do all this with Reformer Dickens, what marvel could a whole troupe create? Deep in the wicked corners of their hearts, the people wondered. And what was more, came the next thought, if it was entirely moral to wear costumes with music, why not wear them for the spoken word? Why was an opera singer acceptable and an actress unacceptable? For in vast stretches of the country, even in the so-called "Bible Belt," that peculiar distinction did exist, rooted somehow in the fact that the church itself had always used music.

Chautauqua's earliest travelling musical companies had put on skits and one-act plays, the "singing bands" and choruses all had worn elaborate costumes. Vawter had dared tie opera singers to one of his first bands and the audience listening to Thaviu render Verdi's *Trovatore* had approved. When the LeBrun Grand Opera Company, with Italian-born Madame LeBrun as its director and soprano, toured in 1911, she so entranced people everywhere that in Hannibal, Missouri, boyhood home of Mark Twain, when rain poured through the top of a leaky tent, women simply had put up their umbrellas, as they had on another occasion with Estelle Gray, and remained where they were, absorbed in melodious drama.

There had been countless other examples. Chicago, which in 1900 had built the first little theatre in the United States for Jane Addams' Hull House Players, also had mothered the Parish Players, the first theatre group in the country to be organized in a church, and on Redpath circuits they had offered a program of one-act plays with Katherine S. Brown as producer. Such companies as the Kellog-Haines Singing Party and the Cavaliers had packed the tents. The Singing Party, in costume, gave selections from such operas as *The Bohemian Girl* and *Lovely Galatea*. The Cavaliers had depicted the music and manners of Queen Elizabeth and if one could listen to songs of Elizabeth's Merrie England, sung in costume, why not to its plays? Again, deep in that wicked corner of their restless hearts, the people wondered.

Chautauqua was ready when the issue finally had to be decided. Ben Greet and his Shakespearian Players had been strolling the land off and on since 1904, when Charles Frohman brought them from England to Broadway to play *Twelfth Night,* with talented Greet as Malvolio and Edith Wynn Matthison as Viola. The next year, with Sybil Thorndike in the cast, they had made their first cross-country tour, giving Americans in the larger cities a taste of a new stage technique. They had played out-of-doors more often than within, on college campuses and rich men's estates and the city hall lawn, against backgrounds of pine branches or autumn leaves. At the invitation of Theodore Roosevelt, they even had performed on the White House grounds.

In the 1860's James Redpath had listened in Boston to Charles Dickens and conceived the idea of a lecture bureau. Similarly now Crawford Peffer, the astute impresario of the New England-Redpath circuit, watched the Ben Greet Players and turned his imagination loose on what might happen if this group of actors should appear on the Chautauqua stage. The name Shakespeare certainly would help such a venture. Generations of American schoolteachers had paved the way for the Bard's introduction to rural audiences and Ben Greet's own fame had currently hopped the continent. In the east, if not elsewhere, the name "New York" had influence and there, at the moment, the legitimate theatre was in a healthy state, with all types of attractions. Sothern and Marlowe were playing Shakespeare repertoire. *Potash and Perlmutter* had started its phenomenal run. Sheldon's *Romance* and George M. Cohan's *Seven Keys to Baldpate* were skyrocketing upward, and more and more conservative people on the eastern seaboard, where Peffer lived, were going into New York to see any or all of them, and take a look, too, at *Poor Little Rich Girl* and a Biblical spectacle, *Joseph and His Brethren,* for which even the religious press spoke a good word.

To Peffer, never a timid man, the time seemed ripe. The Shakespeare Players already had appeared in winter Lyceum. So Peffer talked Greet into letting Redpath send them out across the 1913 summer Chautauqua circuits, and in another stroke of genius, he employed William Keighley as director. Already a success on Broadway, Keighley stayed on a dozen years, training cast after cast, making the hard one-night stands with them, often playing a difficult part. With his helping hand, Peffer now chose *Comedy of Errors* for the Greet Players' first production.

Since opera already was considered "safe," Chicago-Redpath had scheduled Farelli's *Lover's Quarrel* for the 1913 summer run. It was to be the opener in most towns, with Scotch tenor David Duggan, resplendent in white wig and the fanciest of fancy velvet costumes, singing the role of Florindo. There was no doubt that it would be received well, but what would happen, say in the Baptist south, to the Shakespeare Players?

To make doubly sure that *Comedy of Errors* would not offend even the most moralistic audience, Peffer, Keighley and everyone else with money invested in the venture, went over the script line by line, deleting every tart Elizabethan phrase that might wound soft sensibilities. Ben Greet himself did not go on the tour. But in the group, scheduled for one hundred and ten Redpath towns, were seven of the original players the impresario had brought from England; the other six had been trained by him here. Percival Vivian, who that winter had played in the New York production of *Oliver Twist,* took the lead. Opposite him was Grace Halsey Mills, a trouper who thirty years later was still valiantly answering her cues in theatrical productions.

The play was presented before a plain backdrop stretched behind the stage. There were no sets or scenery. In the summer, playing mostly out-of-doors, the strolling Greets had no need for extra scenery; grass, trees, sky and entranced imaginations were enough. In the winter, forced indoors, Greet believed that it was better to continue to do without scenery than to use the creations of a local sign painter, which were all that most "opera houses" or auditoriums offered. This fitted Chautauqua's frugal needs admirably, particularly when the cost of transportation was considered.

As a second play in 1913, partly to break the monotony for themselves, the Ben Greets took along what extra costumes were needed for Goldsmith's *She Stoops to Conquer.* They tried Goldsmith on such metropolitan cities as Birmingham, Chattanooga, Augusta; Shakespeare elsewhere. With hands cupped to ears Redpath waited for the reaction. The storm of moral indignation that had been feared did not materialize. Instead came shouts of praise. By the time the company reached Michigan, northbound, crowds were gathering at the big brown tent two hours before the program. Shakespeare was in. People liked both the play and the players.

Vivian, whose wife was actress Irene Bevans of another Ben Greet company, became a particular favorite with other talent as the years went on. Like Reno, the magician, he gave the crews a willing hand and they quickly passed the word around their fraternity. In Kentucky one June it had rained all week and the tent, arriving at Morgantown on the Ohio River, was wet and heavy. It took two teams of horses to haul it to the grounds and the exhausted crew, trying to use the horses to lift the canvas, had it half up when the cable slipped off the pulley wheel. Running across the lot, Vivian saw the situation, undressed down to his underwear, shinnied up the tall centerpole, and fixed the pulley. The boys made certain afterward that Vivian's pitcher of fresh water was always ready in his dressing room.

Vivian, the summer he was out with the cast of *The Bird Masque*—the play in which he annoyed Director Ernest Baynes by appearing one day in a cat's costume instead of the faun's—was on the stage the night the crew boys found their first humor in this Percy MacKaye fantasy. *The Bird Masque,* which Author-Dramatist MacKaye called *Sanctuary* when he published it, was played behind a curtain of theatrical gauze to make it seem more eerie. The boys, who had to hang the gauze, insisted that nothing, gauze or anything else, could help anybody "understand what it was all about."

The boys also did not like the actor from New York who played the part of the heavy. One evening in Cynthiana, Kentucky, in a scene in which popular Vivian sat by a bird bath, playing shepherd's pipes under a blue spotlight, the unpopular villain in buckskins and moccasins, carrying bow and arrow, was supposed to come out saying, "What ho! The hounds!"

It had rained that day and the canvas top had leaked, leaving a puddle on the stage. The heavy stepped into it, his moccasin slipped and he sat down hard and failed to get up. Vivian continued to play his pipe sweetly, but the heavy could not get to his feet. The electrician handling the spotlight at the back of the tent was a lad named Fertig, from Brooklyn. Even if *The Bird Masque* didn't make sense to him, a pratfall was a pratfall, funny in any man's language. Bellowing with laughter, he turned the spotlight on the floundering villain. The audience joined in while the unhappy performer limped off the stage.

In 1914 the Ben Greet Players, again with Vivian and Miss Mills, took out *Twelfth Night* and *The Merchant of Venice,* admission still fifty cents. Once more the audiences received the company with acclaim, once more Redpath reflected that these people had accepted Shakespeare; but what about other drama? The Ben Greet Players had bridged the old canyon of moral indignation at the stage, but would the bridge hold if a company playing modern theatre travelled over it?

The solution was *The Servant in the House.* In 1908, the same year that Maude Adams scored on Broadway in *What Every Woman Knows,* this modern morality play by Charles Rann Kennedy, had been produced in New York with Walter Hampden and Edith Wynn Matthison in the cast. It had been a solid, long-run hit, with touring companies taking it on the road even before the Broadway run was finished. Kennedy was particularly suited to write this kind of play. A well-born Englishman, he had been destined for holy orders until he met and married Actress Matthison. Between Miss Matthison's arrival with the original Greet company for its first Broadway run and her appearance in *The Servant in the House,* she had played to acclaim, on both sides of the Atlantic, in the revival of the sixteenth-century morality play, *Everyman.* She was a great lady of the theatre and any production she was connected with drew prestige from that connection.

Opposite Hampden in husband Kennedy's play, she possibly had given *The Servant in the House* greater fame than it deserved. It was not a great play, but it was wholesome and highly moral, a sermon on humility as well as a dramatic presentation, in five acts, of the love of a father for his child.

The humble servant, of course, was Jesus, come back to a modern, selfish world. But before the final curtain, the Master had solved the problems and virtue triumphed over selfishness and deceit. Respected religious journals reviewed it enthusiastically. Small-town newspapers in Redpath territory commented smugly on the heartening fact that the Great White Way had searched its gaudy soul at last and rediscovered its lost faith.

With the same independence of spirit that had characterized Bishop Vincent, the Chautauqua Lake management announced Miss Matthison and Mr. Kennedy in a series of recitals for their 1915 season. Not to be outdone, Redpath-Chicago scheduled *The Servant in the House* for the third evening's program on its seven day circuit. Broadway's William Owen was selected as leading man, an actor so seasoned in rich character roles that he could, and did, portray sensitively the great part of Robert Smith, the "drain man." At twenty-three, Owen had been playing Mephistopheles in *Faust.* Supporting him in *The Servant* were Margaret Ulrich, an actress trained in Shakespearian roles, as the vicar's niece; Robert Stevens, another Ben Greet player, as the vicar; Sarah Willey as the vicar's wife; J. W. McConnell as the bishop; William Lindquist as Manson, the butler. Lindquist had started with a juvenile minstrel group; Miss Wiley had played character parts in dozens of road companies.

Uneasily Redpath watched the William Owen Company start out. Its story might be the theme for Sunday sermons, but how would the play itself be received in corn and cotton lands where dancing, cards and theatre still were labeled as tools of Satan? In our advertising we said: "In the beginning, the drama was the handmaiden of the church. Since then it has wandered afar . . . the church today recognizes its power and force for good when rightly directed and looks forward to the time when it will come into its own. The introduction of this play by Redpath this season is, we believe, a long step in the right direction."

The Servant in the House opened April 17 in Jacksonville, Florida, with Dramatist Kennedy, down from New York to take curtain calls with the cast, enthusiastically approving their performance. Kennedy liked to call himself a "clergyman in disguise," so on Sunday afternoon, doing all that he could to help dissipate any churchly disapproval of Redpath's theatrical experiment, he led a mass meeting sponsored by the Y.M.C.A. in the Chautauqua tent. That evening in the Congregational church he gave a program of Bible readings. Jacksonville liked both Mr. Kennedy and Mr. Owen, and after its opening triumph the play moved north.

Again we waited. In spite of a good start, this adventure might have a sad ending. But again it did not. The censorious attitudes of 1905 and 1910 for the most part were gone, snuffed out along with the kerosene lamp. At long last, three centuries after young Will Shakespeare put on his shows beside London River, small-town America was ready to pay hard-earned half dollars, and finally dollars, to see high-class, decent plays, ready to accept the haunting odor of grease paint. The play was in, the reading on the way out. By 1924 Redpath had stopped booking it.

Motion pictures had assisted greatly, just as eventually they were to help spell Chautauqua's doom. The same year that Redpath experimented with *Twelfth Night,* David Wark Griffith had sent his six-reel production of *Birth of a Nation* on tour, with a symphony orchestra for accompaniment. By the time we tried *The Servant in the House,* Miss Mabel Normand and the Keystone Kops were hurling custard pies with vigor and great charm, and a blonde moppet named Smith, who called herself Mary Pickford, was blinking her way into the nation's heart. Rural America, at least segments of it, already had begun to acquire the taste for high adventure, sugary romance and low comedy on celluloid.

After *The Servant in the House,* other plays followed rapidly in the sputtering white glare of Chautauqua's acetylene footlights. To be sure, it was necessary to take certain liberties with the scripts. What had seemed innocuous on the Great White Way still might shock Kansas or Iowa. Playwrights, with tender attachment for their brain children, hesitated at first to let anyone adapt their dramas to such peculiar needs. Play them as written, they insisted, or not at all. It took persuasion and all William Keighley's skill to break down a playwright's solicitude for each blunt word that must be deleted, but we soon discovered that letting an author see the record of royalties paid on *The Servant* was effective. Eventually all our contracts with playwrights and Broadway producers contained a clause permitting us to "Chautauqua-ize the script."

Dramatic companies, some excellent, some not, toured the circuits with a variety of fare. One favorite in the rural reaches was Israel Zangwill's *The Melting Pot,* in which Jewish immigrants in New York slums cast off habits and cultures of forty centuries to become one-hundred-percent Americans.

A million midwest hearts went out to the confused and troubled strangers. Hadn't most Swedish or German, Irish or Polish grandparents had similar experiences before their covered wagon days? And hadn't Jacob Riis visited these same platforms not long before? Veteran Broadway actor Dore Davidson, who had begun his career in support of Edwin Booth at McVickers Theatre in Chicago, took a role in *The Melting Pot,* as did William Keighley.

College players, who were free in summer vacation, were naturals for Chautauqua excursions. Typical of them was the company headed by Clyde Tull, of the Cornell College English department, and his wife, Jewell Bothwell Tull. This group, as talented as they were energetic, some seasons put in an average of one hundred and eighty nights, playing in towns under a thousand in population, often with afternoon and evening shows. They travelled in Model-T Fords, with a Model-T truck to carry costumes and scenery, and in four years they never missed a date.

Crew boys loved the Tulls as they had Percival Vivian. On arrival at the tent, the Tulls set up their own stage, in contrast to the troupe of Equity actors from New York who one summer played *The Gorilla,* by Mrs. Tull, on a Vawter circuit. Equity actors never set up their own stage and so the boys did not care for them. The Tull Company took out *Adam and Eve* one season after giving it the most extensive cleaning ever prescribed by a Redpath moral mop-up squad.

Most casts from college campuses had the freshness of youth, whether or not their acting was a finished product. Stars averaged a hundred and fifty dollars a week, the youngsters forty. At season's end, a few went on to small parts on Broadway, but most of them went back to school.

About the time that Cecil B. DeMille, out in Hollywood, began his series of lavish film spectacles, a Redpath company of eight, headed by a young Canadian actor named Eugene Lockhart, went out on our seven-day circuit with *It Pays to Advertise,* a thistledown comedy so hound's-tooth clean that it seemed to have been written for Chautauqua. Lockhart did a prelude of readings in the afternoon and took the lead in the play at night. He made a sensational hit, the first in the series that led him from Chautauqua tents to Broadway and Hollywood. Carl Backman, who later married impersonator Gay Zenola MacLaren, and who now is manager of the Chicago department of the Redpath Lyceum bureau, was a young superintendent on that circuit that summer.

Lockhart was only one of many for whom Chautauqua was a broad stepping stone to Hollywood. Producer Keighley, shifting first to Broadway, then to the movies, took along many promising youngsters. Among them was Clarence Nash, who having matched his vocal chords against flapping tents and howling winds, became the voice of Donald Duck. Many of the Ben Greet players moved permanently to Hollywood.[1]

[1] Martha Scott, who later would win an Oscar in *Our Town,* and Rhys Williams of *How Green is My Valley,* started in Chautauqua. Emory and Effie Parnell toured as a man-and-wife duo. Jay Tobias worked for both Horner and Chicago and Ohio Red-

The season after Lockhart's performance in *It Pays to Advertise,*
Chautauqua put *Nothing but the Truth* on the road and a year later the
Tarkington-Wilson comedy, *The Man from Home,* which had been meat
over the years for the elocutionists. In 1922 the hills and pastures echoed
with roars of laughter when the Winchell Smith-John Hazard comedy, *Turn
to the Right,* rolled through more than one hundred Chautauqua towns.

The play was pure but excellent corn. The poor old mother, about to be
evicted from her cottage by the rapacious money-lending deacon, and the
mother's noble and falsely accused son, were protected by two agreeable ex-
convicts. One had been a pickpocket, the other a burglar. It was the friendly
burglar who paid off the mortgage, with funds from a recent burglary, and
the pickpocket who immediately lifted the money from the nasty deacon's
wallet and gave it to the young hero—whose money it was, happily, all the
time. The crowds wanted the folks on stage to be friendly, the endings happy.

Chautauqua obliged with *Peg o' My Heart,* without Laurette Taylor, and
Smilin' Through, without Jane Cowl. Clean drama ranged from *The Witch-
ing Hour* to *Applesauce, Three Wise Fools* to *Welcome Stranger,* all sticky
with the rich syrup that had sweetened box offices along the Great White
Way.

Chautauqua did not apologize for "wholesome drama." David Belasco,
Broadway's most successful producer of the era and, later, the great John
Golden could announce at the end of unbelievably successful careers, that
no suggestive word had crept into a single one of their plays. What was
good enough for Belasco in New York was good enough for Redpath in
the tents.

We had our unforeseen and unforeseeable crises, to be sure, and we were
not always able to keep them out of the press. I still remember the shock
with which the entire Chautauqua world faced a Madison, Wisconsin, newspaper headline the morning after a Ben Greet company had put on *Hamlet*
in the capital of Dairyland.

The "distinguished actor," who played the title role, later insisted that it
was only a wee nip that he had taken and that his troubles on stage were
the result of something he had eaten. Whatever the cause, he did trip over
his sword and he did give the Dane comical lines that Shakespeare had
neglected to put into the play.

The newspaper headline was: "Ham-lit!"

---

path, Phil Tongue for Peffer in New England, fat John Bunny with Affiliated. Conrad
Nagle served as an apprentice with Reader Edna Means. Broadway director Charles
Hanna, and Actress Blanche Frederici both had their own companies. Richard B.
Harrison, "de Lawd" of *Green Pastures,* was a Jubilee singer.

Leo S. Rosecrans, now an executive of Jerry Fairbanks Productions, the largest
maker of commercial movies, put in twelve years in Chautauqua, nine of them as a
superintendent with Coit-Alber and Redpath, three with Central as a circuit manager.
Dozens of other names, from Frederick Warde to Edgar Bergen and Dean Jagger, fill
the roster.

The Big Time

17

The Nashville policeman, after the crowd thinned, had walked two blocks up Gay Street before he noticed the sticker glued to his night stick. "Redpath Chautauqua," it read. He smiled and peeled it off. That magician fellow must have stuck it on, the one who pulled the bunny out of the mayor's hat. These Chautauqua folk sure had fun and had they taken over the town! You'd think it was the Fourth of July!

Nashville streets had swarmed with people that May morning. Kryl's band played *Dixie* twice on the steep slope of the Statehouse lawn. A dapper Redpath superintendent in a new straw hat made a rousing speech. This great Chautauqua, now bound south, would be back in Nashville in June with all its marvels. The stop today was only preliminary. Chautauqua would be welcome, the mayor said; it always was welcome in Tennessee and he recited a piece by John Trotwood Moore to prove that Tennessee hospitality was more than skin deep.

The crowd cheered and the band swung into *Dixie* again and the parade started back to the depot dining room. After lunch and a few choice remarks by Nashville-born Opie Read, the *Redpath Special,* waiting in the railroad yards, would resume its southward journey.

The year 1913 saw the Redpath-Chicago circuit go into the big time. The first Special DeLuxe train, flying banners that put Ringling Brothers to shame, roared its way south for the opening in Albany, Georgia. A hundred and twenty-five persons were aboard when the train left Chicago's smoky LaSalle Street Station on May 20. Some of the talent—the New York contingent, including the Ben Greets and the Grand Opera Company—had gone on ahead, but celebrities galore remained: Opie Read with his cigar,

205

and Kryl in his big hat, Magicians Reno and Laurant, the Barnard Orchestra, the Mozart Trio, officers of the bureau, excited Chicago friends, crew men, entertainers, song heisters.

The train would pause a dozen times on its way south, in big towns where a Chautauqua program already had been sold for later in the summer. Each stop would be brief, just long enough for a trombonist to toot, a lecturer to say a few well-chosen words.

After two nights in the crowded Pullmans the party arrived at Albany. It was noon, which was good. People had got downtown. Flags adorned the streets. The new palm trees lining the park across from the hotel were beginning to perk up after a bad winter. Whistles at the cotton mills and the oil presses blew a noisy welcome and performers joined the parade of cars to the Chautauqua park. By some stroke of luck, the timetable had worked; one hour remained before the first afternoon's curtain.

The week before the exodus from Chicago had been strenuous, at times frantic. Talent, some of it weary from winter Lyceum, had gathered from the four corners for the final shape-up. There had been rehearsals, morning, afternoon and night on the stage of McVickers Theatre in the Loop and in smaller halls scattered from Lake Michigan to suburban Oak Park.

Directors had been exacting. Over and over they put companies, orchestras and entertainers through their paces, and, when everybody was about to collapse, had said, "Almost! Let's try it once more." Skits had been cut, singers dropped and other singers substituted. Sets had been rebuilt, costumes fitted and refitted. Lecturers had been drilled, drilled, drilled. "You'll be stepping on your applause!" coaches yelled at them. "Slow down! Give people a chance . . . a pause there and you'll get a hand. . . ."

Dunbar's current crop of college boys, all in high spirits, had been whipped into a professional Hussar troupe. An expert—his name was Howard Tooley and years before he had taken a long jump to the stage from Sullivan, Indiana—whittled the musical comedy to fit the time allotted to it, never, according to Mr. Tooley, time enough. Endlessly, patiently Elias Day coached his young hopefuls. "Now then, just once more. Put the emphasis on that third word . . . not the first. . . ."

And wild Sandor Radanovitz, with the title of "musical director," had gone into fresh frenzies, extracting every drop of sweet melody from duos and quartets. The "mad Russian," hopeful youngsters called this Hungarian-born genius, admiring him at a cautious distance and dreaming that, some glorious day, he might single them out for praise.

Director Radanovitz believed in music for music's sake. He was a big man with a big voice, a big appetite, a big heart and a big nose with a duelling scar across it. The scar had brought him to America. He had been arrested, following a duel in his native Budapest; a court gave him a choice, go to jail or overseas. He was nineteen and one successful year in the Hungarian Royal Opera School lay behind him.

He reached New York eventually; there minor roles in *Babes in Toyland, Robin Hood, The Darling of the Gods* earned bread and cheese. They were hard years. Hearty Radanovitz liked to eat. Next to music he liked to cook. Once, when times were good, he formed the Little Pig Society, in which every member had to learn to roast a pig. But times weren't good as he reached Chicago. Everything he owned went to the pawnshop—piano, rugs, furniture. Then Redpath took the tickets and bailed the goods out and he signed a contract that would be continued all his life.

Sandor came to Chicago the year after our first venture on the road. He died the year Chautauqua died, one evening in 1932, after leaving the Redpath office. In the meantime he was "Mr. Chautauqua."

Money meant nothing. "Bah, who wants it?" he would say, but loyalty was important. When Movie Mogul Tom Ince, worried over the change from silent screen to "talkies," tried to hire the big man, at high wages, to "place" the voices of stars, Radanovitz said, "No," shortly. He was too busy. Hollywood had no allure for him. It was time for Chautauqua's spring rehearsals, time to get ready for big tents on the long road.

"She can't sing! She never will sing!" a distressed coach would cry after struggling for hours with a new girl in a chorus. But brow-beating Sandor would keep at her all day and all night and next day she could sing, passably. She had no alternative. He *made* her sing. Whether or not she wanted to, whether or not she could, she sang. A frustrated Sandor was the terror of any performer. Frustration drove him, first crazy, then to bed. A run of sour notes, an overdone roast pig, a succession of missed cues, and the Hungarian's big hands clasped his big stomach, and like Schumann-Heink, he cried desperately, *"Ach,* I am sick!"

Radanovitz was the best talent scout in the business. Twice he went to Europe to search fairs and concert halls for prospects. Tent Chautauquas were American to their roots. Yet foreign Radanovitz, who to the end spoke with an accent that embraced all Middle Europe, knew by instinct the musical longings of rural America and how to satisfy them. If this was a contradiction, it was perhaps because all Chautauqua was a complex sort of contradiction itself.

A Redpath Special sped down to Dixie every spring after 1913, banners flying, engineers, firemen, brakemen, porters decked to a man in Chautauqua hats. It was a spectacular publicity device, but its original purpose was to save money for the bureau. Railroads, in those days, provided a special baggage car for any theatrical troupe of twenty-five or more persons. So if we bought tickets for one hundred and twenty-five, we were entitled to five cars.

Heavy equipment, canvas, stage, seats, lights and a piano for one tent filled nearly half a car. Thus, in five cars, we could ship all nine outfits, with another half car left over for band instruments, property trunks, personal luggage.

Our arrangement with the railroad for a dining car called for a minimum guarantee on our part for food to be consumed. Talent, the crew boys in particular, who never had much cash in their pockets, always ordered frugally. So that we usually approached the end of the run with the minimum not reached. And then came the last meal, a free dinner for everyone, "to eat up the guarantee."

In 1914 our opening was in Charleston, South Carolina, with Judge Marcus Kavanagh and the Cathedral Choir giving the first program. The Chicago office sent out two circuits for the first time that year, the big seven-day DeLuxe and a new five-day, which, since it started in Louisiana, we named the "Gulf." The next year we were to add the "Atlantic," also a five-day, and in 1920 a three-day.

Nineteen-fifteen was a "wet" Chautauqua year, with no reference to Al Smith or Headliner Bryan intended. Rains, building creeks up to rivers and rivers to flood stage, gave most managements the worst physical troubles they ever had endured. In Ainsworth, Nebraska, the Britt system lost two tents in four days, with the piano finally blown off the stage.

For us, however, it was the year of *The Servant in the House* and Alice Nielsen. Trying *The Servant* on the public might be a gamble. Sending Miss Nielsen on the kind of tour we did was big business for us and hard, weary business for her. In one hundred and eighteen days the dark-haired soprano from the Metropolitan and Boston Opera companies, travelling with her own piano in her own private car, sang one hundred and eighteen consecutive concerts in one hundred and eighteen packed tents, in the most pretentious musical effort any circuit ever had attempted.

It went well. When the season ended in September, in Chicago, on grounds near the Edgewater Beach Hotel, the over-all picture had been excellent. In addition to the one hundred and eighteen towns on Miss Nielsen's route, our new "five-day" had covered one hundred and one. We had dropped Sunday performances as an experiment. Idling the tents the one day had cost a hard-to-lose twenty thousand dollars. But in the larger cities we had charged an unheard-of three dollars for a season ticket. Counting the "morning hour" lecture, this amounted to just fifteen cents a performance, for Alice Nielsen and William Owen in *The Servant* and everybody else.

When the treasurer feverishly counted the last receipts, the seven-day DeLuxe had topped $300,000. Our three circuits together had totalled in the neighborhood of $700,000. For all Redpath systems, Horner's, Vawter's, Vernon Harrison's and Peffer's, gross had topped three million dollars. That was high finance in anybody's language in 1915.

Alice Nielsen received the highest salary ever paid up till then in the tents, a whopping fifteen hundred dollars a week, plus expenses. The private car made her daily life a bit easier though even a plush private car, standing all day in a smoky Chattanooga railroad yard (those were the days when air-conditioning had not yet been dreamt of) left something to be desired. But the car itself also piled up twenty thousand miles worth of publicity. Named the *Mayflower,* it had been used by Theodore Roosevelt and Taft, not to mention Lillian Russell and Sarah Bernhardt, and we saw to it that anybody who could read a newspaper learned all about this historic vehicle.

Miss Nielsen, born in Nashville, had made her grand-opera debut in Naples, as Marguerite in *Faust.* In the early 1900's she had sung opposite Caruso in London's Covent Garden. This was stardom and we made the most of it. She was an artist, she enjoyed fame. But happily for us she had also understood the people who jammed the tents to hear her sing. Her down-in-Tennessee birth gave her a bond with the small town. She never unbalanced her program because she faced a summer audience. Her German and French songs appeared in the same strength as they would have in Boston, but she knew how to oblige with folk songs for encores. At Chattanooga, in a count of "song requests," sixty-three out of two hundred and four were for "Kathleen Mavourneen, the gray dawn is breaking. . . ."

When the trip was over, Miss Nielsen, a little wan, said, "I've sung for every type of audience. Church, stage. Straight comedy, light opera, grand opera. Concert, oratorio. Now Chautauqua. Nowhere have I ever had a more appreciative audience. Often farm families filled the tent. The look on their faces was the same whatever I sang. They loved music."

In the Alice Nielsen Musical Company a few years later a cello player in his very early teens amused himself, as the train rolled along, by making rhythms from the sound of the wheels. Sometimes he scratched them down on paper. Older talent, watching him, wondered: Was this a boy-genius, composing a masterpiece, or was he just bored? They learned later. He was Howard Hanson who became the great composer and conductor, the handsome bearded director of the Eastman School of Music at Rochester, New York.

In 1915 Miss Nielsen's pianist was William Reddick, the assisting violinist Karel Havlicek. These two shared the *Mayflower* with her. The little piano tuner, who took over anxiously the minute the train slid to a halt, rode with less famous talent in a less comfortable car.

Crew boys prayed for heavy dew on "Nielsen Night," to tighten up the tent and make it a good sounding board. All artists objected to noise; Miss Nielsen chafed at small sounds, boiled over at louder ones. The evening express, clearing every grade crossing on ten miles of main line with an admonitory hoot, left her deeply unhappy. Let there be an evening express and a crying baby, too—in that case, even brash crew boys knew enough to keep their distance. They had heard about her angry telegram from Tennessee when the cows mooed outside the tent, everybody had heard of it. Nobody mentioned it.

Unlike Sandor Radanovitz, frustration did not send Miss Nielsen to bed.

It sent her storming, with a chance that something at hand might get thrown. If it were the white roses an admirer in the town just had sent up, why, too bad. She liked white roses. She preferred them to red. But Pianist Reddick had been an eighth note behind in the loveliest part of the Heart's Delight aria from *Figaro*. She had sung that aria in Covent Garden and who was Reddick to mar it? Before she went to bed she flung the fresh roses out the door.

The car stood nearer the station than usual and her admirer discovered his gift wilting on the ground. As might be expected, Redpath had complications over its next year's contract with that town.

In 1916 Alice Nielsen moved her grand piano into another private car on the Ohio circuit, along with Pianist Reddick and Karl Kirk-Smith as cellist. Taking her place in the *Mayflower* was Julia Claussen, mezzo-soprano from Sweden's Royal Opera.

Madame Claussen had been in this country only four years. The European war had halted her Continental concert tours and she had come to the States, to the regret of King Gustaf. At home she held the Jenny Lind Medal and the King's own decoration. She had mastered the contralto as well as the mezzo-soprano parts of almost every standard opera. She would be missed in Stockholm. But the Chicago Grand Opera had been quick to welcome her. Summer Chautauqua would only fill a gap before the New York Metropolitan.

Madame Claussen's assisting artists were both Frenchmen, Violinist Pierre Henrotte and Pianist Marcel Charlier, director of the French Grand Operas. Again there was no preliminary act the evening this high-priced group held the stage, and, as on "Nielsen Night," single admissions cost one dollar.

Travelling with Madame Claussen in the sumptuous *Mayflower* were her husband, Captain Theodore, and their two young daughters. Somehow in the hubbub of travel the four maintained a family life, even had fun. Loafers around the Darlington, South Carolina, cotton warehouse one steaming Sunday watched the prima donna and her children. Dressed in chin-high wool bathing suits, they were cooling off under the hose that Captain Claussen had tied to the roof of the loading shed.

Crew boys joined the family when they finished work. The boys were not afraid of Madame Claussen. She gave them food, even breakfast sometimes. There was the night in Cynthiana, Kentucky, when a switch engine, pushing the *Mayflower* into a siding, jumped the tracks. The boys went to work with the railroaders. They were dirty and dog-tired when the engine was back where it belonged. It was just dawn.

They were asking each other: Had Madame Claussen slept through the racket, when the door opened and she appeared.

"Come in," she said. "Breakfast is ready."

Madame Claussen, like Miss Nielsen, took it for granted that her summer crowds wanted good music. So she opened usually with Schumann's *Wid-mung* and *Frülingsnacht*. At some point she included the contralto aria, "My Heart at Thy Sweet Voice" from *Samson and Delilah*—Delilah was one of her best roles.

The seven-day circuit opened April 20 that year in Jacksonville, Florida, with what we proudly classed as a "big town program." Everything went well. The company had moved northward to Griffin, Georgia, when, on "Claussen Night" there occurred one of those near-catastrophes that could whiten the hair of a superintendent.

Griffin was a cotton town, a county seat. It manufactured towels, stockings and half dozen other cotton products. It was not a large city. Its population was considerably under ten thousand, but that still put it in the top ten cities of the state. "Chautauqua Week" had brought people in from all over the county.

Madame Claussen was in the middle of the *Samson and Delilah* aria when Superintendent Joe Meade, later dean of men at Cornell College, Iowa, sniffed. He smelled smoke. Quietly, very quietly, he snooped around. It did not take long to find the trouble. Electric wire, fastened to the canvas by rings, was burning against the tent roof behind the stage. He leaped up and tore it down. Miss Claussen, unaware, went on with her aria.

Next day she asked solicitously, "Dear Mr. Meade, tell me, why the bandages?"

Accidents to equipment were incessant. But those that involved persons, considering the vast number on the march, actually were rare—although that same summer Contralto Elsie Baker, starting out for ten weeks with the Oratorio Artists on eastern Redpath, broke her ankle the third day and sang all the rest of the season from a wheel chair.

This was anxious 1916. The next year the United States entered the First World War. The declaration of war was signed April 6, the Friday before Easter, and the day after Easter we took uneasily to the road. Dislocations were immediate. Crew boys and platform talent rushed to enlist or found defense jobs. Speakers had to cancel.

Everyone suffered, but as spring turned into summer, those who had the biggest worries were the men who handled the equipment. Normally it was moved in baggage cars attached to passenger trains. These cars were needed now for troop movements, and lucky the superintendent who, to begin with, could get a rickety old freight car, next persuade a railroad to hook such a car to a passenger train in time to make the next date. President Wilson eventually eased our travel restrictions to some extent. Also, under a ruling by the Secretary of War, Chautauqua and Lyceum folk, "because their work was of an educational nature," were not subject to the draft.

After the War Department's Commission for Training-Camp Activities was formed under Raymond B. Fosdick, the Redpath bureaus, together with the Y.M.C.A. and the Klaw Theatre chain, took over the job of entertaining the soldiers in the camps; each group also put physical properties at the disposal of the government.

For admission to an Activities Commission entertainment, the soldier needed only to present his Smileage Book. This device originally was planned to resemble a railroad mileage book. But a young artist in the Globe Printing Company of Philadelphia, drawing the cover, created the word "S-mileage." It caught on. Relatives and friends bought more than two million dollars worth of coupons as gifts for their proverbially penniless soldiers. The Rotary and all Chautauquas handled the sale.

When the war ended, $400,000 worth of these books were unredeemed. To whom did this money belong? No one was quite sure. It took an Act of Congress to get the sum out of a bank and assign it to Walter Reed Army Hospital in Washington, D.C.

In the meantime a new kind of talent had flocked to the platform. Newspaper correspondents, new flying "aces," Red Cross nurses had stories of some kind to tell. John Foster Fraser, England's top newspaper correspondent, was among the first to knock at the lecture-bureau door; Canada's hero, Private Harold Peat, soon followed him.

Fraser, who was knighted next year by King George, first offered a lecture with political overtones, called *The Checkerboard of Europe.* He talked war; Private Peat talked peace. Their approach was so different, their feelings were so high, that as we had done with William Jennings Bryan and Champ Clark, we maneuvered to keep Sir John and Private Peat off the same circuits at the same time.

Private Peat, with his *The Inexcusable Lie*—later he changed to other titles, all with the same idea—was to be a headliner the remainder of Chautauqua's life. He talked with brutal frankness to a people who hated war more than ever and who, as much as ever, apparently liked to be shocked by a realistic narrative. Peat, like Justice Oliver Wendell Holmes returning as a youth from service with the Union troops, was bitter at loose, excited talk on the platform of "gallantry," "cowardice," "courage." He wanted no flags waved. War was a miserable, rotten business. Accounts of battles should not be "tales of a circus."

"War is an organized bore," Holmes had said, refusing to talk about it. Peat was not aloof like Holmes. He called war carnage and preached that it should be prevented.

We booked Britisher Ian Hay and American Arthur Guy Empey. Hay's real name was Major John Beith and he was the author of the first best seller of the war, *The First Hundred Thousand,* the story of the British volunteers who died gloriously trying to stem the German military tide. Hay was one of the handful to live to tell the tale. He was another of the lecturers with a permanent grudge against platform managers.

"I have lectured under five hundred and twenty-eight chairmen," he exploded one day, "and I loathe every one." All five hundred and twenty-eight, it seems, had talked too long in introducing him. All they needed to say was, "Here is Ian Hay."

Captain Empey's fighting remarks, like Sir John Fraser's, were opposite in philosophy to Private Peat's. Captain Empey's were based on his new book, *Over the Top,* which was to be made later into a nine-reel movie. He had been wounded fighting with the British at the Battle of the Somme; in between lectures, now, he recruited for the United States Army, into which the next year he went back to duty.

War hysteria caused a few program shifts. Bias against Iowa sociologist, Edward Steiner, an Austrian by birth, had raised its head before we entered the war; occasional overwrought communities cancelled his lecture, *From Alien to Citizen.* There were other scattered cases of unjust prejudice, and cases, too, of well-meaning lecturers who, in the enthusiasm of their cause, overplayed their acts.

Once, in Sebring, Florida, I chanced to hear Elwood T. Bailey, who had been overseas with a welfare unit, talking to a misty-eyed group of fathers and mothers.

"Just what kind of man is this Jack Pershing who's in charge of your sons?" he asked them. "Well, I'll tell you . . ." and he rushed into a wonderful tale. He had asked a company of Marines, ordered over the top at one A.M., "How many of you boys have written home to your mothers?"

"Not many had," he related, "so I went to Jack and said, 'Jack, will you postpone this attack one hour?' and he said, 'Sure, Elwood, one hour.' "

Bailey appeared on the same circuit with General Pershing's brother James, who offered a speech called *Backing up the Boys.*

A star attraction the first summer proved to be Robert Bowman, a volunteer with the American Ambulance Corps in France, whose speech, we advertised, would tell "the inside story of the resignation of General Joffre." His lantern slides included a close-up of a bursting large-caliber shell. The sight was shockingly new to our public. It terrified, and also fascinated.

Actually, more speakers were available than the circuits could use. Many were women, heroines in both name and fact, with exciting, and often touching, stories. Belgian nurse Marie Van Gastel was one, and a pretty young French girl, Marie Rose Lauler, who had been a German captive, was another. Captain Paul Périgord took off his horizon-blue cap and told of France's last stand at Verdun; next night Captain Norman Knight praised the Scottish Gordon Highlanders. Most of the men lecturing were on hospital leave. All spoke feelingly and at least with some restraint, and then along came Captain George F. Campbell of the Royal Flying Corps.

Had he no other claim to greatness, Captain Campbell could go down in history as the man who introduced the expletive "Hell" to the Chautauqua platform. He didn't speak it, exactly. He shouted it, and with a British accent. And not merely once, but repeatedly.

"We gave that Hun Hell!" he cried, and next minute, again bringing down both fists on the speaker's stand, "And another of the Kaiser's planes went straight to Hell!"

The tent did not collapse. The audience did not march out in a body. No one asked to have his money refunded. No radio engineer, sitting in a cramped control booth, could cut us off the air. Before season's end this handsome young ace, describing *A Soldier in the Sky,* had also hurled a "damn" into the people's ears.

The second summer, with America deep in the war, Ralph Dunbar's new revue was a rousing, flag-waving extravaganza in which the eagle screamed throughout and every line had a patriotic meaning. By the end of the second act, arthritic grandfathers were trying to tear down the tent sides to rush off and enlist.

Dunbar's cast of twenty-three represented the Allies in every glorious attitude. Dressed as American, British, French and Belgian soldiers, as Joan of Arc, Uncle Sam, a Red Cross girl, *La Belle France* in Liberty cap, the Spirit of Verdun and the Statue of Liberty, they sang *Tipperary* and *Over There* and *Keep the Home Fires Burning.* The "Parade of the Allies" that ended the show swept around the tent, and everyone able to totter joined in the grand march.

Other acts hitched their appeal to patriotism that year. Old-time impersonator John Ratto also called his program a "revue." The word was to degenerate gradually until dignified performers let it alone. But in 1917 Ratto's "revue" was so well received that he repeated it for several seasons after World War I ended. He used his old devices. By skillfully daubing his face and shifting wigs, he represented everyone from George Washington and Abraham Lincoln to President Poincaré and King Albert of Belgium.

Programs could not deal with war exclusively. Distraught people with soldier sons had to be amused as well as stirred, and the sons still in camp had to be entertained. All music could not be martial. So it was fortunate that Redpath was ready, as the war started, with light opera.

Shortly after we presented our first plays, we began to experiment with opera. This was less risky, because of the common acceptance of costumes with music; entertaining companies had offered "costumed operas" for many seasons. Two things, unfortunately, made the average light opera unsuited to our tents. First, the casts were so large that no Chautauqua treasurer could pay their salaries. Second, the acts, sometimes three, often four, were so long, with encores added—and every audience insisted on getting its money's worth—that the last curtain would go down too late for children, and local Chautauqua committees depended on the whole family's attendance.

Dunbar and Tooley took over the task, with assistance from Sandor Radanovitz. With their souls bleeding for every character sheared out of the script, every aria left behind, every chorus reduced to a quartet or a trio, they cut good light opera into short lengths. They began with Gilbert and Sullivan.

The pleasant humor of this team of British geniuses was already well known to the Woodrow Wilson generation in America. It was genuinely English, with no tinge of vulgarity. Churchgoers were familiar with the fact that it was Sir Arthur Sullivan who had written the music for *Onward, Christian Soldiers;* many of them had sung his *Lost Chord.* If Chautauqua now had something else to offer by Sir Arthur and his song-writing partner, well and good. The people would listen.

In 1917 the Howard Tooley Opera Company went out with *The Mikado.* They had cut it down to two acts, with Arthur Aldrich in the role of the Minstrel, Nanki Pooh, the disguised son of the Emperor. Aldrich, one of the country's leading light opera tenors, had scored in DeWolf Hopper's [1] recent revival of this most famous of Gilbert and Sullivan's operettas. Big Ed Andrews sang the part of Ko-Ko, the Lord High Executioner. Bertha James Gilbert fitted admirably the part of charming Yum-Yum.

The company numbered only thirty, including the orchestra. The war was giving women a chance to pursue many activities heretofore not accessible to them. The orchestra conductor was tall, talented, high-strung Miss May Valentine, musical protégé of an Indiana heiress. There were a few women among the players, too, and in addition to the opera performance at night, they gave a separate concert every afternoon. We bought a truck to carry the scenery and, for $12,000, a big second-hand, six-wheel bus to transport the cast. We painted *Mikado* in large letters on both sides of the bus, "Redpath" in more modest ones. The fact that the second-hand vehicle was forever breaking down detracted not at all from its advertising value.

Single admissions were seventy-five cents for *The Mikado.* From Florida north to Michigan it was a sell-out, playing everywhere to audiences overflowing into the fields. The sets were simple and colorful, the costumes gay, the airs light and graceful enough to please the most unmusical audiences, from *Three Little Maids,* to *Flowers That Bloom in the Spring.* The story ended happily. The audience, moved though it was by Titwillow, the little bird that died for love, nevertheless went home cheerful and content.

The next year Tooley presented *The Chocolate Soldier,* with Marjery Maxwell in the lead. Bernard Shaw's sardonic *Arms and the Man,* from which this opera was taken, might have been too subtle for our customers. Oscar Straus' pleasant musical adaptation was not.

By the end of the war, light opera, like the play, was established on

[1] Actor William DeWolf Hopper, comedian who at the turn of the century had been playing in musical extravaganzas in Weber and Field's Music Hall, and who from 1912 on starred in many Gilbert and Sullivan revivals, went out for Redpath Lyceum Bureau for several years with his own company. This was in the 1930's, after Chautauqua was gone from the road.

Chautauqua circuits. Companies remained small and orchestra members adaptable. If there were ten players, each one usually could double on an additional instrument. Likewise, members of the cast joined in lustily, when occasion required, to reinforce the chorus which sometimes had as few as four regular singers. Thus the added cost of a dozen or more railroad fares and weekly salaries was avoided.

When Gilbert and Sullivan's *H.M.S. Pinafore* set out to sail the ocean blue on Chicago's DeLuxe circuit, Arthur Deane, who had taken the role of Captain Corcoran in the original London production, led the company. Mildred Rodiger sang "Buttercup," with her tray of ribbons and laces. From the moment the big costume trunks were lifted off the morning train through to the last catchy song, reception of this opera, too, amounted to what the local press called "an ovation." The evening air in a hundred little towns was sweetened by the lilting melody:

> "So buy of your Buttercup, poor little Buttercup,
> "Come of your Buttercup buy."

When Arthur Deane's voice thundered:

> "I am never known to quail
> "At the fury of the gale
> "And I'm never, never sick at sea!"
> "What, never?" . . . "No, never!" . . . "Then give three cheers. . . ."

the audience responded with three cheers and one more. As in New York's Fifth Avenue Theatre in 1879, when Sir Arthur Sullivan conducted an orchestra in the play's American opening, people welcomed it enthusiastically.

Equally well-trained troupes were responsible for successful tours of *The Chimes of Normandy, Robin Hood, The Bohemian Girl,* Puccini's *Madame Butterfly*.

A happy little Japanese soprano who loved to sing, Tamakia Miura, was our star in Puccini's tragic piece. Fortuno Gallo, the dapper impresario of the National Opera Company, had brought her to this country. She travelled for us four seasons, first in Butterfly—"and a little butter ball she is herself," you heard people say—and then with her own formal programs. Her husband was a doctor in Japan. At the time she was the only woman in her country successful in opera.

Redpath booked Christian Zacharias for the male lead in Balfe's gay musical, *The Bohemian Girl*. The gypsy with her tambourine was Hazel Allison. For days after this company left town, postmen, milkmen, boys delivering papers walked the streets whistling, "I Dreamt I Dwelt in Marble Halls." The season that *The Bohemian Girl* showed on Crawford Peffer's New England circuit, there were three other complete theatrical companies on the same six-day program, not to mention a marionette show thrown in for good measure. We had come, indeed, into the big time.

Maidens Fair

18

In his 1915 Chautauqua program, Poet Edmund Vance Cooke recited a four-stanza verse on woman's about-face from pie-baking to politics. He called it *Mother's Gone A-Marching*. It ran in part:

"Mother used to join the 'Dorcas' and the 'Missionary Band,'
"And spent herself from Greenland's ice to India's coral strand,
"She never dreamed of politics, nor cared how they were made,
"But now . . . well, Mother's marching in the Suffraget parade.
    "Hep! Hep!
    "Mother is keeping step,
    "Marching with her chin up and a plenitude of pep!
"She wouldn't pass a corner-store or any loafing spot,
"For fear someone would look at her . . . or heaven alone knows what!
"But now she lugs a yellow sign which shrieks 'I want a Vote!'
"Implying that she'll get it, or else get someone's goat.
    "Hike! Hike!
    "Mother's on a strike!"

The fight for woman suffrage waxed eloquent in the Chautauqua tents. When the Susan B. Anthony amendment finally became law in late August, 1920, echoes of thousands of flaming words settled over the hills. Tired women took off their yellow and white ribbons and went back to neglected kitchens. Since the day almost a half century earlier when a gallant California senator had introduced the resolution, clubwomen in feather boas or militant hats, mannish short skirts or trailing evening gowns, had climbed persistently to any stage and asked for the right to vote.

James Redpath had endorsed woman suffrage; his lecture bureau booked its advocates wherever it could. Mary Livermore, whom he called the "Queen of the Lyceum," had made her first speech by chance, just after the siege of Vicksburg. She had been working on the battlefield and had come north to beg for supplies. Reaching St. Louis on a Sunday, she had asked a clergyman to tell her story. He persuaded her to tell it herself and in her muddy dress she had mounted the platform.

After the Civil War the subject of anti-slavery had given way in conversation and speeches to the problem of Negro suffrage. On this no one was more vocal than Anna Dickinson. As a girl she had scrubbed pavements to earn two shillings for a ticket to hear Wendell Phillips; her own lecture fees later climbed to two hundred dollars a night.

"She is not afraid to say 'shirt' or 'legs,' " Redpath said of Miss Dickinson. "There is not a particle of forced modesty about her. Everyone feels as though he were sitting in the presence of a very chaste and pure-minded woman." Pure-minded, but intense. By 1870 she was speaking so hotly that after hearing her an Ohio editor wrote, "Pants are likely to be worn by a few of the Dickinson converts before the vexed question is laid."

The public had been chilly in its reception of women when they talked anti-slavery and temperance. At least it seemed so to Susan B. Anthony and Elizabeth Cady Stanton; if a woman's words were ever to be taken seriously, she must have the vote. Handsome Mrs. Stanton, who was born before the War of 1812 and lived to see Teddy Roosevelt in the White House, appeared often on the same platform with Miss Anthony. In James Redpath's first season the two launched the *Revolution,* the first printed organ of the feminist movement. Its motto was: "The true republic—men, their rights and nothing more; women, their rights and nothing less."

Everyone respected tall, thin-faced Miss Anthony. A Quaker by birth, she never could be as militant as Miss Dickinson; or as that other headliner, Lucy Stone, who in midcentury dared sound the first call for a women's rights convention. Miss Stone had flouted custom by keeping her maiden name when she married Abolitionist Henry B. Blackwell, and to make another point for her cause, she allowed her property to be sold for taxes, and then published a pamphlet on "taxation without representation." Miss Stone's father had not believed in education for women, let alone the vote. His opposition had not kept her from working her way through Oberlin College, the first school in the country to let women enter as equals with men.

In one of her first public steps, Miss Anthony had launched in New York the first woman's temperance society in the country. Next she had touched off a celebrated case by casting a vote in Rochester, New York, in the Presidential election of 1872. She was arrested and fined one hundred dollars. The following year she said in a speech:

"Webster . . . defines a citizen to be a person in the United States entitled to vote and hold office. The only question left to be settled now is:

Are women persons? And I hardly believe any of our opponents will have the hardihood to say they are not. Being persons, then, women are citizens . . ."

Miss Anthony's fine was still unpaid when she died in 1906. Her steadfast example sparked the suffrage movement.

Taking to assembly stages while Miss Anthony was still in public life, and in 1900 following her as president of the National American Suffrage Association, was Mrs. Carrie Chapman Catt. Tall, handsome, white-haired Mrs. Catt, a midwesterner, saw the fight through with the help of Dr. Anna Howard Shaw.

Through 1915 and 1916 and the war years of 1917 and 1918, pressure for votes for women had been exerted chiefly on Washington. After the Sixty-sixth Congress finally proposed the amendment to the states, in the early summer of 1919, ratification was up to the people at home, and the people at home attended Chautauqua. So our "Women's Days" began to resemble "Bryan Days," with the yellow and white banners rivalling Chautauqua's own. The "suffrage tent" stood just within the gate, and foolish the man who tried to duck by it without taking the piece of literature a determined sister thrust into his hand. Woe, also, to the visiting lecturer if he failed to drop a favorable word in her direction.

Straw ballots livened up many a 1919 program: "Are you for or against women having the vote?" States in the Mississippi Valley and the west were voting on ratification that season. One western town, tired of the argument, signed its Chautauqua contract with a provision, in plain print, that no one should refer on the platform to suffrage, nor to prohibition, even to temperance. Next summer, as the tents on the DeLuxe circuit moved through the south, Tennessee was preparing to accept the amendment, North Carolina to reject it. Tennessee, as the thirty-sixth state to ratify, claimed credit jubilantly in August for making the amendment into law.

Miss Jane Addams, of Chicago's Hull House settlement, who consistently opposed any violence by women in their efforts to win the vote, was vice-president of the National American Woman's Suffrage Association when Dr. Anna Howard Shaw was its president. In 1913 the International Suffrage group met in Budapest and Dr. Shaw gave the "Congress sermon." In telling of it later, in her *Second Twenty Years at Hull House,* Miss Addams said:

"In scholastic cap and gown, Dr. Shaw stood on her raised dias and with the eloquence of which she had been past master since her early days as a pioneer Methodist preacher, she filled the vast arches with a valiant plea for the rights of women, based on the old historic pleas for the rights of the individual." [1]

[1] *The Second Twenty Years at Hull House,* by Jane Addams. Copyright © 1930. Used by permission of The Macmillan Company.

Jane Addams made only a few Chautauqua appearances. She was too busy; too busy in Hull House, in international peace groups, in Chicago's civic affairs, before Congressional committees, in independent politics. At the Bull Moose convention in 1912, Miss Addams was the first woman ever to second a Presidential nominating speech. With convincing words she endorsed Theodore Roosevelt.

Dr. Shaw, however, had no settlement house to run. Her squat, vigorous figure appeared everywhere. She was a Methodist minister and a doctor, but first and last a suffragette. When the nineteenth amendment finally was ratified, determined Dr. Shaw was seventy-three years old; most of the free moments of her life she had spent lecturing and holding office in the movement.

In the late 1870's, the New England conference of the Methodist Episcopal church had refused to ordain Dr. Shaw because of her sex. The General conference had sustained the refusal. But the Methodist Protestants, a splinter branch of the denomination, had welcomed her. She preached, lectured, wrote, argued constantly from then on, the first ordained woman ever to preach in London and half a dozen European capitals. But like other truly great persons, she insisted to the end of her career, "My poor weak knees knock together during the first five minutes of every speech."

Miss Addams and Dr. Shaw and blind Helen Keller, with her teacher beside her, were great names on a program. There were others, not so famous, but equally articulate. Mrs. Percy Pennybacker, a peppery little lady from Texas, appeared repeatedly in the "morning hour" session. She drew attendance partly because of her lively manner, partly because she was president for several years of the growing General Federation of Women's Clubs. After the Suffrage Association was converted into the League of Women Voters, Mrs. Pennybacker went out with a new challenge: *How Should You Use Your Vote, Now That You Have It?* She was a trustee for some length of time of the Chautauqua Lake Institute.

The most vocal suffragette on the Redpath-Chicago circuit was that five feet, four inches of energy, Miss Jeannette Rankin. The public's initial feeling about Miss Rankin was curiosity; she had been the first woman ever elected to the United States Congress—from Montana on the Republican ticket in 1914. Then, in great areas of public opinion, rage followed curiosity. When the resolution for war was being voted on in the House in April, 1917, she at first remained silent. Then "Uncle" Joe Cannon urged her, "You cannot afford not to vote, you represent the womanhood of the country in the American Congress." Thereupon, with forty-nine men, she voted against the resolution. But not only that. She burst into tears as she stood by her chair to tell why. Zealots did not like her explanation. Some women said that she had shamed them. We resisted the pressure and continued to book her. When the war hysteria ended, crowds filed in again to hear her. She had not changed, and did not. When 1941 came and the Second

World War, she was again a member of the House and again voted against war—this time hers was the *only* negative vote.

Miss Rankin's later lecture, *Let the People Know,* filled postmen's bags with letters. "Write your Congressman!" she cried. "Tell him what you think!" Congressmen read the flood of correspondence and didn't know what to think. Matters which they previously had considered only their own affair apparently were very much the affair of the people.

I once heard Jane Addams tell an audience: "The French have a proverb. 'Men make the roads but it is women who teach the children how to walk.' " This, indirectly, is what Miss Rankin and her women friends talked about. Some years before, along with a few men, they had dared mention wormy flour; presently the country got a pure-food law. They talked better schools, and in 1917 Federal grants to education became a fact. They proposed a child-labor amendment; in 1924 such an amendment finally went to the people for ratification. Clean streets, mothers' pensions, eight-hour days, safety in factories, all came within their province. Some dreams went up in smoke. Ideas that were practical became issues, then laws.

Great Britain, over a period of years, sent the American lecture platform the highly dramatic, and highly controversial, Mrs. Emmeline Pankhurst. Each trip, by accident or design and to the benefit of herself and the Pond Lecture Bureau, followed a violent incident in her campaign at home. For she used stones, fists and even arson, if no peaceable way presented itself, to emphasize her conviction that the Liberal Party must enfranchise women.

Mrs. Pankhurst's first visit here was in 1908. She had been arrested for the first time while on her way to the Prime Minister with a petition. Ill health prevented her from serving all of a five weeks' sentence and she recuperated on platforms in the United States. She went to jail again in 1909; two years later her second American trip followed a nine months' sentence. This time, with her daughter Christabel, she had broken windows. In 1913 and 1914 she used arson.

English women were at the height of their campaign of violence. At the Derby, Emily Davison had thrown herself under the feet of a racing horse, to be trampled to death in order to get the attention of the King. Mrs. Pankhurst did not go to quite such extremes. She merely demonstrated her outrage with a bomb at Lloyd George's house and was sentenced to Old Bailey prison for three years. "Hunger striking" brought her release in less than four months. Again there followed excellent performances on platforms in Canada and the United States.

In 1914, when war struck England, Mrs. Pankhurst ceased her militancy and spoke in behalf of recruiting. As with many other extremists, time was sobering, for after English women did acquire the franchise, two years before their American sisters, Mrs. Pankhurst joined the Conservative party. She was sixty years old.

Vawter had one woman lecturer on his pioneer 1904 tour, Maud Ballington Booth, the little "Mother of the Prisons." Another speaker from the independent assemblies followed close on her heels. She was Mrs. LaSalle Corbel Pickett. Her name, like Miss Mary Livermore's, went back to the Civil War, but unlike Miss Livermore, she was not militant.

Fastidious little Mrs. Pickett always stepped out gracefully onto the stage in a clinging black lace gown, yet the only luggage she ever seemed to bother with was her little black handbag. She was the widow of General George B. Pickett, leader of the tragic Confederate charge at Gettysburg, and she kept faith with him for a score of years, by repeating over and over in Chautauqua, "The Confederacy was right!"

"Mother" Booth's lecturing career began before little Mrs. Pickett's ended, and stretched long past it. Steadily, all her life, she pleaded for decent people to help the ex-convict. British-born—and not to be confused with the Redpath bureau's actress Maud Booth—"Mother" Booth had left her original relief work with the Salvation Army while still a fairly young woman. With her husband she had organized the Volunteers of America. Her own name was Maud Charlesworth, her husband was Ballington Booth. Her speeches on the shocking conditions in English and American jails helped whip up the wave of prison reform that swept this nation before the First World War.

We billed "Mother" Booth's speeches just as she wanted them, even though her titles had the ring of a dime novel. *Broken Hearts Mended, After Prison What?* and *Wanted, Antiseptic Christians* are samples. "Every man can be redeemed by Divine Power" she used to say as she ended a speech, "provided he will second that power."

The Redpath systems never booked Carrie Nation, although a few of the smaller circuits did. We did sign Virginia Brooks and "Mother" Lake.

Shortly after the turn of the century, Mrs. Nation had made headlines and headaches by her direct approach to the liquor problem. Armed with a sharp hatchet, she had fought the Demon Rum by chopping any handy saloon or beer garden to pieces and getting arrested for her effort. "Hatchetation," she called her method. There is small doubt that she was encouraged by the press to engage in her forays, and she managed to stay in the headlines for several years.

Young, energetic Miss Brooks was like Carrie Nation, to the extent of believing in direct action. The ballot box, in Miss Brooks' opinion, not only was slow but sometimes corrupt. She wanted women to vote, and men to vote honestly, and her elaboration on these desires filled a good stirring hour.

Miss Brooks was a reformer of the first order, with the zeal of a female Tom Paine. She also was comely, whether riding her white horse at the head of a parade, or driving to the polls at West Hammond, Illinois, in a buggy draped in the Stars and Stripes. The newspapers dubbed her "the Twentieth-Century Joan of Arc"; it was good publicity.

Talent used to quote one remark, in particular, from the speeches of "Mother" Lake: "God never intended man to smoke. If he had, he would have put a smokestack on his head." Being of a positive nature, she pounded the stand as she said it.

Mrs. Lake was an erect, well-groomed woman with sharp black eyes, born Leonora Marie Kearney, in County Cork, Ireland. She first lectured on "temperance." Then women's and children's wretched working conditions challenged her, and eventually she became the author of Pennsylvania's state factory inspection law. She spoke for Redpath, later, on the subject, *The Country Boy in the City.* He was not safe. Of that "Mother" Lake was sure.

In 1919 another Englishwoman arrived, but by no odds another Mrs. Pankhurst. Ada Ward was quiet, earnest, black-haired, witty. Her speech was full of humor, even though its title did not indicate it. She called it *Getting Together,* which meant friendly hands-across-the-sea between the United States and Great Britain. She treated her topic lightly, but she did not consider it so. To her, as to many others, it could be the most important thing in the world. She toured many summers, particularly effective on "opening night." Her 1927 topic, *You Americans,* laughed a little harder at our foibles, but it centered on the same theme, "Stay Friends."

We listed two women, about the time the peacemakers went to Versailles, who properly could be called orators. One was Mrs. Ruth Bryan Owen, later Ruth Bryan Rohde, the other Mrs. Mable Walker Willebrandt. Both were eloquent and handsome, with good stage presence.

Like Representative Rankin, Mrs. Willebrandt stirred enormous curiosity. She had been assistant attorney general under Harry Daugherty in President Harding's administration. Daugherty had been proven one of the dishonest "Ohio gang." What, people wanted to know, could she disclose about its scandalous goings-on? And what could stir up hotter debate than prohibition? Or taxes?

Mrs. Willebrandt had headed the division in the attorney general's office that handled both of these horrid subjects. In California she had been public defender of women. She had married at twenty-one, had been admitted to the bar when she was twenty-six, clung to her legal knitting through the Daugherty scandal, through the Coolidge and into the Hoover administration. Her story was lively and she told it brilliantly, first for Redpath-New England. But to the disappointment of the curious, she never mentioned Harry Daugherty.

Ruth Bryan Owen continued with us until, in 1929, with her children grown, she went to Congress for two terms from Florida. Audiences that had loved the Great Commoner were quick to transfer their affection to his only daughter. In New England, where Bryan, occasionally, had had a less warm reception, Mrs. Owen was unusually popular. She not only had inherited her father's platform presence and his gift for the right word; she also understood plain people and knew how to talk about the plain things that interested them. Her father had used a watermelon to illustrate his ideas in *The Prince of Peace.* She could be as simple and direct. "When you are brushing your teeth," she interrupted herself once to advise a startled audience, "brush your tongue, too. It's just as important."

She had been a nurse with the British Army in the First World War and had served in the Egypt-Palestine campaign, where she married Major Reginald Owen of the Royal Engineers, and her first speech she called *Modern Arabian Knights.* General Sir Edmund H. H. Allenby and his latter-day crusaders to the Holy Land were the "knights."

President Franklin D. Roosevelt, in 1933, was to make a payment on the Democratic debt to the Bryan family by appointing Mrs. Owen United States Minister to Denmark. Before returning home, she married Captain Borge Rohde, gentleman-in-waiting to the King. Indicative of Mrs. Rohde's closeness to the platform is the fact that her first published book was *Elements of Public Speaking.* Many others followed.

Louis Alber, of the Coit-Alber bureau, once told Chautauqua and Lyceum managers, "The most dangerous subject to tackle on the platform is housekeeping. The subject is more thickly covered with a concrete mixture of prejudice and ignorance than any other."

Mrs. Sarah Tyson Rorer, high priestess of the cook book, was lecturing on the New England circuit at the time, preaching efficiency in the kitchen. Mrs. Rorer was plump and pleasant and she came from Pennsylvania, where food was good. She looked important, and women suspected she really was—she was an editor and publisher as well as a cook, and anyone who could have seventeen books published, all on the same general subject, must be important. The book on "made-overs," in particular, would be handy to own, women thought.

But Mrs. Rorer didn't mix bread the way some people had been taught, and her "twenty quick soups" weren't so quick. There was grumbling, here and there in the audience. What *was* efficiency in a kitchen? More cooking or less? And which should one buy first, *Mrs. Rorer's New Cook Book,* or *Mrs. Rorer's Philadelphia Cook Book?*

Blue-blooded Nellie Tayloe Ross, the first woman governor of a state, headlined our 1929 programs. Four years earlier, on January 5, 1925, she had succeeded her husband, William Bradford Ross, as Wyoming's chief executive. Wyoming had hurried with the honor. Fifteen days later Texas inaugurated Governor Miriam ("Ma") Ferguson.

Wyoming, Mrs. Ross took pains to explain, always had been gallant. It had been first among the states with equal suffrage. The men of the Territory had guaranteed women the vote in 1869, a score of years before it entered the Union, and in 1870 Mrs. Esther M. Morris of South Pass City was appointed the first woman justice of the peace in the world. Mrs. Ross, tall and aristocratic-looking, called her lecture *The Governor Speaks*. It was a down-to-earth plea to women, no matter how busy, to work actively in affairs outside the home. Mrs. Ross was to win another "first" later; President Franklin D. Roosevelt appointed her the first woman director of the United States mint.

Spirited little Mrs. Anna Dickie Oleson of Minnesota was another woman Democrat with a "first" to her credit. In 1922—the year the co-operatives in her farming state got exemption from the anti-trust laws—her party nominated her for the Senate. She was defeated, but that did not keep us from stressing the fact in our advertising that no other woman, up to then, had been so honored. The year James M. Cox was nominated for President, Mrs. Oleson had been a delegate to the Democratic national convention. She had served on her party's national committee; in count-less capacities, big and little, she had worked in the new, vocal League of Women Voters. She knew the ins and outs of public life and she discussed them in *Women in Politics*. No matter how hot the night, the people in front put down their fans and listened.

Crowds were thinning in 1929, but they never failed to jam the aisles for the tall girl in a flyer's helmet, Lady Mary Heath of Dublin, who covered a circuit in her own plane. If the town did not boast an airport she landed, without mishap, in a cow pasture and small boys followed her to the Chautauqua grounds. Lady Mary furnished lively material for our pub-licity posters. Typical was her flight to Niagara Falls for Redpath-New England, when she raced a telegram. She started the message as she left the Cleveland airport and beat it to Niagara Falls, which in those days was considered a smart feat, worthy of newspaper space. She talked on the *Conquest of the Air*. Her personal experience with the title had included a solo flight from Cape Town to Croyden Field.

Women travelled all the circuits, in all capacities, lugging their suitcases, sleeping in lumpy beds. In the entertainment ranks they supplied at least half the talent, and no one in the business worked harder than the in-spired young women who signed up to entertain the children.

"Junior Chautauqua" originated with the need to get the children out of the front rows while the "great men" spoke. Ten-year-olds might sit quietly while little Alice Schroeder sang and whistled, but not while Zueblin or Hobson urged freedom of the seas. If the parent, or the lecturer, was to have peace of mind inside the tent, the children must be entertained outside. This was the idea in the beginning. It quickly outgrew the first plan.

Within a few seasons we discovered that in Junior Chautauqua we had a silver mine in our back yard. The dimes and quarters it produced were real. Before long, crew boys no sooner had set up the tent, than they un-packed a swing and filled a box with sand. Four-year-olds arrived first;

next curious older brothers. Soon a crowd of gangling twelve-year-olds sitting in a circle—in knickerbockers, not long pants—were listening, goggle-eyed, to what "Teacher" was telling about a man named Teddy Roosevelt. Nothing about Trusts or Big Business. Just about the American Boy. "Teacher" happened to know that this man had written an essay that ended with the words, "Hit the line hard! Don't foul and don't shirk, but hit the line hard!"

"Read it again!" became a chorus.

The girls in charge of the children at the start were college students. Later we hired trained city-playground workers. At first all they did was read stories—about "Darius Green and his Flying Machine," or Stockton's *Lady or the Tiger*. Was it the lady or the tiger came out of the open door?

"The tiger!" young people would scream.

The playground had to be moved before long, a safe distance from the tent. Shouts and laughter outside could be as distracting as wiggling inside. And if boys and girls were learning a bit about the germ theory by reciting a nonsense limerick, of course they would be shouting.

"Listen," said the teacher. "There is a poet named Arthur Guiterman and he wrote a verse like this:

'The Antiseptic Baby and the Prophylactic Pup
'Were playing in the garden when the Bunny gamboled up:
'They looked upon the creature with a loathing undisguised.
'It wasn't Disinfected and it wasn't Sterilized.' " [1]

The children got the point. It had something to do with washing one's hands and face before eating.

Grade-schoolers laughed hard when they heard about Carolyn Wells' "Tooter who tooted the flute," but they also learned that "Blow, blow, thou winter wind," came from Shakespeare and that *Evangeline* could be pretty good reading.

Because of these stories, the name "Teacher" shifted to "Story-Hour Lady," or some variation of the idea. On the Redpath-Vawter circuit, the word was "Squaw Lady," and sweating nobly under the Nebraska sun, she walked the fields in stout brown denim. The word itself was intriguing. One western cattleman named his new prize calf for the good-looking Squaw Lady whom his wife entertained in their home during Chautauqua week.

These were the days when well-dressed college girls wore long-sleeved white shirtwaists and long dark skirts. Not too long. Skirts already were starting upward; by 1926 they were at the knees and ready to start down again. The Story-Hour Lady wore them half way, and that pleased everyone. After a season or two, she appeared in bloomers, and not in a starched white blouse. A middy was comfortable, and why not, on a summer vaca-

---

[1] From the book *Lyric Laughter* by Arthur Guiterman. Copyright 1939, by E. P. Dutton & Co., Inc. Reprinted by permission of the publishers.

tion in Chautauqua, be comfortable? You could play volley ball without ripping a middy to pieces, teach a crowd archery, go on a hike, watch birds, do all the dozens of things that developed in children's entertainment.

Pet shows created universal excitement. Youngsters on "Children's Day," watched in awe while "Professor Pamahasika," in high patent-leather boots and a costume out of Arabian Knights, exhibited fifty "educated" cats, dogs, monkeys and back-yard sparrows. And then, as a matter of course, they always responded with alacrity when the Story-Hour Lady suggested that they have a pet show of their own.

A show to end shows took place one season in Flint, Michigan. Nice little girls displayed proper pets—dogs in ribbons, cats in doll dresses, a bird in a gilded cage. The boys roamed farther afield. One brought a dead mouse, another an angleworm. A third carried in a pan full of potato bugs. "They are trained," he explained. "When I shake the pan, they dance."

Juvenile entertainment gradually became more formalized. Groups of Camp Fire Girls were organized to match the Boy Scout troops that we had sponsored earlier. One year Redpath-Chicago staged a *Mother Goose Festival* in a hundred towns, another season a moralistic pageant called *Good Fairy Thrift*. Once in Kansas, on the Horner circuit, when a trained horse did not arrive in time for its date, Harry Dunbar and Charles T. Grilley of the Rogers and Grilley team built a trained wooden mule named Maude, who performed nobly to the delight of hundreds of children. No finale ever aroused more cheers than her *Hee-Haw Chorus*.

Stunts like these brought satisfied customers. Often a school-children's parade out-did the suffragettes'. In June, 1914, at Springfield, Ohio, a thousand boys and girls from all over the center of the state, decked in Chautauqua hats and waving pennants, arrived like a cloud of locusts at Chautauqua's opening performance. One photograph left for critical posterity shows President Calvin Coolidge, in 1927 in Rapid City, South Dakota, trying hard to smile as he holds an American flag and the hand of a perspiring five-year-old "Indian" who had just marched his short legs half off in Chautauqua's "Pilgrim-Indian Parade."

The first and most famous Story Lady was Miss Georgene Faulkner. Children on the playground of a Brooklyn settlement house where she worked named her. For several seasons in Chautauqua, Miss Faulkner talked in the mornings to parents and teachers on *How to Tell a Story*. Afternoons, in costume, she presented a program of folk tales and historical episodes. She possessed a remarkably clear, sweet voice. Blind Senator Gore, visiting the Chicago office and wanting someone to read aloud to him, always asked for Miss Faulkner.

Children's programs followed the same pattern as adults'. As the First World War approached, there were "Peace Pageants" and "Peace Parades." If civic reform was the shibboleth, the Story Lady translated it. One Squaw

Lady, with this in mind, presented a pageant once in which six little boys
sang *Town Song,* by Nan Oppenlander:

> "When we work and when we play,
> "Good citizens we will be.
>
> "Then I'll be proud of my own town
> "And I'll make her proud of me!"

I hope that they did. One afternoon, in the mid-twenties, I was on the
grounds in Quincy, Illinois, when I passed a group of young girls sitting in
a circle on the grass listening to the Story Lady read aloud. I stopped to
listen, too. She was a student from Rockford College, the school from which
Jane Addams was graduated, and she had a copy of Dr. Anna Howard
Shaw's *Autobiography, the Story of a Pioneer*.

There is a passage in that book which tells how young fifteen-year-old
Anna, already teaching country school, living with her family on a backwoods Michigan farm, received a proposal of marriage from a twenty-year-
old lad, who was, by an unhappy chance, "the least attractive young person
in the countryside." His costume, when he came to call on Anna, was a
blue flannel shirt and a pair of trousers made of flour bags. On one leg
was the name of the flour manufacturer, on the other leg it said, "96 pounds,"
and holding it all in place was a bright yellow sash.

The youth informed the young girl that his father just had given him
a cabin, a yoke of steers, a cow and some hens, and then he asked solemnly, "Will ye have me?"

The future great Dr. Shaw was flustered. "I can't," she told him. "I'm
sorry, but . . . but . . . I'm engaged."

The Story Lady then went on reading from Dr. Shaw's book: "He arose
quickly, with the effect of a half-closed jackknife that is suddenly opened.
. . . He was six feet, two inches tall and extremely thin. I am very short,
and as I looked up, his flour-bag trousers seemed to join his yellow sash,
somewhere near the ceiling of the room. He put both hands into his pockets
and slowly delivered his valedictory. 'That's darned disappointing to a fellow,' he said, and left the house." [1]

The girls, sitting in a circle on the Chautauqua grounds, shouted. Perhaps they had never learned who Dr. Anna Howard Shaw was. The suffrage
fight was over. But they knew a good story and a pleasant way to spend
an afternoon. This was it.

[1] *Autobiography, the Story of a Pioneer,* by Dr. Anna Howard Shaw and Elizabeth
Jordan. Published by Harper and Brothers.

The Clock Ticks On

19

A new America came out of the First World War, an America tired of issues. Great sections of the country wanted to forget old arguments and stir up no new ones. The "war to end wars" had left a whopping tax bill, 126,000 dead, uncollectable debts of nearly eighteen billion dollars from other nations, and a terror of international alliances.

The people, with women voting for the first time, were about to elect as their President that old Chautauquan, Warren G. Harding, on a platform that promised "normalcy" and little else. To many Americans, normalcy meant minding one's own business, planning one's own future, patching up one's fences and playing in one's own back yard. It meant peace.

Harding typified the moment by campaigning for the highest office in the land while sitting on the front porch of his plain frame house in his own small Ohio town. The "front porch campaign" had a homey, vote-getting appeal to a people tired of having their sons rushed around an unappreciative world on what seemed strangers' business. Harding did leave his old rocking chair long enough to make several brief speaking trips, one of them to Boston in May, 1920. It was there he first mentioned "normalcy."

"America's present need," he declaimed, "is not heroics, but healing; not nostrums but normalcy; not revolution but restoration; not surgery but serenity."

The speech expressed the average middle-class American's simple aspirations. The "heroics" and "nostrums" Harding mentioned were aimed directly at Woodrow Wilson's League of Nations. The League was Wilson's formula for that everlasting peace everyone hoped for more than anything else. Out of it, Wilson made clear, would come international agreements for disarmament.

Chautauqua managers made an honest attempt to give both sides of the picture. Brooks Fletcher, in 1920, was advocating universal military service; so were other regular lecturers. Oppositely the next year, under the leadership of Paul Pearson, managers and talent of both Lyceum and Chautauqua organized a committee to study means of disarmament. The debate in the Senate on the proposed League, stormy as it was and full of sound and fury, became muted by distance before it reached most quiet home towns. Earnest pleas for disarmament did stir controversy. The young, slim American Legion, its members still able to button uniforms worn at Belleau Wood, heeded the sonorous warnings of its orators against "letting down our guard" and came out flat-footed for "peace through preparedness." Legion spokesmen answered Chautauqua's disarmament pleaders by quoting Theodore Roosevelt's "Speak softly, but carry a big stick." The people listened to all the arguments but did not join in the shouting as they had in the Bede-Seidel debates over socialism.

Congressman Bede still toured the tent circuits with his "String of Bedes." He had a large family; of his many children, no two had happened to be born in the same state—so that his youngest, hearing Humorist Opie Read comment on it one night, asked, "How in the world did we ever get together then?" The fact that Chautauqua managers booked Bede continuously for more than a quarter of a century supports, as much as anything can, our claim that the independent speaker kept a permanent place on the programs. Bede, a Republican, had been a Cleveland Democrat; he had opposed Bryan, was an original Bull Mooser, at present was back in the Republican fold; in 1932 he would support Franklin D. Roosevelt.

Right now Bede was devoting his elocutionary talent to the proposed St. Lawrence Seaway. His home folk in Minnesota wanted cheaper freight rates to the seaboard for their wheat. This was something the midwest could understand. It was a home-grown subject, and if on deeper cogitation, it became apparent that Canada also was involved, Canada was just a neighbor, not an "entangling alliance."

Canada was part of the American scene. Chautauqua circuits crossed the border; Canadian talent came south—the Adanac Quartet, a lively musical attraction of the period, was made up of four young men who chose to spell Canada backward.

Entertainers, Canadian or otherwise, still accompanied the lecturers, even those on serious international subjects. Frederick William Wile, Hoosier-born foreign correspondent, tells how, in 1919, he travelled on Paul Pearson's Swarthmore circuit with a lecture called *John Bull and Uncle Sam.* Ninety midsummer nights he mounted the platform, after a melodious prelude by the Boston Beauty Sextette, made up of pretty New England college girls, and talked about international relations. He thought that his audiences were interested in what he said and the Swarthmore management considered him important enough to pay him $5000 for the three months. And then one evening in a North Carolina town the chairman of the occasion, a church deacon, stood with Wile in the wings while the crowd called the Boston beauties again and again for encores.

At last the deacon turned to the distinguished speaker. "Shall I put you on now," he asked, "or let them enjoy themselves a bit longer?"

As had happened often before, lecturers popular in one section of the country drew a smaller gate in others. Seaboard audiences—and this now included the west coast with its eye on Japan—listened to ideas that the midwest found more and more irritating. Speakers from President Wilson's official family, for instance, seldom visited the plains states; even in the east and south people listened to them for many reasons other than mere interest in the content of their speeches. Rear Admiral Cary Grayson had a curiosity value; he had been "Wilson's doctor." Josephus Daniels, Secretary of the Navy for eight difficult years, was highly controversial; friends and critics alike went to hear him at least once. As for Bainbridge Colby, Wilson's third and last Secretary of State, he had participated in many of the ailing President's last official acts and so must have many secrets concealed under his well-brushed hat.

Colby, an original Bull Mooser, in legal tilts often had represented "the people" against "the interests," which in one instance were the insurance companies. He likewise told an occasional good story about Mark Twain. He had represented Twain in court in the settlement of his affairs with his publishing house.

Like Bryan before he left Wilson's cabinet, Daniels even before the war had been lampooned violently in the eastern press—he had denied the Navy its beer and later was to deny it prophylactics. His order in the spring of 1914 forbidding the use of alcoholic liquor in the Navy was "arbitrary." A *New York World* cartoon pictured both Bryan and Daniels as "Pirates," making "Alcohol" walk the plank, while an unhappy sailor hauled up a banner marked "Grape Juice." Cartoonist Nelson Harding, in the *Brooklyn Eagle,* under the title "Dropping the Pint," showed a dejected little "Wine Mess" walking down the ladder that usually dropped the pilot, while Daniels, in black clothes and broad-brimmed slouch hat, watched triumphantly from the main deck. This was a farcical adaptation of Tenniel's famous cartoon in *Punch* entitled "Dropping the Pilot," printed when the Kaiser got rid of his great Chancellor, Otto von Bismarck.

Some people disapproved of Secretary Daniels' enrolling women as yeomen for clerical work in the naval bureaus. In 1920 more headlines blazed when his wartime subordinate, Rear Admiral William S. Sims, fired a charge that as commander of naval forces Daniels had been hostile to the British. In short, he was talked about; therefore liked or disliked, vehemently in the cities, less so in the country, and the crux of the matter was not the political philosophy he represented, but "temperance."

The nation had voted itself bone dry while more than a million of its voteless young men in uniform were making the pleasant acquaintance of the wines of France. The accomplished fact of national prohibition naturally finished off the "temperance lecturer" who had dedicated his life and vocal cords to bringing about the Volstead Act. In his place appeared a new type of "dry" speaker, who told how to enforce the prohibition laws.

In the front ranks of these on the platform was an ebullient crusader, William "Pussyfoot" Johnson, who urged heroic measures to prevent boot-legging and to punish "scofflaws" who defied the new statute. Johnson had gained his nickname, he told audiences, by following "catlike policies" in pursuing the varmints who had tried to sell liquor to reservation Indians while he worked for the government in the southwest. He had gained international notoriety when, soon after the passage of the Volstead Act, he sailed for Europe to help rescue that debauched continent from the Demon Rum. He went first to the Scandinavian countries, where he was accorded a cold reception, later toured England. It was at Reading that an "un-regenerate bloke" heaved a whiskey bottle and put out one of Johnson's eyes. He wore a patch after that, and leaving the British to stew in their own Scotch and soda, he returned to many years of lecturing and editing in America.

Another character who came along to help lighten oratorical fare was Oklahoma's Texas-born governor, "Alfalfa Bill" Murray. Like "Pussyfoot" Johnson, Murray had worked in the old Indian Territory and he, too, told tales of those stirring days. A fearless speaker, who called a spade a spade, Murray was a lank man, with stooped shoulders and unruly handle-bar mustaches. He was famous up and down the Chautauqua circuits as the most astounding coffee drinker of all time. Instead of a pitcher of ice water on the table beside him, crew boys kept a pot of hot coffee. One evening he emptied seven pots. His method of drinking the coffee awed all watch-ers and listeners. To begin with, he strained it through the thicket of his mustache, then with his lower lip squeezed the mustache as he sucked in the last delectable drop with a whoosh of satisfaction. Goggle-eyed crew boys also insisted that he often spoke with a wad of tobacco in his cheek and that sometimes he strained the coffee through the quid as well.

Murray had been a pioneer himself and he refused to believe that the day of the American pioneer had passed. So he had bought, for a small sum, a great tract of land in Bolivia and he urged "red blooded Americans" to help him "strike out for a new life" by settling there. He was entirely honest in the matter and it made interesting listening, but he found few recruits.

The early 1920's brought forth all kinds of "groups." Some of these were selfish in their aims, others sought to contribute to the general welfare. Teachers began to weld scattered local and state organizations into a na-tional association. Farmers started the Farm Bureau Federation. Newspaper editors, actors, truckers, barbers and beauticians, chiropractors and motion-picture producers set up nationwide combinations.

Besides the American Legion, there came into being such diverse bodies as the Better Business Bureau, the Institute of Pacific Relations, the Civil Liberties Union, the radical I.W.W., the bigoted Ku Klux Klan. All had their pleaders and spokesmen and all longed for opportunity to tell their stories from any stage, including Chautauqua's. Some even tried to censor speakers in the tents.

Although it had been organized secretly in 1915 as a reincarnation of the old post-Civil-War "Klan," the Ku Klux Klan did not step into the open until the night of Saturday, October 20, 1920, when it held a masked and hooded parade in Jacksonville, Florida. Its original purpose was in part at least the same as that of its famous forerunner—to inspire terror among southern Negroes—and its determination was to maintain "white supremacy." It grew rapidly, chiefly in the less literate rural regions; by 1922 it had spread as far as Indiana, Iowa and Michigan.

In the north it played down its hatred of the Negro and substituted other hatreds and other fears. It became the bulwark against "the Pope" in Protestant midwest small towns; in the cities it warred against "the Jews."

Except in the south, where they treated the Klan warily, Chautauqua speakers boldly lashed out at the hooded mobs and the evil that they stood for. All preachers and many politicians denounced the night-riding, cross-burning forays. Joseph W. Folk of Missouri, who earlier had attacked dishonest city government, bitterly assailed "The Hooded Empire." There is no record of anyone ever defending the Klan in a Chautauqua tent.

Delegations from the "Imperial Wizard" appeared at various circuit headquarters, demanding the right to tell their side of the story. We once had offered the liquor interests a chance to speak, why not the Klan? We refused. No circuit, no lecturer or entertainer was molested and never was there a hooded picket line at a brown tent. But the Klan occasionally did attempt to boycott Chautauqua by urging its sympathizers to stay away. It failed, chiefly because the people who flocked to the programs were an intellectual cut above the Klan membership lists.

The American Legion, for its part, occasionally tried to censor those Chautauqua speakers who pleaded for peace at any price or who urged disarmament. Chief target of the Legion was Private Peat, with his *Inexcusable Lie,* charging that American children were being misled in their schoolbooks which represented war as glamorous. The Legion never set up a picket line, even against Peat. But at Terre Haute, Indiana, the local post did influence the Chautauqua committee to try to break its contract. We fought back, and won. The circuit played Terre Haute, Private Peat spoke, and the controversy in the newspapers stirred such curiosity that the crowds were good.

No other political convention year in Chautauqua's history, least of all 1920, produced the stirring debates of 1912. But 1924, with the Democrats deadlocked through one hundred and two ballots between Alfred E. Smith and William G. McAdoo, did approach the Bull Moose year in excitement.

John W. Davis, solid, colorless corporation lawyer from West Virginia, finally won the Democratic nomination for President, with Governor Charles W. Bryan of Nebraska as Vice-Presidential candidate. Calvin Coolidge and General Charles Gates Dawes were the Republican standard bearers, urging the voters "to keep cool with Cal."

The reorganized Progressive party, more serious and less spectacular than T.R.'s "hosts at Armageddon," nominated Chautauqua's old "Fighting Bob" LaFollette, with Montana Senator Burton K. Wheeler as his running mate. Wheeler, the previous March, had started the Senate inquiry that led to the exposure of Attorney General Harry Daugherty and the "Ohio gang" of Harding's administration. LaFollette, still "controversial," had been one of that "little group of willful men" who opposed Wilson's foreign policies. He had voted against declaration of war on Germany, fought American entry into the League of Nations, and started the Senate inquiry into the Teapot Dome scandals.

Chautauqua could claim four of the six candidates. Davis and Dawes never had spoken in the tents, but all the others had, either for long weeks or for scattered engagements. Charles Bryan, seven years younger than his brother, William Jennings Bryan, and considerably less gifted as a speaker, was a veteran of Vawter's circuit, talking, in a hesitant way, about good government. Republican politicians, who considered him merely a shirttail-rider, referred to him, lightly, as "Brother Charley."

LaFollette's lecturing days were mostly behind him; he was sixty-nine years old and conserving his strength for the campaign. He died the next summer. But many an old-timer from the seats down in front scratched his ticket that year to vote for Chautauqua's grand old man. He polled nearly five million votes. But the Democrat and the Progressive together did not reach the total of the victorious Coolidge. The country still wanted "normalcy."

The deadlock between Smith and McAdoo in the Democratic convention drummed into the public's mind a name that, while the sessions lasted, overshadowed those of the major candidates. For one hundred and two ballots, Alabama's delegation started the roll call by shouting, "Alabama casts twenty-four votes for Oscar W. Underwood."

Senator Underwood, for a dozen years, had appeared more or less regularly on several of the circuits. His subject, of course, had been the tariff. The Underwood Bill in 1913 had put iron, steel and raw wool on the free list. The same year he also had drawn up, introduced and fought through the Congress the measure that gave America its first Federal income tax.

In 1920, however, he had been American delegate to the International Conference on the Limitation of Armaments which Senator William E. Borah had first proposed, and from then on Underwood contributed hard facts to the discussion of the ways to peace.

Stephen S. Wise, a militant pacifist and a leader in the American League to Enforce Peace, came to the fore as the talk of disarmament swelled. Founder in 1907 of New York's Free Synagogue and its rabbi since that time, Wise already was a "personality," with one of the finest speaking voices on the platform. His crusades up to now had ranged from Zionism —he talked eloquently of the world's moral responsibility to grant the Jews a homeland in Palestine—to reform of prisons, abolition of child labor and the wretched county poor house, and general assistance for old age. The east and the far west both knew Rabbi Wise; he had preached a long time in Oregon.

Another voice discussing disarmament in the west was that of President —later Chancellor—David Starr Jordan of Leland Stanford University. The California educator in 1915 had been president of the World Peace Congress; as early as 1912 he had said hopefully that "the great international wars are already practically at an end," because nations had found their senses and realized the folly of armed conflict. Then came the First World War to prove how little the nations had learned. *War and Waste* was a typical Jordan title.

When Chancellor Jordan did relax in his sober discussion of disarmament, he talked, entertainingly, about fish. He was a naturalist; he liked to discuss "fossil fish," "game fish," and "the evolution of animal life," in all of which he probably skirted close to heresy in the opinion of devout followers of Fundamentalist William Jennings Bryan.

It was Borah, not Jordan, however, whose voice was loudest. He warned the nation about California's constant uneasiness—the west coast feared Japan. From William Randolph Hearst, in his palace facing the ocean, to local labor leaders in grubby union halls, people sensed trouble approaching across the Pacific. A naval race was threatening between the United States and Japan, and Borah's state of Idaho was far enough west to feel the tension. He was a member of the Senate Foreign Relations Committee and in its deliberations was the spokesman for the group trying to halt naval expansion everywhere around the world. He wanted a "naval holiday" during which no ships would be built by any nation, and he used the persuasion of his great oratory in this cause.

Chautauqua personnel stopped everything and sat down and listened the nights that Senator Borah "pulled the feathers out of the eagle." He differed sharply in his subject matter from Bryan. There was no "mother, home and heaven" about him, but a great deal of Bryan's eloquence. Crew boys who had called Bryan "the old Reliable" disrespectfully dubbed Borah "the Unreliable." They claimed, rightly or wrongly, that the busy western senator frequently wired at the last minute that he could not keep the engagement. It was any audience's loss.

"Senator" remained a magic word. An ordinary "John Jones" would not have been booked, but if it were "Senator John Jones," the people bought tickets. We paid a senator five hundred dollars a week in the 1920's; if he were Senate leader, as Oscar Underwood and "Pat" Harrison both were, he got seven hundred dollars.

Pat Harrison, the senator from Mississippi—he was baptised Byron Patton Harrison—was picturesque in his string tie and his Kentucky-colonel hat. His speeches entertained, but they never aroused. When he confessed, "I had more fun as Senate minority leader than I do as majority leader, it's easier to throw brickbats," people smiled, but they didn't expect him to throw any brickbats at them, and he never did. They smiled, too, and affectionately, at gallant, pink-whiskered James Hamilton Lewis of Illinois.

"J. Ham," as his neighbors called him, was a public idol. Like certain ladies in our entertainment lists, the debonnaire senator always failed to include his birth date in his biography. He came out on the platform, good-humored and sartorially perfect, and entertained with a solid speech. The words "entertain" and "solid" are not contradictory. "Safety of the Seas," much talked about in that period, Senator Lewis could make sound like a tall tale of pirates.

Back in 1897, "J. Ham" had sponsored recognition of Cuban independence and supported it by going off himself to the Spanish-American War. He entered Congress first from the state of Washington; in 1913 he went to the Senate from Illinois. He had a ready wit and a Chesterfieldian manner. People rarely got the best of him, but one girl did, and because this was so exceptional, the story lived on in Illinois folklore. He was paying his check in a downstate restaurant and lightly complimented the cashier on her good looks. She answered, "Go on, I've been kidded by experts." Senator Lewis laughed and went out and told the story on himself.

Audiences learned to wait for certain speakers' good stories. Charles Brough, a politician who always asked, "How's the baby?" also made them laugh with a story he told on himself. Brough—an early advocate on the platform of "good roads"—had been governor of Arkansas twice and he always injected a few glowing words about his "wonderful state" into any speech or conversation. One day he was praising its natural resources to a luncheon group in which one elderly man was very deaf and one young woman very beautiful.

Brough was boasting about Arkansas's natural gas, when the deaf man lowered his ear trumpet for a moment's private reflection, and the governor shifted his attention to the beautiful young woman. He enjoyed flattering people and, to her embarrassment, he launched forth, "My dear young lady, what a wonderful picture you make in that beautiful dress, that stunning hat, sitting here like the Queen of the Lakes. . . ." He was stopped by the deaf man, who put his trumpet back up to his ear and re-entered the conversation at exactly the point where he had left it.

"Governor," he asked, "how did you say you pumped that gas?"

Brough laughed the hardest of all. A committee in a Chautauqua town had criticized him, years before, for "not shaking hands hard enough at the gate." After that he found that it paid, on the platform and off, to be a "good fellow."

The "business revivalists," the reformers of civic affairs continued to thrive in the 1920's. Frank Dixon still limped out across the stage on his crutch, still shook it at the audience when he became excited—in what was undoubtedly the most dramatic elocutional gesture ever seen in a Chautauqua tent. Dixon's excitement continued to stem from his zeal for improved municipal government. A few years after World War I, he described to the people a plan being tried here and there for a nonpolitical manager to run the business of a town. Mayors and aldermen, accustomed to paying off political debts with jobs and contracts, and devil take the low bidder, were furious at Dixon's unreasonable idea of a council-manager form of government. Many newspaper editors agreed. The Lansing, Michigan *State Journal* cried out in editorial indignation after Dixon's Chautauqua appearance, that if his revolutionary ideas were accepted, "the individual would be submerged, the state glorified." But as a result of efforts of men like Dixon, some fifteen hundred alert North American communities today are operated under the council-manager plan.

As Lincoln Steffens had done earlier, Dixon emphasized that "honest business men" paid graft money to "dishonest politicians." Those business men, he shouted, deserved to be thrown into the same jails with the men who accepted the graft.

The American climate was ripe for this kind of talk which avoided international complications and concerned itself with matters close to men's hearts and pocketbooks. The Federal income tax was beginning to reach down into lower income groups and local taxes were climbing. The voices in Chautauqua tents and in other forums were teaching citizens that not only must they participate actively in campaigns for better government, but that they could profit from such campaigns.

Thomas Mott Osborne was a "reformer," not of cities but of prisons. Born in 1859 in Auburn, New York, near the old state penitentiary, he probably had long been interested in the grim, rock fortress, but not until he had made his fortune and was ready to retire from business did he become a crusader for prison improvement.

Osborne was a wagon manufacturer, a newspaper publisher, mayor of his home town, a Democratic politician who had held half a dozen state offices. Then in 1913 he managed to get himself locked up in Auburn Prison. Neither guards nor inmates realized that he was not another felon, serving time. After several weeks he came out, loaded with ugly facts.

Appointed warden of Sing Sing the next year, he instituted a humanitarian regime, to the outrage of those who wanted "to lock 'em up and throw the key away." He was indicted by a Westchester County, New York, grand jury for mismanagement and "coddling," but the charge was so flimsy that the case never was tried. On eastern circuits Warden Osborne talked of his own experiences as a voluntary convict and of the pressures still in force to prevent humane treatment of prisoners.

Handsome, white-haired Ole Hanson, Seattle's fighting mayor, also had his say in this period, as did Sociologist Charles Zueblin. In 1919 Zueblin, another expert in municipal affairs, debated government ownership of railroads with Leslie M. Shaw, suave ex-governor of Iowa, who had served as Secretary of the Treasury for Theodore Roosevelt. Shaw was a great talker. On his way to Lexington, North Carolina, in June, with Zueblin and the Rita Rich-Laura Werno "pre-luding" company, the ex-Secretary was talking so hard and so loud that no one heard the conductor call the station.

Two miles beyond it the group, all except Shaw a little annoyed, climbed off with twelve bags and walked back. The two men debated in the evenings. Afternoons Zueblin lectured on *The World's Highway,* another plea for freedom of the seas. Shaw and he both stayed with us for several years.

Mayor Ole Hanson had run unsuccessfully for the Senate in Oregon, on the state issue of rural credit banks. After he was elected mayor of Seattle, he won national prominence somewhat as Calvin Coolidge had in Boston: he settled a strike. Hanson was one of the first to fret on a platform about the high cost of living, and also to warn against Russia. Before 1920 he published *Americanism versus Bolshevism* and incorporated its ideas in many of his speeches.

Russia as a subject leaped excitedly to the fore as soon as World War I ended. Ralph Dennis, an Iowan who became speech professor at Northwestern University, had been American vice-consul in Moscow in 1918 when the Revolution broke out. He had entered Russia through Siberia and with other Americans went out through Finland. His observations provided good, fresh material.

Congressman Henry Rainey, an Illinois favorite Democratic son, also went to Russia to see for himself what Bolshevism was like. He came back with a favorable report. The people had been friendly.

Rainey related how, when his car sank in mud and a kulak with oxen pulled it out, "I had somebody ask the fellow how much I owed him. He said, 'Nothing. Americans are our friends.' " Rainey thought that they would continue to be. He was Speaker of the House later, in Franklin Roosevelt's first administration. His southern Illinois district had elected him to Congress in 1903; by the time our circuit sent him over the trail in the 20's, he had plenty to say. He said it well always and inoffensively.

I did not go to Russia, but I did visit Amtorg, the Russian Purchasing Agency, that for many years had headquarters in Washington. We were

booking Senator Smith Brookhart at the time. Brookhart, an Iowa Republican, had been elected to the Senate first to fill the vacancy caused by
the resignation of ailing Senator Kenyon. He was a Progressive—an early
member of the Farmers' Union—and because he came from farming
Iowa, he was interested in international trade in grains and for that reason
he had conversations with Amtorg.

"You might like to meet a friend of mine from the Redpath Bureau," he
told a Russian.

"Red-path? Ah!" the fellow said. "Of course! Of course! Bring him here
today."

I was greeted by a cordial functionary who eased me past guards and
the doors were relocked. Officials left their desks to welcome me. They
were honored. This "Red-path"—it was a splendid organization dedicated
to the better appreciation of the Revolution—no? And what a charming
name!

No, I explained, "Redpath" had been named for an American patriot.
We were not concerned with revolution. "Redpath" was one word and not
a communist slogan. Wham! I was ushered out.

The incident is significant of the times. No one called me a communist
simply because, by chance, I happened to call at Amtorg. Neither did
anyone, in those less suspicious years, accuse me of improper dealings
with George Brown, head of the Chicago Stagehands Union, convicted
later of accepting bribes. When the Ben Greet Players were touring, with
practically no stage equipment to handle, I approached Brown to ask if
union regulations might be made more reasonable. The Ben Greets did not
need five or six stagehands to get the company into the theatre and as
many to get it out, plus three carpenters, three electricians and three property men. I found Brown affable.

The Ben Greets were playing at South Bend, Indiana, that week. "I'll go
up and look them over," Brown said.

I met him in South Bend.

"You're right," he agreed. "There isn't much to do for this company."
He scaled down all requirements and gave me a yellow card to prove it.

I thanked him and, impressed by his good nature, asked, "What do I
owe you for the trip from Chicago?"

"Nothing," he said.

We parted friendly. Today I probably would be accused of having tried
to grease a palm.

It seemed some seasons that more visitors swarmed from overseas after
the war than had during it. Count Felix von Luckner, the dashing, handsome
German "Sea Devil" whose submarine sank countless Allied ships, announced at war's end, after the Kaiser had taken refuge at Doorn, in Hol-
land, that he never had approved of the Kaiser's heartless terrorism. He
wrote a lively book, based on his marauding adventures. Translated into

English, it became a best seller in America and he followed it across the Atlantic.

One von Luckner story, told with considerable relish from the platform, sometimes shocked his audiences. Theodore Roosevelt, he hinted, was indirectly responsible for the First World War. Roosevelt had been in Berlin several years earlier and Kaiser Wilhelm had put on a great military display in his honor. According to von Luckner, Roosevelt, impressed by what he saw, told the Kaiser, "Great Guns, with an army like this, you can lick the world."

"He believed Mr. Roosevelt," von Luckner added. "The fool thought he could do it."

In Chautauqua the "Sea Devil" used lantern slides of photographs he had taken from his submarine's deck, showing his men in humanitarian rescues of the survivors of sinking ships. His contention was that the people of Germany had been forced into the war by their masters, and that they had no more stomach for the conflict than did the Americans. His lecture, delivered in a throaty Prussian accent, was so convincing that many American Legion posts entertained him after his talks and plied him with illegal beer.

We paid Count Ilya Tolstoy, son of Count Leo, the great liberal Russian novelist, $350 a week for a forty-five-minute talk. He looked like his father, a big, shaggy man, his massive head bald on top but with long hair about the ears. Like Count Leo, he had advanced views on morality and religion and he expressed them. He detested socialism and "the Bolsheviks," and lashed out at them. Count Ilya had icy blue eyes and a taste for tea and paperback novels; he did not like the Chautauqua road and Chautauqua audiences did not like his lecture.

Two foreigners who did find a hearty reception were Chew Ng Poon, the "Chinese Mark Twain," founder of the first Chinese daily newspaper in San Francisco, and Poet-soldier Tom Skeyhill from Australia. Skeyhill, a veteran of the Gallipoli campaign, travelled first with a talk on Mussolini on the seven-day circuit. He painted a gloomy picture of the world. Civilization was in its twilight unless "it scraps the greeds, jealousies and revenges of narrow nationalism and selfish patriotism." In spite of his pessimism, he was extremely popular. Like Private Peat, his text was, "Avoid war as you would poison." The American Legion did not get particularly interested in Skeyhill as it had in Peat.

Chew Ng Poon's discussion of China was one of dozens of lectures on the growing problems of the United States and the Orient. The public liked Chew as a personality, but only the west coast was interested politically in the Pacific, and in Japan, not China.

Remote areas that first had been the province of returned missionaries became rapidly the happy hunting ground of travellers, and the most popular among them was the indefatigable Richard Halliburton. English-born

Carveth Wells might specialize in the Malay Peninsula, Sir Hubert Wilkens in the Arctic—Halliburton took a look at everything.

This enthusiastic young man in his "seven league boots" trotted and slid and coasted around the world. He examined the bones of Columbus in Santo Domingo, rode on an elephant over Hannibal's trail through the Alps, visited the "oldest man in the world" in the Caucasus, and Emperor Haile Selassie in Ethiopia. He made the first ascent, in winter, by one man, of Mount Fujiyama in Japan. He went here, there, everywhere—and died young—but not before he had talked and talked and written and written.

Halliburton had "platform personality." He was handsome. Women were swept off their feet by him. When he sent the manuscript of his first book, *The Royal Road to Romance,* to a publishing house, it was so extravagantly written that serious-minded editors unanimously turned it down. Then he walked into the publishers' office to pick up the rejected manuscript.

"A Greek god walked in," one of the young women reported. "We girls all thought perhaps we had better give the book another reading. We did, and found it wonderful. We worked so hard for it—rather, for Dicky—that we talked the staff into printing a few thousand copies, and soon had a best seller on our hands."

"Going down the line," as talent called a summer tour, took stamina, even if not of the Halliburton quality. Curiously enough, there was one group it never attracted—poets dared the man-killing trips, but not many athletes. Charles Paddock, who could run three hundred yards in thirty and two-tenths seconds, toured one summer, addressing young people on *The Spirit of Sportsmanship.* Baseball owner Branch Rickey discussed *Business and Baseball.* "Farmer" Burns in his hard-muscled eighties talked about wrestling and John L. Sullivan, thirty-four years after he won the bare-knuckled world heavyweight championship, delivered a talk on "temperance." Those were the athletes, in the main, who "went down the line," until one remembers a demon in shirt sleeves, Dr. Charles Barker, hopping over a pile of chairs on the stage.

Barker had been physical adviser to President William Howard Taft and when the latter left the White House, the gymnast took to the Chicago circuit with a lecture we billed as *How to Live One Hundred Years.* Removing his eyeglasses, smoothing back the imaginary hair on his bald head, the good middle-aged doctor demonstrated with chairs, dumbbells and what not, just what exercises he had prescribed for President Taft to take off weight. I never learned how successful they were with President Taft, but Dr. Barker and the audience enjoyed it.

Edgar Bergen, in his personal sketch in *Who's Who in America,* lists his work as "ventriloquist and magician" on the 1922 Redpath-Chicago circuit as the first job he ever held. He was nineteen at the time, and a student at Northwestern University. Reader Adrian Newens claimed credit for discovering Bergen, and we hired Charlie McCarthy's creator the first season at $50 a week to entertain the children in the mornings. Bergen "found" himself that summer, and a delighted management, for its part, found that the parents not only were delivering the children to the tent, but staying themselves. So the pay went up to $75, then to $125, for a morning entertainment and a thirty-minute prelude in the afternoon. Bergen used Charlie McCarthy the first season, along with a girl dummy, but Charlie, needless to say, was the one who clicked.

Trying his talents in Chautauqua about this time was Dean Jagger, who also went to Hollywood to earn an "Oscar." On his first tour Jagger played in *Cappy Ricks* on the Ellison-White circuits in the far west. One day the troupe arrived by train at Needles, on the California-Arizona border, and started by chartered bus for a mountain community in Arizona. The grade was steep. Half-way up, the steering knuckle of the bus broke and the vehicle raced off the road, plunged into a deep wash and turned over.

The "old man" who played the lead in *Cappy Ricks* was killed, two actresses were hurt. The only individuals able to stand on their feet were Jagger and a young baritone, who other seasons had gone on the Chautauqua road as a vocal soloist. After the ambulance had started back to Needles, Jagger said, "Well, I guess the show must go on. That's what I've always heard. Let's get into town and give some kind of performance."

The pair, in soiled torn clothes, Jagger in the white suit he had bought secondhand for $16 in Chicago, hitchhiked a ride to the Chautauqua tent. It was crowded. News of the wreck had reached the village and the audience was tense. Jagger told them the facts. "We'll try to entertain you," he finished.

The baritone sang everything he could remember, from the *Volga Boat Song* to *Hail, Noble Hall* from *Tannhauser*. Jagger, in turn, reached back in his memory for poems he had learned in school, monologues taught him by Coach Elias Day. He recited "Hats off . . . the flag is passing by," and Thomas Paine's "These are the times that try men's souls," passages from Shakespeare, a half dozen of Keats' sonnets. He ended with Mary Roberts Rinehart's *The Perfect Tribute*.

The audience stood and cheered, and the next night and the next, in two other small Arizona towns, singer and actor went on with their impromptu show, until the Ellison-White management could send out a new dramatic group.

Joining Redpath in 1917 was an enthusiastic personality who supposedly was only a scientist, but who on the platform became that phenomenon, a scientist with a broad streak of entertainer in him. From 1917 on, this indomitable man made the trek for twelve to twenty weeks every season. Hilton Ira Jones, "Hi" his friends called him, left a professorship in chemistry at South Dakota's Wesleyan University to start out with three big trunkloads of equipment, for a lecture on sound, electricity and light. He called it *The Harp of the Senses, A Study in Vibrations*. His wife assisted him on the platform and when the fascinated crowd left the tent, it had absorbed more poetry, literature and wit, woven into a fabric of technical remarks, than some specialists in those subjects ever gave. Such nonsense as "Why don't we hear an ant's voice?" "Why do red-headed people never suffer sun-stroke?" intrigued sections of the crowd. But the more thoughtful persons went away contemplating what Lecturer Jones had said about the mysterious atom, or future television, or that "new" metal, beryllium, which he predicted would revolutionize the airplane industry.

Even in those days an occasional town had no electricity. So Jones carried with him an electrical converter that he could hitch to a Ford car to generate enough power to run his apparatus and put a few lights on the stage. A few years later, around 1927, R. B. (Army) Ambrose also went out with electrical apparatus to explain modern broadcasting. Ambrose had one stunt that harked back to the first days of Dinner Pail McNutt. He put an aluminum pan on a cake of ice, over an electromagnetic field, and fried an egg.

Hilton Ira Jones' reputation for humor made his lecture particularly saleable and carried him through many a predicament. One hot May evening in Lakeland, Florida,—his birthday—in the middle of his lecture his trousers split up the back. Unlike Ralph Bingham, years before in a similar situation, Jones couldn't give the rest of his program sitting on the floor. So the genial ex-professor simply faced front carefully while he finished speaking, bowed cautiously but politely to the applause and backed off the stage. He reappeared immediately in a heavy raincoat. It was his custom to shake hands with his admirers and he intended to do it, split trousers or no.

For many seasons Jones drove one of the big Chautauqua busses, carrying six girls and six harps—real ones, not his "harp of the senses." Fortunately for the girls he was of the type that could make quick decisions. If an on-coming car forced him to take to the ditch with his lumbering vehicle, he took to the ditch and then drove out again. In one such incident, he possessed more equanimity than the superintendent who was riding in the back seat with the girls. The superintendent grabbed his umbrella and jumped while Jones drove on.

Once on the Gulf circuit, the Jones group gave the evening program at Hammond, Louisiana, and next afternoon they were scheduled for Holly Springs, Mississippi, by the Tennessee line, almost four hundred miles away. They drove all night and all forenoon. As they arrived at Holly Springs just in time for the afternoon prelude, one of the tired young ladies said, "The nice thing about Chautauqua is that nothing in life can ever seem hard after this."

The remark may explain the scarcity of athletes. Somebody from Jones' company may have told them that it would be easier to run a mile in four minutes flat or wrestle with Strangler Lewis, than to make the rounds on a summer circuit.

Troubles for the Treasurer

20

The bedraggled members of the Blue Danube Light Opera Company stepped from the Southern Pacific Railroad ferry to the New Orleans dock at eleven o'clock that stormy Sunday night in May, 1927. It had taken two tugs to push the ferry against the current. The mighty Mississippi River was in a roaring flood and it was still raining.

This was the second time in seven days that the musicians and their pianist and lecturer had managed to get across the river. Saturday, a week ago, they had stared at the raging yellow water from the high bridge at Memphis; and what distraught audiences, fully one half of which were refugees, they had seen since! They had played Vicksburg on May 20; a sheep had bleated all through that concert. The Chautauqua tent stood next-door to a hospital and the animal, waiting to be used for inoculations, was tied to a post outside.

It had seemed incongruous, under the circumstances, to be singing anything as gay as *In Romany*—30,000 homeless refugees from flooded towns farther north were stranded in Vicksburg's parks. But in spite of the stress, the evening attendance had been good. The Vicksburg committee had re-booked for next year. They asked that Pianist Magdalen Massmann come back, as well as Edward Tomlinson with his South American lecture, *Under Ten Flags,* and Private Peat, who had been the big name the fourth night with his *Inexcusable Lie.*

Private Peat and Orville Bottorff, manager of the unlucky Gulf circuit, had escaped from Vicksburg before the Mississippi bridge went out, but the Blue Danubes and their equipment had not. So to get across into Louisiana for the next date, they had travelled north to Memphis and swung in a crazy circle down through flooded Arkansas and flooded central and southern

244

Louisiana. Now, in New Orleans they piled their luggage into cars and splashed through the streets to the DeSoto Hotel. They were dog-tired. Last night they had played in Crowley, seat of Acadia Parish, the night before that they had been in Jennings. They had left Crowley this morning at 10:15, and all day their eyes had been glued on the unbelievable sights outside the windows of the crawling train.

Town after town was inundated. Boats navigated the streets of New Iberia as the train crawled over built-up tracks. Of the scheduled Chautauqua programs here, only the first and second day companies had managed to appear—Impersonator Ratto with the Adriatic Tamburica Band "pre-luding" him, and next day Baritone Ruthven McDonald and his Highlanders. Water flowed into the tent that second night. At Morgan City the advance man had gone to sleep on dry land and left his hotel the next morning by boat.

There had been a three hour wait for the Blue Danube Company today in Lafayette. With two of the singers, Miss Massmann had wet her feet visiting a refugee camp. The sights were heartbreaking, but show people always had to find a lighter side and Miss Massmann found it. Triplets had just been born to a negro family. Since it was Sunday a priest was performing baptisms, for eleven in all—one pair of twins besides the triplets. The twins, she discovered, were to be named Flood and Overflow.

The five-day Gulf circuit, with its seven "equipments"—tents and pianos, stages and lights—had opened March 11 in St. Augustine, Florida. Everything had gone well, from Florida's east coast over to the west, across southern Georgia and Alabama and on through the state of Mississippi. The troubles began in Louisiana. For a month treacherous water had been rising, levees breaking. Transportation was in a snarl. It was Bottorff's job to keep companies on the march and the right equipment for each day's program in the right spot. Tents had to move, even if in an emergency a lecturer had to cut short his speech. This was difficult when Private Peat was the lecturer. Peat was a man with a mission, and rampaging river or no, the people must hear his message against war.

The two men had left Vicksburg in a hurry in Peat's new Hup-Eight, to cover eight hundred and eighty-five miles to the cotton town of Minden, Louisiana. They had driven continuously, sometimes in a few inches of water, sometimes in a foot, while from overhead came a steady stream of rain. They had reached Minden in time for Peat to change into dry clothes and mount the platform. But again, before he finished, the superintendent rushed in to warn that the roads south would be closed within twelve hours. Peat finished his speech. Then young Crewman Richard Eddy drove the Hup-Eight to New Orleans, three hundred and fifty flooded miles away, while Peat went on to his next date by train. If you had gone through the kind of war Private Peat had, you didn't let high water stop you from talking peace.

Things got worse instead of better, even though Herbert Hoover, Secretary of Commerce then, managing flood relief from the railroad center at Jackson, Mississippi, gave Chautauqua his blessing. It was boosting morale in this demoralized area, he told distracted Bottorff, and in spite of martial law, it should go wherever and however it need. Bottorff thanked him. If he could get tangled equipment straightened out, the blessing meant priorities and companies might move on north. Bottorff, in later years a New York City concert manager, was still a young man that spring, but a Chautauqua veteran. He had joined in 1914, just after his sixteenth birthday.

Redpath's Gulf circuit took the brunt of the trouble that miserable year, but other groups came in for their share. In April, in rain, the five men and women of the Smith-Spring-Holmes Company left Chicago by car for their first date for the Ellison-White circuit in Abbeville, Louisiana. At one point Clay Smith had pushed their big Cadillac, with its built-in property trunk, over a condemned bridge; at another bad spot he had put it on a dray for mules to haul. After five days and nights and sixteen hundred miles, they arrived at Abbeville.

The 1927 Mississippi River flood came toward the end of Chautauqua history. In contrast with it, the rains of earlier years, that at the time had seemed catastrophes, lost their remembered terror—the rains, but not the tornadoes. One could feel miserable in the rain, even laugh when an audience in a leaky tent put up umbrellas and stayed on, but one did not laugh at the wind.

The worst disaster to the public in Chautauqua records came on an eastern circuit in 1915 at Dallastown, Pennsylvania, when a July whirlwind lifted the whole tent and a falling pole killed two persons. Redpath-Vawter's closest call was at Woodbine, Iowa, just before the First World War. A Sunday afternoon program had closed and the crowd had been out of the tent five minutes when a tornado picked up the canvas and the two great center-poles crashed across the seats.

The effect of wind and rain on attendance was less disastrous to the treasury than its damage to the tents. If rips and holes were not too big, patches could be sewn or cemented under almost any condition: Crew boss Eddy tells how, the year following the flood, after a "blow" in Madison, Florida, the men lay on their backs for what seemed eternity, sewing rips directly over their heads. The real problem with the tents, however, was dampness after the rain.

A "tear-down" usually had to be fast. Rain on the final night of a seven-day stand might be only a shower, but if the canvas had to be rolled without any sun, mold often set in before it could be unrolled. And if it were lost on a railroad siding and took three days to reach the next town, then what? After half a dozen such episodes, rot followed mold and tents would whip to pieces in wind. Science-lecturer Hilton Ira Jones, working first at the University of Oklahoma, eventually developed a chemical agent against mold, which not only preserved the canvas, but fire- and water-proofed it as well.

All serious incidents that caused concern for the management did not stem from the elements, of course. There was the terrible day in Tennessee, when a property trunk fell off a truck and killed the drayman's helper, and the terrible night when a new crew boy, heedless of rules against guns, was cleaning one—"I'll be sleeping alone in a tent and may need it," he had thought—and it went off and killed the son of a guarantor. The merciful parents sent the crew boy through college. There was the evening in the 20's in Florida, when, a few minutes before curtain, the hero in a *Nothing but the Truth* company died of a heart attack. The superintendent could not tell the crowd that the actor, with his make-up still on, lay dead behind the stage. He simply reported that one man had been taken sick, and if the play went on, the superintendent would have to read the part, which he did.

Officials responsible for the success of a program had anxious moments when things threatened to go wrong. Managers lay awake nights, worrying over improbable possibilities that once in a long time proved both possible and ghastly. One summer in a Canadian border city, a young lady lecturer with a talk on moral leadership was "pre-luded" by a Hawaiian string quartet. This was deep in the days of national prohibition, for which so many millions of impassioned words had soared from our platforms. Canada had not seen the light; just across the invisible line from the dry United States alcohol was legal.

After the afternoon program, the lady lecturer and the Hawaiian lads took off to see the sights of Canada. Curtain was at eight o'clock, the superintendent reminded them. They would be there, they promised.

At twenty minutes past six, the superintendent received a call from the local police chief. Chautauqua's string quartet and a disheveled lady lecturer had just been returned across the border by Canadian officials. The Hawaiians were taking the situation calmly, but the lady was not. She was resisting arrest. They could be had, in return for modest bail, at the local calaboose.

The superintendent, a quiet young man who had proved his worth against floods and tornadoes, took the affair in his stride. The Hawaiians were particularly effective that night and gave *Aloha O* the full treatment, with variations never heard before or since. Their encores took so much time that the lady lecturer's speech had to be shortened somewhat. She got through it nicely, however. The police chief was sporting; he talked neither to the press nor the local committee, and he forgot the little matter of bail. For that the treasurer was thankful.

Homecomings, baseball, conventions, occasionally a gory murder trial at a county seat, Elks picnics, commencements, all could play havoc with attendance at Chautauqua week. May and June, everywhere, were dedicated to high-school graduation; in the south these months also were the peak of Chautauqua. When the dates conflicted, it had to be Chautauqua that took the loss. One season Chicago's DeLuxe circuit played opposite commencement festivities eight nights out of fourteen. A report, dated May 31, 1923, from Superintendent Earl French in charge at Knoxville, Tennessee, "Rain every day, commencement exercises every night," is typical. As untypical was another daily bulletin, "Rain. But the tent did not leak."

Even labor disputes occasionally cut down attendance. One year at the coal town of Ashland, Kentucky, a strike was on in the mines and hourly, during every program, a pitched battle between mine guards and deputy sheriffs on one side and strikers and their friends on the other, was reported as imminent. Neither a lecturer who had hobnobbed with Hottentots nor a magician pulling rabbits out of a hat could compete with that kind of anticipated drama, and the box office suffered.

The Kentucky coal country posed various problems. Oliver E. Behymer, lecturer and one of the most skilled superintendents and field managers in the business—it was he who ran the big Chicago programs—tells of a night in Harlan, Kentucky, when teen-aged boys climbed the center pole in the midst of his speech and pelted him with peanut shells. In a desperate effort to get their attention, he said:

"Boys, I'll show you something you never saw before, and never will again," and he picked up a peanut shell and ate it. The astonished rowdies became quiet. If this good-looking fellow could eat peanut shells, he must be worth listening to. This "good-looking fellow" stayed fit, to cope with rowdies and everything else, by walking. Often, sending his luggage on by the "pre-luding" company, he walked twelve or fifteen miles between towns.

Long before radio and motion pictures blighted the circuits, the treasurer's office felt the impact of other kinds of competition, from gospel revivals to beer picnics of the *Vorwaerts Turnverein*. One could not fight a revival meeting without being charged with godlessness. But all summer long, particularly in the smaller communities, itinerant evangelists managed to arrive just as Redpath put up its big tents. At Hattiesburg, Mississippi, in April, 1923, four separate tents were offering eternal salvation free of charge, while knowledge, at the Chautauqua grounds down the street, cost thirty-five cents.

Carnivals followed our tents deliberately, we well knew, and how could a lecturer, no matter how loud his voice, make himself heard against a Hindu band ballyhooing a merry-go-round? One summer morning at Logansport, Indiana, Barnes' three-ring circus and a large carnival arrived in the midst of a suffrage speech in our tent. History does not say how the speech came out, but in Norwich, New York, in 1921, Elsie Baker and William Durieux were in the middle of their concert when a Sells-Floto parade blared past. Half the audience ran out to look at the elephant and the maidens on horseback, but having looked, they returned to their seats. Hayden and Handel, for once, had the greater pulling power.

In Charles F. Horner's second year on the road, he suddenly came face to face with the problem of four hundred Sioux Indians camped on the grounds at Valentine, Nebraska. Their noise was damaging enough, but how could he answer their request to do a war dance on the stage? Or how reply, that same year, to the five Oklahoma cowhands who rode up to the tent and asked to stable their horses inside while they watched the show?

Old transportation bills, even as late as 1926, show staggering repair costs. In one fleet we had an Essex, a Reo, a Dodge, a Ford and a Buick. Broken axles and springs and shattered door glass were the most frequent repair items. Axles, of course, snapped when the driver tried to pull out of clinging mud. Rough roads broke the springs and glass. As the size of our venture increased, guiding nearly a million pounds of equipment over the freight lines on three sprawling circuits became a herculean task for any superintendent of transportation. For our circuit L. B. Crotty handled this job from the beginning until 1921, when Carl E. Backman took it over. Each year the Redpath bureau, as a whole, spent a quarter of a million dollars for transportation. For that amount of business, railroad agents beat a path to the door, so, except during the war, there was little real trouble in transporting baggage cars. Shunting them to the wrong siding was another matter, and in that fate certainly had a careless hand.

As for our mail, it might turn up at Kansas City when it was plainly addressed to Nashville, particularly if there was a pay check in it for Strickland Gillilan. In any discussion of things gone fantastically wrong, through the fault of no one in particular, Gillilan is always a good subject. The old files are full of furious or frantic letters, postal cards or telegrams from that unlucky Hoosier humorist, trying to straighten out the latest debacle. A typical wire received in the Chicago office, collect of course, in Gillilan's best angry style reads:

LAST WEEKS SALARY CHECK ALL WRONG WILL NOT FILL THIS WEEKS DATES ON ANY SUCH BASIS OTHERWISE WILL CANCEL GILLILAN

If, after paying freight and fares and salaries for talent, repairs to equipment, overhead and hundreds of unexpected items, there were a few thousand dollars left to meet next year's advance expenses, any system was supremely happy. We faced few springtimes with our cups of financial joy running over.

As an example of profits, let us take the Chicago bureau for the five seasons from 1912 through 1916. Those were top years, sparked by the lively Bull Moose campaign. With three quarters of a million dollars gross income each summer, our average annual profit was $8642. Then came the dislocations of the First World War and by 1924 our office owed one Chicago bank $153,963.41. The situation was not peculiar to ourselves. Only because bankers balanced the hazards of the business against what they called "Chautauqua's moral fibre," could they let us have the money to operate.

Over the years most of us sold Chautauqua to a community as an educational opportunity, not as a money-making scheme. When we discussed a contract, we stressed its cultural impact, never how much profit anyone might make. For this reason only, sponsors were willing to dig down into their pockets for the guarantee necessary for us to set up our tents. Most of these people knew that they would be lucky if on the final night, after the last orator concluded, mopped his brow and left, there was no deficit. They took the chance cheerfully.

This attitude was hard for promotors to understand. In 1915 I went with Alice Nielsen, after her performance in Savannah, Georgia, to a reception at the mayor's home. She had sung to an enormous crowd, a thousand season ticketholders and a thousand single admissions. Among the guests at the reception was a vaudeville manager from New York. He had estimated the gate and was impressed. He inquired now, who put up the money to bring this show to town? Who sold the tickets? Who got the proceeds? The hostess explained that no one in Savannah expected to make money out of Chautauqua, that in spite of hard work, backers would be satisfied if they just broke even.

The man, amazed at "her naivety," went back to New York, built a program around a nucleus of vaudeville acts, called it a "chautauqua," raised $300,000, and set out to sink Redpath, offering half of all income to the locality. To his amazement, he sold not a single date. No one in Savannah had backed Chautauqua for the sake of making money.

Nothing in the history of Chautauqua created so much discussion as the contract. People who construed the movement as an educational influence saw nothing offensive in a binding agreement. But critics asked: If the circus and the theatres come to town without a contract, why doesn't Chautauqua? Or: The bureau is making money, why should the town take the risk?

The bureau itself had to sign agreements, dozens of them, before a tent went into a baggage car. It had to hire talent in advance, sign on the dotted line with its own employees, make a down payment on new equipment, commit itself for the remainder of the investment. If, with this money spent, Wire Corners, Illinois, were free to send sudden word, "Don't come. We'd rather have a Fourth of July celebration," then indeed, the treasurer would have been in hot water.

Bureaus, by and large, used a standard contract form. The "sponsor," representing the town, agreed to pay for a certain number of tickets, at a price set by the bureau, and if that number were not sold, the sponsor paid the difference. In other words, the town guaranteed to pay the bureau a minimum sum. Sponsors might be a group of Main Street merchants, the

Ladies Library Association, a newspaper, a church group, in later years a luncheon club.

Exact dates for Chautauqua week could not be stated in the contract, nor the details of the program; these must be worked out over the winter. The contract did specify the number of programs the bureau would give. It furnished these, the tent and the advertising, the town supplied the grounds.

The size of a town's guarantee ran from $750, in the Chicago circuit's first season, up to $2500 or more in the boom years, depending naturally on the size of the circuit, with $3000 usually set by us as a sum beyond which we divided proceeds equally with the sponsors. In his early days Keith Vawter had encouraged agents to sign up a town for five years in one package. Redpath-Chicago followed an opposite policy. One year at a time was enough. A community needed an annual drive to stir up enthusiasm. We explained this once to a salesman who came up elatedly from Winston-Salem, North Carolina, with a five year contract with minimum guarantee from the Chamber of Commerce. Redpath cancelled it, on the theory that anything for which local people did not have constant, personal responsibility petered out. We were right. Chautauqua died in Flint, Michigan, the year a new millionaire picked up the tab for the whole guarantee.

Getting the contract for the first year was a job for the booking agent; getting it re-signed fell to the superintendent and he began his efforts the day he arrived in the town. Ballyhoo from the platform the last night, with a leading citizen pledging a block of tickets, was accepted practice on most circuits. Talent objected to it; the closing-night company complained, reasonably enough, that it spoiled the effect of a good show. Critics also branded the practice as unpleasantly commercial and eventually Redpath-Chicago used other methods.

Occasionally a rival system tried to stage a price war. All a booking agent could do was to explain patiently that in Chautauqua, as in everything else, one got exactly what one paid for. The country was full of third-rate sopranos and second-string politicians to be bought at a dime a dozen, but William Jennings Bryan and Alice Nielsen, the White Hussars and the Ben Greet Players could not be picked up on any bargain counter. The local committee only could decide which type of talent it wanted.

One opening day in a Georgia city, several dissatisfied committee members approached Superintendent Sam Blackwood and asked sharply why Redpath charged them $3 for season tickets when another bureau was giving another city just across the state line seven days for only $1.50. And what was Redpath going to do about it?

"I'm glad you brought that up," Blackwood replied. "I'll answer it from the stage."

Facing the waving fans that night, he said, "I have been asked why Redpath charges three dollars for a season ticket when certain other cities get certain other Chautauquas for a dollar and a half. The answer is simple. We charge three dollars because Redpath is a three-dollar Chautauqua."

It took a moment for his remark to sink in, then the audience applauded.

Occasionally a town had to cancel, and now and then the bureau did; usually it was by mutual agreement. The 1918 influenza epidemic caused abrupt changes; so, sometimes, did a crop failure. A year or so after the outbreak in Europe of the First World War, we were about to move talent into the Gulf states when town after town sent word not to come. Cotton had dropped to six cents a pound. At that price no one had enough money in his pants pocket to buy side meat and grits, let alone tickets to any kind of show. We hurried down to Alabama and Mississippi. Things looked black. And then we suggested: "How about Redpath taking cotton instead of cash, at ten cents a pound instead of the current six?"

This was a different story. What grower wouldn't be willing to cash in cotton receipts at a fifty percent profit, for a good show or anything else? Tents went up, and the next thing Redpath knew, it owned more cotton than one could shake a loom at. Everywhere the circuit wandered around the sunny southland, we had cotton in warehouses. We held it until midwinter, when the market steadied. The price rose to eleven and twelve cents and we sold at a profit of a cent or two a pound. Sold what was left, that is, for one warehouse at Tupelo, Mississippi, burned to the ground. Redpath's cotton was insured at six cents a pound, so the loss there wiped out the gain on the rest of the season in the south.

The First World War put a heavy strain on our treasury. To finance its share in entertaining troops, our bureau borrowed $50,000 from a Chicago bank; to repay it later we mortgaged our tents. The war tax also hurt us. The ten percent levy on amusements passed in 1917 sent us into a head-on encounter with local committees, most of whom were as shocked as we were to discover that the tax collector considered Chautauqua amusement instead of education. We succeeded, after much effort, in getting the tax computed at a season ticket rate instead of on single admissions, and in 1922 it was finally decided that all tickets were exempt so long as a local committee used any profit for educational, charitable or religious purposes. Since profits were rare, that settled the matter.

The greatest item of expense for any system any year was for talent. The bureau was responsible for getting performers to their dates and therefore for transportation bills. In the contract for salaries we included a modest allowance for board and room, adequate, if a little on the hominy grits side. This allowance was not separately listed. We merely added it to what we agreed was a proper weekly rate of pay and called it all salary.

In the early days when we moved by train, we tried to arrange schedules so that everyone could get from date to date by day coaches. But if an opera singer, an actor or a distinguished senator demanded the soft elegance of a parlor car seat, why object? He could pay the difference. If the schedule required an all-night hop, we still paid day coach rates, but anyone who felt the need of a berth could take one, and we paid half its cost.

As for food, who could control how much talent and crew members ate? Each indulged his own taste and watched his own waistline. All crew boys were at what might be called the "hungry age." For us to have footed their food bills would have been reckless to the point of fiscal insanity. Good citizens, particularly in the small towns, sometimes lessened the crew's hunger pains, but it remained for a superintendent named Lincoln Dickey to make this generosity a common practice.

In one town at a first-afternoon program, Dickey called his four husky young men up to the stage, described their athletic prowess, and added, "Last week in"—and he named the nearest town up the line—"the good people swamped these lads with cakes and pies and home-made bread. My friends, it was a beautiful gesture. . . ."

"Of course," he went on, "that couldn't happen in every community, and please don't misunderstand me, I don't think it should. But the people back there certainly showed a Christian spirit." It worked, and in the next town as well. Pies and cakes filled the boys' tent.

Crew boys' pay over the years ranged from $12 to $21, with $5 extra a week to all who finished the season. There were prizes, too, for condition of equipment, sometimes for personal appearance. Morale was high; each superintendent took pride in his crew.

Superintendents earned from $35 to $75 a week, more for the seven-day circuits than for the five, with various bonuses; there was extra pay, for instance, if a town re-signed. Booking agents, of whom a few were women, at the peak of the era collected $30 per week, plus railroad fare and a share in all contracts, sometimes as much as ten percent. This kind of money appealed to old hands among the talent, and often men like Ratto or Fletcher or Reno used their open time to book programs for the next season. By 1921 the Lyceum and Chautauqua Managers Association had established a minimum wage of $40 a week for entertainment. Outstanding lecturers and musical stars set their own terms from the start.

The same economy that controlled travel also covered newspaper advertising. At first we bought a set amount of space in local newspapers and at the right moment sent along running publicity to accompany the ads. This did not work too well. So instead we simply ordered "Seventy-five dollars worth of advertising and publicity." Occasionally we had a knockdown fight with a local publisher who refused to realize that the coming of Chautauqua was important news, as worthy of headlines as a local hammer murder or a fire at the livery barn.

With talent, too, newspaper advertising was an endless source of discussion. It was a rare actor or musician who was satisfied with what we deemed sufficient space in newspapers or on posters. How could they get along with six inches when they deserved a whole page? Why, the Swiss Yodelers would ask, did we give them that stingy space, lost at the bottom of third page, and run the name of Mr. William Jennings Bryan in letters two inches high on the first page? Didn't we realize that it was they, rather than Mr. Bryan, who packed the tent? Who could argue successfully against such logic?

Scouts for talent had to be constantly alert not to be taken in by those who used the platform to advertise some commodity. An example was the explorer who offered to tour all summer at a surprisingly reasonable fee. One night I decided to slip into the back of a hall where he was appearing. He had magnificent motion pictures and audience attention never wandered.

But at one point he said "When your life depends on the boat you use, make sure it's the most trustworthy boat money can buy." Then the camera panned around to show the boatmaker's trade name on the bow. In the same way he revealed the make of his outboard motor, of all his equipment, even the canned beans that he ate. He never mentioned the name of any product, but his camera told the advertisers' story effectively. We did not hire him.

Commercial groups, watching our representatives welcomed on Main Street, conceived all sorts of clever schemes to convert Chautauqua employees into potential salesmen. Could our men sell insurance? No. Or paint? No. We could also have made money by inserting national advertising in our programs, a legitimate practice among theatres and opera houses whose aim is only to entertain; we were afraid of it. The nearest approach to free advertising we ever made was our use of Kimball Company pianos. We used them only to spare the superintendent the nightmare of finding in each small town a piano that was tuned to suit a musician's temperament.

All managements agreed that the stage in the tent should not be a soapbox, but it took wits, and fortitude, to prevent it. Despite our need to cut costs, we felt constrained to fight off all offers, some of them kindly, to share expenses. If Red Cross nurses spoke, we paid them at regular rates, regardless of the proposal of their national organization to provide them free of charge. In 1920, to keep ourselves free from any charge of political bias, we declined to rent our tents, after the season closed, for use in the Harding-Cox Presidential contest.

Also in the "roaring twenties" the American Legion suggested that it send Sergeant Alvin York, of First-World-War fame, around the circuit as a lecturer. We refused. This straight-shooting hillbilly from Tennessee would have been a great drawing card. A pacifist, he probably had accounted for more Germans than anyone else in the war. He was full of homespun philosophy and boiling patriotism.

The War and Treasury Departments, in efforts to sell Liberty Bonds, had made sure that all America knew about York's battle-field heroism. Alone, so the story went, he had rounded up hundreds of enemy soldiers and marched them back to the American lines. Years later, when a Hollywood studio filmed the Sergeant York story, with Gary Cooper in the lead, the aging mountaineer gave his share of the royalties to a school in his county.

York's speech, when the Legion offered it, would have been patriotic, his viewpoint virtuous. But he would not have been a free agent and Redpath directors could not have altered his speech, even to give it more dramatic punch, had the Legion paid his salary. Chautauqua did book Sergeant York later for a season. He was a member of a team, he came on, said a few words and sat down. Then his partner delivered a patriotic address *about* York and his patriotism.

Only once did our bureau give any time to a speaker somebody else paid for. In that instance, with the Swarthmore system, we allowed space on the programs to the American Public Health Association, for which the Association made a grant. We announced it publicly in advance.

One year when the chill of the coming 1929 depression was already making itself felt, we offered a well-known lecturer what we considered a generous contract. He refused it, demanding more money than he would draw at any box-office. So reluctantly we cast about for someone less expensive to fill the spot, at the same time seeking desperately to raise funds to open the season.

Several weeks later a famous industrialist called on us with a proposition. He had heard of our efforts to get this particular speaker and also that the system was having financial difficulties. Could he help us out on both problems? He did not mention, what we knew, that this particular speaker's point of view happened to be favorable to legislation the businessman's industry needed. Instead he suggested: "Book this man for twenty weeks and it will not cost you a cent. I'll pay, not only his salary, but all his travel expenses and Redpath can cash in handsomely."

"Fine!" I agreed. "We'll put him on as a free lecture, as an additional number on the program, and we'll advertise that he's appearing under your sponsorship."

"Oh, no, no!" the industrialist was shocked. "That must not be known! He will just be one of your regular lecturers."

We explained that Chautauqua did not operate that way. Neither the industrialist nor the lecturer understood.

Later, after the stock-market crash, a Wall Street banker came to us with another offer. His financial grapevine told him that not only Redpath but all circuits were wearing patches on their pants and that probably some of them would not open. So he proposed: If the largest four or five systems would join in a single nationwide organization, the banker would supply a million dollars. Certainly this would be manna from heaven. But after managers had met and discussed the offer, they turned it down. What the hidden motive in this generosity was, we did not know, but we were afraid of it.

The banker countered our refusal with a second offer, this one for two million dollars. In return, we only need name him, or a man of his choice, as president of the new combination. We refused this suggestion faster than we had the first; we all knew that with a president picked by Wall Street, Chautauqua would become a mouthpiece for big money. If we were to go broke, it would have to be "honest broke."

But we weren't broke yet. Whenever the end of the world seemed just around the corner, someone or something came along to remind us that the show must go on . . . and to prove that it *could* go on.

Clyde Tull and the redoubtable Tull Players, with a cast of six, appearing in *The Temporary Husband* one summer in South Dakota, came to the end of the road and then kept right on going. They had played one night in the town of Faith, in the Badlands, and were due next night at Belvidere, one hundred miles to the south. The rains came. Word was flashed back. The roads were out. They were not to attempt the jump.

Director Tull was not easily thwarted. Hearing that the storm was milder to the east, he started out at dawn for the little railroad town of Eagle Butte, near the Cheyenne River Indian Reservation. In spite of the downpour, he reached the town without too much difficulty. Belvidere was straight south and if the main road was impassable there must be back trails. Tull located an old scout who knew them—vaguely—"Go left here," the directions went, ". . . here right."

Eventually, of course, the party got lost. In seventy-five miles only one bridge crossed the Cheyenne River and where was it? Searching this way and that, Director Tull finally sighted an Indian crossing the prairie. He waded out to meet him. The Indian knew no English. Tull tried sign language. The party found the bridge eventually, got over it, found a crossroads store and with new directions ploughed on. The car's engine got hot. But where, in the midst of torrents of rain, was there water clean enough for a car radiator?

An abandoned farm showed up at last. There was no pump. There was a pond, though, and so the men carried water in their hats and the car went on. After a dozen more miles a fence blocked the way. Tull cut the wire and splashed ahead. Ten miles from Belvidere, in the Bad River area, a culvert was out. Bumping across it, they broke a spring in the car. But right ahead lay the village of Belvidere.

The first person to be seen was the Redpath superintendent, out in the road, scanning the landscape. Only a few minutes remained before evening curtain. But the Tulls had arrived and the show went on.

End of an Era

21

The Chicago Male Quartet sang its heart out in 1927. The four men also wore snappy white dinner jackets that gave them a prosperous, big-town air. When, between vocal numbers, they lined up on the stage and lifted their gold-plated trumpets for a Sousa medley, no other troupe on any circuit could touch them.

They were classy, the people out in front said, and wasn't it too bad there were so many empty seats? In the old days this was the kind of company that an audience would have kept up there on the stage half the night, with encore after encore.

Most of the songs were new and some of them had been coming in over the radio. Folks here in the back country—if there still *was* any back country—no longer waited years for Broadway tunes to reach them. Radio sent a hit west in a few days. Light opera still supplied most of the popular songs. There were many good ones to pick from and these handsome singers certainly knew how to pick.

Sigmund Romberg's *Stout-Hearted Men* was only a year old, and just made for quartets. A fellow on the radio named Nelson Eddy had been singing some sweet music from a New York hit named *Rose Marie,* and the audiences recognized it, too. Jazz still was king. But the Chicago Quartet avoided it. It also avoided, to the disappointment of the few young people in the tent, a foolish song about *YES! We Have No Bananas,* which everybody was singing and which somehow seemed made for 1927. Like the year itself, the words just didn't make sense. The tune was all right, older people thought. The *Hallelujah Chorus,* from which the music was adapted, was still the good old *Hallelujah Chorus.*

Before the Quartet had left Chicago in the spring, Sandor Radanovitz had helped plan its program and had drilled the four relentlessly. He had talked about "balance." Just the right amount of new light-opera music, just enough solid old favorites, just the proper proportion of trumpeting, just enough humor—balance, balance, balance, he had insisted, something for everybody, not too much of any one thing.

The Quartet kept its program short. People preferred short programs now. Everyone was in a hurry. There was a feeling of restlessness and uneasiness in the air. The Chicago singers hurried, too, as soon as the concert ended, folded their white dinner jackets carefully, and started for the next town up the line, hoping for a bigger crowd.

The Dumond Light Opera Company, three days behind the Quartet, was presenting a "musical play," long on melody and short on plot. Unfortunately, old in subject matter, too. It was based on the life of Stephen Foster and packed with "old favorites," by the old minstrel man from the Old Kentucky Home. Audiences in the tents didn't want things old; they wanted them new. The Light Opera Company, the Quartet had heard, was playing to even more empty seats than it was.

The people seemed to take better to the two comedies that followed in the course of the week. *The Patsy,* a "great Broadway hit," was by Barry Connors, who, the season before, had supplied Redpath with a wholesome confection entitled *Applesauce.* Advance notices billed the drama as "uproarious comedy . . . fun, laughter, romance, intermingling with a gay play of sunny skies and silver linings."

The second dramatic offering was *The Goose Hangs High.* In 1924 it had enjoyed a fairly long Broadway run. It was good clean fun, and who wanted subtlety?

The entertainers were good, too, all through the week, old headliners most of them, and popular Ruth Bryan Owen was a lecturer. Only one thing was lacking—enough people to fill the tents.

As the 1927 season was about to close, I wrote a pessimistc letter to Manager Paul Pearson of the Swarthmore circuits. Describing what had happened to us on the road that year, and to most other systems in the middle west, I referred to the story of the surgeon whose operation had been a complete success in all respects except one: the patient died.

Chautauqua did not die in 1927, but to say merely that its health was impaired is to understate the facts. Every manager still sending companies across the country had ample reason to suspect that the circuits were very ill. East to west, all were suffering from acute box-office anemia.

The causes were many, and few stemmed directly either from the character of Chautauqua itself or from the changing character of the people. Distractions were going on outside the tents, and not even the best oratory or the sweetest melody could compete with them.

The people were listening to radio. In the seven years since Station KDKA in Pittsburgh had sent its first faint signals over the air, more than two million receiving sets had been bought for American homes. In 1925, WLS, the Sears-Roebuck station in Chicago, had boosted its power to 5000 watts and could be heard from New Orleans to Winnipeg. By 1927 farmers and villagers were storing away their gooseneck "tulip" horn speakers—they already were outdated—and into the parlor instead came new "cabinet sets" with built-in sound boxes.

Columbia Broadcasting System came into existence in 1927. David Sarnoff and Owen D. Young had organized the National Broadcasting Company the year before, and the year before that, in March, 1925, a President, Calvin Coolidge, had delivered his inaugural address direct to the people.

The season that the Mississippi River floods ruined our prospects in half a dozen southern states and nearly washed us, tents, talent and baggage, into the Gulf, airwaves bristled with news, drama and music. Particularly news. In May a quiet youth named Charles Augustus Lindbergh left St. Louis to start from New York's Roosevelt Field on his solo flight to Paris. From the day of his lonely take-off until he was welcomed back on June 13 by Governor Al Smith, Mayor Jimmie Walker, one hundred and sixty policemen with motorcycles and a million shrieking enthusiasts, what red-blooded American dared leave his radio long enough to attend any kind of program, anywhere?

On May 21 a Redpath train, taking a five-day program to its opening date, was chugging over the Big Four Railroad in Indiana. At Lafayette someone shouted from the station platform that Lindbergh's plane had been sighted crossing the French coast. The news spread through the cars. One could feel the anxiety. Would he make it?

As the train pulled into Indianapolis, a railroad employee swung aboard. "He got there!" he shouted.

Indianapolis was not a Chautauqua town that year. No pause had been planned. But our people piled off and ran up the platform to the grimy old Union Station, cheering. Out in the street the Redpath band lined up and actors and actresses, magician and superintendent, vocal soloist and lecturer and crew boys formed ranks. The band stepped off. The leader lifted his baton and music swelled. *Stars and Stripes Forever*. And there went Chautauqua, one hundred and twenty-five strong, marching unexpectedly up Meridian Street, cheering as loudly as Hoosiers cheered on the sidewalks.

"The young fellow made it! What's his name?"

"Lindbergh!"

A crowd was waving flags on the Severn Hotel balcony and the big policeman at Washington Street held up traffic as Redpath marched through. Our parade did not pause until it reached the top of the broad steps at the foot of Soldiers and Sailors Monument, with its statue of Victory on top. Indianapolis swarmed in behind the Chautauqua company. The band, sweating hard, played *Hands Across the Sea* and *The Star Spangled Banner*. The people still were cheering when, back at the station, the superintendent counted the last nose and signalled the conductor that the train could go on.

There were unhappier moments that season, to distract talent and public alike. Clamor in support of Sacco and Vanzetti continued all summer. The two soft-voiced Italian "anarchists," convicted of a murder committed during a pay-roll robbery in South Braintree, Massachusetts, had been sentenced to death. Execution was being stayed, while protests mounted that the trial had been unfair. There had been mass demonstrations, some of them in Chautauqua towns. The Governor of Massachusetts in July had appointed a commission to examine the evidence. Its report sustained the verdict, and late in August the two men were electrocuted. But the argument went on.

Earlier in the season the United States Marines had landed in Nicaragua "to protect American interests," and two months later a force of twelve hundred debarked at Shanghai for the same laudable purpose, but both times they arrived too late to rescue American property from native "revolutionaries." Radio, feeling its green young oats, made the most of both incidents. Breathless news announcers, striving to equal Floyd Gibbons' three hundred words a minute or Graham McNamee's staccato style, talked excitedly of possible war, and again people stayed glued to their receivers.

On the seamy side, but reported in every grim detail, was the New York affair of a corset salesman named Henry Gray Judd and Housewife Ruth Snyder, who finished off Mrs. Snyder's husband with an iron sashweight. The pair's confession, sent across the air waves, introduced the word "paramour" to the smallest Kansas village. Finally, as the Chautauqua season drew to an unprofitable close, a tornado ripped through St. Louis, in the heart of the circuit country, destroying a thousand homes and killing eighty-seven citizens. The debris had hardly been cleared before floods ravished quiet Vermont, with radio bulletins every hour on the hour.

Not only the news, but radio entertainment was available, at home, in a comfortable chair. A team called Sam and Henry, who later were to rename themselves Amos and Andy, went on the air in Chicago. Also available was the silken voice of poet-philosopher Tony Wons, filling a million living rooms with the radio version of mother, home and heaven. And what Chautauqua orchestra could claim half the fame and fans of radio's Cliquot Club Eskimo troupe, conducted by Harry Reser, and paid for by big money?

Radio was still new when Redpath tried to take advantage of it. That was the day of the crystal set and the homemade receiver. We employed a "wireless expert," with five small transmitters, capable of pushing out signals over a radius of twenty-five miles.

Before Chautauqua reached a town, a truck, with a crew boy as announcer, began to broadcast news of the seven exciting days ahead. Local talent lined up immediately to give a hand. Church choirs, music teachers with classes of future Carusos, and American Legion drum and bugle corps all wanted a chance to be heard and soon there was hardly time to get in our own announcements. The opening day, and the second, we broadcast the program from the tent.

It was expensive advertising and did not attract many paid admissions. After six weeks we gave it up. Potential customers were sitting at home, listening to the new marvel, instead of buying tickets. We were competing with ourselves.

Throughout their lifetimes circuits had competed with each other and flourished. Radio was competition of a different kind. Since the start, too, tent Chautauqua had depended on the country and small town. For years it had been an accepted axiom that good crops meant good Chautauqua. If things went well on the farm, they went well with us. But this 1927 summer things were not going well on the farm and had not for several years.

In Florida, the starting point for countless treks north, the real-estate boom collapsed in 1926. Across mid-America, as early as 1924, farmlands which in the war years had brought $400 an acre, $500, sometimes a whopping and unrealistic $1000, suddenly were going begging at $100 an acre. Mortgages began to be foreclosed. When distracted farmers, thousands of whom had been the financial backbones of local Chautauqua committees, cried to Washington for help, they were told, soothingly, to "keep cool with Cal"; but in 1927, and again in 1928, Coolidge vetoed the bipartisan McNary-Haugen farm relief bill. His reason: it included a price-fixing principle and benefited special groups.

As the bottom dropped out of land prices, it also dropped out of thousands of little country banks. These were the banks in which our local committees, by agreement with the bureaus, had deposited their advance guarantees. If the banks and the farmers now had no money, who did? Certainly not the small-town merchants. And if no money was in sight for even a single, fifty-cent admission, how could anyone sell three-dollar season tickets? Asked to sign new guarantees, distraught businessmen threw down their pens and announced that never again would they put their John Hancocks on any dotted line.

Wall Street might not hear about it for a time, but the Great Depression was on the American doorstep.

Vawter, in farming Iowa, had sensed the situation more quickly than other managers. He still respected a dollar. How could he sell those season tickets? He cast about for a means—and in 1925 bought a caliope. All summer its strident, steamy voice echoed along the roads, heralding the arrival of the tents. But few seemed to care.

Next season Vawter sent out Whistling Sue Hueling and Her Rainbow Orchestra in a Ford truck, equipped with bunks. He would use the roads and save train fares and hotel bills. The roads were new and hard and good, so good, in fact, that they were ruining Chautauqua. The whole world was using them, going to town to the new movie, to the next town for an ice-cream soda, on beyond to a dance, driving for fun, here, there and everywhere.

Miss Hueling could whistle charmingly and the girls could sing. This was the year that *Who Stole My Heart Away* captivated the country and hillsides reverberated with its catchy melody.

After the Model-A truck broke down the first few times, the girls slipped another song into their repertoire: "Get Out and Get Under, Get Out and Get Under Your Automobile . . ." It was not new, but it was applicable, and the crowd laughed. The six young ladies also performed on saxophones and trumpets; the dramatic climax came when they played *Down in Chinatown* on a carpenter's saw, with a violin bow.

Whistling Sue and Her Girls were tough competition for Hughie Fitzpatrick, Barnum and Bailey's famous clown, whose antics followed their program.

Vawter's other talent included Ye Olde New England Quartet, harmonizing *A Cottage Small by a Waterfall*—later a popular fox-trot number —and three pretty girls called the Betsy Trio. An awe-struck chairman, introducing the Betsys, announced that they appeared in "pre-historic costume." The lecturer was Andrew Beaushore, with a mother, home and heaven story of his own life. Beaushore was a cripple; he had overcome his handicap so well that his energy wore out the rest of the talent.

Without fanfare, in the middle of the 1926 season, Vawter sold his tents and territory. His profits since spring had been exactly $345. The buyer was W. S. Rupe, an early operator, who recently had re-entered the business. As always, Vawter's timing was good. The old master had started the tent circuits at exactly the right moment; he got out of the business now in precisely the nick of time.

In a letter to a friend Vawter summed up the new, dark world by blaming "dancing mothers." He had found a catchword, at least. In 1924, the Methodist Episcopal church, at long last, had lifted its ban against dancing and theatre-going. The Protestant Episcopal House of Bishops, two years earlier, had removed the word "obey" from its marriage ceremony.

Mother was dancing. Vawter was right in that. She had come out of the kitchen. Sewing circles and missionary societies did not give her room enough to kick up her new high heels. In 1917 she had gone into "war work." She had come from the industrial plants with the vote firmly clutched in her right hand, a new lipstick in her left, and in her handbag a cigarette to smoke in the privacy of her bedroom. Mother not only was dancing. She was turning on her radio and like her husband, she was following the stock market quotations. Like him, she did not have the remotest idea of what they actually meant.

It is incorrect to assume that, in this period between the first wholesale foreclosures of midwest farms and the Wall Street crash of 1929, there was no money in America to be spent on oratory and entertainment. There was loose and ready cash, plenty of it, but unfortunately for businesses like ours, it was not in the right pockets. Most of the available currency was borrowed money. Rich farm land no longer was good collateral; one had to have something really valuable to put up, something like gilt-edged stocks in Sam Insull's midwest utility empire.

Insull was building a forty-five-story opera house in Chicago and picking up the tab for deficits incurred by that city's Civic Opera Company. The smart boys were betting on Insull. How could they guess that ten years later he would elude Federal officers and escape to Greece, dressed in women's clothes?

Chicago could be tolerant. It boasted of its tolerance and most tolerant of all was the city's mayor, Big Bill Thompson, with his slogan, "Throw away your hammer, get a horn." In his city—and Redpath-Chicago's city, too—145,000 spectators one night in 1927 paid more than two million dollars (one estimate is $2,600,000) to see Gene Tunney defend his heavyweight championship against Jack Dempsey. That same fall, in seven weeks, thirty million Americans paid fifty million dollars to watch football.

Al Capone already was a millionaire. In dingy blind pigs, all the way from "bone dry" Kansas to unrepentant Greenwich Village, gullible citizens were paying a dollar a shot for whiskey "just off the boat," cut and re-cut with rot-gut alcohol from ten thousand illicit back-country and city-basement stills. But in the eroded valley of the winding Tennessee and Cumberland Rivers, where Chautauqua always had been welcomed, the lean hogs were dying up dry ravines and children were growing peaked on half-rations of hominy grits.

Hard times on one side, changing times on the other, both hit our particular form of entertainment. And then suddenly all show business felt the jar of "progress." The inventors had kept busy. Redpath tents were in the warehouses for the winter when, on October 26, 1927, an event on Broadway heralded a new era in entertainment. The Brothers Warner, of Hollywood, presented a movie called *The Jazz Singer,* with Al Jolson as the star. Jolson, wearing his floppy white gloves, spoke from the screen. He sang. The talking picture had arrived.

This wedding of cinema sight and sound, at the moment famed Conductor Walter Damrosch was celebrating his fiftieth year in music, was a blow to the legitimate stage as a whole and to scores of movie actors, including Charlie Chaplin. The public, in its picture houses, soon would enjoy the new dimension of the spoken word. And Chaplin and many another actor and actress, whose gestures had endeared them to the people, found that they had unendearing voices.[1]

---

[1] The first Walt Disney cartoon was released the next year, in 1928.

Broadway, where that year two hundred and sixty-four plays had opened in seventy-five theatres, was shaken by the advent of movie sound. One by one, playhouses "closed for remodeling," and became picture palaces. We always had been able to advertise "genuine Broadway actors" in our play casts, but now hundreds, out of work, became hungrily available for the summer road. Available, but inexperienced in the Great Outdoors.

Many of them had much to learn about people and places west of Manhattan's Eighth Avenue; a long, long trail, they discovered, led from a Missouri meadow to Schubert Alley. Among the plays on a smaller circuit one of these years was the Chautauqua perennial, *The Little Shepherd of Kingdom Come,* by John Fox, Jr. It appealed particularly to superintendents and directors; so pristine was its purity that it could be presented exactly as written, without deleting a line.

A former crew boy, responsible for supplying the stage props for this production, remembers that the "Broadway cast" actually did come from Broadway and "not one of them ever had seen a cow."

"In New York," the man recalls, "they'd been used to getting all the props they wanted. For this play the list filled two typewritten columns. The first week out we borrowed stuff everywhere, from hardware stores, furniture stores, local families. Every sort of thing, from a Bible for the hero to a butter churn. It was a terrible job.

"After a few towns, we decided to train these New Yorkers to get along with what was available in the country. By the end of the season we had cut the property list to half a dozen items. We showed Broadway that, out in a tent, one wooden box, borrowed from the corner grocery, could do the work of a couple of dozen fancy props."

Vawter's sale in 1926 shocked us. Already several other outfits, one at a time, had stepped out of the parade. As early as 1922 Redpath's Chicago and Columbus offices and Paul Pearson's Swarthmore had bought what was left of Coit-Alber. Ellison-White's great empire, out of Boise, Idaho, had withdrawn in 1925. One new group had entered. After World War One, Associated Chautauquas, an organization put together by two smart showmen named C. Benjamin Franklin and E. M. Carson, had begun picking up small circuits here and there. To our surprise the pair seemed able to make money, while more experienced managers could not make ends meet.[1]

Older men had borrowed money, more money, re-cut costs. We had experimented by increasing, then decreasing advertising budgets. We had tried small circuits in big cities, big circuits in small towns. We had lengthened seasons, then shortened them, concentrating first on the south, then on the north. We had put more emphasis on music, without startling results. Heart-breaking experience had taught us innumerable things that would

[1] Associated Chautauquas had bought Mutual, Midland, Standard, White and Brown, Cadmean, Acme, and also Vawter's old circuit from Rupe.

not improve the business, and nothing that in these frightening days did improve it.

Talent and local committees, all had tried vainly to help the management. In an effort to overcome higher railroad rates, entertainers who formerly headed companies went out with one-man shows. Adjoining towns doubled up for a week's run. A few, while others frowned, even offered the programs free and passed a hat for contributions at the exits. Swarthmore tried fall circuits, with programs of three days each. It didn't work.

In Ohio and Indiana Coit-Alber in its last season experimented by charging no admissions, passing no hat except on closing night to pay for the next year's program. At Milroy, Indiana, one man startled everyone by giving ten dollars for himself and five dollars for his dog, "to be sure it would have a seat next year." But not enough men or dogs were interested; the scheme had to be dropped.

Van Wert, Ohio, put the following summer's tickets on sale in December, for Christmas presents. Churches teamed up in selling campaigns. Desperate managers promoted "Home Town Days" with exhibits, "Field Days" with athletics. They sponsored a nation-wide contest for a play "best suited to Chautauqua," with Manager Paul Pearson heading the judges—the prize of three thousand dollars went to a New York bank officer for *Crossed Wires,* a good comedy with civic reform its theme. But it failed to revive Chautauqua.

Lecturers sensed apathy even among audiences that did buy tickets. The old "Chautauqua bustle" was gone. What did the people want? Did they know? In 1927 lecturer Harry Hibschman sent out a list of thirty subjects with the question: Which did potential audiences prefer that he discuss? To his surprise, ninety-seven percent chose: "Can a man accept evolution and retain his religious faith?" So Hibschman discussed "evolution," and an indignant ticketholder in New Park, Pennsylvania, peculiarly enough a doctor, kept him from a return engagement because he was "too modernistic."

In the Redpath-Chicago office the financial handwriting on the wall loomed redder and redder, almost as plain to me as the words on a sign hanging beside my desk. Over the years the sign had caused merriment among the talent. It said, "When in doubt, tell the truth."

One day ex-Congressman Bede of Minnesota was entertaining me with a cock-and-bull story when I turned and pointed lightly to the sign. Bede's retort had been, "Trouble is, you never are in doubt."

Examining the financial structure now, I was very much in doubt. What should Redpath-Chicago do? We owned five circuits. We were losing money. Franklin, of Associated Chautauquas, still wanted to expand. Making up my mind, finally, I sold three circuits to him. These were the "Gulf," that had nearly drowned in the flood; the Atlantic, which despite its name operated from Chicago; and a third, smaller and nameless, which we simply had called our "Circuit B," with headquarters in Columbus, Ohio. We kept our seven-day DeLuxe and the Columbus six-day.[1]

Then came 1929.

The country, jittery in some sections, reckless in others, was marking time as spring advanced. In April President Hoover called a special session of the Seventy-first Congress to do something about farm relief. Farmers had been behaving "socialistic." They had taken up shotguns and chased off the sheriffs sent to sell their barns and stock at auction to pay off debts to broken banks.

In the cities the insane stock market speculation went on. The insane drinking of green alcohol, disguised as gin, went on. Al Capone went on. He had reached into Chicago's organized labor, into business, even into entertainment. Any restaurant with an orchestra had to pay the "syndicate" for protection.

On February 14 six men in the "business" of bootlegging were lined up against a wall in a Chicago garage and shot down by rival "business men" with machine guns. Radio and newspapers referred to the affair as "the St. Valentine's Day Massacre." They gave it more time on the air and more space in the press than they did the heartening news, announced by the President in July, that sixty-two nations had signed the Kellogg-Briand pact forswearing war.

That summer Vatican City became a sovereign state, and at a base in Little America, Commander Richard E. Byrd was preparing his tri-motor plane for the first much-publicized flight over the South Pole. In August Henry Ford, in an interview with Samuel Crowther in the *North American Review,* expressed his opinion that the only way to get America out of the doldrums was for all industry to pay higher wages. Wall Street was shocked. But not as badly shocked as it was two months later, when its own house, built on the sands of loose credit to speculators, collapsed.

Variety, the weekly journal of show business, told the story: WALL STREET LAYS AN EGG. The Depression, that was to last forty-two months, was on.

Our DeLuxe circuit had opened the first of May as usual, in Columbus, Georgia. The mayor and the commanding general of Fort Benning, the army's infantry post, had met our special train. It was a warm sunny day— and the ticket sale had been good.

Redpath people felt at home in Columbus after all these years. The city already was on its way to being one of the south's greatest textile centers. It was progressive. Its streets were wide and clean. Visionaries had laid them out double, with broad green parkways down the center.

To talent a town became famous not for anything that ever had happened to it in history, but for what happened to talent in it. Columbus,

---

[1] Rupe bought Horner's holdings in 1929. Pearson's Swarthmore operation was declared bankrupt in 1930.

Georgia, therefore, was where golf player Opie Read, one pleasant day, was practising putting in the wide parkway in the middle of the street, when he felt an urge to swing. He drove his ball two long, busy blocks— fortunately he drove it straight. The town also was the place where Lecturer Ralph Parlette, with his famous jar of beans and its moral, "The big man comes to the top," gave out with another immortal truism.

In 1918, the year we observed the anniversary of James Redpath's opening of his Boston office, we had celebrated in Columbus. There had been speeches and more speeches, all stressing that Pioneer Redpath had "established" a great institution. Parlette had arrived just in time for his own lecture, too late to hear the fulsome praise of what James Redpath had "established." He began, "Nothing is established in this world but the graveyard and taxes." The audience had laughed, and we had laughed too —at ourselves.

Everybody worked hard in 1929, all the way from Georgia north to Wisconsin. The final show in Racine was good. But cars were not parked, hub to hub, around the Chautauqua grounds. In a spirit either of determination or bravado, we had printed on our final program Thomas E. Edison's once hopeful words, "Chautauqua is a movement which has now spread over the whole of our country, in fact over the world." No one argued it. But the tent was half full.

The indestructible Montaville Flowers opened, with a speech aimed at young people—who were not much in evidence. The five Filipino Collegians "pre-luded" him. Single admission, fifty cents.

The directors thought that they had achieved "balance" with the music. The famous Cathedral Choir sang *Chimes of Brittany*. Energetic Edna White, a graduate of the *Aida Opera Company*, presented her three girl trumpeters, who did not play saws. Afternoon and evening, the sixth day, a bejewelled middle-aged Hungarian "cymbalon artist," and a handsome Russian soprano in both jewels and a crown, glamorized the program of the Blue Danube Orchestra. Our star, in the grand concert, admission up to a dollar, was an Indiana girl named Lorna Doone Jackson, a worthy successor to Alice Nielsen and Julia Claussen.

Miss Jackson had begun her professional career in vaudeville, with an act specializing in college songs, known simply as *Rah Rah*. In 1913 she was touring grubby "opera houses" in middle-sized, midwest towns, playing to "ten-twenty-thirty-cent" admirers. Ten years later she had reached grand opera. In 1926 and 1928 she had been prima donna dramatic soprano in the Chicago Civic Opera Company and came to Redpath directly from her triumph in *Carmen*.

In the afternoon of Miss Jackson's big evening, Anne Campbell, "the only American woman to write a poem a day," recited her own verse. In Michigan Miss Campbell was the answer of the *Detroit News* to the "heap o' livin'" with which Edgar A. Guest beguiled poetry lovers in the *Detroit*

Free Press. Naturally a summer season on Chautauqua could not interfere with her daily poetic output, so she wrote when and where she found the time and a scrap of paper. The rest of the day she was the old style of good trouper, getting up early and going to bed late and liking it, liking the little towns and writing pieces about them, reciting:

> "Little towns with just one street,
> "Cities where all highways meet,
> "Early trains and weary feet,
> "Bird baths in a bowl of white,
> "Packing luggage late at night,
> "Pressing clothes by stolen light,
> "That's trouping!" [1]

It was not deathless literature, just pleasant, homey verse that people understood. Crowds liked it as they earlier had liked the simple poems of Fred Emerson Brooks about Calaveras County, California. They liked Miss Campbell's "It isn't the size of a town that counts. It's the folks who are living there."

Edna White's Trumpeters "pre-luded" two lecturers. One was Nellie Tayloe Ross, with *The Governor Speaks,* the other was a tough Irish flyer, Captain Denis Rooke, who had flown solo from London to India, seven thousand miles in a Moth plane. In the British army Rooke had been "a first-class fighting man," and he had not put fighting behind him with the Armistice. The chip he carried on his shoulder was the size of a ten-foot hemlock plank. He had a habit of fighting at the drop of a hat and he succeeded in dropping his hat in every town.

Crew boys, admonished at the start of the season that "a soft answer turneth away wrath," watched Rooke enviously. They could fight mosquitoes and chiggers. That was part of the life. And if local toughs threatened to tear down the canvas, they might parade up and down, in pants and shoes, bare to the waist, in a brawny display of biceps, and look hard. But they were not to fight—unless it became absolutely necessary. At Huntington, Indiana, late in the season, when town boys cut the guy ropes, three crew men, taking a lesson from Rooke, thought it was necessary. After a spirited melee the local forces retreated.

In the 1929 program, the day after the belligerent Rooke's lecture, "Teddy" Graham, a former business associate of Vawter, gave liberal views on the current immigration problem. "Let 'em in," he counselled. "Make Americans of them." Montaville Flowers, fortunately, was several towns up the line by the time Graham spoke. Flowers' ideas were violently opposite: he was a Californian now and the Yellow Peril made him see red.

Our first play, early in the week, was Southern Playwright Lula Vollmer's *Sun-Up*—"a great drama of the Carolina mountains." Miss Vollmer, who

[1] Reprinted by permission of the author.

contributed most of her royalties to educational work among the mountaineers, next year began her radio serial, *Moonshine and Honeysuckle.* In
our presentation at Columbus in 1929, Actress Marie Pavey, who back in
1912 had started her Broadway career in the long run of *Little Women*
with Alice Brady, played the role of old Widow Cagle with her corn-cob
pipe. *Sun-Up* had been on the road since 1923. *Skidding,* which we offered
our final night, was just one year off Broadway. As in all "closing-nights,"
it was good comedy, the germ for the later Andy Hardy films.

We had no "inspirationalist" on our final program, but cartoonist and
magician still were on hand. Artist John Bockewitz, keeping up with the
times, had added "electrical effects" and a Disney touch to his "animated
cartoons." Mardoni, whose talented wife assisted him on the platform,
was our magician.

Earlier, in Eustis, Florida, Mardoni had been the hero, or villain, in an
episode of the kind that always sent temperamental Sandor Radanovitz to
the solace of his bed, crying, "I am sick! Sick!" Director Radanovitz had
arrived at Eustis, in the center of the state, to learn that "Escape Artist"
Mardoni was planning another "stunt."

"Stunts," in the opinion of the musical director, imperiled not only
the man but Redpath. In Chicago Mardoni had tempted Providence by
parachuting in a strait-jacket from an airplane, extricating himself above
Lake Michigan, and Radanovitz had covered his eyes and prayed. He discovered now that the magician and the local sheriff had argued as to how
skillful Mardoni really could be in a tight spot. It had ended by the magician
challenging the sheriff to handcuff him, put him in leg irons and a strait-
jacket, chain him to a hundred pound anchor and drop him into ten feet
of water. Mardoni's name, if I remember correctly, actually was Waite;
Radanovitz thought it "not romantic enough" and changed it.

The local newspaper had given front page attention to the coming test.
A skeptical crowd had already gathered on the shore of Lake Eustis, when
Radanovitz arrived in town to catch the evening program. He raced to the
water. Mardoni and the sheriff were fifty yards from shore in a boat and,
from all appearances, the sheriff was about to toss the hero of the evening
program overboard.

"Stop him!" Radanovitz screamed. "You kill him! He will drown! You
ruin Redpath!"

Mardoni heard him, everyone north of the Everglades did. There was
a chance the Hungarian was right, Mardoni knew. He probably would
drown, two hours before curtain. But he couldn't back out now, his honor
had been challenged. Calmly he went over the side and disappeared.

Writhing with apprehension, the upset Radanovitz was helped to a hotel
to bed. But before he got there Mardoni was back on land, drying off, and
the sheriff was dragging the lake bottom for his discarded irons.

Mardoni got out of his tight fix; we who had money in Chautauqua did not. Redpath-Chicago did not open in the spring. In late winter we sold our last two circuits to W. S. Rupe. We did not unload. Both Rupe and Franklin who also had bought in, were operators who believed that they could succeed. They made down payments and planned to pay the remainder out of later profits. We took that chance with them. There were no more profits.

The world had changed; the hinterland had disappeared. The word "decency" had new meanings. New times had brought new fashions in entertainment, just as they had in clothes, houses and food. Youths who never had ventured beyond the second station up the line had come back from France saying *mercy bo-koo* and *toot-sweet*. The popular song, "How you gonna keep 'em down on the farm, after they've seen Paree," was based on fact. Hard roads and movies and the car standing at the back door were too inviting.

Of the original Redpath managers only Crawford Peffer carried the proud name on the road after 1929, still with high-class programs. Almost to the end this easterner offered good debates on national issues. The country was deep in the depression by 1932; in spite of it, Peffer and Rupe advertised circuits, Peffer a six-day in New York and New England, Rupe a five-day from Des Moines, Iowa. Franklin, of Associated Chautauquas, also presented a modest program; its final show opened at Cornell, Illinois, on August 23, closed four days later.

Peffer and Rupe both used marionettes that last summer, Rupe even a "music box revue," definitely no relation to the Broadway hit of the same title. Drama had come to stay, whether Chautauqua had or not, and both operators offered two comedies. Peffer booked *Six-Cylinder Love* and in what perhaps was a spirit of desperation, he paid high royalties for George Kelley's uproarious Broadway hit, *The Show Off*. For the midwest Rupe resurrected *The Hottentot,* fresh from successful road-company runs, and a not-too-subtle comedy entitled *Laff It Off*.

Redpath-New England's last date was in Laconia, New Hampshire. When the cast of *The Show Off* took its bow the night of September first, the Redpath tent came down for good. Persevering Franklin made one more try. In 1933 he booked three plays in Keota, Iowa.

A few independent assemblies were to continue. The one at Fountain Park, Indiana, carries on after sixty-odd years. Winona Lake annually presents a program in Billy Sunday's old haunts. A few others were to re-remain, with the "mother" institution at Chautauqua Lake still the guiding star. But the circuits were dead and no requiem sounded, not even from the ghost of Keith Vawter's caliope.

Heritage

22

Chautauqua left its indelible mark on the communities which knew it best. I am sure that in the years it flourished it spelled out the meaning of democracy. Certainly it was among the first agencies in America that taught townspeople to work together.

If it is true that in the over-all picture the guarantee harmed circuit Chautauqua, it also was one of the things that made it great. It was this agreement that brought rival merchants, teachers, farmers, Democrats and Republicans, around the same table to sign their names on the same piece of paper. It made churches get along with other churches, it spanned the railroad tracks, welded village to farm. In that day, before any Improvement Associations or PTA, before drives for community chest and national charity, that little, hard-working, earnest Chautauqua committee was often a town's only all-embracing unit.

In 1914, when Chautauqua week was over in Clinton, Indiana, its *Saturday Argus* said: "Clinton never again can be what it was. Gone are the narrow petty persecutions. The old order has passed. The Chautauqua did it."

I still remember a speech made from the stage at Paducah, Kentucky, when the question of whether or not to undertake a Chautauqua series for the next year was put to its citizens. The mayor asked to be heard. "I hope we have a good program next year," he began, "but whether it is good or not doesn't particularly matter. I think the one we're closing today is the finest we ever have had, but that isn't important either. What *is* important is the work we did together this year, before the tent went up. For the first time in my memory, all the people in this town got together for a common purpose. We raised three thousand dollars to put this Chautauqua

on, but if we had sent that money to the heathen and had no program at
all, Paducah would have been a better city because our people learned to
work together. The program itself was just that much bonus."

There in the south any lecture by a Catholic priest was attended by an
audience ninety-five percent Protestant. Even in a rare instance when a
community showed religious intolerance, a manager did not need to com-
ply with intolerant dictates. When one town in Pennsylvania objected to
a Catholic speaker, Quaker Paul Pearson released it from its financial contract and presented his speaker anyway. When the Ku Klux Klan tried to
show its head in New England, Manager Crawford Peffer hired a Roman
Catholic lecturer to cover his whole circuit. If Senator Frank Cannon in
the 1912 period created sentiment against the Mormons as charged, out
in his home state of Utah a western Chautauqua is credited with being
the first agency to bring Mormons and Gentiles into double harness on a
committee. Seeds of tolerance sowed in this way certainly took root and
sprouted.

Chiefly because of Chautauqua, religious opposition to drama ended in
small towns everywhere. That fantastically unreasonable attitude of wide
stretches of back country toward all forms of the theatre, bureau managers
attacked skillfully and successfully. They put good plays on the road and
succeeded in getting preachers and Sunday-school teachers to attend. The
early elocutionist, memory of whose stylized presentations makes a modern critic shudder, was only paving the way for Ben Greet and *It Pays to
Advertise*. The Swiss yodeler who entranced audiences in the early years
was gradually shouldered aside by symphony ensembles and operettas as
Chautauqua made classical music commonplace. The entertainer who jug-
gled while playing the piano prepared a welcome for the prima donnas of
the peak years. True, the circle turned in the end and some entertainers as
light in substance as the juggler came back, but thousands of middle-
class audiences, in the meantime, had learned to ask for Beethoven, Bach
and Brahms. Cities all over the nation, once just small towns whose music-
hungry people filled the big brown tents on hot summer afternoons, today
enjoy their own symphony orchestras, their own little theatres. Even the song
heister made the informal community sing a national institution.

Speakers like Folk, Lindsey, Wiley stirred the American conscience and
curiosity in countless fields. No people can vegetate long while it is arguing
political, social and moral causes vigorously, and the summer get-together
left a long trail of healthy argument in its wake. When the movement was
in its prime, Professor Irving Fisher of Yale wrote:

"The success or failure of Democracy depends on public opinion. The
Chautauqua movement has probably done more toward keeping American
public opinion informed, alert and unbiased than any other movement.
The press has come to be regarded, like advertising, as warped by special
interests. The pulpit is restricted as to subject matter and manner of treatment. The moving picture screen . . . offers possibilities as yet unknown

for good or ill. But the Chautauqua platform has kept above suspicion as the greatest agency of popular education."

Certainly it quickened the social spirit and helped create a public opinion that, in turn, produced leaders who dared take creative action. More often than not it was the lecturer under the canvas at a muddy crossroad who first introduced the pros and cons of high or low tariff, prohibition, juvenile courts, votes for women. Parents heard talk of supervised playgrounds, school lunches, free milk for babies, warnings that the little red schoolhouse no longer was good enough. Neglect, not by conscious intent, perhaps, but neglect, nevertheless, in using Chautauqua to the full as an open forum, may have helped its decline.

Although Chautauqua audiences were made up chiefly of rural and small-town folk, they were not yokels. They were hard to fool, as an occasional lecturer who tried to put something over on them quickly discovered. They wanted an honest picture of any disputed subject, listened just as respectfully to Atheist Clarence Darrow as they did to Fundamentalist Bryan and, after they had heard both sides, they went home and made up their own independent American minds. Peddlers of buncombe came and went on the programs. But masters of oratory and political thought followed them, and most of the men and women on the plank seats learned to distinguish between the two kinds of speakers. How many grass-roots orators counted their votes and went to Congress because as boys they had heard LaFollette or J. Adam Bede? Or how many musicians did the Claussens and the Estelle Grays encourage, or warm-hearted Sam Schildkret unearth, with their belief in music for the masses? In this particular field the impact was tremendous.

One might argue that the travel talk so popular before the First World War was ineffective, since isolationism long remained a dominant force in the Chautauqua belt. But who can judge how much more stubborn that isolationism might have been without the explorer and traveller, foreign or American, stressing the fact that the plain peoples of India and Turkey, for all their incomprehensible habits and tongues, under the skin were very much like the neighbors across any American farmer's line fence?

Small boys kicked up the dust running to the depot when the tents unloaded, and after the last of the talent left town they rushed to join the Scouts or the new Bird Club. Twenty years later their wives joined book clubs that plainly have more than one tie to Bishop Vincent's Chautauqua Lake Reading Circles. And what, after all, is the whole modern adult education movement but an extension of the Bishop's classes by the Lake, or of the morning-hour lectures in the circuit tent?

Again and again Chautauqua's methods have been found good, from ways of booking talent to selling tickets en masse. The circuit program disappeared like the circuit rider. Its last oratorical echo died, the last quartet sang its last sweet note, the tents moldered. But something has endured, something more than memory remains.

Index